The Scriptures of Mankind

AN INTRODUCTION

Books by the Author

RELIGIOUS ASPECTS OF THE CONQUEST OF MEXICO

MODERN TENDENCIES IN WORLD RELIGIONS

VARIETIES OF AMERICAN RELIGION, Editor

PROCESSION OF THE GODS, with Gaius G. Atkins

THE WORLD'S RELIGIONS

MAN'S QUEST FOR SALVATION

THESE ALSO BELIEVE

THE SCRIPTURES OF MANKIND

The Scriptures of Mankind

AN INTRODUCTION

by

CHARLES SAMUEL BRADEN, Ph.D.

Professor of History and Literature of Religions
Northwestern University

————◆————

New York
THE MACMILLAN COMPANY
1952

To
The memory of my wife,
Grace McMurray Braden

1888–1951

Acknowledgments

One who writes on as many different religions and their literatures as are included in this book must perforce depend heavily
upon the labors of others who have specialized in the several faiths.
The author, therefore, desires to record his deep indebtedness to
the devoted scholars who have spent years in the study and translation of these literatures. Most of them are specifically mentioned in
the footnotes scattered through the book. After reading and study-
ing the published work of specialists, the author still felt it desirable
to submit what he had written to men well versed in each separate
area, for their criticisms and suggestions. He desires here to record
his deep appreciation of the service of these men: Dr. Henry E.
Allen, University of Minnesota, read the chapter on Moslem Sacred
Literature; John Clark Archer of Yale University, on the Sikh Scriptures; Swami Akhilananda of the Ramakrishna Vedanta Society of
Boston, and Swami Vishwananda of the Vedanta Society of Chicago, on Hindu Scriptures; Dr. Chan Wing-Tsit (W. T. Chan),
Dartmouth College, on the Chinese Literature; Dr. Clarence H.
Hamilton, of Oberlin Graduate School of Theology, on Buddhist
Scriptures; Dr. D. C. Holtom, on the Japanese Sacred Books; Dr.
Charles F. Kraft, of Garrett Biblical Institute, on the Old Testament; Dr. George E. Mendenhall, of Hamma Divinity School, on
the Babylonian Literature; Dr. Ernest W. Saunders of Garrett Biblical Institute, on the New Testament; and Dr. John A. Wilson of the
Oriental Institute, University of Chicago, on the Egyptian Literature. Final responsibility for what went into each chapter rests not
upon these esteemed colleagues but upon the writer, who greatly
profited by their corrections and suggestions.

In the preparation of the manuscript he has been greatly helped by various students and secretaries. Mrs. Louise Baldanzi read the entire typescript and the proofs, and gave invaluable help in making it more readable. To Ruth Glenn and Marguerite Williams, my secretaries during the past year, and to Miss Myrtle Myer who again and again gave freely of her time to further the work, my heartiest thanks.

But most of all I owe to my wife, Grace, who did not live to see the final completion of the book; for her inspiration and encouragement, as well as practical suggestions. The summer in our cottage by an inland lake in the North woods, where she painted, or worked, or later, lay prostrated by illness, but uncomplaining, while I wrote a substantial portion of the volume, is a precious memory time will not dim.

CHARLES S. BRADEN

Northwestern University
Evanston, Illinois
January 3, 1952

Preface

For a long time the writer, whose task it has been to teach the history and literature of the world's religions to college students, has felt the need for just such a book as this one. During the whole of his teaching career in the field there have been available scholarly translations of considerable quantities of sacred literature from the greater religions; for example, the great fifty-volume series, *Sacred Books of the East*, each volume of which contains a learned discussion of the particular segment of the literature presented. This has been of inestimable value to all teachers and workers in the field for two generations. But it is very heavy reading for the undergraduate student with little technical acquaintance with the field. Then, too, there are admirable translations, such as those of the Pali Text Society, covering a very wide range of Buddhist literature, and others of similar nature, useful to the scholar, but not easily available for the ordinary college student.

In more recent years have appeared important anthologies in which the translation is accompanied by a minimum of introductory material which might help explain the text, which is usually printed with few or no notes of explanation. Here the outstanding example is the fourteen-volume *Sacred Books and Literature of the East,* a magnificently printed, well selected anthology of the best in all the great sacred literatures. Smaller, single-volume anthologies containing excellent selected material continue to appear, but most of them present only the text with almost nothing by way of explanation of its origin or meaning. In many ways admirably selected, they leave the reader with a great many questions, the answers to which would make the reading vastly more intelligible and probably more valuable.

There are, of course, separate volumes discussing these literatures;

e.g., on the literature of India there are at least four or more excellent, scholarly studies in existence, made by competent scholars: Winternitz, Hopkins, Farquhar, Macdonell, and others; but they are found in comparatively few libraries outside the larger centers. The same could be said concerning the literatures of other religions. What is needed by the ordinary student, it seems to the writer, is a single volume which will provide an adequate, if not an exhaustive, discussion of the great sacred literatures in non-technical language, so that he may better understand and appreciate what the anthologies so generously provide him.

One book which, for many years, served precisely this purpose was A. W. Martin's *Seven Great Bibles;* but it has long been out of print, and it covered by no means all the literatures. Halliday's *Dawn of Civilization* is a partial fulfillment of this need, but only partial. Furthermore, it was published many years ago, though still in print.

For years the writer has given a course which he has called "The Literature of the World's Religions," in which he has supplied his students with much of the material here presented, while they read extensively in the literatures themselves. His students have—so many of them said—found such introductory matter helpful in an understanding of the nature and the outlook of the several literatures. It is his hope that a greatly widened circle of readers will find it equally helpful. Owing to limitations of space, not a great deal of illustrative material is included in the body of the text. However, page references will be found to some of the more popular anthologies where additional selections may be found. It may, therefore, well serve as a reading guide to be used with any one of the better known selections from the world's religions.

The question may very well be raised as one reads through the book: Why was there no chapter on the Greek and Roman religions? The answer is in part that these religions developed no sacred books of a canonical sort. But then neither did the Babylonians or the Egyptians, in a strict sense, and they are included. The rest of the answer is that the author fully intended to include a chapter to be called Graeco-Roman Sacred Literature. But before it was written, the outside limit set by the publishers for the size of the book had already been exceeded, and rather drastic cutting was indicated, even if no Graeco-Roman chapter were added. Hence it was omitted. Had one been written it would have included some discussion at least of the following with brief selected passages. Among the Greeks, the *Homeric Epics*, the *Theogony of Hesiod*, which pretty well fixed the stories of the Olympian gods and their relationships; something from the extant hymn and prayer literature including the Orphic, something from Plato and possibly some of the other philosophers. From the Romans, probably much less, for much of their later religion was borrowed largely from the Greeks, but certainly selections from some of the great Roman Stoics; Seneca and Marcus Aurelius would have been included. For selections see Ruth Smith, *The Tree of Life*, pp. 279–306; Grace Turnbull, *Tongues of Fire*, pp. 291–375.

Although detailed suggestions for further reading are made at the end of each chapter, it is worth while to insert here at least a partial annotated list of the available anthologies in which the reader may find ample selections from all of the great religions. Some one or more of these volumes may be found even in most small libraries, and several or all of them in the greater university or city libraries.

MULTIPLE-VOLUME ANTHOLOGIES

Sacred Books of the East, ed. by Max Müller. 50 vols., Oxford University Press, London. Contains at least one volume for most of the world's religions. Highly scholarly. Not too readable for the layman.

Sacred Books and Early Literature of the East. 14 vols., Parke, Austin, and Lipscomb, N.Y., 1917. Contains extensive selections from all the world's religions, a volume or more for each one. Beautifully printed, very readable.

The Wisdom of the East Series, ed. by L. Cranmer-Byng and Dr. S. A. Kapadia. John Murray, London. Numerous small, well printed volumes of about 100 pp. each, one to several on each religion. Well edited, usually with a good introduction. Very readable. Pocket size.

Harvard Classics, Vols. 44 and 45. P. F. Collier & Son, N.Y.

ONE-VOLUME GENERAL ANTHOLOGIES

Containing Selections from All or Most of the Sacred Literature

The Bible of the World, ed. by Robert O. Ballou. 1415 pp., Viking, N.Y., 1939. This popular anthology has been condensed to 600 pp. and published under two titles with identical text as *The World Bible* (Viking, 1944) and *The Pocket World Bible* (Routledge, London, 1948).

The Bible of Mankind, ed. by Mirza Ahmad Sohrab. 743 pp., Universal Publishing Co., N.Y., 1939. Good selection, topically arranged. Very few long passages from any faith.

The World's Great Scriptures, ed. by Lewis Browne. 559 pp., Macmillan, N.Y., 1946. Selections primarily concerned with ethics rather than religious teachings.

The Tree of Life, ed. by Ruth P. Smith. 496 pp., Viking, N.Y., 1942. Very much briefer selections than in *The Bible of the World.* Purportedly for young people.

Tongues of Fire, compiled by Grace H. Turnbull. 416 pp., Macmillan, N.Y., 1929. Excellent but fragmentary selections.

The Sacred Writings of the World's Great Religions, ed. by S. E. Frost, Jr. 410 pp.; Garden City Publishing Co., N.Y., 1949. Very brief selections. Costs less than a dollar.

Treasure-House of the Living Religions, ed. by Robert E. Hume. 493 pp., Scribner, N.Y., 1932. Very brief but numerous selections, topically arranged.

LIMITED ANTHOLOGIES
Covering One or More Particular Religions

The Harvard Oriental Series. Many vols., Harvard University Press, Cambridge, Mass. Very scholarly and magnificently printed.

Sacred Books of the Buddhists. Highly scholarly translations with critical notes, by leading Buddhist scholars, issued by various publishers.

Publications of the Pali Text Society. Very scholarly translations, with critical introductions and notes, by leading Buddhist scholars, issued by various publishers.

The Wisdom of China and India, ed. by Lin Yutang. 1104 pp., Random House, N.Y., 1942. Excellent selection, good introductions, especially to the various sections of Chinese literature. Some of the translations are by Lin himself. Very readable.

Hindu Scriptures, ed. by Nicol Macnicol. 293 pp., Everyman's Library, Dutton, N.Y., 1938. Costs only a little more than a dollar. Good and representative selection.

The Gospel of Buddha, compiled by Paul Carus. 275 pp., Open Court Publishing Co., Chicago, 15th ed., 1915. Excellent and well varied selection, popular and readable. Not so easy to identify sources.

Some Sayings of the Buddha, transl. by F. L. Woodward. 356 pp., Oxford University Press, London, 1925. Pocket size. Wide and representative selection. Each selection documented for easy reference to original sources.

Contents

Contents

The Scriptures of Mankind

AN INTRODUCTION

CHAPTER I

What Is Sacred Literature?

It is interesting to note that the one subject which, more than any other one, is held to be necessary for graduation from college in the United States, is English. English A is required work for freshmen in almost every college in America, unless the freshman is able to pass a proficiency examination in the subject. Even then, usually, he is only accorded the privilege of electing a more advanced course in English, and preferably in the field of literature. Why is this?

To be sure, composition usually forms a substantial part of English A, and it is conceivable that the colleges are mainly interested in making certain that one who bears its diploma is capable of writing good English. But it is always more than composition; it always requires a substantial amount of reading in English and American literature. And most advanced English courses concern themselves with literature. In a typical university, 58 per cent of the students enrolled in English were in advanced courses. Here literature was the principal subject of study. Why is this? In this same university no other single subject is required of all students of whatever school.

Evidently it is felt that even in an age of science and technology there is something in the study of literature which is imperative. Is this simply a hold-over from an earlier day which the general

1

conservatism of the educational world perpetuates because it has become a sacred tradition, or is there something in the study of literature which, regardless of the field of specialization into which one goes, makes it of vital importance? If so, why?

One may venture to suppose that perhaps the major reason is that in literature, as nowhere else, man is revealed to himself; that what one gets out of literature—great literature—is an understanding of man himself. In poetry, the drama, the story, the novel, the essay, man mirrors his own soul. Here are expressed the desires, the urges, the hopes, the dreams, the successes, the failures of man in his struggle to make himself at home in his world. Here are exhibited the heights and the depths to which man can rise or fall. Here one lives vicariously the life of every man, and out of it all comes a large measure of understanding of mankind in general, and of oneself, perhaps, in particular. Surely great literature well taught, that is made really to come alive for the student, can be one of the great formative experiences of his college years. Alas, that so often it does not live! And the student emerges from his literature courses with a permanent prejudice against literature as something dull, uninteresting, and certainly to be avoided henceforth. The author recalls the long years it took to recover from a Shakespeare course to a love of Shakespeare, awakened, it may be said, by a masterly stage presentation.

Of course, much could be said for a study of literature as a basis for the understanding of any particular period of history. The literature of a given age reflects it perfectly. Who cannot recognize the writings of the Victorian Age? And if one would get the feel of the hectic twenties, just before the great depression, he need only read the novels of the times. There is much to be said for the current resurgence of interest in the great epochal books as reflected in the widespread Great Books courses as an educational venture. Much of the history of the world can be understood through this approach to history; and this is to say also that man, in this our own day, can better understand himself and his own day as he sees how his own problems were met by men of an earlier day.

Great literature, then, forms a most important part of the cultural heritage of any age. But what shall be meant by such a term? What constitutes great literature? It is instructive to ask a group of people, a class for example, to list what they consider the ten greatest books in the world. Sometimes the writer has made this a class assignment. Usually he has asked each member of the class to state specifically his criteria of greatness, and then to pick out those that rank highest on this basis. What a variety of criteria! and what a varied list of books! Of course, there is no one single authoritative criterion, or a definitive ten greatest. Shall greatness be judged by literary style, size of circulation, influence, depth, emotional power, what? Lists of the greatest have varied all the way from *Gone with the Wind* to Hans Andersen's *Fairy Tales*, to Karl Marx's *Das Kapital*, to Plato's *Republic*, to *In His Steps* by Charles M. Sheldon. Almost always Shakespeare appears in the lists. And unless instructions have been given deliberately to omit all sacred writings, one or more of the great Bibles of the world are likely to appear.

Without here attempting to define fully what is meant by "great literature," at least these qualities usually are found to appear in the discussion of what is agreed upon as great if not the greatest literature: It must have unusual power to stimulate readers to thought, feeling or action; it must be in some sense universal in its appeal. By this is not meant that every person can read it; for obviously Plato's *Republic* is not for popular reading, nor is *Das Capital*, nor Bacon's *Novum Organum*. But it is meant that to people of requisite mental capacity to read and appreciate it, a work of this character makes its appeal across boundaries of race, nation, and language, and likewise across the barriers of time. That is to say, there is a timeless, spaceless quality about really great literature that makes its appeal to men of every age and of every race who are capable of understanding it. It is no accident that Shakespeare is translated into most of the major languages of the world, because the characters that stalk through his plays, though they wear the costumes of Englishman, Italian, Dane, or Jew, are timeless human figures whose loves, hates, ambitions, fears, weaknesses, courage, and heroism are those of every man. In the end it is the ability of a work to "find" men, wherever or whenever they live, that makes it truly great.

It is the presence, in large measure, of this quality, in the Bibles of the world, which places them securely among the great literatures of the world. It is for this reason that they deserve to be read much more widely than they are today. To be sure, the Christian Bible is the most widely circulated book in the world. If circulation were to be made the test of greatness, it would unquestionably top all the rest and stand as the greatest of all time. It has been translated in whole or in part into more languages than any other book. A few years ago when the number of languages into which it had been rendered was approaching the one thousand mark, it was decided to publish a volume in celebration of that event, to be called *The Book of a Thousand Tongues,* based doubtless upon the old hymn, "O, for a thousand tongues to sing my great Redeemer's praise." But before the book reached the publication stage in 1938, the number of languages was one thousand and eighteen. Today it is eleven or twelve hundred. A list of these languages runs all the way from Latin, through German, Ancient Armenian, Bengali, Inpougme Dmyene, Koi Gondi, Mopudungu, to Luolaba Ngwana. At the same time it was estimated that there yet remained five hundred to a thousand other language groups spoken by substantial numbers of people into which translations should be made, and many of them will be. The story of these translations is one of the most romantic ever told. Fascinating beyond words, for example, is the story of John Paton's translation into the Tonga tongue. Starting with no grammar or dictionary, indeed not one written word to aid them, missionaries have learned the oral language, often without benefit of any interpreter—definitely the hard way—worked out an alphabet, reduced it to writing, prepared a grammar and dictionary, translated some portions into the newly written tongue, then had to teach the natives to read their own language in order to read the Bible.

The number of Bibles or portions thereof—sometimes the Old Testament, sometimes the New, sometimes the New Testament and Psalms, or just the Psalms, or perhaps the four gospels, or more often only some one of the gospels—that circulate every year is almost incredible. Last year it reached the total of twenty-eight millions. Now this, of course, is done to a considerable extent by great Bible societies who act for the churches—one of the early inter-denominational activities of the various divisions of the church. That the Bible would circulate in such vast numbers without this world-wide activity in its behalf may be open to question. Bibles are produced cheaply, are sold at very low prices, often below cost, and are frequently given away. This is an advantage which most other books of large circulation do not enjoy. It may therefore be asked whether it is the merit of the Bible which secures for it so over-whelming a circulation over that of other books. However, a prior question is, Why do people feel it incumbent upon them to give of their money, time, and effort to secure its distribution? Evidently, they have found in it values which they prize beyond words, and are glad to share it with those who do not know it.

But the true test of its greatness is that, into whatever language it is translated, it has a message for the people which they can understand and which, in constantly increasing numbers, they ac-cept. The timeless, spaceless qualities of this book have a universal appeal to peoples at every stage of culture when it is made available to them. It speaks, of course, the language of the universal human heart, so it speaks to every man.

But if this may be said about the Hebrew-Christian Bible, some-thing of the same kind can be said about the other great Bibles of the world. Not everything that is found in them is of the same high order, of course, but this could likewise be said of the Christian Bible. There is much in it that is dated, or that is applicable to a particular people; for example, some of the legal lore in Leviticus, or a detailed description of the tabernacle or the temple. But each of the great scriptures contains some—some more, some less—time-less passages which speak to peoples of widely different ages and cultural backgrounds. They, too, deserve to be better known. And certainly a knowledge of them is a vast help in understanding the people who have been nourished upon them and hold them sacred;

for example, the sacred writings of Japan. Had Western nations been better acquainted with them, they might have understood the Japanese people better, and there might then have been no Pearl Harbor tragedy!

What constitutes sacred literature? How does it differ from ordinary literature? Well, first of all, not in its being religious. For there is much religious literature that is not regarded as sacred; and a great deal of the content of so-called sacred literature is not necessarily directly religious at all, though indirectly it is usually in some way linked up with religion. In sacred literatures are found history, legislation, poetry, letters, fables, myths, drama, genealogies, prophecy, visions, laments, martial songs, indeed almost the whole gamut of literary variety is to be found. Often specific passages taken out of their setting would bear no marks of religion or of sacredness, yet the whole has somehow come to be regarded as sacred. In what way this has come about we shall attempt to see in later chapters. There are several marks of sacred, as against general, literature.

First, sacred literatures are, as a usual rule, regarded as in some sense the word of God or the gods, revealed to man. In other words, to use the technical term employed commonly by scholars, they are regarded as "inspired" books. The degree of inspiration, or the nature of it, varies among the religions and within any given faith. Sometimes the words of the sacred text are thought to be the very words of God himself, *ipsissima verba*, the human element in the situation being merely instrumental. Verbal inspiration is believed to be infallible, letter for letter, word for word, perfect. This is a belief found among Fundamentalist Christians, Orthodox Jews, Moslems, Hindus of some schools, and others, with reference to their scriptures or at least certain parts of them. This will appear in greater detail in connection with each separate scripture. Sometimes the inspiration is of less absolute character, human men or women who are filled with the divine spirit interpret the will of God, but not infallibly; and sometimes there is no definite theory of inspiration, but the belief exists that in some way the writings do express the will of God. Men were inspired, just as poets write under some kind of inspiration, and in the intrinsic values communicated through the writings lies the evidence of divine inspiration. All alike, however, of the sacred scriptures purport to be in some degree divine in origin.

As a natural corollary of this view, sacred literatures stand in a class apart from other literature. Since they are of divine origin, they are not treated in the same way that other literatures are treated. They are inviolable. Other literature may be studied critically, every method of literary analysis and criticism may be employed, but not so in the case of the sacred. What a furore was created when first, under the influence of the scientific spirit of the times, men began to study the Bible critically just like any other book. It seemed to many to be sacrilege to apply the ordinary canons of historical and literary criticism to the Bible, and to many even yet this is the case. Especially the so-called "higher criticism," which was nothing but the application of the historico-literary critical method to Biblical study, drew the fire of defenders of the faith who believed it an attempt to destroy the Bible. In Japan when certain modern scholars undertook to study their sacred books upon which was founded the belief in the divine descent of the royal house, they were summarily dismissed from their university teaching positions, and so elsewhere.

Second, being the word of God, the sacred scriptures became the foundations upon which the several religions were erected. They are the authoritative sources from which the truths held by the various faiths are drawn. They became the basis of the organization and teachings of the respective religions. To know what is true or required by God, one must go to the scriptures. If support for a given idea can be found in the Bible, it suffices. Proving something by the Bible is a familiar technique in most religions. A good example in Christianity is the Westminster Confession, the declaration of faith of Presbyterians, where one or more scripture texts are cited in support of every detailed affirmation of belief. Conservative Christians make much use of the proof-text method, e.g., Jehovah's Witnesses. Taking five pages at random in one of their widely circulated books, I found that the author had averaged five scriptural citations per page. This is not unusual. Taking a Moslem book from one of my shelves, I discovered about the same frequency of use of Moslem scripture.

Of course, every religion has within it a variety of attitudes toward scripture. Some hold that there is but one proper interpreter of the Bible, e.g., the Roman Catholic Church. Others, like Protestantism, allow the individual freedom in its interpretation; but in some sense, among all it is the sacred scripture to which appeal must be made if one desires to know the truth. This differentiates sacred literatures from most other types of literature.

Third, the scriptures are almost always strictly limited. Only certain books are regarded as sacred and authoritative. To these nothing can be added, nor may anything be taken away. The word used to describe this limited set of writings is "canon." Most religions have a sacred canon. Non-canonical books may be of great value, but they have not the same authority or value as the canonical. For example, the Bible as held by Protestant Christians contains sixty-six books, no more, no less. Catholic Christianity adds a few books, called "Apocrypha" by Protestants; but for each division of Christianity its sacred list is irrevocably fixed. Sometimes Protestants have wanted to exclude some books. Martin Luther thought that Esther had no proper place in Holy Writ, but not even so powerful a figure as Luther could dislodge a book from the canon. How canons are determined will be described in the case of each religion, but once fixed they are not subject to change. The existence of a sacred canon, then, is peculiar to sacred literature.

Fourth, although there is a fixed canon in most religions, it is also true that there is often a body of supplementary literature which, while theoretically less sacred, does nevertheless constitute a highly important source of direction for faith and practice. Usually these are regarded as simply extensions of the really sacred books, although in actual fact they may add to or modify in no small degree the content of the canonical books. An example here is the Jewish Talmud, which among Orthodox Jewish Rabbis requires far more study than does the Old Testament itself. Among Moslems, the Traditions are of enormous importance. Other examples will appear in connection with the study of the separate scriptures.

To sum up, sacred literature is distinguished from the non-sacred, not by any criteria of style, literary form, or even content, but by the fact that in some way or other it has come to be thought of as divine in origin, and therefore set apart from other literatures and given an authority for faith and life quite surpassing that accorded to any other writings. Supplemented it may be by other literature, but it stands apart, sacred, relatively inviolable, abiding, unchanged across the centuries as the basis of religious faith and practice, as do no other writings.

Not all the literatures studied in this book fulfill all these conditions, notably the Chinese who do not attribute their authoritative writings to divine origin, but in most other respects they are like the rest. We turn now to see how scriptures arise. We can best do this by looking at what we like to call the pre-literate sacred scriptures.

CHAPTER II

Pre-literate Sacred Scriptures

Not all religions have a body of sacred scriptures such as that described in the preceding chapter, not even all of those which had reached the stage of writing. For example, neither the Greeks nor the Romans, the Egyptians nor the Babylonians—all highly literate cultures—had what may be termed sacred books with a definitely limited canon, held to be the exclusive basis of religious faith. But they did all of them have writings which corresponded closely to various portions of sacred books as found in other religions. These were never collected, regarded as of divine origin and hence as the basis of the several religions. Why this was may be conjectured, but perhaps never certainly known. To this question we shall recur later.

And of course those religions which had not achieved the art of writing had, in a strict sense, no fixed sacred book. But even here there existed all the "makings" of sacred literature, and in some cases they had gone far toward collecting these materials and handing them on verbally from generation to generation. It is amazing what a mass of material can be preserved in the human memory and passed down for centuries by word of mouth.

We may look for a moment at the Bible, our best-known scripture, to see of what it is composed. We discover there the story of

10

the beginnings of the world, the creation of man, the explanation of the origin of many of his institutions; the history or legends of the ancestors of the Hebrew people, the stories of their kings and heroes, the laws by which they lived and whence they were derived; their martial songs of victory and lament over failure; the prescriptions for the cult practices; prayers for help and thanksgiving, for vengeance on enemies; their explanation of suffering; tales for moral instruction; stirring prophecies, their dreams of a future in this life and beyond—all this and very much more. Is there anything like this to be found among pre-literate peoples? The answer is "Yes," almost everything.

Before a sacred literature of the kind we know emerges, many conditions must be fulfilled.

First of all, there must be a relatively long tribal history during which legends may grow up, institutions arise, religious faith take form, and the emergence of a desire to perpetuate this by transmitting it verbally to succeeding generations. Then the art of writing must be developed. This is a long, slow process. But even this is not enough. Many peoples that have reached this stage have left us no sacred literature because they wrote on easily destructible materials which have not survived the vicissitudes of time. Only those who discovered an enduring medium on which to write are known to us today, and there are very few such media. Stop and reflect on how little that is being written today is upon durable materials. Paper is highly destructible. Even the rag-paper editions of newspapers disintegrate in a comparatively short time, and wood-pulp papers are very soon gone. It may be that some durable kind of film will be elaborated on which, in microfilm form, books may be produced and preserved; but so far the film that is used requires very favorable conditions of storage if it is to endure. Perhaps of all materials that have been used, hard stone is the most enduring, though even this is subject to destructive erosion if exposed to wind and weather. Very little, except inscriptions on monuments, is being written on stone today, and even stone inscriptions are highly vulnerable in a climate such as ours in the United States. We shall see later how Egypt was favored in this respect by her climate.

Or again, even when writing has been achieved, and on durable materials, military conquest may destroy what has for long endured. Conquerors are often highly destructive. Here an eloquent example is the conquest of Mexico by the Spaniards. The Aztecs had achieved a high stage of culture. They had learned to write in hieroglyphic form, and there existed at the time of the conquest a vast body of writing, as well as stone carvings, but it was almost entirely destroyed. Eager missionaries, fearful that the memory of the old gods of Mexico might be kept alive if the writings which pictured them were preserved, destroyed almost all the books, or codices as they were called, and for the few that remain, the clue to their understanding no longer exists. Fortunately, some of their ideas were preserved by the ancient padres, so that we can see that there did exist among them not a little of the sort of writing which appears in the sacred books of other peoples.

In the modern age an interest has been awakened in the study of existing lower cultures, and as a result much of their legendary lore, their songs, their rituals, their laws, are being translated into modern languages and published. These materials, that would otherwise have been irrevocably lost, are preserved and made available to students of culture. In the United States, for example, recordings have been taken of the songs of the Indians, and the stories are told by native story tellers in their own tongue, then translated. We have thus done for the Indians what they could not, or might never have done, for themselves. In so doing we have discovered a vast wealth of beauty and wisdom which we had hardly thought to find among backward peoples. We have found almost every element that goes into the making of sacred scriptures. Much the same thing has been done for the African peoples, the South Pacific Islanders, and other relatively primitive peoples. It will be worthwhile looking at some of this material, as a phase of what we call pre-literary sacred literature.

Look, first of all, at the creation story as told by various peoples. The Omaha Tribe of American Indians described it thus in what seems a veritable first chapter of Genesis:

At the beginning all things were in the mind of Wakonda. All creatures, including man, were spirits. They moved about in space between the earth and the stars. They were seeking a place where they could come into a bodily existence.

They ascended to the sun, but the sun was not fitted for their abode. They moved on to the moon and found that it also was not good for their home. Then they descended to the earth. They saw that it was covered with water.

They floated through the air to the north, the east, the south, and the west, and found no dry land. They were sorely grieved. Suddenly from the midst of the water uprose a great rock. It burst into flames and the waters floated into the air in clouds.

Dry land appeared; the grasses and the trees grew. The hosts of spirits descended and became flesh and blood. They fed on the seeds and grasses and the fruits of the trees, and the land vibrated with their expressions of joy and gratitude to Wakonda, the Maker of all things.[1]

The Maoris of New Zealand have a creation poem which details the creative activity through six successive periods. It is in part as follows. (The explanatory phrases inserted within the poem are the work of the transcriber, not a part of the creation poem itself.)

The first period may be styled the epoch of thought—

From the conception the increase,
From the increase the swelling,
From the swelling the thought,
From the thought the remembrance,
From the remembrance the consciousness, the desire.

The second period is that of night or darkness—

The word became fruitful;
It dwelt with the feeble glimmering;
It brought forth night:
The great night, the long night,
The lowest night, the loftiest night,
The thick night, to be felt

[1] Alice C. Fletcher, *27th Annual Report of the Bureau of American Ethnology,* p. 571.

The night to be touched, the night unseen,
The night following on,
The night ending in death.

This, we are told, is all we have to do with night; during these periods there was no light—there were no eyes to the world.

The third period is that of light—

From the nothing the begetting,
From the nothing the increase,
From the nothing the abundance,
The power of increasing, the living breath;
It dwelt with the empty space,
It produced the atmosphere which is above us.

The fourth period, the creation of the moon and sun—

The atmosphere which floats above the earth.
The great firmament above us,
　　　the spread out space dwelt with the early dawn,
Then the moon sprung forth;
The atmosphere above dwelt with
　　　the glowing sky,
Forthwith was produced the sun,
They were thrown up above as the chief
　　　eyes of Heaven:
Then the Heavens became light,
The early dawn, the early day, the mid-day,
　　　The blaze of day from the sky.

The fifth period, the creation of land—

The sky which floats above the earth,
Dwelt with Hawaiki,
And produced
　　Taporapora,
Tauware nikau and Kukupara,
Wawauatea and Wiwhi te rangiora.[2]

The sixth period contains the formation of gods and men.

[2] Richard Taylor, *New Zealand and Its Inhabitants*, London: William Mac-Intosh, 24, Paternoster Row, n.d., pp. 109–111.

Earth Magician makes the mountains.
    Heed what he has to say!
He it is that makes the mesas.
    Heed what he has to say.
Earth Magician shapes this world;
    Earth Magician makes its mountains;
Makes all larger, larger, larger.

Into the earth the Magician glances;
    Into its mountains he may see.

I have made the Sun!
    I have made the Sun!
Hurling it high
    In the four directions.
To the East I threw it
    To run its appointed course.

I have made the Moon!
    I have made the Moon!
Hurling it high
    In the four directions.
To the East I threw it
    To run its appointed course.

I have made the Stars!
    I have made the Stars!
Above the earth I threw them.
    All things above I've made
And placed them to illumine.[6]

No people is without its proverbial wisdom, which gathers up in brief, pointed, epigrammatic fashion the accumulated wisdom of its past. Anonymous, for the most part, these sayings sometimes may be attributed, as in the case of Proverbs in the Bible, to some famous wise man of the tribe. Here are a few, for example, from the Omaha American Indians. If it be remarked that these are not

[6] Frank Russell, *26th Annual Report of the Bureau of American Ethnology,* p. 272.

religious in character, the same may be said of many Biblical Proverbs. A casual glance reveals that in five of the first fifteen chapters of the Book of Proverbs, there is no direct religious reference. Much of that book is made up of plain, common-sense advice concerning conduct, without appeals to any non-human sanction, though of course this may well have been taken for granted, so permeated was the whole of Israel's life with the sense of dependence upon God.

Among the Omaha Indians these sayings are in common use:

Totem food never satisfies hunger.

A poor man is a hard rider.

All persons dislike a borrower.

No one mourns the thriftless.

The path of the lazy leads to disgrace.

A man must make his own arrows.

A handsome face does not make a good husband.[7]

Here are some examples from Surinam folklore:

When you eat with the devil, then you must have a long fork.

A bad name is a woman's winding sheet.

The inquisitive sheep is the tiger's food.

Faces were there before mirrors.

Cunning is more than strength.[8]

[7] From Alice Fletcher, *The Omaha Tribe*, Bureau of American Ethnology, Vol. 27, p. 604.
[8] M. J. and Frances Herskovitz, *Surinam Folklore*, Columbia University Press, New York, 1936, pp. 455 ff.

These are proverbs of the Saramacca Bush-Negroes:

Hide today's anger until tomorrow.

Still water has a deep bottom.

If you love the bud, you must love the fruit too.

When a child does evil, you should forgive him.[9]

Some peoples have a memory of a long migration before reaching their permanent home, very much as in the Old Testament is recorded the migration under divine direction of Abraham who went out, he knew not whither, and his descendants. An interesting record is that of the wanderings of the Nahua tribes of Mexico who came out of some not certainly known region of the Northwest into the Valley of Mexico to found the great Aztec Empire. So much did these wanderings resemble those of Israel that one of the early Franciscan Fathers wrote this of them:

They affirm that it was this idol that had commanded them to leave their own country, promising them that they would be the rulers and the chiefs of all the provinces which had been settled by the other six tribes; of a land greatly abounding in gold, silver, precious stones, feathers, and rich shawls, and every costly thing conceivable. . . .

Thus did the Mexicans set out, just as the children of Israel had done, in search of the promised land, taking with them their idol enclosed in an ark, made of rushes, just as the others had taken with them their Ark of the Covenant. They took along with them four principal priests, who made their laws and instructed them in their rites, and ceremonies and in the most superstitious, cruel, and bloody sacrifices ever known, as will be seen farther on in this account, where the sacrifices are described in detail. Under no conditions did the Mexicans ever move an inch without the advice and command of this idol. . . .

The first thing they did whenever they wished to stop at a particular place, was to erect a tabernacle or temple to their false god for the duration of the time they expected to stay there, and they built this temple in the middle of the site on which they had established themselves, the ark being placed upon an altar such as is used in a church, for the idol

[9] *Id.*, pp. 475–481, *passim.*

wished to imitate our religion in many ways, as we shall afterwards show.[10]

But the Nahuas, quite like the Hebrews, were willful and did not always heed the directions given them by their divine guide:

The Mexicans, quite oblivious to what their idol had told them, namely that this place was merely an imitation and pattern of the land they were to be given, stayed in this delightful place (a long time) and began to feel that it was quite satisfactory, some even saying that they desired to stay there permanently, and that this was really the place selected by their god Huitzilopochtli; that it was from that place that they were all to follow their desires, being the rulers of the four parts of the world, etc.

Their idol, seeing this, waxed so angry that he said to the priests, "Who are these who thus wish to transgress and put obstacles in the way of my orders and commands? Are they perhaps greater than myself? Tell them that I will take vengeance before tomorrow and that they should not dare to give advice about matters which are for me to determine. Let them know that all they have to do is to obey."

Having said this, those who saw assert that the idol looked so ugly and frightful, that all were terrified and frightened. On that very night, it is said, when everything was quiet, a loud noise was heard in part of the camp and when the people rushed there in the morning, they found that all those who had spoken in favor of remaining in this place were dead with their breasts torn open and their hearts torn out. In this way it was that they were taught that most cruel of sacrifices, a custom they always practiced after that, which consisted of cutting open a man's chest in order to tear out his heart and offer it to their idols.[11]

The bitter lesson taught them,

. . . On the following night Huitzilopochtli appeared in a dream to one of his ministers and said, "Now you are satisfied that I have not told you anything that did not turn out to be truthful and you have seen the thing that I promised you would find in the place where I was going to take you. . . .

"Go there in the morning and you will find the beautiful eagle on the

[10] Paul Radin, *The Sources and Authenticity of the History of the Ancient Mexicans,* Berkeley, California: University of California Press, 1920, p. 71.

[11] *Ibid.,* pp. 73, 74.

nopal tree and around it you will see a great quantity of green, red, yellow, and white feathers of the elegant birds on which the eagle sustains himself. To this place, where you will find the *nopal* with the eagle above it, I have given the name Tenochtitlan."[12]

On the morning of the following day the priest had all the people, old and young, men, women, and children, gathered together, and standing before them he began to tell them about the revelation he had received, dwelling on the great manifestations of regard and the many acts of kindness they had received day after day from their god. After a long harangue he concluded, saying, "The site of this *nopal* will be the place of our happiness, peace, and rest. Here we will increase in numbers and add prestige to the name of the Mexican people. From this home of ours, shall be known the force of our valorous arms and courage; our undaunted hearts by means of which we shall conquer all the nations and countries in the world, subjecting even the remotest provinces and cities, extending our rule from sea to sea.". . .

Proceeding in this way they finally came to the site of the *nopal* on top of which was perched the eagle with wings spread out to the rays of the sun, absorbing its heat and holding in its claws a gorgeous bird that had very precious and gleaming feathers. When they beheld this, they knelt down and did reverence as to a divine object. The eagle saw them and he also knelt, lowering his head in the direction in which he saw them. When they noticed that the eagle was kneeling before them having now seen what they had so earnestly desired, they all began to weep and utter shouts of joy and happiness. Then as an expression of gratitude they exclaimed, "How have we merited this? Who is it who has made us worthy of so much excellence, greatness, and grace? We have beheld that which we so earnestly desired and we have now obtained that which we were seeking. We have found our city, our abode. Let us give thanks to the lord of creation and to our god Huitzilopochtli."[13]

Is it not strikingly like the story of Israel? Indeed, some believe that it was the Hebrew story learned from the Spaniards which led them to recast their legends in this fashion. But this is by no means certain.

Almost every people has its prayers and rituals for use in the cult. These become fixed and formal and are handed down from genera-

---

[12] *Ibid.*, p. 79.
[13] *Ibid.*, p. 80.

tion to generation. Some of them are of singular beauty. They form part of what may correspond to the Hebrew Psalms. Here for example is a prayer of the Omahas. On the eighth day after the birth of a child, the Omaha priest chanted it at the door of the tent where the child lay:

> Ho! Ye Sun, Moon, Stars, all ye that
>   move in the heavens,
>   I bid you hear me!
> Into your midst has come a new life.
>   Consent ye, I implore!
> Make its path smooth, that it may reach
>   the brow of the first hill!
>
> Ho! Ye Winds, Clouds, Rain, Mist, all ye
>   that move in the air,
>   I bid ye hear me!
> Into your midst has come a new life.
>   Consent ye, I implore!
> Make its path smooth, that it may reach the
>   brow of the second hill!
>
> Ho! Ye Hills, Valleys, Rivers, Lakes, Trees,
>   Graces, all ye of the earth,
>   I bid you hear me!
> Into your midst has come a new life.
>   Consent ye, I implore!
> Make its path smooth, that it may reach the
>   crown of the third hill!
>
> Ho! Ye Birds, great and small, that fly
>   in the air,
> Ho! Ye Animals, great and small, that dwell
>   in the forest,
> Ho! Ye Insects that creep among the grasses
>   and burrow in the ground,
>   I bid you hear me!
> Into your midst has come a new life.
>   Consent ye, I implore!

Make its path smooth, that it may reach the
brow of the fourth hill!

Ho! All ye of the heavens, all ye of the air,
all ye of the earth,
I bid you all to hear me,
Into your midst has come a new life.
Consent ye, consent ye all, I implore!
Make its path smooth—then shall it travel
beyond the four hills![14]

The Haida Indians of Queen Charlotte's Island, B.C., in the
Pacific Northwest pray earnestly to the Sun for good weather, because upon it depend the hunting and fishing. They also petition
for peace within the tribe and with all enemies:

O good Sun,
Look thou down upon us:
Shine, shine on us, O sun,
Gather up the clouds, wet, black, under thy arms—
That the rains may cease to fall.
Because thy friends are all here on the beach
Ready to go fishing—
Ready for the hunt.
Therefore look kindly on us, O Good Sun!
Give us peace within our tribe
And with all our enemies.
Again, again, we call—
Hear us, hear us, O Good Sun![15]

The Hako, an elaborate Pawnee ceremony, contains a number of
fine prayers and hymns. The first two are to "Our Father, the
Sun":

Father, unto thee we cry;
Father thou of gods and men;
Father thou of all we hear;
Father thou of all we see;
Father, unto thee we cry.

[14] Alice Fletcher, *op. cit.,* p. 115.
[15] George W. Cronyn, *The Path on the Rainbow,* pp. 158–159.

> Father! Thou above, father of gods,
> They who can come near and touch us,
> Do thou bid them bring us help.
> Help we need. Father, hear us![16]

An expression of gratitude to Mother Earth, reminiscent of some of the Hebrew Psalms of Thanksgiving, forms a part of the Hako:

> Behold! Our Mother Earth is lying here.
> Behold! She giveth of her fruitfulness.
> Truly, her power gives she us.
> Give thanks to Mother Earth who lieth here.
>
> Behold on Mother Earth the growing fields!
> Behold the promise of her fruitfulness!
> Truly, her power gives she us.
> Give thanks to Mother Earth who lieth here.
>
> Behold on Mother Earth the spreading trees!
> Behold the promise of her fruitfulness!
> Truly, her power gives she us.
> Give thanks to Mother Earth who lieth here.
>
> We see on Mother Earth the running streams;
> We see the promise of her fruitfulness.
> Truly, her power gives she us.
> Our thanks to Mother Earth who lieth here![17]

In an Iroquois ritual of fire and darkness, the note of thanksgiving is also struck and an offering is made. In the presence of a certain society among them, the medicine man throws a bit of sacred tobacco on the altar fire and chants in a low voice:

> Great Spirit who puts us to sleep in darkness,
> We thank thee for the silences of darkness.
> (Singer)
> Now I ask blessing and make prayers.
> (He sprinkles sacred tobacco on the fire.

[16] Alice Fletcher, Bureau of American Ethnology, Vol. 22, part 2, p. 334.
[17] *Ibid.*, p. 335.

Then he speaks to the Invisible):
Now I give you tobacco,
You, the great Darkness!
(To the Thunder Spirit)
Now we act as we offer you tobacco!
You love it most of all offerings.
With it you will hear us better
And not tire of our talking
But love us with all power
Beyond all treasures
Or spreading of words through the air!
All men traveling under great heaven,
You have invited, your grandchildren and all nations;
Oh you, maker of noise,
You, the great Thunderer!
Your grandchildren wish to thank you!
All your grandchildren have asked me
To offer this tobacco upon the mountain to you!
(Speaking to the Great Spirit)
You the All-maker,
Above-all-high
Best Friend of people!
We ask you to help us!
We implore your favor!
I have spoken.
(The lights are extinguished, leaving the assembly in
total darkness.)[18]

To Huitzilopochtli, mighty war god of the Aztecs, their leader
to the promised land, a typical hymn is sung:

1. Huitzilopochtli is first in rank, no one, no one is like unto him: not
vainly do I sing (his praises), coming forth in the garb of our ancestors;
I shine: I glitter.

2. He is a terror to the Mixteca; he alone destroyed the Picha-
Huasteca, he conquered them.

3. The Dart-Hurler is an example to the city, as he sets to work. He
who commands in battle is called the representative of my God.

[18] George W. Cronyn, *The Path on the Rainbow*, p. 7.

4. When he shouts aloud he inspires great terror, the divine hurler, the god turning himself in the combat, the divine hurler, the god turning himself in the combat.

5. Amanteca, gather yourselves together with me in the house of war against your enemies, gather yourselves together with me.

6. Pipiteca, gather yourselves together with me in the house of war against your enemies, gather yourselves together with me.[19]

To the Mother of Gods, Teotenantzin, a divinity much adored by the Aztecs long before the coming of the Europeans, obviously a goddess of fertility who dwelt of old on the precise hill where the Virgin of Guadalupe later appeared to Juan Diego, is addressed the following hymn:

1. Hail to our mother, who caused the yellow flowers to blossom, who scattered the seeds of the maguey, as she came forth from Paradise.

2. Hail to our mother, who poured forth flowers in abundance, who scattered the seeds of the maguey, as she came forth from Paradise.

3. Hail to our mother, who caused the yellow flowers to blossom, she who scattered the seeds of the maguey, as she came forth from Paradise.

4. Hail to our mother, who poured forth white flowers in abundance, who scattered the seeds of the maguey, as she came forth from Paradise.

5. Hail to the goddess who shines in the thorn bush like a bright butterfly.

6. Ho! she is our mother, goddess of the earth, she supplies food in the desert to the wild beasts, and causes them to live.

7. Thus, thus, you see her to be an ever-fresh model of liberality toward all flesh.

8. And as you see the goddess of the earth do to the wild beasts, so also does she toward the green herbs and the fishes.[20]

The Zuñi Indians of Arizona have some magnificent hymns. One of the most noteworthy is this hymn to the sun. Of course, all these come to us through the medium of a translator, and one may not know whether it has gained or lost in the process of translation. At all events, here it is definitely beautiful:

[19] Daniel G. Brinton, *Rig Veda Americanus*, Philadelphia: D. G. Brinton, 1890, pp. 16–17.
[20] *Ibid.*, pp. 28–29.

Early in the morning,
We waken, we waken.
When mother Sun-god rises,
We welcome her with joy.
She greets us with a radiant face,
She meets us with a warm embrace,
So sweetly, so sweetly.
Merrily we sing and dance;
In happy spirit we advance;
Merrily we sing and dance;
In happy spirit we advance.
We are children of the sun,
Arm in arm together run,
Round a ring we steady move:
Our hearts will faithful prove,
As the sun comes near to us,
Near to us, near to us.
Listen! just listen!

What a wondrous shower of sounds,
Countless beats in rapid rounds,
Ever changing, ever new,
Constant strains of high and low.
They are messengers of love,
Spirit voices from above,
Bringing light and life and joy
Telling us of bliss on high,
Listen! just listen!

Whence come all these distant sounds?
Echoes, where the light abounds:
Crystal streams in murmurs faint,
Bursting forth without restraint.
They are golden grains of thought,
Silent whispers faintly caught,
Filling us with joy content,
Pathways of our souls' ascent,
Souls' ascent, souls' ascent.
Listen! just listen!

Glory to the sunlight rays,
Glory to the Sun-god's ways,
Sunlight rays, Sun-god's ways.
They command us: to endure,
To be silent, chaste and pure,
To be faithful, true and brave,
To the laws our fathers gave.
O harken to the Sun-god's voice
Beckoning your soul to rise:
In radiant light, the source of song,
The origin of thought has sprung:
As light and song in one unite,
Let us forever seek the light,
We seek the light, we seek the light.
Listen! just listen![21]

A Polynesian divinity, Lono, is approached with a sacrifice by the priest, chanting:

Oh Lono, of the blue firmament!
Here are vegetables, here is meat,
An offering of prayer, a sacrifice,
An offering of fat things to you, Oh Lono!
Let the crops flourish in this ahu-puaa (district)!

The following quotations reveal the fact that Lono, the god of crops, was a rain god:

Send gracious showers of rain, Oh Lono.
Life-giving rain, a grateful gift,
Symbols of Lono's blessing. . . .

Oh Lono, of the broad leaf,
Let the low-hanging cloud pour out its rain,
To make the crops flourish,
Rain to make the tapa-plants flourish,
Wring out the dark rain-clouds
Oh Lono in the heavens.[22]

[21] "Awakening at Dawn," from *Traditional Songs of the Zuñi*, by Carlos Troyer; published by Theodore Presser Co.; used by permission.
[22] Handy, *op. cit.*, pp. 110–111.

Now and then there is a song which seems to be individual just as some of the Hebrew Psalms are, and registers some profound experience or hope or aspiration. One wonders in the following, which is called a ritual song of the Pawnees, what has happened between the first and second stanzas:

> I know not if the voice of man can reach to the sky;
> I know not if the mighty one will hear as I pray;
> I know not if the gifts I ask will all granted be;
> I know not if the word of old we truly can hear;
> I know not what will come to pass in our future days;
> I hope that only good will come, my children, to you.
>
> I now know that the voice of man can reach the sky;
> I now know that the mighty one has heard as I prayed;
> I now know that the gifts I asked have all granted been.
> I now know that the word of old we truly have heard;
> I now know that *Tira wa* hearkens unto man's prayers;
> I know that only good has come, my children, to you.[23]

No more poignant human utterance is to be found anywhere than in the "Lament of a Man for his Son." The most remarkable thing about the song is its origin. It is a Paiute Indian who sings it; and in all the literature about Indians, none is represented as more "ornery" than the Paiute. But it is the father-heart of humanity that we hear echoing David's lament over Absalom:

> Son, my son!
> I will go up to the mountain
> And there I will light a fire
> To the feet of my son's spirit,
> And there will I lament him;
> Saying,
> O my son,
> What is my life to me, now you are departed!
>
> Son, my son,
> In the deep earth

---

[23] Alice Fletcher, *Bureau of American Ethnology*, Vol. 22, pp. 343–344.

We softly laid thee
In a Chief's robe,
In a warrior's gear.
Surely there,
In the spirit land
Thy deeds attend thee!

Surely,
The corn comes to the ear again!
But I, here,
I am the stalk that the seed-gatherers
Descrying empty, afar, left standing.
Son, my son!
What is my life to me, now you are departed?[24]

These all too few illustrations of the psalm literature of the pre-literate groups of the world do not register the full height nor breadth nor depth of that vast unwritten sea of song and prayer. It may well be said here that we have gleaned the best; much is repetitious, meaningless (to us at least), superstitious, crude, even savage and licentious, but if God is where the Good, the True, the Beautiful are found, who can deny that among these people there were those who saw something of His face as they "sought after if haply they might find him?"

It is not unusual to find among non-literate people, as among the literate, a feeling of world-weariness or disillusionment, and despair. Some of them, like the ancient Babylonians, developed a *carpe diem* philosophy; others found nothing to lighten their melancholy. From Mexico come some excellent examples of this type of literature, not unlike the book of Ecclesiastes in the Bible. Two or three of these must suffice.

1. Weeping, I, the singer, weave my song of flowers of sadness; I call to memory the youths, the shards, the fragments, gone to the land of the dead; once noble and powerful here on earth, the youths were dried up like feathers, were split into fragments like an emerald, before the face

---

[24] From *The American Rhythm* by Mary Austin, 1923. Used by permission of Houghton Mifflin Co.

and in the sight of those who saw them on earth, and with the knowledge of the Cause of All.

2. Alas! alas! I sing in grief as I recall the children. Would that I could turn back again; would that I could grasp their hands once more; would that I could call them forth from the land of the dead; would that we could bring them again on earth, that they might rejoice and delight the Giver of Life; is it possible that we His servants should reject him or should be ungrateful? Thus I weep in my heart as I, the singer, review my memories, recalling things sad and grievous.

3. Would only that I knew they could hear me, there in the land of the dead, were I to sing some worthy song. Would that I could gladden them, that I could console the suffering and the torment of the children. How can it be learned? Whence can I draw the inspiration? They are not where I may follow them; neither can I reach them with my calling as one here on earth.[25]

But perhaps the most notable example of this kind of literature is one from the great King Nezahualcoyotl, who ruled only a little while before the coming of the European conquerors. The king himself had reached nearer perhaps to a monotheistic conception of God than any of his people, but he was oppressed by the fleeting character of life, and uncertain of what lay beyond this life.

1. The fleeting pomps of the world are like the green willow trees, which aspiring to permanence, are consumed by a fire, fall before the axe, are upturned by the wind, or are scarred and saddened by age. ·

2. The grandeurs of life are like the flowers in color and in fate; the beauty of these remains so long as their chaste buds gather and store the rich pearls of the dawn and, saving it, drop it in liquid dew; but scarcely has the Cause of All directed upon them the full rays of the sun, when their beauty and glory fail, and the brilliant gay colors which decked forth their pride wither and fade.

3. The delicious realms of flowers count their dynasties by short periods; those which in the morning revel proudly in beauty and strength, by evening weep for the sad destruction of their thrones, and

[25] Daniel G. Brinton, *Ancient Nahuatl Poetry*, Philadelphia: D. G. Brinton, 1890, p. 73.

for the mishaps which drive them to loss, to poverty, to death, and to the grave. All things of earth have an end, and in the midst of the most joyous lives, the breath falters, they fall, they sink into the ground.

4. All the earth is a grave, and nought escapes it; nothing is so perfect that it does not fall and disappear.

. . . That which was yesterday is not today; and let not that which is today trust to live tomorrow.

5. The caverns of earth are filled with pestilential dust which once was the bones, the flesh, the bodies of great ones who sat upon thrones, deciding causes, ruling assemblies, governing armies, conquering provinces, possessing treasures, tearing down temples, flattering themselves with pride, majesty, fortune, praise and dominion. These glories have passed like the dark smoke thrown out by the rude skins on which they are written.

6. . . . first and last (all) are confounded in the common clay. What was their fate shall be ours, and of all who follow us.

7. Unconquered princes, warlike chieftains, let us seek, let us sigh for the heaven, for there all is eternal and nothing is corruptible. The darkness of the sepulchre is but the strengthening couch for the glorious sun, and the obscurity of the night but serves to reveal the brilliancy of the stars. No one has power to alter these heavenly lights, for they serve to display the greatness of their Creator, and as our eyes see them now, so saw them our earliest ancestors, and so shall see them our latest posterity.[26]

Nor are there lacking among most peoples some legal requirements established by the gods, as in the case of the Mosaic and Levitical law in the Bible. Hero stories abound, moral tales told for the instruction of childhood and youth are common to most cultures, but space forbids lengthening this chapter. Enough here if we have established the fact that many, if not all, peoples even at the pre-literate stage have already developed most of the kinds of material that are found in the Bibles of literate peoples. And probably it serves very much the same functions among them as do the Bibles among those whose scriptures were preserved to them in written form.

[26] *Ibid.*, pp. 45–46.

PRE-LITERATE SACRED LITERATURE
Sources for Further Reading

George W. Cronyn, *The Path on the Rainbow,* Boni and Liveright, N. Y., 1918.

Nellie Barnes, *American Indian Love Lyrics,* Macmillan Co., N. Y., 1925.

Natalie Curtis Burlin, *The Indian's Book,* Harper & Brothers, N. Y., 1907.

There is a great mass of this material scattered through the *Annual Reports of the Bureau of American Ethnology.*

See footnotes for other suggestions.

CHAPTER III

Egyptian Sacred Literature

In a strict sense, Egypt has no sacred book. The Egyptian people never reached the stage at which they formed a definitive canon of writings which served as the basis of their faith. But they did have a very extensive sacred literature which was highly influential in the expression of their faith, and to some extent in the determination of that faith. Why she never reached the point of canonization of her scripture can be a matter of conjecture only. Certainly she had materials of the sort that compose sacred scriptures in other faiths, and certainly she had a priesthood who might have been thought of as interested in crystallizing Egypt's religion by means of a preferred set of sacred books. Possibly the shifting of capitals, due to the political changes, and the corresponding shifts in the centers of religious authority, may have played some part in the prevention of the crystallization of a true sacred book.

Egypt has had perhaps as long a period of literacy as any area in the world. Even before the dynastic period she had achieved the art of writing, using the picture or hieroglyphic method. She had immediately at hand a most durable medium on which to record her thought, and both political and climatic conditions were unusually favorable to the preservation of her writings. Politically,

34

she was relatively isolated from the rest of the world for many, many centuries of her earlier history. There was a brief invasion in about 1700 B.C. by the Hyksos kings, and there were imperial wars fought with the nascent Babylonian and Assyrian empires at a later time; but few cultures have enjoyed a longer, more uninterrupted period of development than did Egypt.

Furthermore, her climate because of its extreme aridity was highly favorable to the preservation of what was written. For, of course, Egypt would be completely desert were it not for the Nile which furnishes irrigation for her fields. This climate makes anything written in Egypt almost eternal in its enduring quality, particularly if it has become covered over so as to escape the cutting effect of sand storms.

For many centuries there lay side by side in one of the famous archaeological sites two enormous obelisks, cut with great skill out of the living rock of Egypt, dressed down to the proper shape, then deeply inscribed with hieroglyphic characters. In the course of time, these were overturned and became at least partly covered by the sand. Something over seventy years ago it occurred to certain Americans to bring one of these obelisks to America so that it could be seen by those who could not make the journey to Egypt. Accordingly, at no small cost in money and effort, it was towed across the Atlantic Ocean on a specially constructed barge, unloaded, and transported through the streets of New York City on a specially built, very wide-tired truck, to its present site in Central Park near the Metropolitan Art Museum. There it was mounted, and has stood for roughly seven decades only, but already the eroding effect of cold and heat, moisture and dryness, has taken its toll, and the sharply cut figures have begun to lose their edges. It is certain that within a comparatively short time the inscription on the obelisk will become practically illegible. Meanwhile, a like monument in Egypt is said to be the same as it was the day the New York obelisk was borne away. Even writings on so perishable a medium as papyrus, the ancestor of paper, have survived for nearly three thousand years with almost no serious deterioration, a thing which could never happen in a climate like our own.

But there was a third factor which made for the preservation of Egypt's writings which must be considered; namely, the fact that much of the material was written on the inside of, or deposited within tombs. During most of Egypt's history it was customary, for important people at least, to be buried in rock-hewn tombs. On the interior walls of these burial places were carved religious texts as well as many other things that tell of the life and thought of the ancient Egyptians. Once sealed, the tombs were perhaps the least likely of all places to be disturbed, for in Egypt as elsewhere, there was a superstitious dread of the dead and anything connected with them. On the walls of some tombs were written words to this effect: "Cursed be he who does damage to this tomb." Egyptians believed very definitely in the spirit world, and only the most courageous would venture to violate such a tabu. One has only to recall the dread which modern people have of cemeteries, particularly at night, to understand how the Egyptians felt about this.

Some years ago an unusually rich find was made in the rock cliffs along the Nile Valley. It was obviously a royal tomb. Naturally there was a great deal of interest in its discovery and in its opening. The sensational press wove a fabric of unbelievable but dramatic tales about the affair. Lord Carnarvon, the financial backer of the work of excavation, was said to have been stung by something that darted out of the tomb when the closed opening was finally broken through. Much was made of the fact that on the face of the mummy there was a mark similar to that on Lord Carnarvon's cheek—and that the latter suddenly died. Furthermore, it has been frequently alleged that one after another of those who had either directly or indirectly had anything to do with the affair died, some naturally, some tragically, all as a result of an implied curse.

The facts are that Lord Carnarvon was stung by a mosquito not there, but at another site, that the wound became infected and that he died some five months later, at the end of twenty years of invalidism, at the age of fifty-seven. Responsible scholars, checking on the facts, assert that of eight persons in the working party that opened the tomb, six were still alive fourteen years later, while two were still living twenty-eight years after the event, which was longer than the period of their average life expectancy. Howard Carter, who was in charge of the excavation, lived to be about seventy years of age and died only shortly before World War II. No wonder an Egyptologist cried, "We all die ultimately. How long does a curse take anyhow?"

While, therefore, the popular stories have no solid basis in fact, they do, nevertheless, illustrate in some measure the feeling people have about tombs; and to a considerable degree, help account for the preservation of so much that was placed in the burial places of the Egyptians. To this fact we owe a great deal, for much of Egyptian literature, particularly concerning their religion, has come to us from the tombs.

It may be, of course, that just because so much of the religious literature was from this origin, so much attention was focused upon death and the after life. No other single idea seemed so to preoccupy the mind of the Egyptians as this. Possibly if we had more general preservation of the writings which, lacking the protection of the tombs, have been lost or destroyed, we might have a better balance of interest. Certain it is that no people in the world, seemingly, have been so deeply concerned about what was to happen to them after death. It was a near obsession with them. Kings spent much of their time and effort, as well as the economic resources of their country, in building burial places that would defy the ravages of time, and so guarantee to them immortality. It was for this that the pyramids were built, hundreds of them, and literally thousands of mastabas, which were the more primitive forms of the developed pyramid. These latter served as the burial places of the wealthy and powerful who could not aspire to truly great pyramids, as their bid for immortality.

It is with this concept of the life hereafter that a great deal of the literature has to do. The very oldest writings known in Egypt, and indeed in all the world, were certain writings found on the inner passages of a group of pyramids at Sakkara, along the Nile, which date from about 2700 to 2600 B.C. They are known as the pyramid texts. At the present time nothing older than these in written form is certainly known. Yet, that these were not the earliest writings of Egypt is apparent from the fact that in the course of writing these pyramid texts, their authors quote from books written much earlier, perhaps many hundreds of years previously.

The purpose of the pyramid texts was to enable the king to reach the realm of the dead (at that early time not in the underworld, but in the sky, and in the East rather than the West, as in later times) and to insure his happiness there. To reach that abode it was necessary to ferry over certain bodies of water. Charms were therefore furnished to compel the ferryman, called "Look-behind," to bear him over the waters. Sometimes if he proved obdurate, the god Re was besought to command the boatman to serve him: "O Re, Commend King Teti to Look-behind, the ferryman of the Lily-Lake, that he may bring that ferry-boat for King Teti, in which he ferries the gods to yonder side of the Lily-Lake, to the east side of the sky."[1]

If these means fail he may fly to the sky. A charm is provided for this: "Thy two wings are spread out like a falcon with thick plumage, like the hawk seen in the evening traversing the sky."[2] Or men and gods are called on to lift him to the sky. "O men and gods! Your arms are under King Pepi! Raise him, lift ye him to the sky, as the arms of Shu are under the sky and he raises it. To the sky! To the sky! To the greatest seat among the gods!"[3]

Then there were the doors of the celestial fields to be opened and for this also charms were required. As he faces the gates he cries: "O lofty one (gate), whom no one names! Gate of Nut! King Teti is Shu who came forth from Atum. O Nun (the primeval waters), cause that this gate be opened for King Teti."[4]

At last, of course, the Pharaoh is admitted and becomes one with the gods.

This literature is fairly extensive, running to something over two hundred printed pages in translation. It contains rituals for the

---

[1] Pyr. 88599–60, reprinted from *Development of Religion and Thought in Ancient Egypt,* by James H. Breasted; copyright 1912 by Charles Scribner's Sons, 1940 by Charles Breasted; used by permission of the publishers. Page 106.

[2] Pyr. 81048, Breasted, *op. cit.* p. 109.

[3] Pyr. 1101, Breasted, p. 113.

[4] Pyr. 603, Breasted, p. 114.

funerary offerings at the tomb, charms, very old rituals for use in worship, hymns, myths and prayers. "The chief note," says Breasted, "in all this mass of material is that of protest against death." He calls it "humanity's earliest supreme revolt against the great darkness and silence from which none returns."[5] Again and again is repeated the assurance that the dead lives: "King Teti has not died the death, he has become a glorious one in the horizon."[6]

Although primarily of the character thus indicated, pyramid texts are highly revealing as to the general outlook of the people of that time, particularly with reference to the life hereafter. In the earlier period, it should be noted, this seemed to be chiefly the prerogative of kings, at least there is no comparable literature as expressive of the hopes of the common man. There are, however, indications that go far back of any of the pyramids, in the simple burials found in the desert sands, that there was a hope of an after life, and that one would evidently need there very much the same kind of things he needed here. This at any rate appears to be the case, from the sort of utensils and tools and other objects found in the graves.

The funerary literature, of which the pyramid texts are simply the earliest phase, was a constant element in Egyptian literature from the time of the pyramid texts until very late in the pre-Christian era. At a somewhat later time the writing was done, not on the walls of pyramids, but on the inside of coffins in which the mummies were placed. In this form the writings were known as the coffin texts, their purpose being essentially that of the pyramid texts, only there are now evidences that the after life is a concern, not alone of rulers, but also of people of lesser social stature.

The final phase of this literature is what is known as *The Book of the Dead,* a very extensive literature which is found written on papyrus rolls and placed within the coffins. At this stage it is quite clear that "Everyman" entertains the hope of immortality, and these numerous texts are the means by which the soul is supposed to be able to make its way through the nether world.

[5] P. 91.
[6] Pyr. 8350, Breasted, *op. cit.,* p. 91.

The Book of the Dead is sometimes called the Bible of the Egyptians. It is true that it is the one book which does have some semblance of a canon, but, aside from this, it would be a mistake to regard it as a Bible. As a matter of fact, there are various recensions of the book which are similar, but by no means identical, either in the number of the chapters included or in the content of the chapters. It is true also that it does form what, perhaps, for the first time, may be called a book, but it was certainly never the fixed and unchanging kind of a book that most Bibles have become.

The writing was done on long papyrus rolls, some of them reaching a length of something like 150 feet. They are written very much as the Hebrew scrolls are written, in columns a few inches wide. Some of them were written with great care, some of the chapters being headed by illustrations in color indicating the content of the chapter.

But even in death there is a difference among people. The wealthy and powerful were able to employ able scribes and use high-grade materials, while the poor had to content themselves with cruder, cheaper work of less capable scribes, some of it written almost illegibly. Dr. John A. Wilson says that probably the really poor (the great mass of the people) could afford no *Book of the Dead* at all. "Such privilege may have run down through the merchants, artisans and minor priests, but not to servants and peasants."[7] Toward the close of Egypt's history, the book grows shorter and shorter, possibly due to a changed view of its value, or to a conviction that it was primarily magic, and that a token book would work quite as effectively as a much more elaborate and expensive one. The result is that in lesser burials, the book comes to be only a small, single sheet of papyrus written in demotic script.

Each chapter as translated and published by Budge has a title, and from a study of these titles the general purposes of *The Book of the Dead* may be gathered. Chapter XV, for example, is a group of hymns to various gods, a hymn of praise to Ra[8] at rising; a hymn and litany to Osiris; a second hymn to Ra at rising, followed by

[7] Personal correspondence.
[8] Ra same as Re (p. 38). Ra is the spelling preferred by Budge, Re by Breasted.

three hymns to Ra at setting. These are similar to, but yet different from, the several hymns to Ra at rising which form part of the Introduction to *The Book of the Dead*. Other chapter titles are: "Of not letting the deceased do work in the underworld"; "Of making the Shabti figure to do work," the Shabti (Ushebti) being a molded figure of a slave placed in the tomb to serve the deceased. This was a late substitute for the earlier actual slaying of a slave to serve his master in the other world. Others are: "Of giving a mouth to the deceased"; "Of giving a heart to the deceased in the underworld"; "Of not letting the heart of the deceased be driven away from him in the underworld"; "Of not letting the deceased be bitten by serpents"; "Of not suffering corruption in the underworld"; "Of sitting among the great gods"; "Of causing the Soul to be united to the body in the underworld"; "Of providing the deceased with food in the underworld"; "Of forcing an entrance into heaven"; "Of not dying a second time"; "Of entering in the company of the Gods." These are but a few, but they furnish something of an indication as to the value of *The Book of the Dead* to the deceased.

Many of the chapters are quite lengthy and there is not space to quote them at great length, but a few excerpts will give an idea of their general nature. Here is part of Chapter 68, "Of Coming Forth by Day."

The overseer of the house of the overseer of the seal, Nu, triumphant, saith:

"The doors of heaven are opened for me, the doors of earth are opened for me, and the first temple hath been unfastened for me by the god Petra. Behold, I was guarded and watched, (but now) I am released; behold, his hand had tied cords round me and his hand had darted upon me in the earth. Re-hent[9] hath been opened for me and Re-hent hath been unfastened before me, Re-hent hath been given unto me, and I shall come forth by day into whatsoever place I please; I have gained the mastery over my heart; I have gained the mastery over my breast (?); I have gained the mastery over my hands; I have gained the mastery over my two feet; I have gained the mastery over my mouth; I have gained

---

[9] Re-hent: the entrance to one of the great celestial canals.

the mastery over my whole body; I have gained the mastery over sepulchral offerings; I have gained the mastery over the waters; I have gained the mastery over the air; I have gained the mastery over the canal; I have gained the mastery over the river and over the land; I have gained the mastery over the furrows; I have gained the mastery over the male workers for me; I have gained the mastery over the female workers for me in the underworld; I have gained the mastery over the things which were ordered to be done for me upon the earth, according to the entreaty which ye spake for me (saying), 'Behold, let him live upon the bread of Seb.' That which is an abomination unto me, I shall not eat, (nay) I shall live upon cakes (made) of white grain, and my ale shall be (made) of the red grain of Hapi.[10] In a clean place I shall sit on the ground beneath the foliage of the date palm of the goddess Hathor, who dwelleth in the spacious Disk as it advanceth to Annu (Heliopolis), having the books of the divine words of the writings of the god Thoth."[11] . . .

"I shall lift myself up on my left side, and I shall place myself up on my right side, and I shall place myself (on my left side). I shall sit down, I shall stand up, and I shall place myself in (the path of) the wind like a guide who is well prepared."

"Rubric: If this composition be known (by the deceased) he shall come forth by day, and he shall be in a position to journey about over the earth among the living, and he shall never suffer diminution, never, never."[12]

Also part of Chapter 154:

. . . "Homage to thee, O my divine father Osiris, thou livest with my members. Thou didst not decay. Thou didst not turn into worms. Thou didst not waste away. Thou didst not suffer corruption. Thou didst not putrefy. I am the god Khepera, and my members shall have an everlasting existence. I shall not decay. I shall not rot. I shall not putrefy. I shall not turn into worms. I shall not see corruption before the eye of the god Shu. I shall have my being, I shall have my being. I shall live, I shall live. I shall flourish, I shall flourish. I shall wake up in peace. I shall not putrefy. My inward parts shall not perish. I shall not suffer injury. Mine eye shall not decay. The form of my visage shall not disappear. Mine

[10] Hapi: the Nile.
[11] E. A. Wallis Budge, *The Book of the Dead,* Open Court Publishing Co., Ltd. Chicago, 1901, Vol. 2, pp. 231–233.
[12] *Ibid.*

ear shall not become deaf. My head shall not be separated from my neck. My tongue shall not be carried away. My hair shall not be cut off. Mine eyebrows shall not be shaved off. No baleful injury shall come upon me. My body shall be established, and it shall neither crumble away nor be destroyed in this earth."[13]

Quite the most notable of all the chapters is the 125th, which describes the famous judgment scene through which every soul must pass before the entrance into the other world. The chapter is preceded by a graphic picture of the judgment scene, clearly showing the characters who participate in it. There is Osiris, god of the under-world; there is Anubis, the jackal god, who appropriately enough conducts the souls to the judgment hall; there are depicted the famous scales on which the heart of the person being judged is weighed in the balance against Maat, or justice, represented by a feather. Standing beside the scale with what appears to be a stylus and a writing pad is Thoth, god of learning and patron of all literature, who is the secretary always present to note the outcome of the judgment. And most fearsome of all stands a curious beast compounded of parts of a hippopotamus, a lion, and a crocodile, the latter furnishing the mouth, which stands with fearful jaws open, ready to receive the hearts which do not weigh out properly against justice. The figure is known familiarly as the "devouress."

Before proceeding to the weighing of the heart, however, the soul must appear in a great judgment hall in which are seated forty-two gods, each representing one of the ancient city states of which Egypt was compounded. Before each separate god, the soul must prostrate itself and deny having committed some particular sin. In the list of these denials of specific sin may be found an excellent index of what the Egyptian evidently thought was sin, and it proves to be a most interesting list indeed. It is too long to copy entirely, but here are some of the things which the soul must affirm that it has not committed. The negative confession here given is addressed to Osiris, Lord of the hall of judgment. It is given again in slightly different form to the several forty-two gods in the same 125th chapter.

[13] E. A. Wallis Budge, *The Literature of the Ancient Egyptians*, p. 55.

Text; (1) (The following) shall be said when the overseer of the house of the overseer of the seal, Nu, triumphant, cometh forth into the hall (2) of Double Maati so that he may be separated from every sin which he hath done and may behold the faces of the gods. The Osiris Nu, triumphant, saith:—

(3) "Homage to thee, O Great God, thou Lord of Double Maati, I have come to thee, O my Lord, and I have brought myself hither that (4) I may behold thy beauties. I know thee, and I know thy name, and I know the name(s) of the two and forty gods who exist with (5) thee in this Hall of Double Maati. . . . I have not oppressed the members of any family, (8) I have not wrought evil in the place of right and truth. I have had no knowledge of worthless men. I have not wrought evil. I have not made to be the first (consideration) of each day that excessive labour (9) should be performed for me. (I have) not brought forward my name for (exaltation) to honours. I have not ill-treated servants. (I have not thought scorn of God.) I have not defrauded the oppressed one of his property. I have not done that which is an abomination (10) unto the gods. I have not caused harm to be done to the servant by his chief. I have not caused pain. I have made no man to suffer hunger. I have made no one to weep. I have done no murder. (11) I have not given the order for murder to be done for me. I have not inflicted pain upon mankind. I have not defrauded the temples of their oblations. I have not (12) purloined the cakes of gods. I have not carried off the cakes offered to the *khus*. I have not committed fornication. I have not polluted myself (in the holy places of the god of my city), nor diminished from the bushel. (13) I have neither added to nor filched away land. I have not encroached upon the fields (of others). I have not added to the weights of the scales (to cheat the seller). I have not mis-read the pointer of the scales (to cheat the buyer). (14) I have not carried away the milk from the mouths of children. I have not driven away the cattle which were upon their pastures. I have not snared (15) the feathered fowl of the preserves of the gods. I have not caught fish (with bait made of) fish of their kind. I have not turned back the water at the time (when it should flow). I have not cut (16) a cutting in a canal of running water. I have not extinguished a fire (or light) when it should burn. I have not violated the times (of offering) the chosen meat-offerings. I have not driven off (17) the cattle from the property of the gods. I have not repulsed God in his manifestations. I am pure. I am pure. I am pure. I am pure." etc.[14]

14 E. A. Wallis Budge, *The Book of the Dead*, Vol. 2, pp. 360–362.

If there remained no other inscriptions or written material concerning Egypt, it would be possible to reconstruct, to a very considerable degree, the life and thought of ancient Egypt from this important book, for in the process of preparing for death and immortality, almost everything that is important in life itself is considered in one way or another. It is thus a priceless document, telling of Egypt's life and faith.

The ethical development indicated in the "Negative Confession" does not seem particularly remarkable from the standpoint of modern Christian civilization; but it is necessary to recall, as one reads it, that this antedates by hundreds of years the time of Moses and the earliest possible date given for the Ten Commandments. Evidently here man had already achieved a high degree of moral insight. Some think that there may have been some influence of the Egyptians upon the Hebrew people through the contact of Moses with the Egyptian court, but that lies in the realm of conjecture and is not to be taken too seriously. Reference will be made to it again a little later.

As in most scriptures, there appears in the literature of Egypt eventually not a little of disillusionment and pessimism. Life deals hardly with men; they seem unable to cope with it; they fall into moods of hopelessness and melancholy, not unlike that found in the Book of Ecclesiastes in the Old Testament. One of the most interesting of the poems depicting this mood is one called the Song of the Harper, a reflection upon the transitory nature of life and fame, prompted by the contemplation of tombs of ancestors.

> There is none who comes back from over there
> That he may tell their state
> That he may tell their needs
> That he may still our hearts
> Until we (too) may travel to the place
>   where they have gone.

This gloomy reflection led them as we shall see in a number of other cultures to a "Carpe diem" philosophy—"Eat, drink, and be merry," for "You can't take it with you."

Put myrrh upon thy head. . . .
Let not thy heart flag
Follow thy desire and thy good. . . .

Make holiday, and weary not again
Behold it is not given to a man to take his
      property with him.
Behold there is no one who departs who comes back again.[15]

Still another, which has been entitled "Dialogue of a Misanthrope with his own Soul," Breasted calls our earliest Book of Job.[16] By a succession of misfortunes a man is brought to the depths of despair from which death in the end seems to offer a glad release. Though in the first half of the poem the same note of "carpe diem" appears, in the latter part life is seen to be utterly intolerable and death offers the only way out.

In the first of four poems which the Misanthrope addresses to his own soul, his name is unjustly abhorred by men, more than the odor of birds, or the stench of fish or crocodiles. He uses the strongest possible similes to express the depth of the abhorrence. In the second he is oppressed by the utter corruption of men about him, not unlike the psalmist who on one occasion says in his heart, "All men are liars." Even brothers are wicked, men seize their neighbor's goods, the gentleman suffers while the bold-faced flourishes. It seems that none is righteous, and endless evil afflicts the land.

So unhappy and so hopeless of any happy outcome of life is he that he welcomes death as a glad release. It appears to him as a recovery from illness, as the odor of myrrh or of lotus flowers, as a release like that of a man who has returned from war, or from long years spent in captivity.

But in the fourth poem there is a forward look. There the dead will inflict punishment on the wicked ones, and shall cause the

[15] J. B. Pritchard, *Ancient Near Eastern Texts Relating to the Bible,* Princeton University Press, 1950, p. 467. Translation of John A. Wilson.

[16] Breasted, *Religion and Thought in Ancient Egypt,* p. 188. The entire poem is given in translation, pp. 191–197. It is also found in Pritchard, *op. cit.,* pp. 406–407, translated by John A. Wilson.

choicest of offerings to be made to the temples, and he shall be as a wise man, praying to Re when he speaks.

The tone is so different in the last poem, that one cannot help wondering if it may not have been the thought of one who lived later, interpolated into the total poem, very much as seems to have been true in the case of the Biblical story of Job and Ecclesiastes.

There are likewise documents preserved which, in almost prophetic vein, depict the evils of the period in which the writer lived. One of these, that of Ipuwer, arraigns the social and political life of his time as sharply as Amos:

"A man smites his brother." . . . "A man looks upon his son as an enemy." . . . "Blood is everywhere." . . . "A few lawless men are endeavoring to despoil the land of kingship." . . . "Some of the provinces make civil war and pay no revenue." . . . "The economic situation is desperate: No craftsmen work. . . . The scribe sits idle in his office. . . . Cattle are left straying. . . . Grain has perished on every side. . . . The store house is laid waste." . . .

Public safety no longer exists: "Men are plundered and beaten." . . . "He who was a robber is a lord of wealth." . . . Even "royal tombs are not respected." . . .

Society is topsy-turvy: "He who had no yoke of oxen is now possessor of a herd. . . . He who had no grain is now an owner of granaries." . . . "The owner of wealth now begs." . . . "The possessors of robes are now in rags." . . . "Mirth has perished." . . . "Great and small say, I wish I might die. . . . Little children say, He ought never to have caused me to live. . . . Life is no longer worth living."[17]

Unlike a number of other somewhat similar documents of despair, Ipuwer is unwilling to let things rest as they are. On the other hand, he exhorts his fellow countrymen to destroy the enemies of their king, and looks forward to a recovery of the land. This is compassed by an ideal king who stands in sharp contrast to the reigning sovereign. Of this ideal king he sings:

He brings coolness to that which is hot. It is said he is the shepherd of mankind. No evil is in his heart. When his herds are few, he

[17] The translation is that of Alan H. Gardiner, *Admonitions of an Egyptian Sage*, Leipzig, 1909, pp. 9–12, *passim.*

passes the day to gather them together, their hearts being on fire. Would that he had perceived their nature in the first generation. Then would he have suppressed evil. He would have stretched forth his arm against it. He would have destroyed their inheritance. . . . Where is he today? Is he sleeping? Behold his might is not seen.[18]

What is here seen in vision is apparently a return to the Golden Age, not unlike that seen by the Hebrew prophets who look back upon the Davidic age as the golden period, and long for a return to it. Here, says Breasted, we have a reference to Messianism.[19] The writer is definitely prophetic in character, although the predictive element may not actually have appeared in his writing. He goes ahead in somewhat the manner of Nathan condemning David, to condemn the line of sovereigns upon whom he puts the responsibility for the evil conditions which he has exposed. The end of the long document is a final picture of joy and prosperity, again not unlike some of the Hebrew prophecies.

In somewhat different vein is a remarkable document known as *The Eloquent Peasant,* which may be said, perhaps, to be the oldest literature of social protest in the world. It is the plea of a peasant who has had his donkeys taken away from him by a covetous, wealthy neighbor on a vicious pretext. The peasant seeks their restoration, finally carrying his plaint to the highest authority. It is too long to quote here, but the reader will do well to seek it out and follow *The Eloquent Peasant* through to the end. Finally the covetous neighbor is punished, and his possessions bestowed upon the eloquent peasant. Breasted thinks that *The Eloquent Peasant* was in the nature of a pamphlet issued by some members of the court of Pharaoh as a bit of propaganda for justice and kindness toward the poor.[20]

Most striking of all of the literature of this character, perhaps, is the "Wisdom" type; that is, the advice of the sage to his people, very similar in character to the Book of Proverbs in the Old Testa-

[18] Alan H. Gardiner, *op. cit.,* p. 13.
[19] *Op. cit.,* p. 212.
[20] This may be found in *Sacred Books and Literature of the East,* Vol. 2, on Egypt, pp. 115–132. Also J. B. Pritchard, *Ancient Near Eastern Texts,* pp. 407–410. Translated by John A. Wilson.

ment. There are a number of these extant, but the most notable of them all is the *Wisdom of Ptah Hotep,* which purports to be the utterances of a governor of a city to his son, who, the father hopes, may be appointed as his successor as governor and vizier. It is dated in the Fifth Dynasty, according to John A. Wilson, about 2450 B.C. It is much too long to quote at length here, but a sampling at least is necessary:

Be not puffed up because of thy knowledge; be not confident because thou art a wise man. Take counsel with the ignorant as well as the wise.

If thou art one to whom petition is made, be calm as thou listenest to the petitioner's speech. Do not rebuff him before he has swept out his body or before he has said that for which he came. A petitioner likes attention to his words better than the fulfilling of that for which he came.

Do not be greedy. . . . Do not be covetous against thy own kindred. Greater is the respect for the mild than for the strong. . . . It is only a little of that for which one is covetous that turns a calm man into a contentious man.

If thou art a man of standing, thou shouldst found thy household and love thy wife as is fitting. Fill her belly; clothe her back. Ointment is the prescription for her body. Make her heart glad as long as thou livest.

If (thy friend) should do something with which thou art displeased, behold he is still a friend. Do not answer in a state of turmoil; do not remove thyself from him. Do not trample him down.[21]

Below are a few selections from *The Instructions of Ani,* written by a scribe Ani for the instruction of his son:

Do not talk a lot. Be silent and thou wilt be happy. Do not be garrulous. The dwelling of god, its abomination is clamor. Pray thou with a loving heart, all the words of which are hidden, and he will do what thou needest, he will hear what thou sayest, and he will accept thy offering.

Thou shouldst not eat bread when another is waiting and thou dost not stretch forth thy hand to him. A man is nothing. The one is rich; another is poor. . . . The man rich last year is this year a vagabond.[22]

These may or may not have been written by the persons to whom

[21] J. B. Pritchard, *Ancient Near Eastern Texts,* pp. 412–414, *passim.* Translation of John A. Wilson.

[22] *The Instructions of Ani,* Pritchard, *Ancient Near Eastern Texts,* pp. 420–421, *passim.* Translation of John A. Wilson.

they are attributed but, like the wisdom literature of most peoples, probably represent the accumulated wisdom of the time in which they appeared, which is exactly what occurs in the wisdom literature of the Old Testament.

The Instructions of Amen-em-Opet, which is variously dated by scholars from the tenth to the sixth century B.C., is thought to be quite similar to the Hebrew book of Proverbs—particularly 22:17–24:22

> Do not neglect a stranger with thy oil jar
> That it be doubled before thy brethren.
> God desires respect for the poor
> More than the knowing of the exalted.

> For man is the clay and straw,
> And the god is his builder.
> He is tearing down and building up every day.
> He makes a thousand men poor as he wishes
> Or he makes a thousand men as overseers.
> When he is in his hour of life,
> How joyful is he who reaches the west
> When he is safe in the hand of the god.

> Better is poverty in the hand of the god
> Than riches in a storehouse.
> Better is bread when the heart is happy
> Than riches with sorrow.

> The ship of the covetous man is left in the mud
> While the boat of the silent man has a fair breeze.

> Do not spend the night fearful of the morrow.
> At daybreak what is the morrow like?
> Man knows not what the morrow is like.[23]

There is an extensive hymn literature in Egypt which may be said to be, in some sense, parallel to the Book of Psalms in the

[23] From *The Instructions of Amen-em-Opet.* Translation of John A. Wilson. Pritchard, *Ancient Near Eastern Texts,* pp. 422–424, *passim.*

Hebrew-Christian Bible. Some of these we have already noted as appearing in the *Pyramid Texts* or *The Book of the Dead,* but apart from these there have appeared many hymns of high order in praise of one or the other of the gods. A few examples of these are as follows:

A hymn prayer addressed to the Lady of the West—from a Stela dating from the 19th Dynasty (*c.* 1350–1200 B.C.):

> Praised be thou in peace, O Lady of the West,
> The Mistress that turns herself toward mercy!
> Thou causest me to see darkness by day.[24]
> I will declare thy might to all people.
> Be merciful to me in thy mercy![25]

A hymn to Luna-Thoth—A Stela from the 19th Dynasty (*c.* 1350–1200 B.C.):

> Giving praise to Luna-Thoth:
> Homage to the Merciful One.
> I give him praise to the height of heaven:
>
> I adore thy beauty.
> Be thou merciful to me,
> That I may see that thou art merciful:
> That I may observe thy might.
> Thou causest me to see a darkness of thy making;
> Lighten me that I may see thee.
> In that health and life are in thine hand
> One liveth by the gift of them.[26]

Still another is addressed to the Nile, which plays such an important role in Egyptian life:

I

> Adoration to the Nile!
> Hail to thee, O Nile!
> who manifesteth thyself over this land,
> and cometh to give life to Egypt!

[24] Darkness by day seems to indicate that the suppliant is blind.
[25] *Sacred Books and Literature of the East,* Vol. 2, p. 317.
[26] *Id.,* p. 323.

Mysterious is thy issuing forth from the darkness,
on this day whereon it is celebrated!
Watering the orchards created by Re
to cause all the cattle to live,
thou givest the earth to drink, inexhaustible one! . . .

II

Lord of the fish, during the inundation,
no bird alights on the crops.
Thou createst the corn, thou bringest forth the barley,
assuring perpetuity to the temples.
If thou ceasest thy toil and thy work,
Then all that exists is in anguish. . . .

VIII

He shines when he issues forth from the darkness,
to cause his flocks to prosper.
It is his force that gives existence to all things;
nothing remains hidden from him.
Let men clothe themselves to fill his gardens.
He watches over his works,
producing the inundation during the night. . . .

X

Establisher of justice! mankind desires thee,
supplicating thee to answer their prayers;
thou answerest them by the inundation!
Men offer the first-fruits of corn;
all the gods adore thee!
The birds descend not on the soil.
It is believed that with thy hand of gold
thou makest bricks of silver!
But we are not nourished on lapis lazuli;
corn alone gives vigor. . . .

XII

When thou shinest in the royal city,
the rich man is sated with good things,

the poor man even disdains the lotus;
all that is produced is of the choicest;
all the plants exist for thy children.
If thou hast refused to grant nourishment,
the dwelling is silent, devoid of all that is good
the country falls exhausted.

XIII

O inundation of the Nile,
offerings are made unto thee,
oxen are immolated to thee,
great festivals are instituted for thee.
Birds are sacrificed to thee,
gazelles are taken for thee in the mountain,
pure flames are prepared for thee. . . .

XIV

Come and prosper! come and prosper!
O Nile, come and prosper!
O thou that makest men to live through his flocks
and his flocks through his orchards!
Come and prosper, come,
O Nile, come and prosper![27]

But perhaps the greatest of all the hymn literature belongs to
the Imperial Age, particularly to the time of Akhnaton. As Egypt
evolved from a body of separate city states into upper and lower
Egypt and finally into a united Egypt, the religious concepts were
also modified and certain gods became more and more important
and far-reaching in their sway. It was therefore perhaps natural
that precisely at the moment that Egypt became a world empire
and sought, by conquest, to enlarge her borders, her gods should
also tend to transcend their local, limited character of the earlier
period.

It is a fact that at this time, under the noted sovereign, Akhnaton, there did appear, perhaps for the first time in the history of

[27] *Sacred Books and Early Literature of the East,* Vol. 2, Egypt, pp. 300–305.
Translation of M. Paul Guieysse.

the world, a concept of monotheism, of a universal god subject to no limitations of time or space.

Akhnaton was an innovator in various fields. Although he came to the throne very young, married and reared a family, and passed off the scene in his early thirties, perhaps no monarch of Egypt or any other country came to stand out so sharply against the background of his own people. Students of ancient Egypt, particularly Breasted, grow lyric in singing the praises of Akhnaton. Breasted calls him the world's first individual. Certainly he was unique in many respects.

First of all, students of the history of Egyptian art know well that from his period dates a new epoch in Egyptian art. As king, he required that he be represented with a crude naturalism that was little flattering to his person. He was definitely an innovator with respect to his attitudes toward his family, and the way in which he permitted himself and his family to be pictured for future generations, not as divine, but as very human, enjoying the most intimate relationships with his wife and children. He was likewise different in his attitude toward war. He was clearly the world's first pacifist. Convinced of the evil and destructiveness of war, he refused to use violent means to hold his empire together, and, as a result, during his time it began to crumble. Living as he did nearly fourteen hundred years before Jesus, and over three thousand years before our own time, which pays little attention to pacifists, it was to be expected that few would follow him in his refusal to use force. So the decline of the political power of the Egyptian Empire began.

But perhaps his greatest claim to fame rests on his theological innovations. Already there had been some tendency in the direction of a unified view of the world, but it remained for Akhnaton to espouse a monotheistic concept of god and to give it prestige. He simply declared Aton, originally only the sun's disc, but under his grandfather made one of the sun gods, to be not only the god of the sun but the universal divinity of the world, to whom men everywhere ought to give their allegiance. This set him in rivalry with the ecclesiastical powers of his day whose chief god was

Amon, and his attempts at theological reform were made increasingly difficult by the opposition of the prevailing theological leaders.

It may well be confessed that he did not use the most tactful methods in seeking to get his ideas accepted. To escape from the immediate presence of the rival divinities, he created a new capital in which Aton alone was worshiped, and provided him with rich temples and a priesthood. But it was his attempt to erase from the minds of his contemporaries the rival god Amon that perhaps stirred up the deepest resentment against him. He sent out men to chisel off the tombs, including those of his own ancestors, the hated name of Amon. This was a violation of something very sacred in the minds of the people; so it is little to be wondered at that soon after his own early death a reaction against the reform developed, and that finally his own name and the name of the god Aton, whose name he had incorporated in his own when he had it changed from Amen-hotep to Akhnaton, were likewise erased from public monuments.

Akhnaton was himself a poet of no mean stature. If it be true that the great hymn to Aton is his own composition, then he must be rated very high indeed, for here is one of the truly great poems of all time. It is much too long to be given in its entirety, for it describes the universal splendor and power of Aton, the sources of night and day, man and animals, the waters, the seasons, etc. But a few characteristic portions follow:

UNIVERSAL SPLENDOR AND POWER OF ATON

Thy dawning is beautiful in the horizon of the sky;
O living Aton, Beginning of Life!
When thou risest in the eastern horizon,
Thou fillest every land with thy beauty.
Thou art beautiful, great, glittering, high above every land,
Thy rays, they encompass the lands, even all that thou hast made.
Thou art Re, and thou carriest them all away captive;
Thou bindest them by thy love.
Though thou art far away, thy rays are upon earth;
Though thou art on high, thy (footprints are the day).

NIGHT

When thou settest in the western horizon of the sky,
The earth is in darkness like the dead.

DAY AND MAN

Bright is the earth when thou risest in the horizon.
When thou shinest as Aton by day
Thou drivest away the darkness.
When thou sendest forth thy rays ...

DAY AND THE ANIMALS AND PLANTS

All cattle rest upon their pasturage,
The trees and the plants flourish,
The birds flutter in their marshes,
Their wings uplifted in adoration to thee.
All the sheep dance upon their feet,
All winged things fly,
They live when thou hast shone upon them.

CREATION OF MAN

Creator of the germ in woman,
Maker of seed in man,
Giving life to the son in the body of his mother,
Soothing him that he may not weep,
Nurse (even) in the womb,
Giver of breath to animate every one that he maketh!
When he cometh forth from the body ... on the day of his birth,
Thou openest his mouth in speech,
Thou suppliest his necessities.

THE WHOLE CREATION

How manifold are thy works!
They are hidden from before (us),
O sole God, whose powers no other possesseth.

Thou didst create the earth according to thy heart
While thou wast alone:
Men, all cattle large and small,
All that are upon the earth,
That go about upon their feet;
(All) that are on high,
That fly with their wings.
The foreign countries, Syria and Kush,
The land of Egypt;
Thou settest every man into his place,
Thou suppliest their necessities
Every one has his possessions,
And his days are reckoned.
The tongues are divers in speech,
Their forms likewise and their skins are distinguished.
(For) thou makest different the strangers.

WATERING THE EARTH IN EGYPT AND ABROAD

Thou makest the Nile in the Nether World,
Thou bringest it as thou desirest,
To preserve alive the people.
For thou hast made them for thyself,
The lord of them all, resting among them;
Thou lord of every land, who risest for them,
Thou Sun of day, great in majesty.
All the distant countries,
Thou makest (also) their life,
Thou hast set a Nile in the sky;
When it falleth for them,
It maketh waves upon the mountains,
Like the great green sea,
Watering their fields in their towns.

How excellent are thy designs, O lord of eternity!
There is a Nile in the sky for the strangers
And for the cattle of every country that go upon their feet.
(But) the Nile, it cometh from the Nether World for Egypt.

THE SEASONS

Thy rays nourish every garden;
When thou risest they live,
They grow by thee.
Thou makest the seasons
In order to create all thy work:
Winter to bring them coolness,
And heat that (they may taste) thee.

REVELATION TO THE KING

Thou art in my heart,
There is no other that knoweth thee
Save thy son Akhnaton.
Thou hast made him wise
In thy designs and in thy might.
The world is in thy hand,
Even as thou hast made them.
When thou hast risen they live,
When thou settest they die;
For thou art length of life of thyself,
Men live through thee,
While (their) eyes are upon thy beauty
Until thou settest.
All labor is put away
When thou settest in the West.[28]

The hymn is sometimes thought to have influenced certain of the Hebrew psalmists, particularly the writer of Psalm 104; but whether this is true or not, it is certain that it breathes the spirit of the Hebrew idea of God and his creative activity. It is just possible that the emergence of Hebrew monotheism is due in part to the influence of the great Egyptian philosopher-king.

[28] Reprinted from *Development of Religion and Thought in Ancient Egypt* by James H. Breasted; copyright 1912 by Charles Scribner's Sons, 1940 by Charles Breasted; used by permission of the publishers.

EGYPTIAN SACRED LITERATURE
Sources for Further Reading

James H. Breasted, *The Development of Religion and Thought in Ancient Egypt,* Charles Scribner's Sons, N. Y., 1912.

Lewis Browne, *The World's Great Scriptures,* Macmillan, N. Y., 1945, pp. 27–53.

E. A. Wallis Budge, *The Book of the Dead,* three volumes, Translation of the Complete Book of the Dead, Open Court Publishing Co., Chicago, 1901.

Adolf Erman, *Egyptian Literature,* Aylward Blackman, Methuen, London, 1927.

Grace H. Turnbull, *Tongues of Fire,* Macmillan, N. Y., 1929.
Book of Wisdom, pp. 13–27.
Psalms, pp. 37–73.

Janet Mayer, and Tom Prideaux, *Never to Die, The Egyptians in Their Own Words,* Viking Press, N. Y., 1938. Some, but not much religious literature included.

Sacred Books and Literature of the East, Vol. II, entire.

James B. Pritchard, Editor, *Ancient Near Eastern Texts Relating to the Old Testament,* Princeton University Press, Princeton, 1950.

B. Gunn, Translator, *The Instruction of Ptah Hotep and the Instruction of Ke' gemni,* Wisdom of the East Series, London, 1909.

CHAPTER IV

Babylonian Sacred Literature

Archaeology seems to be of perennial interest to modern man. Probably as many articles on the subject appear in the Sunday supplements as on any other topic except those which are of romantic interest. Men of this age seem to be very much interested in either digging up the remains of past civilizations, or reading of the work of those who have themselves done so. Of all of the civilizations uncovered by the archaeologists probably that of the Babylonians and Assyrians has been of greatest interest. Why should this be?

Well, one reason for the interest of western civilization in ancient Babylonia and Assyria, lies in the close connection of that part of the world with the Bible. Indeed, a major incentive to archaeological discovery lay precisely in the desire of students of the Bible to find in the records of this ancient culture some support for their faith in the Bible. Concerning the Bible there was very little skepticism until about a hundred years ago, when the impact of the modern scientific age began to make itself felt. With the beginning of critical study of the Bible many questions were raised as to the accuracy of the historical record. It was in no small degree the desire to find corroboration for the Biblical narrative that led scholars to carry on their excavations in the Near East. Archaeology has now largely outgrown this primary interest, but there is no doubt that it played an important part as an incentive to widespread digging in the Babylonian and Assyrian area.

It was of course known from the Bible that there had been a very close relationship between the civilizations of the Hebrews and the Babylonian-Assyrian people. Abraham himself had gone out from Ur of the Chaldees, a migrant toward the West. The Assyrians and Babylonians had long been a political threat to the independence of the Hebrew people before the latter finally succumbed to superior force and were either destroyed or dispersed, in the case of the ten northern tribes, by Assyria, or continued, in the case of Judah, in a vassal relationship even after their return from the Babylonian captivity. Might there not therefore be left among the buried cities of the Mesopotamian region some records which would tell of these relationships and so confirm the Biblical stories?

So they dug in dozens of sites. Excavation at one site uncovered eleven different cities superimposed one upon the other. In a great many, there were as many as six or seven that had been built upon the same site; and out of these great mounds there came a vast wealth of information disclosing the nature of the great civilization that had flourished there. Incidentally, among these ruins were found many things which did indeed tend to confirm the story of Israel's past. Old inscriptions of imperial movements did make mention of Israel and corroborate some of the assertions found in the books of the Kings and the Chronicles.

But other things were found which served not so much to confirm the Bible as to raise a question about it and its uniqueness. For amid the debris of these ancient cultures there were found remnants of literature so similar in general character to stories found in the Bible that at once the question was raised as to whether the Hebrew writers had not borrowed from their Eastern neighbors.

To suggest such a dependence of Hebrew upon Babylonian thought in the present day occasions no shock, and raises no serious question, but in an earlier day it proved very shocking indeed. If the Bible were the infallible word of God, in every respect, as was being constantly asserted, how could it have borrowed anything? Was God dependent upon any outside sources for his revelation? The finding of two things in particular, the Story of Creation and the Story of the Flood, stirred up a tempest which was long in subsiding, and which, even yet, in some circles, causes not a little difficulty. With the passage of time and more mature study of the nature of scripture, as disclosed by the application of the modern historico-critical method of investigation, it is seen that the possible borrowing of Bible writers from another source in no way affected its intrinsic worth, or even the belief that these writers were inspired in their writing. For the whole conception of inspiration has undergone a change.

In all the discoveries made through extended archaeological research, there has never appeared what might be called a sacred scripture of the Babylonians or Assyrians. Apparently they, like the Egyptians, never arrived at the point where they set aside certain books as of divine origin and accorded them an authoritative place in the regulation of their religious beliefs or practices. Why they did not do this, we can no more say than we could in the case of the Egyptians. Possibly, they might, in time, have done so had outside influences not deflected their interest and changed their religious outlook. But the fact remains that they do not have a canonical scripture. To be sure so distinguished a scholar as Robert W. Rogers[1] does affirm that they had sacred books, that indeed they had little else in their literature. But they had no Sacred Book. What probably he means, for it is certainly true, is that they did have a great many writings which are of the nature of scripture, and might very well have been a part of a canonical selection, had one been made. That is, they had a very substantial amount of literature of varied kinds which corresponds closely with the kind of thing that is to be found among the scriptures of other people, notably those of the Hebrews and Christians. Whether the Hebrews are actually indebted to the Babylonians for anything found in their own scripture will always remain a question on which scholarly opinion may

[1] *The Religion of Babylonia and Assyria,* Eaton and Mains, N. Y., 1908, p. 143.

differ, but that there might have been some borrowing of one from another, there can be no doubt. That the dependence of either upon the other, if any, is probably that of the Hebrew upon the Babylonian, is indicated by the fact that the Babylonian is, in almost every case, obviously earlier than the Hebrew.

We shall mention five types of Babylonian writings: (1) The Creation Story and the Flood Story, that is, the story of mythological beginnings; (2) hymns and prayers, including their penitential psalms; (3) ritual texts; (4) their legal code; and (5) omens, all of which find some correspondence in the Bibles of most people.

The Babylonians did not, like the Egyptians, have at hand durable material in the form of stone upon which to carve their inscriptions. But they did have clay, and they early learned to write on it while it was still damp, then bake it in the fire, thus rendering it relatively permanent. Nor did they have the stones for building purposes that Egypt enjoyed. They built largely of sun-dried brick. This is very durable so long as it is protected from the rain, but once the roof falls in and the protective surface is worn away, the rain quickly erodes the buildings. It was in part this gradual eroding of the buildings that formed the mounds in which archaeologists now dig up the ancient culture. When enough of the eroded walls has been washed down it forms a covering of the lower part of the building, and this protecting layer preserves the remainder of the building from further erosion. So, into these mounds they have dug, and found innumerable clay tablets, shaped usually somewhat like a shredded wheat biscuit, in all sizes, from thumb-nail up to as large as an adobe brick. On these were written, in what is known as cuneiform, that is wedge-shaped characters, the texts they wished to communicate or preserve. Literally thousands of them have been dug up containing everything from profound moral and religious treatises to receipts for money paid; contracts for the sale of articles; personal letters; business letters; letters from fathers to sons, and sons to fathers; and interestingly enough, they contained very much the same kind of material that such letters contain today. There are textbooks of mathematics, books on astronomy, and a great many other things. Indeed, almost every kind of writing is found.

For a long, long time nobody could read these. They did not, as in Egypt, have the good fortune to find a Rosetta Stone where a single text was found in Egyptian—two scripts—and in Greek, which was easily understood. The account of the decipherment of the Babylonian text is one of the most interesting and romantic stories of scholarship. It is to be found very interestingly told in Robert W. Rogers, *The Religion of Babylonia and Assyria*,[2] and in *They Wrote on Clay* by Edward Chiera.[3] It is well worth reading. Eventually the problem was solved, and specialists now read these ancient records with almost the same ease with which one reads a modern foreign language. Found in one of the ancient libraries one day was a group of rather better tablets of large size, which, when deciphered, turned out to be the story of creation. This aroused a veritable furor in the world of scholarship and of religion, for, as indicated above, it proved to be very similar in some respects to the story in Biblical Genesis.

The text is by no means complete, despite the fact that more than one set of tablets has been found containing the story, for most of the tablets have suffered some breakage; but its main lines can be discerned very well. If it proved to be alike in some respects to the Biblical story it proved very different in other respects. Over against the Hebrew creation story, "In the beginning God created the heaven and the earth," the Babylonian story begins:

> When on high the heaven had not been named
> Firm ground below had not been called by name.[4]

When none but the primordial Apsu and Mummu-Tiamat, mother of all, existed, then were the gods created one after another. But Apsu was not happy about his offspring and resolved to destroy them utterly that he might have rest.

> Verily their ways are loathsome unto me.
> By day I find no relief, nor repose by night.[5]

[2] Chapter I.
[3] Chapters 4 and 5.
[4] J. B. Pritchard, *Ancient Near Eastern Texts,* Princeton University Press, 1950, pp. 60–61. Translation of E. A. Speiser.
[5] *Id.,* p. 61.

Tiamat sought to dissuade him, but to no avail. Learning of the plot to destroy them, Ea, one of the gods, slew Apsu. Tiamat, angered, created a host of monsters to do battle with the gods. The gods chose Marduk as their champion. He was probably not the god originally mentioned in the telling of the story, but by this time he had become chief god of the city of Babylon and therefore greatest of the gods, so his name was substituted as champion. He drove a bargain with the other gods to recognize him as supreme if he led the battle. The story of the killing of Tiamat is dramatic in the extreme.

> Marduk spread out his net to enfold her,
> The Evil Wind, which followed behind, he let
>   loose in her face.
> When Tiamat opened her mouth to consume him,
> He drove in the Evil Wind that she close not
>   her lips.
> As the fierce winds charged her belly
> Her body was distended, and her mouth was wide open,
> He released the arrow, it tore her belly
> It cut through her insides, splitting the heart.
> Having thus subdued her, he extinguished her life.
> He cast down her carcass to stand upon it.
> Her power was broken, her army scattered.
> With his unsparing mace he crushed her skull
> He split her like a shell fish into two parts;
> Half of her he set up and ceiled it as the sky.[6]

Presumably, the other half became the earth. Then he fixed the responsibilities of the various gods, before proceeding to the creation of life upon the earth. The particular tablet on which this is described is badly broken. Fortunately the account of man's creation is preserved.

> When Marduk hears the words of the gods
> His heart prompts him to fashion artful works.
> Opening his mouth, he addresses Ea
> To impart the plan he had conceived in his heart:
> "Blood will I mass and cause bones to be.

[6] *Id.*, p. 67.

> I will establish a savage; 'man' shall be his name
> Verily savage-man will I create
> He shall be charged with the service of the gods
> That they might be at ease!"

He then took Kingu who had led the uprising against the gods, severed his blood vessels and

> Out of his blood they fashioned mankind.[7]

Babylonia also has its flood story, which, in some points of detail, is much closer to the Biblical account than the creation story. It occurs in the Gilgamesh Epic, found upon twelve large tablets in the great library of Ashurbanipal, though much older than that in origin. It too is much broken, but significant features of the story are still intact. Gilgamesh, lamenting the death of a loved companion, and fearful lest a like fate await him, goes away in search of an ancestor, Ut-Napishtim, who had been carried away to the life beyond. He is advised that the way to him leads over the sea of death, but with the help of a sailor of Ut-Napishtim he may be able to cross. Thus aided, he comes to the place of his ancestor, and there is told the story of Ut-Napishtim, the Babylonian Noah, in which appears the story of the deluge. In part it is as follows: Ea, god of waters, warns him to prepare for the flood.

> Pull down thy house, build a ship,
> Leave thy possessions; take thought for thy life,
> Thy property abandon, save thy life,
> Bring living seed of every kind into the ship.

This he must do because of the hatred of Bel, or Enlil, god of Nippur.

> The ship was built.
> 120 cubits high were its sides.
> 140 cubits reached the edge of its roof.

[7] Pritchard, *op. cit.*, p. 68.

I traced its hull, I designed it.
I built it in six stories. . . .
Its interior I divided into nine parts. . . .

When it was finished he moved in. With all of his silver and gold, living things, cattle, beasts of the field, his family and household he filled it. Then

The senders of the rain in the evening sent heavy rain.
The appearance of the weather I observed.
I feared to behold the weather.
I entered the ship and closed the door.

The rains came, the water reached high
And brought destruction upon men.

No man beheld his fellow
No more were men recognized
The gods feared the deluge
They drew back. They climbed up the heaven of Anu. . . .

The gods sat bowed and weeping
Six days and nights,
Blew the wind, the deluge and the tempest overwhelmed the land.

On the seventh day the tempest spent itself and the sea rested. The flood ceased.

I looked upon the sea. There was silence come.
And all mankind was turned to clay.
I sat down. I wept.
And over my face ran my tears.

Twelve days later an island arose, and to it the ship was fastened. Day after day the waters went down, and on the seventh day he sent forth a dove. The dove flew away and came back, for there was no resting place. He then sent forth a swallow which likewise returned, finding no resting place. Then he released a raven which flew away to show that the waters were receding and she came not back. The ark settled down, apparently on solid ground. He left the ship and immediately made sacrifice.

> The gods smelled the savor,
> The gods smelled the sweet savor,
> The gods gathered like flies over the sacrifices.

Later the God, Ea, drew near and caused Ut-Napishtim and his wife to kneel before him, then blessed them saying:

> Formerly Ut-Napishtim was only a man but
> Now let Ut-Napishtim and his wife be like the gods, even us.
> Let Ut-Napishtim dwell afar off at the mouth of the rivers.
> They took me there afar off. At the mouth of the rivers
>   they made me to dwell.[8]

With this, the story of the deluge ends. There is more to the epic than this, but we need not follow it further. In the end the search of Gilgamesh for eternal life was not successful, but he did find confidence in the assertion of the gods, that in the next world men find themselves among those whom they have known on earth.

Here is undoubtedly close parallelism to the Old Testament story at certain points. If one reads the entire story as found in both sources it is probable, however, that the differences rather than the likenesses will impress him most.

There is a great wealth of hymns, prayers, psalms of one kind or another in Babylonian literature, very much the sort that is found within the limits of the Hebrew Old Testament. Sometimes there are songs and prayers addressed to a score or more of divine beings; but they do seem to be the authentic, prayerful expression of the human spirit in varying moods. One thinks for example of the long prayer to Ishtar, much too long to quote here, but from which the following are brief excerpts.

[8] The translation is that of Robert W. Rogers taken from his *Cuneiform Parallels to the Old Testament*, pp. 91–101, *passim*, and *The Religion of Babylonia and Assyria*, p. 20. It is translated also in Pritchard, *op. cit.*, pp. 73–98.

Thou judgest the cause of men with justice and right;
Thou regardest with mercy the despised man, thou
      settest right the down-trodden every morning.
How long wilt thou tarry, O lady of heaven and
      earth, shepherdess of pale-faced men?
How long wilt thou tarry, O lady whose feet are
      unwearied, whose knees do run?
How long wilt thou tarry, O lady of conflict and
      all battles?[9] . . .

Where thou dost regard the dead live, the sick arise.
The unjust become just, beholding thy face,
I invoke, sorrowful, sighing, suffering thy servant.
Look upon me, O my lady, and accept my supplication,
Pity me in truth, and hearken unto my prayer,
Speak deliverance unto me, let thy heart be appeased.
Deliverance for my suffering body, full of troubles
      and disorders?
Deliverance for my afflicted heart, full of sorrow and
      sighing?
Deliverance for my suffering bowels, troubled and confused?
Deliverance for my troubled house, pouring forth complaints?
Deliverance for my spirit, full of sorrow and sighing?[10] . . .

My heart hath taken wing, it hath flown away like
      a bird on the heavens.
I moan like a dove, night and day.
I am made desolate, and I weep bitterly.
In pain and sorrow my soul is distressed.
What have I done, O my god and my goddess?
Is it because I feared not my god or my goddess
      that trouble has befallen me?
Sickness, headache, ruin and destruction are come upon me;
Miseries, turning away of countenance, and fullness of
      anger are my lot,
Indignation, wrath, anger of gods and men. . . .

[9] R. W. Rogers, *Cuneiform Parallels to the Old Testament*, p. 155.
[10] *Op. cit.*, pp. 156–157.

But unto my lady do I give heed, my ear is turned
My prayer is unto thee, dissolve my ban.
Blot out my sin, my fault, my mockery and my offence!
Forgive my mockery, accept my supplication,
Free my breast, send me comfort,
Guide my footsteps that happily and proudly among
   the living I may pursue my way.
Speak the word, that at thy command the angry
   god may be favorable.
And that the goddess who is angry may be gracious.[11]

From the Assyrian literature which is very closely similar to the Babylonian, comes a prayer to the chief of gods of which the following is a part:

O Lord Chief of the gods Who alone art exalted on
   earth and in Heaven, . . .
O Merciful Gracious Father in Whose hands rests the
   life of the whole world,
O Lord, Thy divinity is full of awe, like the far-
   off Heaven and the broad ocean
O Creator of the land . . . begetter of gods and men
   who dost build dwellings and establish offerings . . .
O mighty Leader whose deep inner being no god
   understands . . .
O Father, begetter of all things, who lookest upon all
   living things . . .
What god reaches thy fullness
Who is exalted in Heaven? Thou alone art exalted.
Who is exalted on earth? Thou alone art exalted.
O Lord, there is none like unto Thee in sovereignty. . . .
O Lord . . . whose word has no rival, whose divinity
   is beyond concern.[12]

Included in the psalm literature, of which there is not a little, there are many penitential psalms in which the penitent seeks forgiveness for his sins. They are addressed variously to Marduk, chief

[11] R. W. Rogers, *Cuneiform Parallels to the Old Testament*, p. 159.
[12] R. W. Rogers, *The Religion of Babylonia and Assyria*, pp. 163–165, *passim*.

of the gods, Shamash, god of justice, Ishtar, and others. One there is which names no specific divinity. Apparently it might be used in addressing any one or all of them. We can here give only a small excerpt, but who can fail to see that in this psalm the human heart speaks sincerely out of a sense of guilt and a desire for pardon.

> The anger of the Lord may it be appeased.
> The god that I know not be appeased.
> The god known or unknown be appeased. . . .
> The god who is angry against me be appeased.
> O Lord, my transgressions are many, great are my sins.
> My God, my transgressions are many, great are my sins. . . .
>
> I sought for help, but none took my hand,
> I wept, but none came to my side,
> I cried aloud, and there was none that heard me.
> I am full of trouble, overpowered, and dare not look up.
> To my merciful god I turn, and utter my prayer.
> Forgive my transgression, for I humble myself before Thee,
> Thy heart like a mother's may it return to its place.
> Like a mother that hath borne children, like a father
>   that hath begotten them. May it turn again
>   to its place.[13]

In a magic incantation text which does not rise to the moral level of these great psalms of penitence, there is nevertheless to be found a remarkable list of what must evidently have been regarded as wrong by the best Babylonian thought. Like the Hebrews, the Babylonians seem to have believed that sin brings punishment in the form of bodily suffering, loss of goods, friends, misfortune of many kinds. When one has suffered loss, or is in bodily misery he is certain that he has sinned. Here, apparently, a man has come to an exorciser to be freed from his affliction. The exorciser or priest desires to know the source of his guilt. He therefore inquires of the suppliant as recorded in the text—here given only in part, separate lines chosen almost at random:

[13] R. W. Rogers, *The Religion of Babylonia and Assyria*, pp. 182–184, *passim*.

> Has he offended his god, has he offended his goddess?
> Has he spoken evil? . . .
> Has he spoken hatefully?
> Has he set a son at variance with his father?
> Has he set a father at variance with his son? . . .
>
> Has he not set free a prisoner or loosed a captive?
> For No, said Yes?
> For Yes, said No?
> Has he used false weights?
> Has he set up a wrong landmark?
> Has he approached his neighbor's wife?
> Did his mouth consent but his heart deny?
> Did he vow, promise, but not fulfil?
> Has he mixed with magic and witchcraft?[14]

There is in it, to be sure, an apparent lack of discrimination between moral and ritual evil as possible causes of suffering and penalty, but this is not without parallel in other religions, including Judaism and Christianity, at times.

Finally there is one poem which has sometimes been called the Babylonian Job. It is not at all comparable in length, or in the completeness with which the problem of suffering is handled in Biblical Job, but it does voice complaints similar to those of Job.[15]

> Wherever I turn there is evil.
> I have cried unto my god but he showed not his face. . . .
>
> The magician by his sorceries did not loosen my ban. . . .
>
> If I look behind me, trouble pursues me,
> Prayer was my rule, sacrifice my order
> The day of gods honoring was my heart's joy.

But

> That which seemeth good, that is evil with god
> That which in its heart is rejected, that is good with god.

[14] R. W. Rogers, *Cuneiform Parallels to the Old Testament,* pp. 170–175 *passim.*

[15] *Id.,* pp. 165 ff. *passim.* See also Pritchard, *op. cit.,* pp. 434 ff.

Who can understand the counsels of the gods in Heaven?
The plan of the gods full of darkness, who shall establish it? . . .

He who lives in the evening is in the evening dead.
Quickly is he in trouble, suddenly he is smitten.
In a moment he is singing and playing
In an instant he is howling like a complainer. . . .

My house is become a prison for me.
In the chains of my flesh are my arms laid. . . .

The god helped me not, he took me not by the hand

Before I was dead the death wail was finished. . . .

When mine enemy heard, his face glowed. . . .

Like all other religions, that of Babylonia developed an elaborate cult. There were magnificent temples, a numerous and powerful priesthood, and a wealth of ritual and ceremonial. Not a little of this is preserved on clay tablets and has been deciphered. It runs closely parallel to what is found in those portions of the Old Testament which describe the tabernacle and the temple, and the sacrifices and ceremonies which the Hebrew faith developed in the course of time. These do not make very interesting reading. A few lines from a Temple Program for New Year's Festivals at Babylon will suffice:

On the second day of the month Nisannu, two hours of the night (remaining) the—priest shall arise and wash with river water. He shall enter into the presence of the god Bel, and he shall . . . a linen *gadalu* in front of Bel. He shall recite the following prayer.

> Oh Bel, who has no equal when angry—
> Grant mercy to your city Babylon!
> Turn your face to the temple Esagil, your house!
> Establish the liberty of the people of Babylon,
>   your subordinates!

Then follow some 400 lines of direction as to the further conduct of the ceremony with occasionally interspersed hymns or prayers. A typical sentence is: These two images shall be of seven finger widths high. One shall be made of cedar, one of tamarisk, etc., etc. Very little is left to the imagination, everything specifically ordered. It is the way of all highly ritualized religions from that day until now.[16]

Other rituals included are that to be followed by the priest when covering the temple kettle drum; Ritual for the Repair of the Temple; daily sacrifices to the gods of the city of Uruk, etc.[17]

The discovery, in the year 1901–1902, of a black diorite stele covered with column upon column of cuneiform characters, was an epoch-making event in the study of ancient Babylonia. On examination, this column, which stands over two meters high and is engraved on all sides, proved to be a legal code, to which the name *The Code of Hammurabi* has been given, since it was collected under the reign of the great Babylonian king, Hammurabi.

At once it claimed the eager attention of Biblical scholarship. Would they find here, as they already thought they had found in the creation story and that of the flood, evidence of dependence of Hebrew culture upon Babylonia? Long familiar with the various Hebrew codes, the Covenant code, the Deuteronomic code, the Levitical code, the Priestly code, they turned to this newest find to see what, if any, similarity existed between them and the Babylonian discovery. There is still not entire agreement among scholars as to just what the influence of the Babylonian code has been. It seems quite apparent that there must have been some carry-over from the early Babylonian to the later Hebrew legislation. Anyone wishing to go into the matter will find lengthy and highly scholarly works on the subject.[18]

The code itself consists of two hundred and eighty-two laws covering a wide range of subject matter. It is all introduced by a discourse written just below a scene picturing the giving of the law by

[16] Pritchard, *op. cit.*, pp. 330 ff. Translation of A. Sachs.
[17] Pritchard, *op. cit.*, pp. 330 ff. Translation of A. Sachs.
[18] W. W. Davies, *The Codes of Hammurabi and Moses*, Cincinnati, 1903. S. A. Cook, *The Laws of Moses and the Code of Hammurabi*, London, 1903.

Shamash, god of justice, to the King. This at once suggests a parallel to the Hebrew decalogue, which Moses, purportedly, received directly at the hands of God. It declares in substance, "When the gods named me Hammurabi to cause righteousness to prevail in the land, to destroy the wicked and the evil, to prevent the strong from plundering the weak, to enlighten the land and to further the welfare of the people . . . I established law and justice in the land and promoted the welfare of the public."[19] Lack of space prevents giving more than a few brief examples of laws taken from the Code, but these may serve to give the flavor of the whole. It begins with the declaration:

1. If a man accuse a man, and charge him with murder, but cannot convict him, the accuser shall be put to death.[20]

A considerable number of other laws deal with the securing of justice before the court. Even the judge is under a control not usual in our own time.

3. If a judge pronounce a judgment, render a decision, deliver a sealed verdict, and afterward reverse his judgment, they shall prosecute the judge for reversing the judgment which he has pronounced, and he shall pay twelve fold the damages which were (awarded) in said judgment; and publicly they shall expel him from his seat of judgment and he shall not return, and with the judges in a case he shall not take his seat.[21]

There is here, and throughout, a very definite assessment of guilt according to the status of the one who does the injury, or that of the injured. For example:

8. If a man steal an ox or sheep, ass or pig, or boat—if it belonged to a god or palace, he shall pay thirty fold; if it belonged to a common man, he shall restore tenfold. If the thief have nothing wherewith to pay, he shall be put to death.[22]

[19] J. M. P. Smith, *The Origin and History of Hebrew Law,* University of Chicago Press, 1931, pp. 181–183, *passim.* Translation of D. D. Luckenbill, edited by Edward Chiera.
[20] *Ibid.,* p. 183.
[21] *Ibid.,* p. 184.
[22] *Ibid.,* p. 184.

Public authorities are made responsible for good order. If a robber is not captured, the city and the governor in whose land the robbery was committed shall compensate the victim for his loss.[23] Protection is thrown about property as well as about the person of the individuals. There are laws covering the obligation of landlords to tenants, and of tenants to those from whom they rent. One who rents a field and is negligent in cultivating it, must give produce to the owner of the field on the basis of production in adjacent fields.[24] Since much of the land was under irrigation, strict laws applied to the use of water. Evidently money-lending was common, for a number of laws deal with putting out money at interest. The rate of interest was under control, as were prices and wages. The modern New Deal is not so modern as many people apparently think. Women are protected and likewise regulated. Some of the laws at this point resemble closely those of the Hebrew codes. Divorce was easy for a man, and next to impossible for a woman. Children were subject to rigid parental control. If a man struck his father, his hand should be cut off. Indeed, the principle of *Lex Talionis* is invoked throughout.

196. If a man destroy the eye of another man they shall destroy his eye.
200. If a man knock out a tooth of a man of his own race they shall knock out his tooth.[25]

The principle is carried to an utter extreme in the case of a builder who wrecks a house which collapses and kills the son of the owner of the house. In such a case:[26]

230. If it cause the death of a son of the owner of the house, they shall then put to death the son of that builder.

An amazing indication of medical skill is to be found in the law regulating the operation, with a bronze lancet, upon the eye

[23] Sec. 23, Smith, *op. cit.*, p. 186.
[24] Sec. 42. *Id.*, p. 189.
[25] *Id.*, pp. 209–210.
[26] *Id.*, p. 213.

socket. The physician is made responsible for any mistake he makes.

218. Should a physician make a deep incision upon a man with his bronze lancet and cause the man's death or operate on the eye socket of a man with his bronze lancet and destroy the man's eye they shall cut off his hand.[27]

The penalty was less if the operation was upon a man's slave. A man is ordinarily responsible for anything that he has hired during the time of his possession, but,

249. If a man hire an ox and a god strike it and it die, the man who hired the ox shall take an oath before God and go free.[28]

There are a number of laws that deal with slaves and their rights. Included is the right to buy their own freedom. There is a lengthy conclusion of the Code in which the King declares, in part: "By the command of Shamash, the great judge of Heaven and Earth, may I make righteousness to shine forth on the land...let any oppressed man who has a cause come before the image of me, the king of Righteousness! Let him have read to him the writing of my monument! Let him give heed to my weighty words! And may my monument enlighten him as to his cause and may he understand his case. May it set his heart at ease."..."In the days to come, for all time, let the king who arises in the land observe the words of righteousness which I have written...let him not alter the judgment...which I have pronounced"....etc.[29]

We conclude the discussion of Babylonian sacred literature with only a brief mention of the omen texts, of which a great many have been unearthed. The Babylonians, like most peoples, believed that the gods were concerned about what man did. Both in the conduct of private and public affairs they believed they should seek divine guidance. What was the will of the gods in any specific undertaking? How could it be discovered? The answer lay in omens through

---

[27] Smith, *op. cit.*, p. 211.
[28] *Id.*, p. 215.
[29] *Id.*, pp. 219–221, *passim.*

which their will was made known to man. Sometimes divination was by the reading of the stars, astrology, sometimes by reading the livers of sacrificial victims, or other means. There were special diviners, who were skilled in interpreting the omens. A recently translated document recording the restoration of the chief temple of the national god of Assyria, Ashur, illustrates the importance of the role of omens in the conduct of affairs. The temple had fallen into disrepair. Essarhadon, the king, was reluctant to do anything about it,

until by the implements of the haruspices, Shamash and Adad returned a true affirmative and for the rebuilding of the temple and the renewing of its cella they caused a liver omen to be written.

Then he, "the obedient lord," called the people and put them to work. He himself made bricks and carried them, and "the people of the land formed bricks in delight, joy and jubilation."[30]

Unfortunately, few of the omen texts are available in English. A Hittite omen text is included in Pritchard's *Ancient Near Eastern Texts,* pp. 495–496.

This, it must be remarked, does not find a very close parallel in the Hebrew Bible, though there are not a few stories of the casting of lots, which is a form of divination of the will of the gods. But the desire to square conduct with the divine will is certainly there.

BABYLONIAN SACRED LITERATURE
Sources for Further Reading

Robert W. Rogers, *The Religion of Babylonia and Assyria,* Eaton and Mains, N. Y., 1908.

Id., *Cuneiform Parallels to the Old Testament,* Eaton and Mains, N. Y., 1912.

Morris Jastrow, *Civilization of Babylonia and Assyria,* J. B. Lippincott, Philadelphia, 1915.

Id., *The Religion of Babylonia and Assyria,* Ginn and Co., Boston, 1898.

J. B. Pritchard, Editor, *Ancient Near Eastern Texts Relating to the Old Testament.* Princeton University Press, 1950.—An excellent translation of well selected material illustrating every phase of Babylonian

[30] *Journal of the American Oriental Society,* Vol. 71, 1, pp. 5–6.

sacred literature. Covers much the same ground as Rogers, *Cuneiform Parallels,* but enjoys the advantage of forty additional years of archaeological and scholarly investigation.

Sacred Books and Literature of the East, Vol. I.

The Hammurabi code appears in several editions by different translators.

CHAPTER V

The Sacred Literature of Hinduism

"Mother" India, as she is lovingly called by her sons, has indeed been a mother of religions. Four of the eleven principal living faiths of the world were born in India: Hinduism, Buddhism, Jainism, and Sikhism, and all have extensive sacred literatures. Hinduism itself, from which all the others have sprung, has a vast and highly variegated set of scriptures. In general there are two types of scripture that are regarded as authoritative in Hinduism: (1) *sruti:* that which may be regarded as the *ipsissima verba,* the very, very word of God. It was given by verbal inspiration to the rishiis or seers, and gathered into a closed canon. From this nothing may be taken away and nothing may be added. This type of sacred writing has, in the course of time, come to be thought of very much as the Bible is thought of by Christian Fundamentalists: as infallible, incapable of error, because of its non-human character.

The second type of scripture is known as *smriti.* While admittedly of human origins, it has come to be thought of as authoritative also, in the expression of religious faith, and of very high value in the teaching of religion and morals. Though of less exalted origin, and not of equal value with *sruti,* as a basis of religious dogma, it is perhaps quite as influential in the lives of the people in inculcating and nourishing religious faith and practice. If all the books which are comprised within these two classes of sacred literature were to be brought together in a single collection, as has nowhere yet been done, they would fill many thousands of pages. While there is rather general agreement as to what may be considered as *smriti,* there is no closed canon. Sectarian groups differ to a considerable degree as to what may be so considered. Certainly they differ as to which particular books of this category are to be emphasized within their own groups. The rather generally tolerant attitude of Indians toward the religious beliefs of others inclines them to admit as sacred for others what they might not accept for themselves. As a matter of fact some sectarian groups make, practically, much greater use of non-*sruti* literature, as the basis for present belief and practice than they do of the recognized *sruti* writings. Indeed for them some books generally regarded as *smriti* have actually become *sruti.* There is nothing in Hinduism to prevent this from happening.

Within Hindu sacred literature may be found, as in most scripture, almost every type of writing. There is both poetry and prose. Examples of nearly every variety of poetic expression may be found. Some of it is lyric, some elegiac, some epic, some dramatic. Love songs abound. There is poetry of praise, poetry of lamentation, heroic verse, and poetry of despair, poetry of thanksgiving, poetry of devotion, poetry that is light, airy, fanciful, and poetry that seeks to express the most profound philosophic insight. Of prose there is every kind, the short story, the drama, the fable, legal lore, philosophic essays, history, drama. Only the epistolary, which is so important in the New Testament, seems to be lacking. There are prose passages of unusual beauty and strength; there are innumerable pages of dry dialectic material, without grace or charm, but none the less important for an understanding of Hinduism.

This Hindu literature like that of most other religions represents the work of many, many hands over a long period of time. It records the hopes, aspirations, ideals, triumphs, failures, strivings after meaning of a great people, across the centuries, as they developed from barbarism to the highly cultured society which is India today at its best. Out of the struggle upward the literature was born and by it India's life has been shaped and controlled to a remarkable degree, for India's sacred literature is no mere museum piece. The daily routine of the orthodox Hindu is probably much more determined by some part of his scriptures than that of the people of the West by the Bible, or for that matter than that of any other people by its scripture, save only the Moslems.

India's sacred literature divides itself logically and to some extent chronologically, into four main groups: (1) Vedic literature, (2) Legal literature, (3) Epic literature and (4) Puranic literature. The exact chronology of some writings it is difficult to fix, and there is often a difference in time between the beginnings of a given body of literature and its final completion. The beginnings of the Epics may well have been within the late Vedic age, their completion more than a millennium later. The earliest formulation of legal codes may go well back into the past; the final fixing of the codes is comparatively late, and of course some codes are much earlier than others. Some of the Puranic lore is old. The Puranas, as now found, are the latest of all Hindu sacred writings. We consider first Vedic literature.

VEDIC LITERATURE

Vedic literature is *sruti*, the infallible, verbally inspired word of God. It is the most sacred of all. So sacred was it held to be at the time of the making of the Code of Manu, greatest of the law books, that it was therein decreed that a lowly *Sudra*, i.e., low caste man, who so much as listened to the sacred text would have molten metal poured into his ears, and his tongue cut out if he pronounced the sacred words of the holy Vedas.[1] Whether such laws were ever actually enforced may be doubted. Certainly there is no evidence that they were, but they do serve to accentuate the degree of sacredness which attached to the Vedic literature.

Vedic literature comprises much more than the Vedas. These give their name to an extensive literature which grew out of them. Specifically regarded as part of the Veda are (1) the Brahmanas,

[1] This is given by Winternitz, Vol. I, p. 35, f.n., as from law book of Gautama XII, 4–6.

(2) the Aranyakas, and (3) the Upanishads. It has become a dogma generally accepted that all that is found in these later writings is simply an outgrowth of the Vedas, the making explicit of what was therein implicit. They are therefore regarded as equally sacred. There is another reason—perhaps the primary reason—for considering them as Vedic, namely, that these writings, except the Vedanta Sutras, were physically attached to the Vedas in their written form.

Most basic of all Hindu sacred writings are the Samhitas, generally called the Vedas themselves, of which there are four, and most basic of the four is the Rig-Veda. The others, the Sama-Veda, the Yajur-Veda and the Atharva-Veda, all derive to a considerable extent from the Rig. Most of our attention will therefore be given to this highly important sacred book.

The name of the book, Rig-Veda, means probably "Verse Wisdom." It is a collection of hymns, 1017 in all according to Griffith. In bulk it is longer than the combined *Iliad* and *Odyssey* of Homer. Translated into English, and with some notes, the hymns make two quite substantial volumes.[2] In the original there are some 20,000 metrical verses in the whole collection.

For the Rig-Veda is just that, a collection, the work of a great many writers, or in some cases, guilds of writers. It consists chiefly of hymns to one or another of the numerous Vedic gods, designed for use in the worship of these divinities. It represents the oldest stratum of Hinduism of which very much is known. In recent times archaeological discoveries in the Indus valley have brought to light evidences of a highly developed culture in India long before the coming of the invading Aryans. Whereas, earlier, it had been believed that the Aryans found only peoples of relatively undeveloped culture, now it is known that at least some of these early Indians had developed the arts to a high degree, that they even had a kind of hieroglyphic writing, not yet deciphered, and probably an equally well developed religion which, suppressed for a time, gradually reasserted itself and greatly modified Vedic religion, gradually transforming it into the Hinduism as practiced in India today. (For an

[2] R. T. H. Griffith, *Hymns of the Rig-Veda*.

interesting account of this civilization see Sir John Marshall, *Mohenjo-daro*, 3 volumes.)

Reference has been made to the Aryan invasion of India. Who were the Aryans? There is much that is not known concerning them, but it is known that long, long before they arrived in India they were part of a great migratory movement of people, sometimes identified incorrectly as a race, probably better as a people of a common culture. To this people, eventually, the name Indo-European came to be attached, since sure signs of their presence are to be found all the way from the British Isles on the West, to the Bay of Bengal on the East, and from the Scandinavian countries on the North to the Mediterranean on the South. Though possessing many common cultural traits found also in Europe and the West, the much closer similarities between the cultures of Iran or Persia and India have led scholars to distinguish an Indo-Iranian branch of the larger whole as having early separated itself from the central or original Aryan migration, perhaps moving eastward from the, as yet, not certainly located origin of the Aryan group. Later this segment again separated into two branches. One of these entered the Iranian plateau, amalgamated with the native populations and eventually gave rise to a new faith, Zoroastrianism, which developed its own sacred literature. The other crossed the Khyber pass and entered the land of India, gradually fanning out to cover the greater part of that vast subcontinent, but losing, in the course of its southern movement, much of its original character.

It was of this Aryan migration that the Vedic hymns were born. In a real sense they, at least the older of them, are not really Indian in origin at all, but were produced either before the Aryans had set foot on Indian soil, or were composed by Aryans, i.e., the foreign invaders, before India had had time to put her own impress upon them. When this invasion took place it is impossible to state with any certainty. It is rather generally supposed to have occurred some time within the period 2500–1500 B.C., though some Indian scholars put it at a much earlier date, even as early as 5000 B.C.

In modern times the term Aryan has become a racial term, as in Germany under the Nazis, when a sharp distinction was made between the Aryan and the Semitic elements in the population. But beyond the probable fact that the Aryan invaders were light rather than dark of skin, little can be alleged as to their racial character. This is evidenced by the lighter complexions of the present-day Indian in the northern parts of India where the Aryans mingled in largest proportion with the indigenous population, in contrast to the much darker complexion of southern Indians where the Aryan influence is least. Also it is an easily recognized fact that modern-day Indians, particularly of the northern half, or more, appear to have European features despite their darker color. Modern anthropologists and ethnologists give no support to the existence, now or at any time, of a pure Aryan race. They do attest to an Aryan culture widely spread over most of Europe, Persia and India, on the basis of evidences drawn from language, the archaeological discovery of artifacts and objects of art, and certain similarities of religious ideas to be found in the areas overrun by these far-ranging migrants.

Whatever the nature of the Aryans, it is a proudly held word in contemporary India. One vigorous modern reform movement in Hinduism which seeks to recapture the best of India's religious heritage calls itself the Arya-Samaj, the Society of Aryans; another publishes a religious journal which it calls *The Aryan Path*. To behave as a true Aryan comes to have something of the meaning of the Confucian term, "the Superior Man," or the old English phrase of "the true gentleman."

The hymns of the Rig-Veda are much older, of course, than the collection itself. Most of them were composed for use in the cult, although there are hymns which seem to be the more or less spontaneous expression of the individual human spirit. At first this cult, or worship was conducted by the father of the household, but in time there arose a specialized priesthood for the performance of the appropriate sacrifices and rituals, and the hymns were probably largely produced by them and for their use in the cult. Not many hymns can be assigned to specific authors, though the Rig-Veda contains seven groups of hymns attributed to seven families, the Gritsamada, Visvamitra, Vamadeva, Atri, Bharadvaja, Vasistha, and Kanva. These may represent separate schools of poetry—the hymns in any one group are certainly not all by the same individual. The collection was not made all at one time, as seems evident also in the Hebrew book of Psalms.

There are ten books in all. Of these, Books II through VII contain the greater number of the oldest hymns and were the first to be brought together, possibly at the command of some famous chief. Here a uniform arrangement appears. Hymns are grouped by families and within each family group they are arranged according to the gods to whom the hymns are addressed; and within these groups according to the number of stanzas, in descending order. Conjecturally, there were then collected and added what is now the second half of Book I, then the first half of Book I and Book VIII, then Book IX which is dedicated entirely to the god Soma, the intoxicant deity, and, finally, the latest of all the books, the tenth and last. Book IX, while collected later than most of the others, contains hymns which may well be as old as any.

From these hymns can be discovered much concerning the life and thought of the ancient Vedic Indians. It is a rare source book for the study of their culture. Here are disclosed not only their religious ideas, their deepest longings, their sins and failures, their ideas of good and evil, their hopes and fears; but also how they worked, how they played, how they fought, what they ate, how they dressed, the pattern of their domestic and public life. Indeed, all we can know about this people is here preserved, for they left no monuments, or buildings, or inscriptions from which the archaeologist might recapture their ancient civilization. It is not only the *sacred* literature of the period, it is the only literature that has been preserved, and it was preserved only because it became sacred.

From the older hymns it is clear that they were still an invading, conquering people, dependent upon military skill and power to make their way ever more deeply into India. Proof of this is the prominent place given to Indra who was their god of war. Much can be inferred as to the character and activity of people from the gods who hold positions of principal importance. In war times there has always been, and still is, a need for a god of battles to spur men on to fight. In modern times when men believe in but one god, his militant character always comes to the front in war time, and his more pacific character is played down. Nearly one-fourth of all the hymns of the Rig-Veda are to Indra. Of course he is more than a war god; he is also god of storm, beneficent, life-bringing storm, which makes grass to grow. The ruder, more destructive aspects of storm are assigned to Rudra, father of the Maruts, who are often associated with Indra in his hymns.

The Vedic people are still pastoral to a large degree. Cultivation of the soil has not yet become a primary source of their living. It is a cattle culture, as only a very cursory glance at the hymns will quickly disclose. Their prayers—to Indra, and to others as well—are largely for rich pasturage, great herds of cattle, long life, big families, and of course success in battle. Rain is a necessity if pastures are to be green. Indra is the slayer of the demon Vritra who herds the cloud cows into a cave and prevents the rains from coming. Prayers rise to Indra. He prepares himself by consuming ponds of Soma, the intoxicant, then sallies forth to slay the monster Vritra. This is all recalled in one of the hymns.

1. Let me tell out the manly deeds of Indra,
   Which he accomplished first of all, bolt-weaponed:
   He slew the serpent, opened up the waters,
   And cleft in twain the belly of the mountains.

3. With bull-like eagerness he sought the soma;
   Out of three vats he drank the pressed out liquor;
   Maghavan took in hand his bolt, the missile,
   And smote therewith the first-born of the serpents.

6. For, like a drunken weakling, Vritra challenged
   The mighty hero, the impetuous warrior;
   He did not meet the clash of Indra's weapons,
   Broken and crushed he lay, whose foe was Indra.

13. Lightning and thunder profited him nothing,
    Nor mist nor hailstorm which he spread around him;
    When Indra and the serpent fought their battle,
    Maghavan won the victory forever.

15. Indra is king of that which moves and moves not,
    Of tame and horned creatures, too, bolt weaponed;
    Over the tribes of men he rules as monarch;
    As felly spokes, so holds he them together.[3]

Indra's close relationship to the preservation of cattle—and therefore to wealth and prosperity of the people—is seen in this hymn
which reflects the naive character of a simple pastoral people:

The Kine have come and brought good fortune: let them rest
    in the cow-pen and be happy near us.
Here let them stay prolific, many colored, and yield through
    many morns their milk for Indra.

Indra aids him who offers sacrifice and gifts; he takes not
    what is his, and gives him more thereto.
Increasing ever more and ever more his wealth, he makes the
    pious dwell within unbroken bounds.

These are ne'er lost, no robber ever injures them: evil-
    minded foe attempts to harass them.
The master of the Kine lives many a year with these, the Cows
    whereby he pours his gifts and serves the Gods.[4]

But Indra also comes to be thought of at times as more than just
a fertility and war god. In one of the hymns he assumes almost the
character of a monotheistic creator god. If no other hymn of the
whole collection had been preserved it would be easy to assume that
Indra had indeed become the one god of the world. This is but an
example of the habit of Vedic people to elevate momentarily first
one divinity, then another to supremacy. To describe this attitude,
Max Muller proposed a new synthetic word, henotheism. Here is a
part of a hymn too long to quote entire:

1. He who as soon as born keen-thoughted, foremost,
    Surpassed the gods, himself, a god, in power;

[3] H. D. Griswold, *The Religion of the Rig-Veda*, Book I: 32, pp. 178–179.
[4] Ralph T. H. Griffith, *Hymns of the Rig-Veda*, Vol. 1, Book VI: 28, pp. 589–
590.

Before whose vehemence the worlds trembled
Through his great valour; he, O men, is Indra.

2. He who the quivering earth hath firm established,
   And set at rest the agitated mountains;
   Who measured out the mid-air far-extending,
   And sky supported: he, O men, is Indra.

3. Who slew the snake and freed the seven rivers,
   Drove out the cattle by unclosing Vala;
   Who fire between two rocks hath generated,
   In battles victor: he, O men, is Indra.

13. Even the heavens and earth bow down before him,
    And at his vehemence the mountains tremble;
    Who, bolt in arm, is known as Soma-drinker,
    With hands bolt-wielding; he, O men, is Indra.[5]

Fire plays an important role in the life of any people, and is commonly worshiped throughout the world. In Vedic India this element whether as in the hearthfire, in the lightning stroke, or in the blazing sun was an object of constant worship as Agni.[6] It is not easy in many of the hymns to say whether the object of cult is the fire itself or a god behind it; perhaps they themselves were not always sure either. Fire is a servant, fire is a friend, it is a purifier, a cleanser, and perhaps most important of all, it is that which transmutes the sacrifice into a holy food for the gods. Easily Agni becomes a mediator or priest god. One of the many hymns reads thus:

HYMN XVIII

Agni, be kind to us when we approach thee, good as a friend
   to friend, as sire and mother.
The races of mankind are great oppressors: burn up malignity
   that strives against us.

[5] H. D. Griswold, *The Religion of the Rig-Veda*, pp. 192, 193.
[6] Cf. Latin *ignis* for fire.

Agni, burn up the unfriendly who are near us, burn thou the
     foeman's curse who pays no worship.
Burn, Vasu, thou who markest well, the foolish: Let thine
     eternal nimble beams surround thee.
With fuel, Agni, and with oil, desirous, mine offering I pre-
     sent for strength and conquest,
With prayer, so far as I have power, adoring—This hymn
     divine to gain a hundred treasures.
Give with thy glow, thou Son of Strength when lauded, great
     vital power to those who toil to serve thee.
Give richly, Agni, to the Visvamitras in rest and stir.
     Oft have we decked thy body.
Give us, O liberal Lord, great store of riches, for, Agni,
     such art thou when duly kindled.
Thou in the happy singer's home bestowest, amply with arms
     extended, things of beauty.[7]

The entire ninth book consists of hymns to Soma. Soma is sometimes the plant, from which juice is extracted to become, when properly strained and mixed, Soma, the intoxicant, the food of the gods,
the elixir of immortality, and finally Soma is one of the chief Vedic
divinities. Nowhere in literature has the intoxicant been more lyrically described and exalted than in this ninth book. The writers
never tire of describing the process of preparation of the divine
drink. Every literary art is laid under tribute to glorify it. The press,
the filter, or straining cloth, the utensils which contain it are described in loving detail. Soma is the drink of the gods. All seem to
be entitled to a libation at intervals, and their standing within the
pantheon can be pretty well determined by the amount and frequency of the offering of Soma to the different divinities. Indra
more than all of them loves it. Three times each day he must have
his meed of Soma, and for his major exploits in man's behalf he
quaffs unbelievable quantities of it, not measured by cups but by
vats or ponds or lakes. To none of the intoxicant gods in the
religions of the world have greater virtues or powers been attributed. Space limits permit only a few illustrations:

[7] Ralph T. H. Griffith, *Hymns of the Rig-Veda*, Vol. I, pp. 335–336.

1. Sent forth by men, this mighty steed,
   Lord of the mind, who knoweth all,
   Runs to the woolen straining-cloth.

2. Within the filter hath he flowed.
   This Soma for the gods effused,
   Entering all their various worlds.

3. Resplendent is this deity,
   Immortal in his dwelling place,
   Foe-slayer, feaster best of gods.

4. Directed by the sisters ten,
   Bellowing on his way this bull
   Runs onward to the wooden vats.

5. This Pavamana made the sun
   To shine and all his various worlds,
   Omniscient, present everywhere.

6. This Soma filtering himself,
   Flows mighty and infallible,
   Slayer of sinners, feasting gods.[8]

Here is a prayer for immortality, addressed appropriately enough to the god who represents, in physical form, the drink of immortality (although the god of the dead and of whatever other-worldly dwelling place awaited them was not Soma but Yama).

7. Where radiance inexhaustible
   Dwells, and the light of heaven is set,
   Place me, clear-flowing one, in that
   Imperishable and deathless world.
   (O Indu, flow for Indra's sake.)

8. Make me immortal in the place
   Where dwells the king Vaivasvata,
   Where stands the inmost *shrine* of heaven,
   And where the living waters are.

[8] H. D. Griswold, *The Religion of the Rig-Veda*, p. 222.

9. Make me immortal in that realm,
   Wherein is movement glad and free,
   In the third sky, third heaven of heavens,
   Where are the lucid worlds of light.

10. Make me immortal in the place
    Where loves and longings are fulfilled,
  · The region of the ruddy (sphere),
    Where food and satisfaction reign.

11. Make me immortal in the place
    Wherein felicity and joy,
    Pleasure and bliss together dwell,
    And all desire is satisfied.[9]

One more quotation must suffice. A graduate student, reading it, was impressed and, being employed as a youth director in one of the local churches and in charge of a weekly worship service, undertook to modify it at certain points and use it as a litany in the Sunday morning service. It so happened that the pastor of the church visited the group that morning, and, impressed by the beautiful litany, inquired where she had found it. He was not a little surprised to learn that it was out of an ancient book of hymns of a pagan people dedicated to an intoxicant divinity. It reads in part:

O Soma flowing on thy way, win thou and conquer high renown;
And make us better than we are.
Win thou the light, win heavenly light, and, Soma, all felicities;
And make us better than we are.
Win skilful strength and mental power, O Soma, drive away our foes;
And make us better than we are.
Ye purifiers, purify Soma for Indra, for his drink;
Make thou us better than we are.
Give us our portion in the Sun through thine own mental power and
    aids;
And make us better than we are.
Through thine own mental power and aid long may we look upon the
    Sun:

[9] Griswold, *The Religion of the Rig-Veda*, pp. 241–242.

Make thou us better than we are.
Well-weaponed Soma, pour to us a stream of riches
    doubly great;
And make us better than we are.
As one victorious, unsubdued in battle pour forth
    wealth to us;
And make us better than we are.
By worship Pavamana! men have strengthened thee to prop the Law:
Make thou us better than we are.
O Indu, bring us wealth in steeds, manifold, quickening
    all life;
And make us better than we are.[10]

It is in the hymns to the great god Varuna that the Vedas reach their highest point, judged from the standpoint of a Christian culture. Here they come closest in moral and spiritual insight to the Hebrew Psalms and the New Testament. Most of the Vedic religious aspiration moves at the level of the satisfaction of physical needs—long life, food, shelter, protection, large families—but in these hymns one finds a consciousness of sin and guilt and the need for forgiveness, as well also as guidance and direction in living.

1. Wise are the generations through the greatness
    Of him who propped the two wide worlds asunder;
    Pushed forth the great and lofty vault of heaven,
    The day-star, too; and spread the earth out broadly.

2. With mine own self I meditate this question:
    "When shall I have with Varuna communion?
    What gift of mine will he enjoy unangered?
    When shall I happy-hearted see his mercy?"

3. Wishing to know my sin I make inquiry,
    I go about to all the wise and ask them;
    One and the self-same thing even sages tell me;
    "Varuna hath with thee hot indignation."

[10] Ralph T. H. Griffith, *Hymns of the Rig-Veda,* Vol. II, Book IX: 4, pp. 271–272.

4. O Varuna, what was my chief transgression,
   That thou wouldst slay a friend who sings thy praises?
   Tell me, god undeceived and sovereign, guiltless,
   Would I appease thee then with adoration.

5. Set us free from the misdeeds of our fathers,
   From those that we ourselves have perpetrated;
   Like cattle-thief, O king, like calf rope-fastened,
   So set thou free Vasistha from the fetter.

6. 'Twas not mine own will, Varuna, 'twas delusion,
   Drink, anger, dice, or lack of thought, that caused it;
   An older man has led astray a younger,
   Not even sleep protects a man from evil.

7. O let me like a slave, when once made sinless,
   Serve him the merciful, erewhile the angry.
   The noble god has made the thoughtless thoughtful;
   He speeds the wise to riches, he a wiser.

8. May this my praise-song, Varuna, sovereign ruler,
   Reach unto thee and make thy heart complaisant;
   May it be well with us in rest and labour,
   Do yet protect us evermore with blessings.[11]

Or, again in another hymn:

> Against a friend, companion, or a brother,
> A fellow-tribesman, or against a stranger,
> Whatever trespass we have perpetrated,
> Do thou, O Varuna, from that release us.
> If we, like those that play at dice, have cheated,
> Have really sinned, or done amiss unwitting,
> Cast all these sins away, as from us loosened;
> So may we, Varuna, be thine own beloved.[12]

One is reminded of Psalm 139 by the following hymn which reveals Varuna as all seeing, even to the inward thought of a man.

[11] Book VII, 86, Griswold, *Religion of the Rig-Veda*, pp. 121–122.
[12] *Ibid.*, Book V. 85, 7–8, p. 124.

7. He knows the path of birds that through
   The atmosphere do wing their flight,
   And ocean-dwelling knows the ships.

8. He knows, as one whose law is firm,
   The twelve months with their progeny,
   Knows too the month of later birth.

9. He knows the pathway of the wind,
   The wide, the high, the mighty wind,
   And those that sit enthroned above.

10. Enthroned within his palace sits
    God Varuna whose law is firm,
    All-wise for universal sway.

11. From there the observant god beholds
    All strange and secret happenings,
    Things that are done or to be done.

12. Let him the all-wise Aditya
    Make all our days fair-pathed for us;
    May he prolong our earthly lives.

13. Wearing a golden mantle, clothed
    In shining garb, is Varuna;
    His spies are seated round about.

14. He whom deceivers do not dare
    Try to deceive, nor injurers
    To harm, nor th' hostile to defy.[13]

The tenth book is the latest of all, and in it are found at least the beginnings of speculation concerning the nature and origin of the world, which occupies so important a place in the later sacred literature of India. Take, for instance, the hymn to the Unknown God. If at the end the answer is given that it is Prajapati who has created everything, this is thought by many to have been a later addition.

1. The Golden Germ arose in the beginning,
   Born the sole lord of everything existing;
   He fixed and holdeth up this earth and heaven,—
   Who is the god to worship with oblation?

[13] H. D. Griswold, *op. cit.*, Book I, 25, p. 128.

2. He who gives breath and strength, he whose commandment
   All beings follow, yea the gods acknowledge;
   Whose shadow immortality and death is,—
   Who is the god to worship with oblation?

3. He who through greatness hath become sole monarch
   Of all the moving world that breathes and slumbers;
   Who ruleth over quadrupeds and bipeds,—
   Who is the god to worship with oblation?

5. He through whom sky is firm and earth is steady,
   Through whom sun's light and heaven's vault are supported;
   Who in mid-air is measurer of the spaces,—
   Who is the god to worship with oblation?

8. He who in might surveyed the floods containing
   Creative force, the sacrifice producing;
   Who 'mid all gods has been and is alone god,—
   Who is the god to worship with oblation?

10. Prajapati, apart from thee no other
    Hath all these things embraced and comprehended;
    May that be ours which we desire when off'ring
    Worship to thee; may we be lords of riches.[14]

The great hymn of creation which in some sense foreshadows the pantheism of later Hinduism is evidently quite late, for it describes the origins of caste, of which nothing is known in any of the other Vedic hymns. Only a few verses of it can be given here.

1. A thousand heads has Purusa,
   A thousand eyes, a thousand feet;
   He holding earth enclosed about,
   Extends beyond, ten fingers length.

2. Whatever is, is Purusa,
   Both what has been and what shall be;
   He ruleth the immortal world,
   Which he transcends through sacred food.

[14] H. D. Griswold, *Religion of the Rig-Veda*, Book X, 121, pp. 348–349.

3. As great as this is Purusa,
   Yet greater still his greatness is;
   All creatures are one-fourth of him,
   Three-fourths th' immortal in the heaven.

4. Three-fourths ascended up on high,
   One-fourth came into being here;
   Thence he developed into what
   Is animate and inanimate.

6. When gods performed a sacrifice
   With Purusa as their offering,
   Spring was its oil and Summer-heat
   Its fuel, its oblation Fall.

8. From that completely-offered rite
   Was gathered up the clotted oil;
   It formed the creatures of the air,
   And animals both wild and tame.

10. From that were horses born and all
    The beasts that have two rows of teeth;
    Cattle were also born from that,
    And from that spring the goats and sheep.

11. Then they dismembered Purusa;
    How many portions did they make?
    What was his mouth called, what his arms,
    What his two thighs, and what his feet?

12. His mouth became the *Brahmana,*
    And his two arms the *Ksatriya;*
    His thighs became the *Vaisya*-class,
    And from his feet the *Sudra* sprang.

13. The Moon was gendered from his mind,
    And from his eye the Sun was born;
    Indra and Agni from his mouth,
    And Vayu from his breath was born.

14. Forth from his navel came the air,
And from his head evolved the sky;
Earth from his feet and from his ear
The quarters: thus they framed the worlds.[15]

There are hymns to many different gods in the Rig-Veda, almost a fourth of them to Indra alone, and over two hundred to Agni, but to lovely Ushas, goddess of dawn, one of the very few goddesses of any independent character in the whole of Vedic religion, there are only twenty-one. Most goddesses are merely given the feminine form of the name of their more important consorts. Thus Indrani is the wife of Indra. There are hymns to numerous sun gods, Vishnu, Surya, Pusan, Mitra, who later appears in Mithraism as a rival of Christianity in the Mediterranean area; to Rudra, god of destructive storm, to Yama, god of the dead, and many others, from which it would be pleasant to quote if space allowed.

Only about thirty hymns are not concerned with the worship of some one or another of the gods. Two of these have already been cited. There are a dozen magical hymns: I, 191; II, 42, 43; X, 145, 162, 163, 166, 183. Two are riddles. Four are didactic, IX, 112; X, 71, 117, and X, 34. This latter has to do with gambling which was apparently very common in Vedic times, as later we shall find it recurring in the Epic literature.

The date of the completion of the collection of the Rig-Vedic hymns cannot be fixed with certainty. Scholars differ in their conjectures from as early as 1200–1000 B.C. to as late as 800–600 B.C. All are agreed that it took place before the appearance of Buddha in the sixth century. But since also they are agreed that the later Vedic literature is also pre-Buddhist, and that these presuppose the existence of the Rig-Veda and indeed depend upon it, it would seem to this writer that a substantial lapse of time must be allowed for the very considerable development of religious thought to take place. Thus it would seem that a date not far from 1000–800 B.C. would be called for. That there were various rescensions of the original collection is doubtless true. The one which has come down to us is that of the Sakalaka school. The remarkable thing is that it

[15] H. D. Griswold, *Religion of the Rig-Veda*, Book X, 90, pp. 344–346.

was preserved and transmitted orally for centuries before it was reduced to writing, passed on from teacher to pupil. When the first written edition was made is not certainly known. I-tsing, Chinese traveller in India in the seventh century A.D., states that the Vedas were still transmitted orally.[16] This does not mean necessarily that there were no written copies, but only that dependence for authoritative transmission was not on the written copies which are so very much subject to error, but upon the painstaking oral transmission from teacher to pupil. It is probable that they were not consigned to written form until sometime not far from the beginning of the Christian era.

If this feat of memory seems almost incredible to the modern student, dependent upon his notebook and pen, let him recall that this was the work of specialists whose primary business it was to cultivate their memories, and who had a profound sense of the importance of transmitting, without error, the sacred text. Furthermore special devices were employed to insure that no word or line slipped out of place as so easily happens in copying a written text by hand, or setting it up in type. In general, the schemes were designed so that each separate word was linked with the word or words before and following it, so that it would be almost impossible either to omit anything from the text or add anything to it. Three separate schemes are known to have been employed.

The first was known as the step text, most easily seen if we designate the first word by the letter "a," the second by "b," and so on. The text was then learned thus: ab—bc—cd—de. Employing this scheme in relation to Genesis 1:1 in the Bible it would read: In the, the beginning, beginning God, God created, created the, etc. etc. The next method, called the woven text, was more complex. It ran thus: ab—ba—ab; bc—cb—bc; cd—dc—cd; etc. "In the—the in—in the; the beginning—beginning the—the beginning; etc. etc." One would think that any mistake with this system would be almost impossible, but just to be quite sure, an even more complicated system for learning the text was worked out. It was known as the *Ghana-patha*, the two previously given, respectively, as *Krama-patha*

---

[16] Winternitz, Vol. I, p. 36, f.n. Takakusu translation, p. 182.

and *Jata-patha*. It reads as follows: ab—ba—abc—cba—abc; bc—cb—bcd—dcb—bcd; or in Biblical terms: "In the—the in—in the beginning—beginning the in—in the beginning, etc."

Could error possibly creep in with this arrangement? The chances are that the Vedic text has been much more correctly transmitted than has the text of ancient holy writ of the Hebrew-Christian tradition, which came to us via the copyists and the printers.

The Rig-Veda is by far the most important of the four Vedas, and is to a large extent the source from which much of the content of the others, particularly the Sama-Veda and the Yajur Veda, is derived. Each of these two Samhitas, or collections, as they are called, arose as the cult developed and are of interest chiefly as revealing the nature of the Vedic cult. Both are essentially priestly documents.

As the cult developed it outgrew the simple household ministration of the father, and a priesthood arose. At first a single priest could perform all the rites. Even so, his various functions were given special names. At one time he was the *Udgatri*, or the singer of hymns, at the Soma-sacrifice. Again, he was the sacrificer, at the animal sacrifice or *Hotri*, performing himself the manual parts as well as reciting the ritual. As the cult became more complex an assistant was required to take care of the manual part of the sacrifice, leaving the *Hotri* free to give his whole attention to the reciting of praises. Eventually there were three ranks of priests, the *Udgatri*, the *Hotri*, and the *Adhvaryu*.

It was for the *Udgatri* that the Sama-Veda or "chant" Veda as it is sometimes called, was formed. All but seventy-five of its more than fifteen hundred verses are taken directly from the Rig-Veda. It is the musical Veda, created for the instruction of the *Udgatri* priests. The first part of it, the Archika or book of praises, consists of 585 single stanzas each to be sung to a separate tune. In ancient times the tunes were taught orally, but in written editions the music accompanies the words. Winternitz says that this part is like a songbook in which only the first stanza of the song is printed as an aid to the recall of the melody. The songs taken chiefly from the Rig-Veda are arranged according to the deities to which they are dedi-

৭৭৭৬

cated. The second, or Uttararchika, contains 1225 stanzas, usually three to each strophe, arranged according to the order of the principal sacrifices. Winternitz compares it to a songbook in which the words are given, assuming that the melody is already known.[17] Of importance in the study of Indian music, and as throwing light on the Vedic cult, it is of little popular interest, and adds nothing essential concerning Vedic life and belief to what is afforded by the Rig-Veda.

The Yajur-Veda was the Veda of the assisting priest or Adhvaryu, whose duty it was to perform the manual part of the sacrifice. From early times it was customary for the priest, while performing various manual acts of the sacrifice, to utter appropriate formulas. These may have been of the nature of magic or incantations. This became a part of the function of the specialized manual priest, leaving the more formal and public ritual utterances to the Hotri or sacrificing priest. Later to these utterances were added also certain praises and prayers derived from the Rig-Veda. It is this material for the use of the Adhvaryu that constitutes the Yajur-Veda collection. It is found in various versions as taught in differing schools. Some of these versions in addition to the above mentioned formulas have incorporated also a certain amount of theological material or *Brahmana* directly into the text. These constitute the so-called Black Yajur-Veda. The other, better known, White Yajur-Veda, has the Brahmana separated out from the formulas and prayers and carries it as an appendix at the end. Brief examples of phrases used by the Adhvaryu are as follows: When a piece of wood with which the sacred fire is to be kindled is dedicated, this formula is recited: "This, Agni, is thy igniter; through it mayst thou grow and thrive. May we also grow and thrive." He addresses the halter by which a sacrificial victim is bound to the stake thus: "Become no snake—become no viper." To the razor with which the sacrificer's beard is about to be shaved he says: "O knife, do not injure him."[18]

Of the forty sections contained in the Yajur-Veda, the first twenty-five, and earliest, contain the prayers for the most important

[17] *Op. cit.,* I, p. 66.
[18] Quoted by Winternitz, II, p. 178.

sacrifices, e.g., the sacrifices of the New and Full Moon, the Soma
sacrifices in general, the Building of the Fire Altar, which requires
a year, and the great Horse Sacrifice. The remaining fifteen are
much later, and are more or less an appendix to the main body of
the work. It is obvious that here is a highly specialized priestly
literature of little popular interest. Nevertheless, it is of very great
importance in the study of Vedic Hinduism.

The fourth of the Vedas, the *Atharva,* is of a still different kind.
It has been characterized as a late book, but as containing a great
deal of very ancient material, reflecting the folk religion of the
early Aryans, and as carried along, it represents the cultural lag of
the Vedic people. For, it is, to no small degree, a book of magic
and charms. It is one of the most interesting books of antiquity and
a very valuable source for an understanding of the folk religion of
the Vedic period. A glance at the table of contents reveals a fascinating list of charms. There is, for example, a charm against a
cough. It runs as follows:

1. As the soul with the soul's desire swiftly to a distance flies, thus do
thou, O cough, fly forth along the soul's course of flight.
2. As a well sharpened arrow swiftly to a distance flies, thus do thou,
O cough, fly forth along the expanse of earth.
3. As the rays of the sun swiftly to a distance fly, thus do thou, O
cough, fly forth along the flood of the sea."[19]

Here is a clear use of mimetic magic. As the soul's desire, as a
sharpened arrow, as the rays of the sun swiftly to a distance fly—
so let cough fly also. But just to help out there are certain things
to be done besides repeating the charm. While reciting the sutra
the patient takes several steps away from the home, again sug-
gestive to the cough, but all this *after* being fed with a churned
drink or hot porridge, i.e., making prudent use of a home remedy,
like drinking hot lemonade, to make a cure doubly sure. A graduate student of English on reading this recalled the following from
the Diary of the famous Samuel Pepys apparently quite soberly
intended.

[19] *Sacred Books of the East,* Vol. 42, p. 8.

> O cramp, be thou faintless
> As our Lady was sinless
> When she bare Jesus.

A charm for finding lost objects recalls practices of the writer's own boyhood days. The formula is this:

> On the distant path of the paths Pushan was born . . .
> He knows these regions all. . . .
> Pushan shall from the east place his right hand about
>   us and shall bring again unto us what has been lost.

Those who seek lost property first have their hands and feet anointed. This is rubbed off and again they are anointed with *ghi* (clarified butter). Then twenty-one pebbles are thrown scatteringly upon a crossroad. These symbolize the lost objects and at the same time are supposed to counteract their lost condition.[20]

We boys of a later day found lost objects sometimes by catching a daddy long-legs, saying over him a formula which unfortunately can no longer be recalled, when the great insect would solemnly point one of his long legs in the supposed direction of the lost object. Sometimes it was by the much less elegant method of spitting in the palm of the hand, striking it with a finger and seeking the lost object in the direction in which the largest spit ball flew. Innumerable examples of like folk beliefs and practices may be found in any so-called advanced culture.

Then there is a charm to promote the growth of hair (6:136); to obtain a husband (2:3); to obtain a wife (6:82); to secure the love of a woman (6:8); and to secure the love of a man (7:38); a charm to secure harmony (3:20); and one to procure influence in an assembly (3:30); a charm to ward off danger from fire (6:106); another to stop an arrow in its flight. There are prayers too, one on building a house (3:12); one for success at gambling (4:38); and particularly in playing at dice (7:50); an incantation for the exorcism of evil dreams (6:46), etc. etc.

In addition there are repeated not a few hymns from the Rig-Veda, and still other theosophic and cosmogonic hymns of rare

[20] *Sacred Books of the East,* Vol. 42, pp. 159–160.

beauty and insight which do not seem to fit in with the cruder concept of religion apparent in the magical portions of the book.

Any anthology which presents only the high and noble points of a sacred literature really misrepresents that literature, for it is not all by any means of equal beauty or interest or of equal moral or religious insight. Most religious literatures have their high spots and their low. From the standpoint of general reader interest the Brahmanas represent the all-time low of Hindu sacred literature, and probably of all the sacred literatures of the world. The Bible has sections that are hard going. Many who bravely set out to read the Bible through from Genesis to Revelation bog down in Leviticus or sooner, and never finish. Well, Leviticus, in comparison with the greater part of the Brahmana literature, is far more interesting and intelligible to the nonpriestly reader. It has the advantage, too, that it is much shorter. Julius Eggeling, translator of the Satapatha Brahmana, says of them, "For wearisome prolixity of exposition, characterized by dogmatic assertion and a flimsy symbolism rather than serious reasoning, these works are perhaps not equalled anywhere unless indeed it be by the speculative vaporings of the gnostics, than which nothing more absurd has probably ever been imagined by rational beings."[21]

The Brahmanas are strictly priestly books and are concerned primarily with the sacrifices which, with increasing complexity, had developed within Vedic Hinduism. Sacrifice had become of enormous importance. By sacrifice the gods could be at first won over to grant favors sought after; then as time went on, it became magical in its powers, and the gods themselves could not resist the prayer spell; indeed, what power they had they owed to the sacrifice.[22] It became a matter of primary importance that the sacrifice be properly performed, for in this its efficacy rested. The Brahmanas provide precisely that detailed direction. Nothing is left to the imagination or the discretion of the priest. Where he shall stand, which way he shall turn, either to right, or left, whether he shall

[21] *Sacred Books of the East,* Vol. 2. Introduction p. ix.
[22] Winternitz I, p. 96.

use right hand or left, in what exact order the various ritual acts must be performed, all this is given in minutest detail.

Typical of the general character of the Brahmanas is the description of the horse sacrifice which occurs in the Satapatha Brahmana. This to be sure was the most complex as well as most important of all the Brahmanic sacrifices. It requires 166 pages in translation in the *Sacred Books of the East,* including extensive footnotes designed to explain the more obscure references in the text. It is much too long and involved to include here—even a detailed description of the sacrifice, much less of the ritual associated with it. But a sample paragraph will suffice to reveal its general character. This one chosen at random, will do.

(He puts the halter on the horse, with Vag. S XXII, 3, 4,) "Encompassing thou art,"—therefore the offer of the Asvamedha conquers all the quarters;—"the world thou art," the world he thus conquers;—"a ruler thou art, an upholder,"—he thus makes him an upholder; "go thou into Agni Vaisvanara," he thus makes him go to Agni Vaisvanara (the friend of all men);—"of wide extent,"—he thus causes him to extend in offspring and cattle;—"consecrated by Svaha (hail!)," this is the Vashat—call for it;—"good speed (to) thee for the gods!"—he thus makes it of good speed for the gods; "for Prajapati,"—the horse is sacred to Prajapati: he thus supplies it with his own deity.[23]

If it is obscure to you, do not be troubled. Even if you read it in its context it would be but little more clear. Indeed, even with the learned translator's detailed footnotes it still does not hold much meaning for one of our time and our culture. Reflect on the fact that this is less than one of some 160 pages of only one *Kanda* describing only one sacrifice, and that the Satapatha-Brahmana of which it is a part is but one of many Brahmanas, all of which were regarded as sacred by the early Hindus, and transmitted orally from priest to priest for centuries. Not only are directions given as to what to do and how to do it but, as appeared in the sample above, some explanation, of either the origin or significance of the act. This often

[23] Satapatha-Brahmana XIII, 1, 2, 3. *Sacred Books of the East,* Vol. 44, pp. 276–277.

runs into rather profound speculations, or often into very obscure symbolism. Indeed, Eggeling calls them "theological treatises composed chiefly for the purpose of explaining the sacrificial texts as well as the origin and deeper meaning of the various rites."[24] Happily also in the midst of tiresome, repetitious instruction are to be found at least the beginnings of some important aspects of India's later culture, philosophic speculation, grammar, astronomy, logic, and also a considerable amount of legend and myth.

Here are to be found, for example, a number of creation myths, not at all in agreement with each other. India never conceived of one single myth of the world's creation, as found in the Bible and many other cultures. Here is a rather delightful account of the creation of night:

"Yama had died. The gods tried to persuade Yam (a twin sister) to forget him. Whenever they asked her, she said: "Only today he has died." Then the gods said: "Thus she will indeed never forget him; we will create night!" For at that time there was only day and no night. The gods created night; then arose a morrow; thereupon she forgot him. Therefore people say: "Day and night indeed. Let sorrow be forgotten."[25]

Most scriptures have somewhere within them a flood story. Hindu literature is no exception, and it is found in the Brahmanas:

> There lived in ancient time a holy man,
> Called Manu, who by penances and prayer
> Had won the favor of the Lord of Heaven.
> One day they brought him water for ablution;
> Then as he washed his hands a little fish
> Appeared, and spoke in human accents thus:
> "Take care of me, and I will be your savior."
> "From what wilt thou preserve me?" Manu asked.
> The fish replied, "A flood will sweep away
> All creatures. I will rescue thee from that."

[24] *Sacred Books of the East,* Vol. 12. Introduction, p. xxii.
[25] Maitrayani-Samhita I, 5, 12. Quoted by Winternitz I, 219.

"But how shall I preserve thee?" Manu said.
The fish rejoined, "So long as we are small,
We are in constant danger of destruction,
For fish eat fish. So keep me in a jar;
When I outgrow the jar, then dig a trench
And place me there; when I outgrow the trench
Then take me to the ocean; I shall then
Be out of reach of danger." Having thus
Instructed Manu, straightway rapidly
The fish grew larger. Then he spoke again,
"In such and such a year the flood will come;
Therefore construct a ship and pay me homage;
When the flood rises enter thou the ship
And I will rescue thee." So Manu did
As he was ordered, and preserved the fish.
Then carried it in safety to the ocean.
And in the very year the fish enjoined
He built a ship, and paid the fish respect,
And there took refuge when the flood arose.
Soon near him swam the fish, and to its horn
Manu made fast the cable of the vessel.
Thus drawn along the waters Manu passed
Beyond the northern mountain; then the fish,
Addressing Manu said, "I have preserved thee.
Quickly attach the ship to yonder tree,
But lest the waters sink from under thee,
As fast as they subside, so fast shalt thou
Descend the mountains gently after them."
Thus he descended from the northern mountain,
The flood had swept away all living creatures;
Manu was left alone. Wishing for offspring,
He earnestly performed a sacrifice.
In a year's time a female was produced;
She came to Manu; then he said to her,
"Who art thou?" She replied, "I am thy daughter."
He said, "How, lovely lady, can that be?"
"I came forth," she rejoined, "from thine oblations
Cast upon the waters; thou wilt find in me

A blessing; use me in the sacrifice."
With her he worshiped, and with toilsome zeal
Performed religious rites, hoping for offspring.
Thus were created men called sons of Manu.
Whatever benediction he implored
With her, was thus vouchsafed in full abundance.[26]

But if lacking in interest for the general readers, these dry, uninspired priestly directions are of very great importance to the student
of India's religion. Already may be seen a notable shift away from
the old simple Vedic conceptions. The Vedic gods had largely lost
their power and significance. New deities, particularly Prajapati,
Lord of creatures, stand as the central figures. In the end, as may
well be imagined, this luxuriant over-emphasis upon the power of
the sacrifice, leading naturally to an exaltation of the power of the
priests, who alone possessed the secrets of their proper performance,
were the undoing of Vedic religion, and it finally disappears. New
forms of religious faith take its place and new gods arise to replace
the older ones, as we shall presently see. It represents a stage in
transition from Vedic religion to the philosophic Hinduism and the
sectarian, theistic Hinduism which has come down to our own time.

The date of the Brahmanas cannot be fixed with exactness, but
they follow after the Vedas and precede the rise of the Upanishads
which in turn are, the older ones, definitely pre-Buddhistic. The
Brahmanas are found in connection with the various Vedas. As indicated above in the Black Yajur-Veda, the Brahmana material is
interspersed throughout the Veda, while in the White Yajur-Veda
the Brahmana forms an appendix to the Veda. They were undoubtedly at first designed for the training of priests. The earlier instruction
may have been quite informal, but gradually it became stereotyped
and finally unchangeable. There were, however, differences in the
Brahmanas as taught in different schools.

But not all the development of religious thought was of priestly
origin. Indeed, it may well have been that as the cult grew more

[26] Monier-Williams' Translation, *Indian Wisdom*, p. 32.

complex and overgrown, lay members of the community became impatient with it and with the ideas behind it, and began to think about religion themselves. By this time, the stratification of society into fixed castes, a thing unknown in the Vedas, save in the late tenth book, was complete. The preferred position of the priest or Brahmin had been securely fixed. His was definitely the top ranking class, quite above the Kshatriya, the ruler-warrior class, and the Vaisya or farmer-merchant group, and his supremacy has continued into our own times. These three classes, known as the twice-born castes, were sharply set off from the lowly Sudra who was non-Aryan in origin, and carried on the heavy unpleasant work of the world. But by no means all the intelligence was to be found among the Brahmins. Even in the Brahmanas and again and again in the Upanishads there are stories of teachers seeking enlightenment on points of religious thought from kings or nobles. Nor were all members of the Brahmin caste priests. Buddhism very definitely arose out of the experience and ponderings of a prince, one of the Kshatriyas. And it is conjectured that much of the impulse to the profound religious and philosophical speculation which forms the basis of the Upanishads was from the non-Brahmin ranks.

Certain it is that before the time of the Upanishads, men of the non-Brahmin castes had undertaken to become ascetics and hermits and give themselves to contemplation of the great problems of religious and philosophic thought. The Brahmins, if they did not originate the custom, ultimately embraced it and integrated it into a system of Ashramas, or the four stages of life. The first stage was that of the student. Those of the twice-born castes were to begin early the study of the Vedas, which meant to live in the home of a teacher and serve him while learning the wisdom of the sacred texts. At an appropriate time the student was to become a householder, marry, rear a family, and perform the proper sacrifices to the gods. Then, when past middle age, he was to go apart from the common life, and to dwell in the forest, passing the time in contemplation and meditation. When at last old age had come he was supposed to abandon all connections with home, with family, and the common life, and become a *sannyasin,* or holy man, a wandering beggar for God.

Of course not every male of the twice-born castes followed this program, but many did. Upon what should these forest dwellers meditate? At first this may have been left wholly to the individual but in time it also became formalized, and there came into being what are known as the Aranyakas or Forest Treatises. These were sometimes included in the Brahmanas or appended to them, but they were of a different kind. No longer is the concern with the rules of sacrifice and ceremonies, but with mysticism and the symbolism of sacrifice, and with the more philosophic aspects of religion. There had grown up a body of secret doctrine, an esoteric type of thought; not to be taught to the uninitiated in the villages, but to be meditated upon in the forest. This all in time became a part of the Veda. There are Aranyakas belonging to the various schools, thus the Aitareya-Aranyaka, which contains the Aitareya-Upanishad, is attached to the Aitareya-Brahmana of the Rig-Veda. There is no clear line of distinction between the Aranyakas and the Upanishads which the non-specialist can easily discern.

The Upanishads, which, with the Aranyakas, form the Vedanta, or the end of the Veda, are probably the most important parts of the Veda. They are the basis of Indian philosophy and philosophic Hinduism, the religion of the intelligentsia of India, and have affected the thought of all India with reference to religion.

Save in the tenth book of the Rig-Veda, the Vedas in general, like the Old Testament, take the gods for granted. There is little or no reflection upon them. In the Brahmanas there is the beginning of questioning about the world and its origins. In the Aranyakas to a still greater degree it goes forward, but in the Upanishads it comes to flower.[27] Here the chief concern is to ask ultimate questions concerning man, and his world, and his final destiny. It represents both an intellectual and a religious interest. Concerned with the nature of the world ground, it is also interested in how man must relate himself to this ultimate reality in order to achieve

[27] Some scholars make no distinction between the Aranyakas and the Upanishads.

what, in Christianity, is called salvation. To the Hindu it was *Moksha*.

It would be a mistake to think of the Upanishads as formal books of philosophy, abstruse discussions of highly profound and difficult subjects. They are, first of all, tied on bodily to the Vedas, Brahmanas and Aranyakas, sometimes contained within the latter. There is in them a great deal that has to do with sacrifice and the cult in general. There is also a good deal of myth and legend. There are long, tiresome, repetitious discussions of what seem, on first reading, to be puerile matters. One who has heard of the vast importance of the Upanishads, and has read scattered excerpts of rare beauty and insight, is likely to feel a sense of shock as he sits down to read through the whole collection of the 12 or 13 principal Upanishads. Some of it is crude, childish, and in such passages as give only the list of names of the teachers through whom the teachings have been handed down, one finds it about as inspiring as the "begatting" or genealogical chapters of the Old and New Testament. But if the reader persists he will come upon passages of deep insight, beauty of expression and profound understanding of the great problems of religion and human thought. One's first excursion into these basic philosophic texts would best be through some modern expurgated edition or anthology, which has carefully weeded out the crudities, the repetitiousness, and contradictions that so much abound in the original.[28]

The word Upanishad seems to mean "secret doctrine." It is also defined as meaning, literally, that which dispels darkness or ignorance completely. It may be written in prose, or in poetry. There are, all told, over 100 Upanishads in existence, many of them quite late. But of the earlier ones which may be surely said to be Vedic there are only a few, some recognize twelve, some fourteen. R. E. Hume's book, *The Thirteen Principal Upanishads*,[29] contains a

[28] Selections will be found in *The Bible of the World*, pp. 38–77; Lewis Browne, *Scriptures of the Great Religions*, pp. 66–96; Lin Yutang, *The Wisdom of China and India*, pp. 31–53; *The Ten Principal Upanishads*, put into English by Shree Purohit Swami and W. B. Yeats, The Macmillan Co., N. Y., 1939.

[29] Oxford University Press, 2nd ed., 1931.

translation of those which are rather generally accepted as basic to a study of Hindu religion and philosophy.

A great deal of the material of the Upanishads is in dialogue form. A seeker after knowledge comes to a recognized teacher to inquire about some phase of religion or thought. A somewhat Socratic dialogue ensues, in which the answer is finally given. It is interesting to note the variety of people who ask the questions, kings and commoners, some of very humble birth, both men and women. Apparently women enjoyed a relatively high status at that time.

As an example of dialogue that between Yajnavalkya, a famous teacher, and a woman, Gargi, may be cited. She approaches the teacher and begs permission to ask a question. Yajnavalkya replies graciously:

She said: "That, O Yajnavalkya, which is above the sky, that which is beneath the earth that which is between these two, sky and earth, that which people call the past and the present and the future—across what is that woven, warp and woof?"

He said: "That, O Gargi, which is above the sky that which is between these two, sky and earth, that which people call the past, and present and future—across space is that woven, warp and woof."

She said: "Adoration to you, Yajnavalkya, in that you have solved this question for me. Prepare yourself for the other."

"Ask, Gargi."

She said, "Across what then, pray, is space woven, warp and woof?"

He said: "That, O Gargi, Brahmans call the Imperishable (Aksara). It is not coarse, not fine, not short, not long, not glowing (like fire), not adhesive (like water), without shadow and without darkness, without air and without space, without stickiness (intangible), odorless, tasteless, without eye, without ear, without voice, without wind, without energy, without breath, without mouth, without personal or family name, unaging, undying, without fear, immortal, stainless, not uncovered, not covered, without measure, without inside and without outside.

"It consumes nothing soever.

"No one soever consumes it.

"Verily, O Gargi, at the command of that Imperishable the sun and the moon stand apart. Verily, O Gargi, at the command of that Imperishable the earth and the sky stand apart. Verily, O Gargi, at the command of that Imperishable the moments, the hours, the days, the nights, the fortnights, the months, the seasons, and the years stand apart. Verily, O Gargi, at the command of that Imperishable some rivers flow from the snowy mountains to the east, others to the west, in whatever direction each flows. Verily, O Gargi, at the command of that Imperishable men praise those who give, the gods are desirous of a sacrificer, and the fathers (are desirous) of the Manes-sacrifice.

"Verily, O Gargi, if one performs sacrifices and worships and undergoes austerity in this world for many thousands of years, but without knowing that Imperishable, limited indeed is that (work) of his. Verily, O Gargi, he who departs from this world without knowing that Imperishable is pitiable. But, O Gargi, he who departs from this world knowing that Imperishable is Brahman.

"Verily, O Gargi, that Imperishable is the unseen Seer, the unheard Hearer, the unthought Thinker, the ununderstood understander. Other than It there is naught that sees. Other than It there is naught that hears. Other than It there is naught that understands. Across this Imperishable, O Gargi, is space woven, warp and woof."[30]

On another occasion when Gargi had pushed Yajnavalkya back step by step, a device often used in the Upanishads and known as the regressus, to Brahman as the ultimate reality, she still persisted in asking what lay behind Brahman. Yajnavalkya said:

"Gargi, do not question too much, lest your head fall off. In truth, you are questioning too much about a divinity about which questions cannot be asked. Gargi, do not over-question."

Thereupon Gargi Vacaknaivi held her peace.[31]

Another regressus throws not a little light upon the shifting away from the old Vedic gods to the One, Brahman. It is given in slightly abbreviated form:

1. Then Vidagdha Sakalya questioned him. "How many gods are there, Yajnavalkya?"

[30] Reprinted from *Thirteen Principal Upanishads*, by Robert E. Hume; 2nd ed. copyright 1931 by Oxford University Press; used by permission of the publishers. Pp. 118–119.
[31] R. E. Hume, *Thirteen Principal Upanishads*, p. 113.

He answered in accord with the following *Nivid* (invocationary formula): "As many as are mentioned in the *Nivid* of the Hymn to All the Gods, namely, three hundred and three, and three thousand and three (= 3306)."

"Yes," said he, "but just how many gods are there, Yajnavalkya?"
"Thirty-three."
"Yes," said he, "but just how many gods are there, Yajnavalkya?"
"Six."
"Yes," said he, "but just how many gods are there, Yajnavalkya?"
"Three."
"Yes," said he, "but just how many gods are there, Yajnavalkya?"
"Two."
"Yes," said he, "but just how many gods are there, Yajnavalkya?"
"One and a half."
"Yes," said he, "but just how many gods are there, Yajnavalkya?"
"One."[32]

There is space for only one final dialogue dealing with the Atman, which, together with Brahman, constitute the two major concepts dealt with in the Upanishads. Their ultimate identification in Brahman-Atman is the culmination of the long time trend toward the monistic or pantheistic world-soul which began in the tenth book of the Rig-Veda. Also the realized identification of the Atman, or self, or soul of man, with Brahman, constitutes *moksha* or salvation for some schools of philosophic Hinduism.

King Janaka of Videha once asked of Yajnavalkya:

2. "Yajnavalkya, what light does a person here have?"
"He has the light of the sun, O king," he said, "for with the sun, indeed, as his light, one sits, moves around, does his work, and returns."
"Quite so, Yajnavalkya.
3. "But when the sun has set, Yajnavalkya, what light does a person here have?"
"The moon, indeed, is his light," said he, "for with the moon, indeed, as his light, one sits, moves around, does his work, and returns."
"Quite so, Yajnavalkya.
4. "But when the sun has set, and the moon has set, what light does a person here have?"

[32] Hume, *The Thirteen Principal Upanishads*, pp. 119–120.

"Fire, indeed, is his light," said he, "for with fire," etc.

"Quite so, Yajnavalkya.

5. "But when the sun has set, Yajnavalkya, and the moon has set, and the fire has gone out, what light does a person here have?"

"Speech, indeed, is his light," said he, "for . . . when a voice is raised (even in the dark) then one goes straight towards it."

6. "But when the sun has set, Yajnavalkya, and the moon has set, and the fire has gone out, and speech is hushed, what light does a person here have?"

"The soul (atman), indeed, is his light," said he, "for with the soul, indeed, as his light, one sits, moves around, does his work, and returns."[33]

The famous phrase *tat tvam asi*, "that art thou," expressing the identity of the self of man with Brahman-Atman occurs over and over again in a long dialogue between Svetaketu and his father, for example:

Said the father:

1. "Place this salt in the water. In the morning come unto me."

Then he did so.

Then he said to him: "That salt you placed in the water last evening —please bring it hither."

Then he grasped for it, but did not find it, as it was completely dissolved.

2. "Please take a sip of it from this end," said he. "How is it?"

"Salt."

"Take a sip from the middle," said he. "How is it?"

"Salt."

"Take a sip from that end," said he. "How is it?"

"Salt."

"Set it aside. Then come unto me."

He did so, saying, "It is always the same."

Then he said to him: "Verily, indeed, my dear, you do not perceive Being here. Verily, indeed, it is here.

3. "That which is the finest essence—this whole world has that as its soul. That is Reality. That is Atman (Soul). That art thou, Svetaketu."

[33] Hume, *The Thirteen Principal Upanishads*, p. 133.

"Do you, sir, cause me to understand even more."

"So be it, my dear," said he.[34]

But how shall this *moksha* which is release from the round of rebirth be accomplished? To the authors of the Upanishads, Vedic sacrifice was unable to help one here. It could come only through knowledge or realization of the truth of the identity of the Atman of living man with Brahman-Atman. The Upanishads themselves suggest the way of meditation under direction of a teacher, but have little to say with regard to the precise methods to be employed. Later thinkers were to develop elaborate schemes whereby man might achieve this end. In general Yoga practice in one form or another, i.e., disciplined meditation, was the answer.

Here in the Upanishads come to full expression two doctrines unknown in the Vedas, that of Karma, or the law of sowing and reaping, and that of reincarnation. Both are expressed in the following:

3. Now as a caterpillar, when it has come to the end of a blade of grass, in taking the next step draws itself together towards it, just so this soul in taking the next step strikes down this body, dispels its ignorance, and draws itself together (for making the transition).

4. As a goldsmith, taking a piece of gold, reduces it to another newer and more beautiful form, just so this soul, striking down this body and dispelling its ignorance, makes for itself another newer and more beautiful form like that either of the fathers, or of the Gandharvas, or of the gods, or of Prajapati, or of Brahman, or of other beings.

5. Verily, this soul is Brahma, made of knowledge, of mind, of breath, of seeing, of hearing, of earth, of water, of wind, of space, of energy and of non-energy, of desire and of non-desire, of anger and of non-anger, of virtuousness and of non-virtuousness. It is made of everything. This is what is meant by the saying "made of this, made of that."

According as one acts, according as one conducts himself, so does he become. The doer of good becomes good. The doer of evil becomes evil. One becomes virtuous by virtuous action, bad by bad action.[35]

[34] Hume, *The Thirteen Principal Upanishads*, p. 248.
[35] *Ibid.*, p. 140.

Though the doctrine of reincarnation was worked out in much greater detail in subsequent Hindu sacred literature, it is expressed in the Upanishads in rudimentary form thus:

15. Those who know this, and those, too, who in the forest truly worship (upasate) faith (sraddha), pass into the flame (of the cremation-fire); from the flame, into the day; from the day, into the half month of the waxing moon; from the half month of the waxing moon, into the six months during which the sun moves northward; from these months, into the world of the gods (devaloka); from the world of the gods, into the sun; from the sun, into the lightning-fire. A person (purusa) consisting of mind (manasa) goes to those regions of lightning and conducts them to the Brahma-worlds. In those Brahma-worlds they dwell for long extents. Of these there is no return.

16. But they who by sacrificial offering, charity, and austerity conquer the worlds, pass into the smoke (of the cremation-fire); from the smoke, into the night; from the night, into the half month of the waning moon; from the half month of the waning moon, into the six months during which the sun moves southward; from those months, into the world of the fathers; from the world of the fathers, into the moon. Reaching the moon, they become food. There the gods—as they say to King Soma, "Increase! Decrease!"—even so feed upon them there. When that passes away for them, then they pass forth into this space; from space, into air; from air, into rain; from rain, into the earth. On reaching the earth they become food. Again they are offered in the fire of man. Thence they are born in the fire of woman. Rising up into the world, they cycle round again thus.

But those who know not these two ways, become crawling and flying insects and whatever there is here that bites.[36]

Parts of the Upanishads are in verse. Here we have space for only three brief poems on Brahman, favorite theme of the writers of the "secret doctrine."

As oil in sesame seeds, as butter in cream,
As water in river-beds, and as fire in the friction-sticks,
So is the Soul (Atman) apprehended in one's own soul,
If one looks for Him with true austerity (tapas).

[36] Hume, *The Thirteen Principal Upanishads,* p. 163.

> The Soul (Atman), which pervades all things
> As butter is contained in cream,
> Which is rooted in self-knowledge and austerity—
> This is Brahma, the highest mystic doctrine (upanishad)!
> This is Brahma, the highest mystic doctrine![37]

The second illustrates the way in which the Brahman concept gathers up into itself the old Vedic gods.

> Thou art Brahma, and verily thou art Vishnu.
> Thou art Rudra. Thou art Prajapati,
> Thou art Agni, Varuna, and Vayu.
> Thou art Indra. Thou art the Moon.
> Thou art food. Thou art Yama. Thou art the Earth.
> Thou art All. Yea, thou art the unshaken one!
>
> For Nature's sake and for its own
> Is existence manifold in thee.
> O Lord of all, hail unto thee!
> The Soul of all, causing all acts,
> Enjoying all, all life art thou!
> Lord (prabhu) of all pleasure and delight!
>
> Hail unto thee, O tranquil Soul (santatman)!
> Yea, hail to thee, most hidden one,
> Unthinkable, unlimited,
> Beginningless and endless, too![38]

And finally, from the Mundaka comes this summing-up of the whole in Brahman:

> Brahma, indeed, is this immortal. Brahma before,
> Brahma behind, to right and to left.
> Stretched forth below and above.
> Brahma, indeed, is this whole world, this widest extent.[39]

The Upanishads have had an extraordinary influence on all subsequent religious and philosophic thought. No writer on Indian

[37] Hume, *The Thirteen Principal Upanishads*, pp. 396–397.
[38] *Ibid.*, p. 423.
[39] *Ibid.*, p. 373.

philosophy would think of beginning anywhere but in the Veda, meaning primarily the Upanishads. Out of them have grown six historical schools of philosophic thought, and each of these has had its effect upon Indian religion. Best known in the West is the Vedanta school. Others are the Nayaya, the Mimansa, the Sankhya, the Yoga, and the Vaiseshika.[40]

Religiously, the concept of Brahman has had a very profound effect on Indian religion. Since Brahman is the one and only real—all the gods of whatever sectarian group can have no reality other than they have in Brahman. They can only be regarded as manifestations, at various levels, of the neuter world soul. Thus a cloak of unity is thrown over all kinds of religions which have appeared in India. Indeed, this concept provides Hinduism with an absorptive quality which enables it to accept any religion from any source as simply a phase of the ultimately real Brahman—so long as it does not make exclusive claims for its deity as do Christianity and Islam. Here the resistance is rather on the part of the representatives of these aggressively exclusivist faiths to such an acceptance.

The Upanishads have been quite influential throughout the west. Schopenhauer, among European philosophers, has spoken of them in terms of high esteem:

In the whole world there is no study except that of the originals, as beneficial and so elevating as that of the Upanishads (in translation). It has been the solace of my life; it will be the solace of my death.

From every sentence deep original and sublime thoughts arise, and the whole is pervaded by a high, holy and earnest spirit.[41]

Emerson got the inspiration from their reading for his great poem, *Brahma*. Thoreau read them and was influenced by them. The whole atmosphere of New England thought in the latter part of the nineteenth century was affected by them. In more re-

[40] A very brief, rather oversimplified discussion of the main features of each of these schools is to be found in Theos Bernard, *Hindu Philosophy*, The Philosophical Library, New York, 1947. Two great treatises by contemporary Indian philosophers are S. N. Dasgupta, *History of Indian Philosophy*, 3 vols., Cambridge University Press, 1922–1940, and S. Radhakrishnan, *Indian Philosophy*, 2 vols., George Allen and Unwin, London, 1927.

[41] Quoted in *Sacred Books and Early Literature of the East*, Vol. 9, p. 67.

cent times, as translations have been multiplied, they have been read by vast numbers of people. A recent book, *Vedanta for the Western World* interprets them to an increasing circle of intelligent readers. Theosophy has taken over some of the basic ideas of the Upanishads and popularized them in the West, and their indirect influence is to be seen in a number of small modern religious movements in America.[42]

The Upanishads are the source of the doctrines which furnish the basis for the Vedanta-Sutras of Badarayana, which are by some considered to be *sruti* literature. On this are based the commentaries of Shankara and of Ramanuja whose writings have influenced and are still influencing the religious thought of countless millions of Indians.

With the Upanishads we come to the end of the Veda, and also the end of the *sruti* sacred literature, with the exception of the Bhagavad Gita, which if not universally so recognized is, by great numbers of Indians, ranked along with the most sacred Vedic literature. To that we shall come back later. But we are only at the beginning of the discussion of literature of the *smriti* type, which, for all practical purposes, is quite as important in the religious life of the Indian people as the older *sruti*. Indeed, rather more so, for actually Vedic religion no longer exists. The old Vedic gods are gone, with the exception of a very few—chiefly Vishnu. Orthodox Indians regard their later literatures as growing out of and fulfilling the Vedas, but in no sense as abrogating them. Typical of the attitude of modern Hindu thought is the statement of D. S. Sarma in his *Primer of Hinduism*, written for the instruction of young Hindus in this faith:

Q. Why, if the Veda is our primary scripture, should we not go direct to it without caring for any of the secondary scriptures?

A. The Veda is like a mine of gold, and the later scriptures are like the gold coins of the various ages. When you want to procure things that would make you comfortable, you should have ready money and not a piece of rock with veins of gold in it straight from the mine. Of course every gold coin that is in the country is

[42] See my *These Also Believe*, Macmillan, N. Y. (1949).

ultimately derived from the mine; but has undergone various processes that make it useful to us at once. The ore has been smelted, the dross has been removed, the true metal has been refined, put into moulds and stamped. Similarly the golden truths of the Veda have been refined by the wisdom of the ages and presented to us in a useful form, in our later scriptures. That is why I recommend to you the Gita, rather than the Upanishads.[43]

While the application was in this case specifically to the Bhagavad Gita, note that he says "presented to us in our later scriptures."

Supplementary to the Vedas there grew up a great body of what is known as *sutra* literature. The name comes from the practice, adopted for mnemonic reasons, of couching what was to be remembered in very terse, almost telegraphic form, which then needed to be expanded, to make complete sentences. Thus: "four castes; Brahmans, Kshatriyas, Vaisyas, and Sudras," requires adding "There are." "Of these the preceding one (is) always better, according to birth (than the succeeding one)." The words in parentheses must be supplied.[44]

The oldest of these sutras are found in connection with the Aranyakas and Brahmanas. Eventually there emerged the *Kalpa* or ritual sutras. Those dealing with the great public sacrifices are called Srauta sutras; those with the domestic rites the Grihya sutras. These latter deal with the simple household sacrifices and observances connected with such things as building a house, cattle breeding, farming, also rites for the prevention of disease, love rites, the ancestral and funeral rites. They constitute a veritable mine of information as to the home and family life of the people and also throw a great deal of light upon the way the Vedas were interpreted and used in actual practice.

There are also sutras concerning the Dharma. Dharma is a word not easily translated. It is sometimes rendered as law, custom, usage, and even religion. The Dharma sutras were, then, sutras covering a great variety of obligations, all the way from personal etiquette to formal law. These were formulated by different Vedic

---

[43] Sarma, *Primer of Hinduism*, p. 24.
[44] Apastamba, I. 1, 1, 4–8. *Sacred Books of the East*, Vol. II, p. 1.

schools and purportedly based upon the Vedas. There are several important books of this character, some earlier, some later, the Apastamba—the Baudhayana, the Institutes of Vishnu, and most important of all that of the Manavan School, the Manavan sutras, or, when, put into poetic form, as was actually done, the Manavan Dharma Sastras, better known as the *Laws of Manu*. These books have been of enormous importance in Indian life, even down to the present time. For example, until recently a British magistrate in India, where an Indian citizen had to be judged on the basis of the law of his particular religious community, had to be instructed in Hindu requirements as set forth in the Code of Manu, as well as in the Koran, which is the basis of Moslem law. When reforms have been pressed, for example with reference to child marriage, or the problem of permitting divorce, a strong appeal has been made by Orthodoxy to the Laws of Manu as having permanently fixed these relationships. They charge the government with infringement of religious freedom in setting aside what was therein written.

The Laws of Manu is a fascinating law book, comparable in many ways to the Code of Hammurabi or to the Hebrew codes found in Exodus, Leviticus, and Deuteronomy. If one desires to know caste rules, or how women should be regarded, or the obligations of servant to master, or wife to husband, or children to parents, or king to people, or people to ruler, or concerning almost any question of social relationship, here may be found what, until quite recent modern times, was the characteristic Indian answer.[45]

Ordinarily one would not regard the great national epics as scriptures though, in the case of the *Iliad* and the *Odyssey*, they come close to forming at least an equivalent of scripture for the Greek people, and to students of Greek religion they provide a rich mine of material with reference to the gods of classical Greek religion. But in India, if not *sruti* they are at least *smriti*, and play a highly

---

[45] It is translated in Vol. 25, *Sacred Books of the East*. Other law books are: The Institutes of Vishnu, Vol. VII, *Sacred Books of the East*. The Apastamba and Baudhayana, Vol. XI; Gautama and Vasishtha, Vol. XIV; Grihya Sutras, Vol. XXIX, XXX. Briefer selections of some of these are to be found in the *Sacred Books and Literature of the East*, Vol. 9.

significant role in Indian religion. D. S. Sarma in his *Primer of Hinduism* so classifies them along with the Puranas, the Agamas and Darsanas. This is an indication of how modern Indians regard them.[46]

In his introduction to the Mahabharata of which he is the supposed author or compiler, Vyasa says: "The reading of the Bharata is sacred: all the sins of him who reads but one portion of it shall be obliterated without exception. He who in faith shall persevere in listening to the recital of this sacred book shall obtain long life, great renown and the way to heaven."

Romesh Dutt, translator of the Epics in Everyman's Library says of them: "The Hindu scarcely lives, man or woman, high or low, educated or ignorant, whose earliest recollections do not cling to the story and the character of the great Epics. Even the traditions and tales which spoil the Epic have themselves a charm and an attraction; and the morals inculcated in these tales sink into the hearts of a naturally religious people, and form the basis of their moral education. Mothers in India know no better theme for imparting wisdom and instruction to their daughters, and elderly men know no richer storehouse for narrating tales to children, than these stories preserved in the Epics. No single work except the Bible has such influence in affording moral instruction in Christian lands as the Mahabharata and the Ramayana in India. They have been the cherished heritage of the Hindus for three thousand years; they are to the present day interwoven with the thoughts and beliefs and the moral ideas of a nation."[47]

The longer of the two great Indian Epics is the Mahabharata. Indeed, it is the longest epic in the world, consisting of about 220,000 lines. In comparison, the *Iliad* and *Odyssey* combined have some 30,000. It is not all strictly epic in character but a combination of epic and didactic material which has been incorporated into it. Modern scholars distinguish between the epic and the didactic epic.

The real epic consists of some 24,000 stanzas, almost twice the

[46] D. S. Sarma, *Primer of Hinduism*, p. 10.
[47] *The Ramayana and the Mahabharata*, pp. 332–333.

length of the Greek epics, but even this is not all of a piece, for in the epic itself there is reference to the fact that it originally had only 8,800 stanzas.

The original epic had its historic basis in the ancient conflict between two tribes—the Kurus and Pandavas. This probably occurred at some time prior to 1000 B.C., though exact dating is impossible. Around this historic struggle grew up a collection of songs celebrating the prowess of outstanding leaders and this was handed down orally. This may then have been woven into a brief epic by some poet. The fact that in this epic, Brahma is the chief god is evidence to some scholars that it is still early, before the rise to prominence of the great divinities Vishnu or Shiva, who figure in the later stage of growth as on a par with Brahma. Here mention of the Greeks appears which would require a date as late as 300 B.C. or later. Macdonell assigns it to the period between 300 B.C. and the beginning of the Christian era.[48] The final stage in the development of the epic was the inclusion of a vast mass of didactic material in the epic—doubtless in order to get it known. For the Epic was popular, and if some teaching matter could be incorporated into it, it might get attention which it would otherwise fail to receive. The process is comparable to the modern effort of teachers of religion and morals to attempt to get their material into the movies, on the radio, or in television, which are the media of mass appeal of today. So one thing after another was added, designed, says Macdonell, "to impress the people, especially kings, with the doctrines of a priestly caste. It thus at last assumed the character of a vast treatise on dharma in which the divine origin and immutability of Brahman institutions, the eternity of the caste system, and the subordination of all to the priest is laid down."[49]

This was probably completed by about 400 A.D. In the end it comes out as a Vishnuite document in which the worship of Vishnu and his divine incarnations, especially Krishna, is promoted. This

[48] A. A. Macdonell, *History of Sanskrit Literature*, p. 286. It should be said that, in general, Indian scholars incline to assign the Epics to an earlier date than do western scholars.

[49] *Op. cit.*, p. 286.

reaches its climax in the Bhagavad Gita which was one of the didactic sections included.

Sometimes the included material fits. There may be, after all, some appropriateness in inserting a lengthy discussion on immortality by two survivors of a dreadfully destructive battle as they survey the corpse-strewn battlefield. The Bhagavad Gita seems somewhat less appropriately placed. It interpolates at the precise moment when the battle lines are drawn and the warriors await only the blowing of the conch shell as signal to charge upon the enemy, a discussion running through eighteen chapters on very profound religious themes between Arjuna the warrior and Krishna the god, disguised as a charioteer. But to the Gita we will return later.

Only a very brief and inadequate summary of the Epic can be given here.

Of the house of Bharata there were two sons, Pandu and Dhrita-rashtra. Pandu had five sons called the Pandavas, by name Yudhisthira the eldest, Bhima, Arjuna, Nakula and Sahadeva. Dhrita-rashtra, who was blind, had several sons of whom Duryodhana was the eldest and Duhsasana the bravest. This family was called the Kauravas.

On the death of Pandu, Dhrita-rashtra, the blind king, took his brother's five sons into his own home to rear, and they were trained in the manly arts along with his own sons, by Drona. Arjuna proved the favorite. When they were all well trained Drona suggested a tournament in which they might exhibit their skill. This was a mistake, for Arjuna excelled all in his mastery of the bow, the sword, the spear, and aroused jealousy in the minds of his cousins, the Kauravas. The tournament ended in a general fight between the cousins. King Dhrita- rashtra saw the necessity of separating the rivals, so divided his kingdom, giving a distant section of it to the Pandavas. Yudhisthira, as eldest, exercised rule and soon won the love of his subjects.

Then one day the father of Draupadi, a very beautiful princess who had come to the age to wed, announced a *swayamvara*, at which a husband would be chosen for her, and all neighboring kings and princes were invited to contest for the hand of the lovely princess. This is quite a common literary device and recurs frequently in the epics and other Indian literature. It brought together a colorful company, not wholly unlike the tournaments associated with the knights of the Round Table in English lore. The particular test on this occasion was to shoot an arrow through a revolving wheel and strike the eye of a golden fish. The five Pandavas attended the event disguised as Brahmins. When none of the contestants could even bend and string the bow, Arjuna stepped forward in his Brahmin's garb, to the surprise of the crowd which scorned the notion that a Brahmin could perform a feat of physical prowess. But Arjuna, putting aside his Brahmin's robes, easily bent and strung the bow, then sent the arrow straight to its mark and by so doing won the beautiful princess, Draupadi. Returning home with the bride, one of the brothers called out to the mother on approaching the house: "We have made a fine acquisition today." She, not having seen what it was, replied: "Share it equally among yourselves, my sons." And the mother having spoken, her words could not be set aside. So, Draupadi became the wife of all five brothers. The irrevocability of a parent's word is a widespread belief—it will appear again in the Ramayana. In Hebrew custom the granting of the blessing to Jacob by Isaac is a good example.

The jealousy felt by the Kauravas was not lessened by this success of the Pandavas. They plotted their downfall. They invited them to a festival, and challenged them to a game of dice. Yudhisthira had a weakness for gambling. He lost steadily until he had staked all his possessions, his kingdom, his brothers and finally his wife—and lost them all. This meant slavery for the cousins, but the blind king would not permit this. Instead, they were exiled to the forest for fourteen years. This, too, is a familiar motif in Indian literature. It appears again and again, notably in the Ramayana.

While they were in the forest saints came to visit them and, in order to entertain and encourage them, told a number of stories, among them the Ramayana itself, indicating that it is the older of the two. In this way there are introduced into the epic some re-

markable stories which have no other connection with the epic than
that they were recounted to the Pandavas. One of them, *Savitri and
Satyavan* or *Love Conquers Death*, may have been introduced for
didactic purposes, but aside from its teaching it is a good story,
beautifully told. Briefly it is as follows:

Savitri, a beautiful princess, was the only daughter of King
Asva-Pati. (The Indians, too, like stories of beautiful princesses
and brave noble princes, just as English and American children
do.) When she reached the age to marry instead of calling the
usual *swayamvara* and inviting the princes to contend for her hand,
she was permitted by her father to set out on a search for a husband
—certainly from the standpoint of the India of more recent times
a very unusual thing for a woman to do. But she found no one
who suited her. One day she came upon a hermit and his wife in
a forester's cottage and at first sight fell in love with their son
Satyavan, a young woodsman. Really they were a royal family, de-
prived by wicked men of their rule. The king consented to their
marriage. The sage Narada warned her that Satyavan was doomed
to die in a year, but she braved widowhood, and insisted on the
marriage.

So they were wed—lived in a humble way in the forest, and were
both very happy, but she with a secret dread. On the fateful day
on which he was to die, she went with him to his wood-cutting,
against his wish. He was suddenly stricken. She attempted to re-
vive him, but to no avail. Yama, god of the dead, came to take his
soul away. Savitri followed after him, unwilling to turn back,
though importuned to do so by the ruler of the realm of the dead.
"Wherever my lord is borne there shall I surely go; he is my all,
I cannot leave him. I must go with thee." Yama offered her boon
after boon if she would cease following him. Still she followed. To
his insistent demand that she return she only replied, "I would go
back if I could, but in your arms you carry my own life."

Finally, Yama, moved by her love, cried, "Thou art innocence
itself, and tenderness and truth. Thou hast taught me lessons new
of woman's fidelity. Ask any boon thou wilt and it shall be thine."
This time she cried: "I ask not wealth nor throne, nor heaven itself;

I crave my heart, my life, give me my Satyavan." So Yama restored her beloved to her, and all was well. The parents were restored to their throne—and they all lived happily ever afterward, we will suppose.[50]

Another story told them was *Nala and Damyanti*. Both are princes. A swan carries to Damyanti the princess, word of Nala whom she has not seen, and she falls in love with him. When a *swayamvara* is set for her to choose a prince, four gods declare that Damyanti shall be for one of them and they send prince Nala as their messenger to woo for them, like John Alden in the *Courtship of Miles Standish,* despite the fact that he declares that he too loves her. Reluctantly he goes and pleads for them. She declares that it is him she loves and that she will reject the gods. They must all appear one day and she will choose him before them. On the given day princes and kings arrive, among them Nala and the gods, but they have all made themselves to appear exactly as Nala so that she may not be able to distinguish him from the rest. But she prays them so earnestly that at last they reveal themselves. She chooses Nala and the gods grant him eight boons. They are married and are very happy.

But Kali, another god (no connection with the goddess Kali, now so widely worshipped) is angered and swears vengeance. After several years of happy married life, two children having been born to them, Kali seeks to break up this home. He does so by means of gambling. Playing at dice, Nala, like Yudhisthira, gambles away everything, but refuses to throw for his wife. So he too is exiled.

She with true wifely devotion refuses to leave him, as Sita refuses to leave Rama. Under the spell of Kali, Nala abandons her. She, left alone and wandering in the forest, is about to be killed by a serpent, but is saved by a hunter who makes violent love to her. She calls down a curse upon him and he falls dead. Finally she becomes servant to a queen, and Nala the charioteer of the king. She eventually returns to her father but keeps up a constant search for Nala. At last she discovers his whereabouts. Then she

---

[50] This poem is to be found in Dutt's translation of the epic, in *The Ramayana and Mahabharata*, pp. 217–230, Everyman's Library, E. P. Dutton & Co., N. Y.

asks her father to call a *swayamvara* for her to choose a husband. Nala comes as charioteer to the king he serves. They are reunited. He wins back his kingdom by a throw of the dice, the demon leaves him, and they live happily ever after. There is no moral not to gamble implied in the story.

After the long exile was ended preparations were made for a war between the two houses—although attempts were made to effect a reconciliation between the rival clans. When these failed, before beginning the battle they drew up a set of rules of warfare— perhaps the first "London Conference" in the history of the human race. The provisions were most interesting, designed clearly to maintain good sportsmanship throughout. In what striking contrast they stand to the current practices in modern warfare. First, there must be no strategy or treachery. It must be a straightforward, honorable combat, everything above board! In intervals, between active fighting there was to be friendly intercourse between the camps. Since they were not to fight at night, this left time for fraternization. It must have made war so much pleasanter! Before they had finished they did fight at night also. Rules are so hard to keep in wartime! Fugitives were not to be killed. (Remember how in the last war prisoners were often machine gunned en masse.) Horsemen must fight only with horsemen, foot-soldiers with those likewise on foot. There must be a sporting chance given. No submarines attacking passenger ships, no airplanes bombing civilians. When fighting only with words—it was the custom to hurl insults at each other endlessly before beginning to fight (cf. the Philistines and the Hebrew armies in the story of the slaying of Goliath[51])—arms must not be taken up against the enemy. Nor should any attack be made without fair warning, no Pearl Harbors, no sudden air attacks on cities! And finally, when two were engaged in combat no third party should intervene. War was to be a fair contest of skill and prowess.

It need not be said that the rules were not always kept. There were acts of treachery, there was fighting at night, more than one did attack an enemy—this is all related in the poem. Rules of war

[51] I Samuel 17:1–49.

worked then about as well as now when it is the control of atomic weapons that is the desired goal of those who would make war more humane.

Finally the battle was joined and raged for eighteen days and some nights. There are recounted stories of valiant combat, individual and collective. Probably no stories of mortal struggle were ever more vividly told. One is reminded on page after page of the *Iliad* of Homer. Enormous numbers were engaged. Even chariots were counted by the millions. But at the end of the struggle only eleven survivors remained. The Pandavas were victorious but it was a tragic triumph. Yudhisthira, conscience-stricken at the vast sacrifice of life and property is about to abdicate his throne and become an ascetic. He is persuaded rather to perform the horse sacrifice and so relieve himself from his guilt. This he does. After he has given enormous quantities of gold to the priests he is freed from his sins and rules his kingdom justly and well.

But Krishna, who until now has been a warrior and friend and helper, becomes involved in another war and is killed by an arrow which struck him in the sole of the foot, his only vulnerable spot. He is to appear in the Bhagavad-Gita as god as we shall later see. Inconsolable for the death of their friend, Yudhisthira and his wife and brothers abandon the kingdom and set off on their last journey, wandering forth to the Himalaya mountains to the divine mountain Meru.

It is one of the most fascinating sections of the Great Epic, beautifully translated into English by Sir Edwin Arnold under the title *The Great Journey*. They set out walking, but one by one failed and died. First Draupadi, the wife of the five brothers; then Bhima and the rest, until only Yudhisthira alone, followed by a dog, at last reached heaven's gate. He was warmly welcomed but the dog was not permitted to enter with him:

Yudhisthira protested:

> "O Most High,
> O Thousand-eyed and wisest! can it be
> That one exalted should seem pitiless?

> Nay, let me lose such glory: for its sake
> I cannot leave one living thing I loved."[52]

But "he is unclean," asserted the gods, and unfit to pass through heaven's portal. Unconvinced, the hero, Yudhisthira, still refused to enter without the dog. Thereupon the king of heaven smiled and said:

> "There be four sins, O Sakra, grievous sins:
> The first is making suppliants despair,
> The second is to slay a nursing wife,
> The third is spoiling Brahmans' goods by force,
> The fourth is injuring an ancient friend.
> These four I deem not direr than the crime,
> If one, in coming forth from woe to weal,
> Abandon any meanest comrade then."[53]

As he spoke, the hound vanished and there stood in his stead the Lord of Death and Justice, Dharma. Then said Indra:

> ... "Because thou didst not mount
> This car divine, lest the poor hound be shent
> Who looked to thee, lo! there is none in heaven
> Shall sit above thee, King!—Bharata's son!
> Enter thou now to the eternal joys,
> Living and in thy form. Justice and Love
> Welcome thee, Monarch! thou shalt throne with us!"[54]

But entering heaven, Yudhisthira did not find his brothers nor his lovely wife whom he had expected to discover already there. So he cried:

> ... "I will not live
> A little space without those souls I loved.
> O Slayer of the demons! let me go
> Where Bhima and my brothers are, and she,
> My Draupadi, the Princess with the face
> Softer and darker than the Vrihat-leaf,

---

[52] Edwin Arnold, *Indian Idylls,* p. 292.
[53] *Ibid.,* p. 294.
[54] *Ibid.,* p. 295.

And soul as sweet as are its odors. Lo!
Where they have gone, there will I surely go."[55]

The gods besought him to remain, but he refused:

. . . "Show me those souls!
I cannot tarry where I have them not.
Bliss is not blissful, just and mighty Ones!
Save if I rest beside them. Heaven is there
Where Love and Faith make heaven. Let me go!"[56]

So, forth he went from heaven. Guided by a golden Deva, and descending by a path evil and dark, he entered through the "Sinners' Road" into one of the hells. Some idea of the grim nature of the Hindu concept of these hells may be seen in the following passage:

. . . The tread of sinful feet
Matted the thick thorns carpeting its slope!
The smell of sin hung foul on them; the mire
About their roots was trampled filth of flesh
Horrid with rottenness, and splashed with gore
Curdling in crimson puddles; where there buzzed
And sucked, and settled, creatures of the swamp,
Hideous in wing and sting, gnat-clouds and flies,
With moths, toads, newts, and snakes red-gulleted;
And livid, loathsome worms, writhing in slime
Forth from skull-holes and scalps and tumbled bones.[57]

While in this dreadful place, he suddenly heard the voices of those he loved:

. . .—words of woe
Humble and eager! and compassion seized
His lordly mind.[58]

Then Yudhisthira called aloud, "Who speaks with me?" Out of the darkness came the voices of Karna and Bhima, Arjuna and the other brothers, and finally the voice of his wife, Draupadi. This

[55] Edwin Arnold, *Indian Idylls*, p. 298.
[56] *Ibid.*, p. 305.
[57] *Ibid.*, p. 306.
[58] *Ibid.*, p. 309.

angered him, for only recently he had seen in heaven men against whom he had fought in the great war, and he could not understand how such as they were accorded paradise, and those he loved consigned to hell. Every instinct urged him to turn back toward heaven, but to his angel guide he said:

> . . . "Go to those thou serv'st;
> Tell them I come not thither. Say I stand
> Here in the throat of hell, and here will bide—
> Nay, if I perish—while my well-belov'd
> Win ease and peace by any pains of mine."[59]

Whereupon the angel returned with the message to the gods. Then the gods answered Yudhisthira:

> "King Yudhisthira! O thou long-armed Lord,
> This is enough! All Heaven is glad of thee.
> It is enough! Come, thou most blessed one,
> Unto thy peace, well-gained. . . ."[60]

> "Come thou to see! Karna, whom thou didst mourn,—
> That mightiest archer, master in all wars,—
> He hath attained, shining as doth the sun;
> Come thou and see! Grieve no more, King of men!
> Whose love helped them and thee, and hath its meed.
> Rajas and maharajas, warriors, aids,—
> All thine are thine forever. Krishna waits
> To greet thee coming, 'companied by gods,
> Seated in heaven, from toils and sorrows saved.
> Son! there is golden fruit of noble deeds,
> Of prayer, alms, sacrifice. The most just gods
> Keep thee thy place above the highest saints,
> Where thou shalt sit, divine, compassed about
> With royal souls in bliss, as Hari sits."[61]

So everything ends happily:

> . . . the rejoicing King
> (Thy ancestor, O Liege!) proceeded straight

[59] Edwin Arnold, *Indian Idylls,* p. 311.
[60] *Ibid.,* p. 314.
[61] *Ibid.,* pp. 315–316.

Unto that river's brink, which floweth pure
Through the Three Worlds, mighty, and sweet, and praised.
There, being bathed, the body of the King
Put off its mortal, coming up arrayed
In grace celestial, washed from soils of sin,
From passion, pain, and change. So, hand in hand
With brother-gods, glorious went Yudhisthir,
Lauded by lovely minstrelsy, and songs
Of unknown music, where those heroes stood—
The princess of the Pandavas, his kin—
And lotus-eyed and loveliest Draupadi,
Waiting to greet him, gladdening and glad.[62]

Unlike the Mahabharata, the Ramayana is traditionally supposed to be the work of a single poet, Valmiki. The story of its composition and recital before King Rama himself is told in the twelfth book of the poem itself. This is really a supplement to the real epic which properly ends with the happy return of lovely Sita to her lord after her long captivity by the Rakshasas. But first the story, one of the most interesting ever told. Very briefly, it is the story of King Rama and his faithful queen who was abducted by a demon and carried away to Lanka (Ceylon) where, despite all his blandishments, Sita remained unmoved and scrupulously loyal to Rama. Meanwhile Rama had for a long time vainly sought to find her, until aided by his monkey friend, Hanuman, he discovered her whereabouts and after a bitterly fought war he was victorious and rescued his beloved wife.

Rama was a prince of the Kosalas, eldest son of King Dasa-ratha and, as such, the heir apparent to the throne. Came a day when the good king decided to abdicate the throne and place his eldest son upon it. Great preparations were made for the event and with much enthusiasm the people awaited the crowning of their well-loved prince. But behind the scenes trouble stalked. Dasa-ratha had more than one queen and one of the younger ones coveted the throne for her son rather than for Rama. By a ruse Dasa-ratha was tricked into offering her any boon she might ask, and the beautiful,

[62] Edwin Arnold, *Indian Idylls*, p. 318.

but wicked, Kaikeyi at once demanded that her son be enthroned instead of Rama, and that Prince Rama be banished for fourteen years to Dandak's forest. The king was heart-broken by the cruel request, but having given his word, there was nothing he could do about it—(cf. the story of Jacob and Esau, and the word of the mother of the Pandavas telling the brothers to share their prize, Draupadi. Isaac could not restore the inheritance to Esau, even though it had been secured by deceit. It must remain with Jacob, the supplanter, because the father had spoken.) This is a frequent motif in stories out of the ancient world.

Rama might have refused to accept this cruel reversal of the plan for his coronation. He might have lifted the standard of revolt and won by battle what had been snatched out of his grasp. But he did nothing of the sort. He quietly accepted his father's word as law, and began to prepare for his exile in the great forest.

But Rama was married. He had won in a great tournament, described in the first book of the Epic, the princess of the Videhas, "soft-eyed" Sita. She must not accompany him in his banishment. She must remain at court, serve his mother, even his rival Bharat, half-brother, now crowned king, and await faithfully the day of his return. The rigors of forest life were not for her. However, Sita was of sterner stuff. She will not listen to him but cries:

"Lightly I dismiss the counsel which my lord hath lightly said,
For it ill becomes a warrior and my husband's princely grade.
For the faithful woman follows where her wedded lord may lead.
In the banishment of Rama, Sita's exile is decreed.
If the righteous son of Raghu wends to forest dark and drear
Sita steps before her husband wild and thorny paths to clear."[63]

Here speaks Indian womanhood, for Sita is the prototype of all that is lovely and virtuous in woman. She is the ideal woman of India, sweet, compliant, loyal, humble in the presence of her lord, utterly devoted to him and to his service. This ideal is breaking down at some points in modern India, but for centuries and even today in most respects Sita embodies the Indian ideal of feminine

[63] Romesh Dutt, *The Ramayana and the Mahabharata*, Everyman's Library, E. P. Dutton & Co., N. Y., 1929, p. 34.

charm and loveliness and character. She was eventually deified, as was Rama, and is very widely worshipped by India's women today.

Rama's brother, Lakshman, also begged to accompany him in his exile, so the three set off, lamented by parents and by the citizens of Kosala, for their fourteen years in Dandak's forest. Even when Bharat, the son for whom Kaikeyi had demanded the throne but who himself had had no part in the plot, came to beseech Rama to return, he would not do so, for "a righteous father's mandate duteous son may not recall."

Bharat returned to rule but vowed to wear hermit's garb for the duration. He besought Rama that he might have his sandals with which to decorate his throne, and if at the end of the fourteen years Rama should not return alive he declared he would die upon the pyre.

While dwelling in the forest there appeared a Rakshasa maiden, sister of the king of the Rakshasas who, when she saw Rama, fell violently in love with him and besought him to forsake Sita and marry her. Repulsed, she attacked Sita to kill her. Lakshman defended her, cutting off the Rakshasa's nose and ears. This brought on a bloody struggle with other evil demons. These were vanquished but sought revenge. They had the power to assume any shape they desired. One of them became a lovely deer and wandered near where Sita one day sat. She at once wanted the deer captured or killed. Rama set out to do so, bidding Lakshman remain with Sita. Unable to overtake or trap the deer, Rama shot the animal, which as it fell sent out a piercing cry, imitating Rama's voice. "Speed my faithful brother, Lakshman, helpless in the woods I die." Reluctant to leave Sita he, nevertheless, urged by her insistent plea, left her for a moment to rescue Rama. This gave the opportunity which Ravan, the Rakshasa king, awaited, and taking the form of a hermit he appeared before Sita. Seeing her surpassing beauty he fell madly in love with her. Passionately he sought to woo her, but was vigorously repulsed. Undeterred by her piteous pleadings and her unheard calls to Rama, Ravan seized her and entering his celestial car was borne swiftly to Lanka, Ravan's home.

Rama was heart-broken at the loss of his faithful wife and sought her, helped of course by Lakshman.

The monkey king Surgriva[64] had also had the misfortune to have been robbed of his wife and kingdom by his brother. Rama agrees to help him against his brother if Surgriva will aid him in finding Sita. Successful in a battle with his evil brother, by Rama's aid, Surgriva commissions Hanuman, one of his counsellors and son of the Wind-god, to find Sita. He locates her in Lanka by the aid of a vulture who had witnessed the abduction. Arriving at the ocean, he is at first dismayed, but with a mighty leap he sails through the air for four days, reaches Ceylon, and finds Sita who, because she had repulsed Ravan's advances, had been confined in an Asoka grove. He reassures her of her deliverance, takes to the air again and returns to report the success of his mission. Follows then the battle with Ravan. The monkey army is enabled to cross the straits by building a bridge and after fearful slaughter Ravan is slain in mortal combat with Rama. Like Hydra, he seems to have grown a new head when Rama's sword severed one from his body. But at last Rama's sword finds its way to the Rakshasa's heart and he falls. Thus is Sita liberated.

But strangely enough, from our viewpoint, Rama will not receive her back as his wife. She, after bitter complaint, requests to die on a funeral pyre and Rama consents. Invoking the fire as witness of her innocence, she rushes into the flames, but Agni the fire-god arises out of the burning pyre and rescuing Sita, gives her to Rama. Rama, who now declares that he never had entertained doubts of her purity, receives her back, asserting that it was only to prove her innocence to the people that he permitted the ordeal. So they are reunited and rule happily over their kingdom.

Here scholars think probably the real Epic ended, but a final Book VII is added. In this it is recounted that suspicion was abroad concerning Sita, and the morals of the women of the land were being endangered. Unable to bear the reproach that he is setting a

[64] Dutt explains that this reference to monkeys is only the result of "that contempt for aboriginal races which has marked civilized conquerors in all ages." This led the poet to describe the indigenous peoples among whom Rama found himself as monkeys and bears, or as the monkey people and the bear people. *Op. cit.*, p. 89.

bad example to his people, Rama has Lakshman take Sita into the forest and desert her—nice man! Here she finds shelter in the hermitage of Valmiki, an ascetic. Shortly after, she gives birth to twin sons, Kusa and Lava. Years pass; the twins, now grown, have become pupils of Valmiki. Rama organizes a horse sacrifice. Valmiki and his pupils attend and before Rama himself they recite in 500 cantos the story of Rama and Sita which Valmiki has composed.

Rama learns that the two young men are sons of Sita, and sends word by Valmiki asking her to purify herself by an oath before the whole assembled company. On the following day Valmiki brings Sita and the two boys, and solemnly declares that they are true sons of Rama. Rama declares himself satisfied, but still desires that Sita purify herself by means of an oath. Sita thereupon says, "As truly as I have never, even with so much as a single thought, thought of another than Rama—may Goddess Earth open her arms to me! As truly as I have always, in thought, word and deed, honored only Rama—may Goddess Earth open her arms to me. As I have here spoken the truth and never known another than Rama—may Goddess Earth open her arms to me!" Whereupon, Mother Earth appears and vanishes with her into a furrow.

So Sita whose very name means "the field-furrow" returns to her own element whence, as told in the first book, she had been miraculously born. Rama is greatly distressed and begs Mother Earth to restore her to him, but only god Brahma comes to comfort him with the hope that he will be reunited with her in heaven. Soon thereafter, Rama gives over his kingdom to his two sons and resumes his place in heaven as Vishnu, as whose incarnation he had been born, according to Book I.

It seems obvious on reading the entire Ramayana that both the first and last books are not real parts of the Epic, but later additions. In the Epic proper there is no indication that Rama is other than a hero. It was apparently after the deification of Rama that the other books were added. In the main part of the work it is Indra who is invoked wherever religion or mythology enters in. How long a time would be required for the process of deification to take place? Certainly a matter of centuries. Winternitz thinks that the poem had assumed its present form by about the end of the second century B.C., at least two centuries earlier than the Mahabharata. There is no agreement among specialists in the field. On the whole, however, the central core of the Mahabharata is generally considered older than the real epic story of the Ramayana.

What is significant from the standpoint of religion is that by the time these great poems were completed there had come about a very important set of changes in the religious outlook. Vedic religion was pretty well gone. The old gods, certainly in the didactic parts of both epics, had lost their power and a new group were now central, especially Vishnu, who had been but a minor sun deity in the Vedic period, was now a supreme God, who along with Brahma, the creator God, and Shiva the destroyer, was regarded as the Preserver—and worshipped chiefly through his incarnations. The two most important of these were Krishna, found in the Mahabharata, and Rama in the Ramayana, first as hero, then as god incarnate in the later portions.

The Krishna incarnation, perhaps the most widely worshipped of all of them, finds his highest development as divinity in a portion of the didactic epic, known as the Bhagavad Gita or the Lord's song. This excerpt from the Mahabharata has become perhaps the most widely read and best loved of all the scriptures of India. It is found in cheap editions, even vest pocket editions, of the sort almost anyone can own, and is avidly read by multitudes of Indians. It has also become the most widely diffused of the Indian sacred writings in the western world. It has been translated more frequently into English than any other Indian sacred work. Some years ago I found that it had been translated thirty-six times into English, and a number of editions have since appeared. Some of the more widely read translations are indicated on page 144. The writer's own favorite version, is that of Sir Edwin Arnold which, while not as scholarly as many versions, has caught the spirit of the poet author and rendered it into very beautiful English poetic form.

The poem is a dialogue between Arjuna the great epic hero, and Krishna disguised as his charioteer, just on the eve of the great battle of the Bharatas. The foes are drawn up ready and waiting for the

signal to attack. Then the warrior Arjuna, reflecting on how kinsmen were about to destroy each other in battle, suddenly speaks—
and in his speech gives utterance to one of the noblest protests
against war ever uttered by a soldier. He says, in the translated
version of Edwin Arnold:

> "Krishna! as I behold, come here to shed
> Their common blood, yon concourse of our kin,
> My members fail, my tongue dries in my mouth,
> A shudder thrills my body, and my hair
> Bristles with horror; from my weak hand slips
> Gandiv, the goodly bow; a fever burns
> My skin to parching; hardly may I stand; . . .

> "It is not good, O Keshav! nought of good
> Can spring from mutual slaughter! Lo, I hate
> Triumph and domination, wealth and ease,
> Thus sadly won! . . .

> "Shall I deal death on these
> Even though they seek to slay us? Not one blow,
> O Madhusudan! will I strike to gain
> The rule of all Three Worlds; then, how much less
> To seize an earthly kingdom!"[65]

But Krishna replies, and it is interesting that here it is the god,
not the warrior, who is defending war and justifying the slaughter
of his enemies. He says:

> "How hath this weakness taken thee? Whence springs
> The inglorious trouble, shameful to the brave
> Barring the path of virtue? Nay, Arjun!
> Forbid thyself to feebleness! it mars
> Thy warrior-name! cast off the coward-fit!
> Wake! Be thyself! Arise, Scourge of thy foes!"[66]

The basis of that defense is that man cannot be killed. Only the
body can be destroyed, the spirit lives on.

[65] Edwin Arnold, *The Song Celestial,* pp. 17–19.
[66] *Ibid.,* p. 21.

"He who shall say, 'Lo, I have slain a man!'
He who shall think, 'Lo, I am slain!' those both
Know naught. Life cannot slay. Life is not slain! . . .

"Nay, but as when one layeth
His outworn robes away,
And taking new ones, sayeth
'These will I wear today!'
So putteth by the spirit
Lightly its garb of flesh
And passeth to inherit
A residence afresh.
I say to thee that weapons reach not the Life."

Then cried Krishna:

. . . "Do thy part
Be mindful of thy name, and tremble not!
Nought better can betide a martial soul
Than lawful war; happy the warrior
To whom comes joy of battle—comes as now
Glorious and fair, unsought, opening for him
A gateway unto Heaven. But if thou shunn'st
This honorable field—a Kshatriya—(member of warrior caste)
If knowing thy duty and thy task, thou bidd'st
Duty and task go by—that shall be sin!
And those to come shall speak the infamy
From age to age; but infamy is worse
For men of noble blood to bear than death!"[67]

In this statement is found the very heart of Indian ethics. To
perform the duty or dharma, corresponding to one's position—that
is to fulfil the requirements of ethics as Indians today see it.

The poem contains eighteen chapters, each treating of some special theme; one, of the way of salvation by work, another by knowledge—but throughout there is emphasis upon salvation by faith or
devotion to Krishna. There are passages here that seem to come
right out of the New Testament. Only the name of Jesus would

[67] Pp. 26–28, *passim.*

have to be substituted for that of Krishna to make it sound exactly like the gospels.

> "Who cleave, who seek in Me
> Refuge from birth and death, those have the Truth."[68]

> "Thou too, when heart and mind are fixed on Me
> Shalt surely come to Me. All who cleave
> With never-wavering will of firmest faith
> Owning none other gods: all come to Me."[69]

Perhaps the reason for its almost universal appeal is the fact that it is eclectic in its religious approach. One may seek salvation and find it by various paths. It becomes every man's book. But it is pre-eminently a book of devotion. It has been compared to the Gospel of John, which, more than any other of the Gospels, has served as a devotional guide for Christians through the centuries. One writer says that if Christianity is ever to make an appeal to the educated Indian it will be through the Gospel of John, because it makes an appeal similar to that of the Gita. It is noteworthy that to many in the west who are no longer held by the ties of orthodoxy, the Gita has become a favorite bedside table book. Perhaps the thing that made it appeal to so many in India was its universalism. Salvation was for every man of every class—for women as well as men. Krishna throws open the road to whosoever will come.

> "Be certain none can perish, trusting Me!
> O Pritha's Son! whoso will turn to Me,
> Though they be born from the very womb of Sin,
> Woman or man; sprung of the Vaisya caste
> Or lowly disregarded Sudra,—all
> Plant foot upon the highest path; how then
> The holy Brahmans and My Royal Saints?
> Ah! ye who into this ill world are come—
> Fleeting and false—set your faith fast on Me!
> Fix heart and thought on Me! Adore Me! Bring
> Offerings to Me! Make Me prostrations! Make

[68] P. 77.
[69] P. 81.

> Me your supremest joy! and, undivided,
> Unto My rest your spirits shall be guided."[70]

In India many stories and legends have grown up about the Gita. Margaret Noble relates this one:

In the Gita is found a word of Krishna which says: "They who depend upon me, putting aside all care, whatsoever they need, I myself carry it to them." A Brahmin one day, copying the verse, hesitated when he came to the word "carry." This seemed to him somehow to be irreverent. How should Krishna "carry" anything? For in India to carry a load is a menial task. So he substituted for it the word, "send." A little later his wife said: "There is no food in the house." Then said he, "Let us ask the Lord to fulfil his promise." Meanwhile he went to bathe.

Soon a youth came to the door with a basket of food. "Who sent this?" the wife asked. "Your husband asked me to carry it," he replied, giving it to her. As she took the basket she noted cuts and gashes on the youth's breast above his heart.

"Alas, who wounded thee?" she cried.

"Your husband, before he called me, cut me with a small sharp weapon." Then the youth vanished. The husband being reproved by his wife for his ill treatment of the young man, declared that he had not left the house. Then they knew. And they restored the word "carry" to its rightful place.[71]

Mahatma Gandhi had the highest regard for the Gita. And, strangely enough, despite the defense of killing in war given by Krishna the god, he finds in it a support for his doctrine of satyagraha or soul-force by which non-violent means he achieved such signal victories and finally won the independence of India. He wrote of it on occasion:

Nothing elates me so much as the music of the Gita or the Ramayana by Tulasidas, the only two books in Hinduism I may be said to know. When I fancied I was taking my last breath, the Gita was my solace.[72]

The literary problems raised by the Gita are numerous, and

[70] Edwin Arnold, *The Song Celestial,* pp. 93–94.
[71] *Web of Indian Life,* p. 211.
[72] Gandhi, *Young India,* pp. 800–801.

scholars are not at all in agreement as to its origin or the date. By some it is regarded as an original poem setting forth Krishnaism based upon the Sankhya-Yoga philosophy, but modified later by the additions in which the Vedanta is taught.[73] Others think that it is an old verse Upanishad worked over by a poet in the interest of Krishnaism, after the beginning of the Christian era.[74]

S. Radhakrishnan, latest and perhaps most eminent of the translators and commentators on the Gita, thinks that "from its archaic construction and internal references we may infer that it is definitely a work of the pre-Christian era. Its date may be assigned to the fifth century B.C., though the text may have received many alterations in subsequent times."[75]

For our purposes it does not greatly matter. It will be enough to say that somewhere, not far from the beginning of the Christian era it attained its present form and has been since that time the highest expression of the essentially devotional type of Hinduism at its best. It is a tribute to its worth that in the course of time it should have taken its place alongside the Veda as *sruti*.

"Is the teaching of the Gita[76] as authoritative as that of the *Sruti?*" runs a question asked in D. Sarma's *Primer of Hinduism*.

"Yes, the Gita being the essence of the Upanishads is considered as authoritative as the *Sruti*."[77]

[73] R. Garbe, *Encyclopedia of Religion and Ethics*, Vol. 2, p. 53.
[74] Farquhar, *Outlines of Religious Literature of India*, p. 92.
[75] *The Bhagavad Gita*, Harper and Brothers, N. Y., 1948, p. 14.
[76] Some of the better known translations of the Gita are the following:
S. Radhakrishnan. *The Bhagavad Gita*, with an introductory essay, Sanskrit Text, English translation and notes. Harper and Brothers, N. Y., 1948.
Franklin Edgerton, *The Bhagavad Gita*, translated and interpreted. 2 vols. Harvard University Press, Cambridge, 1946. The first volume contains the Sanskrit text and Edgerton's translation. Vol. 2 contains his interpretation and also Edwin Arnold's translation.
Sir Edwin Arnold, *The Song Celestial*, published in many separate editions. To be found also in *Sacred Books and Literature of the East*, Vol. 9.
Swami Paramananda, *The Blessed Lord's Song*, in Lin Yutang, *Wisdom of China and India*, pp. 57–114.
Swami Prabhavananda and Christopher Isherwood, Marcel Rodd Co., Hollywood, Cal., 1946, *The Bhagavad Gita, The Song of God*. Excerpts included in Lewis Browne, *The World's Great Scriptures*, pp. 99–119.
Mrs. Annie Besant, *The Bhagavad Gita, The Lord's Song*. Excerpts included in Ballou, *The World Bible*, pp. 85–101. Mrs. Besant was a Theosophist leader.
[77] P. 13.

The Puranas have had much less attention from scholars than has the literature of India thus far studied. Yet contemporary Hinduism is perhaps more influenced by them than by the other scriptures. They are the scriptures of the sectarian branches of Hinduism which, while paying lip service to the Vedas as most precious, draw much of their belief about the gods of their own primary devotion and worship from these books. For most of the gods which now are popularly worshipped[78] in India are gods of little importance, or quite unknown to the Vedas. Vishnu is, to be sure, a not very important sun-god in the Rig-Veda, but Rama, Shiva, Sita, Kali, Durga, Uma, Parvati, Ganesha, Lakshmi are strangers to the Veda. They are, some of them, known in the Epics, but these in religious belief if not in time, are closer to contemporary religions than they are to the Veda.

Puranic literature which by very definition of the word Purana means old or ancient, is purportedly the record of the very beginnings of the world, i.e., they are books of origins like Genesis in the Old Testament. Certainly they are the source of the popular ideas of the creation of the world, the gods, and early history of the race. They are, it need hardly be said, largely legendary. Theoretically a Purana is supposed to deal with five subjects: (1) the creation; (2) re-creation, the periodical destruction and renewal of the worlds; (3) the genealogy of the gods and the ancient Rishis; (4) the great time periods, each of which has a primal ancestor or Manu; and (5) the history of the early dynasties which trace their origin to the sun or the moon. Actually the existing Puranas do not all follow this scheme. This may have been the stereotyped form of ancient Puranas to which reference is made in very early literary sources, but certainly not of the Puranas of today.

The Puranas themselves mention eighteen Puranas which are the generally recognized ones today. Strangely enough each lists them as though no one is older than any other. Obviously this listing would be a late addition. They are, usually listed in this order: (1) Brahma (B); (2) Padma (V); (3) Vishnu (V); (4) Shiva

---

[78] Many modern Hindus, of course, regard these all as but different aspects of the same reality.

(S) or Vayu; (5) Bhagavata (V); (6) Narada (V); (7) Markandeya (B); (8) Agni (S); (9) Bhavisya (B); (10) Brahmavaivarta (B); (11) Linga (S); (12) Varaha (V); (13) Skanda (S); (14) Vamana (B); (15) Kaurma (S); (16) Matsya (S); (17) Garuda (V); (18) Brahmananda (B).

They are generally sectarian in content. The particular divinity to which each is partial is indicated in the above list by the initial letter following the name of the Purana—"V" for Vishnu, "S" for Shiva and "B" for Brahma. It should be said that, in general, Brahma here means not the "neuter world soul," but the personal creator god who with Vishnu and Shiva forms the Hindu Trimurti, sometimes translated Trinity.

A typical legend establishing one of the gods as the preferred divinity of worship is found in the Padma Purana, and incidentally reveals the strong sectarian bias of that Purana which is clearly Vishnuite.

Once a quarrel arose among the Rishis as to which of the three great gods, Brahma, Vishnu or Shiva, was most deserving of worship. Accordingly the great ascetic Bhrgu was commissioned to go to the gods and judge for himself personally which was best. He first goes to the mountains Kailasa to visit Shiva. But Shiva is enjoying the love of his wife and doesn't admit him at all. Bhrgu thereupon pronounces a curse upon Shiva, condemning him to take the form of the generative organs—thus apparently accounting for the worship of the Yoni and Linga.[79]

He goes then to the world of Brahma but he is seated upon his lotus throne surrounded by all the gods, and, filled with pride, does not even acknowledge the homage of Bhrgu. He too is cursed by the Rishi, to the effect that no one shall worship him—an explanation, doubtless, of the fact that almost no worship is actually accorded Brahma.

Coming to the abode of Vishnu, the Rishi finds the god asleep. Roughly kicking him in the chest, Vishnu is awakened, only to stroke gently the sage's foot and express his gratitude and honor at his visit. He rises and with his wife does honor to the guest. Whereupon Bhrgu bursts into tears of joy, and cries: "Thou alone shalt be worshipped by the Brahmans. No other of the gods is worthy to be worshipped." He then returns and makes his report to the assembled Rishis.[80]

[79] The female and male sex organs.
[80] As given in Winternitz, *History of Indian Literature*, I, pp. 542–543.

In this same Purana, Shiva, talking with his wife, himself declares the power and glory of Vishnu and his incarnations. In the course of his eulogy he tells the Rama story. He further declares, in answer to a question of Parvati, that the adherents of the Shivite sect are heretics. Undoubtedly equally sectarian proof of the superiority of Shiva occurs in the Shivite Puranas.

In the fifth book of the Vishnu-Purana which is given up wholly to stories of Krishna, chief avatar or incarnation of Vishnu, is to be found some of the most interesting material for the general reader. The stories are almost exactly like those found in the Harivamsa, usually considered by Indians as an appendix to the Mahabharata, but hardly to be distinguished from the Puranas in general style, character, or content. Here we can only sketch a few of the Krishna stories.

First of all the manner of his birth. A prophecy was made to an evil king Kamsa that the eighth son of Devaki his aunt, and wife of Vasudeva, would kill him. Accordingly he determined that the child should be destroyed. But immediately after Krishna's birth he was exchanged for a child of a cowherd, Nanda and his wife. This child was slain by Kamsa, and Krishna grew up as a child of humble cowherd folk. Remarkable stories are told of his childhood which remind one of some of the stories told of the child Jesus in the apocryphal gospels.

One day his foster mother left him lying asleep under a wagon. Awakening and impatient for food, little Krishna with one foot upset the wagon. Another time to keep him from running away, she tied a rope around his waist and secured it to a heavy mortar. "Now get away, if you can," she said. But Krishna simply walked off with it. When it caught between two trees, he tore the trees out by their roots.

He became a trickster and played all sorts of jokes not only upon his playmates, but upon older folk as well. On one occasion he came upon a group of *gopis* or milkmaids bathing in a pool. He seized their robes and hid them.

As a youth he was handsome and amorous. The *gopis* all fell in love with him. The amorous exploits of the youthful bucolic lover, told in this and in other Puranas, were later to become the basis of an erotic phase of Krishna worship in which the sports of Krishna were taken all too literally as cult practices. Others, less literal-minded, made them symbolic of mystic experience of the soul with god.

He slays monsters and dragons, and overcomes evil rulers. He rebels at the worship of Indra, and bids his followers arrange a mountain sacrifice instead. Indra is infuriated and sends upon them a terrible storm. Krishna lifts a mountain and holds it over them as an umbrella and they are protected. He attends a festival arranged by Kamsa, the bad king, bends and breaks a bow which not even the gods could bend, tears out the tusk of a great elephant which sought to trample him, and kills the beast, and finally slays Kamsa himself. He even descends into the realm of the dead, overcomes Yama, the god of death, and restores the son of a teacher who, as his fee, had required that Krishna bring back the son who had drowned at sea.

Space forbids further indication of the detailed content of these books. In their legendary accounts of the world and the gods they are the basis of much of the religious faith of India. In their regulations for daily living, in their glorification of sacred places and acts of worship they are a great stimulant to the religious practices of the people.

While it is generally agreed that there were some very ancient Puranas, upon which, to some extent, the Puranas as we have them are based, they are the latest of all the sacred writings. Puranas or at least writings that purport to be Puranas, usually called Upa-puranas, have continued to appear until within relatively recent times. They all purport to come from Vyasa, reputed author of the Mahabharata, but obviously they represent a slow growth across the centuries. In literary style they stand far below the great earlier writings. They are diffuse, confused, and contradictory both within and among themselves, but India has never been primarily concerned with consistency in her literature. Indeed, there is found in one of the sacred law books this statement in effect: "If within this book there are found contradictory statements they are both to be taken as true."

Thus we come to the end of this very sketchy, yet relatively lengthy, account of Indian sacred literature. In it is to be found heights and depths of spiritual understanding that compare favorably with the best that have been found anywhere. Its vastness, its diversity, on the whole, its lack of discriminating judgment as to what may be called sacred—so that it includes both the highly moral and the base—make it a literature difficult for peoples of Hebrew-Christian backgrounds to appreciate fully. But that it is interesting to study, challenging to scholarship, and not without great interest in many of its parts for the general reader, there can be no doubt. To Hindus it contains the clue to salvation and the good life as at various levels they apprehend it.

SACRED LITERATURE OF HINDUISM
Sources for Further Reading

References have been made to specific books on the several divisions or books of Hindu sacred writings. Here are mentioned sets, or series of volumes, or single volumes which contain translations of some parts of that literature.

ON THE VEDAS
Sacred Books of the East, Vols. 32 and 42 and 46 (42 Atharva Veda).
Sacred Books and Literature of the East, Vol. 9.
A. A. Macdonell, *Hymns of the Rig-Veda*, Association Press, Calcutta, 1922.
R. T. H. Griffith, *Hymns of the Rig-Veda*, E. J. Lazarus, Benares, 2nd Edition, 1896–1897.

ON THE BRAHMANAS
Sacred Books of the East, Vols. 12 and 44.
Harvard Oriental Series, Vol. 25.
Sacred Books and Early Literature of the East, Vol. 9.

ON THE UPANISHADS
Sacred Books of the East, Vols. 1 and 15.
R. E. Hume, *Thirteen Principal Upanishads*, Charles Scribner's Sons, N. Y.

ON THE EPICS
Romesh Dutt, *The Ramayana and the Mahabharata*, Everyman's Edition, E. P. Dutton and Company, N. Y., 1929.

Sir Edwin Arnold, *Indian Idylls*, Roberts Brothers, Boston.

The Ramayana, translated by R. T. H. Griffith, 5 Vols.

ON THE BHAGAVAD GITA

Sir Edwin Arnold, *The Song Celestial,* Roberts Brothers, Boston, 1885. It has appeared in many editions.

Franklin Edgerton, *The Bhagavad Gita,* 2 Vols., Harvard University Press, 1946.

S. Radhakrishnan, *The Bhagavad Gita* with Sanskrit Text and English translation and notes, Harper and Brothers, N. Y., 1948.

There are nearly two score English translations in circulation.

ON THE LEGAL LITERATURE

Sacred Books of the East, Vols. 2, 7, 14 and 25. The last is the most famous Laws of Manu.

ON THE PURANAS

H. W. Wilson, *The Vishnu Purana,* 5 vols., London, 1864–1877.

IN THE ANTHOLOGIES

Hindu Scripture, edited by Nicol MacNicol, Everyman's Library, J. M. Dent & Sons, London, 1938.

The Wisdom of China and India, edited by Lin Yutang, Random House, Inc., New York, 1942, pp. 1–315.

Harvard Classics, Vol. 45, pp. 799–884.

Lewis Browne, *The World's Great Scriptures,* pp. 57–132.

Ruth Smith, *The Tree of Life,* pp. 71–114.

Ballou, *The Bible of the World,* pp. 3–180.

Grace Turnbull, *Tongues of Fire,* pp. 27–42, 245–267.

Frost, *Sacred Writings of the World's Great Religions,* pp. 9–68.

Sohrab, *The Bible of Mankind,* pp. 31–90.

CHAPTER VI

The Sacred Literature of Buddhism

The first thing to be said about Buddhist sacred literature is that it is very extensive. In Japan over four thousand books are reckoned as canonical. Contrast this with the sixty-six books of the Protestant versions of the Bible. A complete edition of the Buddhist scriptures was published in Japan some twenty years ago, and it ran to fifty substantial sized volumes. This, to be sure, included some scholarly notes also, but it indicates something as to the quantitative aspects of Buddhist scriptures. If one wishes a copy of the entire Christian Bible it can be bought in a single volume, well printed and bound, for as little as fifty cents. The price of the above mentioned set of Buddhist sacred writings, in terms of pre-inflation money, was two hundred and fifty dollars. This is not a wholly fair comparison, the writer well understands, for the quality of printing and binding of the compared Bibles varies greatly, and besides, the cheapness of the Bible is due to a heavy subsidy to the Bible Societies, enabling them to sell the Bible at a very low price. Yet it does tell something about the Buddhist scriptures. They are vast, and as yet no one has felt moved to subsidize their publication, at least as a whole, to the point of making them available to everyman.

Of course, Buddhism is a world religion. It is found all over eastern Asia. Originating in India in the sixth century B.C. as an heretical reform movement in Hinduism, it, unlike the mother faith, spread widely over Asia and even, to some extent, into Europe, though no permanent result of its teaching can be surely detected. It eventually almost entirely disappeared from India proper, but not until it had made itself at home in Tibet, China, Japan, and all southeastern Asia and Ceylon. In the course of time it developed two major divisions, one known as the Mahayana or the Great Vehicle and the other as Hinayana or Lesser Vehicle, roughly comparable to the two major divisions in Christianity, or Protestant and Catholic. In general the Mahayana spread northward and is often called northern Buddhism, while the Hinayana spread south and southeastward. The latter represents the more nearly original type of Buddhist thought and practice. Each developed special scriptures of its own although there is much that is held by them in common. In this respect again they somewhat resemble Protestantism and Roman Catholicism which have each a different canon, although the great part of the Bible is held by both.

The Hinayana canon or, as it is called, the Pali or Theravada canon has come down to us through the Pali language, a vernacular derived from the Sanskrit and closely akin to the native language of Gautama, the founder of Buddhism, which was Magadhi. The Mahayana scriptures have been preserved chiefly in the Sanskrit, although some Mahayana books, while possibly originally in Sanskrit, are known to us only through Tibetan or Chinese translations. The Pali canon is a very definite one as we shall presently see. The Mahayana scriptures form no hard and fast canon. Sects of the Mahayana, of which there are a considerable number, differ as to the scriptures they accept and particularly emphasize.

The history of the sacred literature of the Buddhists is really a part of the history of the sacred literature of India, for it was all produced either on Indian soil, or by Indians who carried the new faith to other lands. But Buddhism having been for so long a religion, reaching far beyond India, and having almost entirely disappeared from India itself, Buddhist scriptures may very fittingly be treated separately.

It will be necessary, however, to go back to the beginnings of the new heretical movement in Hinduism and see how it arose and what therefore these new scriptures have to say on the great central themes of Hindu scripture.

Buddhism arose in the sixth century B.C. It will be recalled that in treating of the Upanishads mention was made of the fact that the older priestly religion of the Vedas and Brahmanas had lost its appeal to many who were not of the Brahmin or priestly caste. There was in the years from perhaps the seventh century B.C. the beginning of reflection by non-Brahmins and in particular by men and women of the Kshatriya or warrior-ruler caste concerning the great questions of God, the world, and man's origin and final destiny, and Gautama himself was, according to tradition, of that class, and was not out of character in seeking the way out of the round of rebirth, which by his time had become a matter of common belief. People of that period believed in Karma, the law of the deed, the law of retribution which inexorably operated to keep one on the wheel of rebirth. How should one escape the evil and misery and suffering inherent in life, as the wheel of birth endlessly turned?

The whole story of Buddha's life, told over and over again in Buddhist scriptures, is concerned chiefly with this problem. There is much that is legendary in the numerous tellings of his life story, but the basic facts seem to be clear. Prince Buddha, despite the happy circumstances in which his life was set, became oppressed with the evil of the world and its suffering, and early became obsessed with a passion to be freed from this round of birth. Everything possible was done to keep his mind off the subject and to make him happy. But after he had seen, despite every effort to keep him from doing so, the ugly facts of sickness, poverty, old age and death, he finally renounced his princely home and comfort, even a new-born son and his much loved wife, Yasodhara, and went out into the world to become, first, a wandering mendicant seeking by austerity and ascetic practices to find release. When this proved of no avail he abandoned it and sought by meditation the way of knowledge to find peace. Ultimately this brought him to the state of enlightenment, and he became the Enlightened One or the Buddha. What that meant precisely, we shall see a little later.

Having found it for himself he now sought to help others find the same release he had himself found. Soon he was surrounded by disciples who craved release also, and through his teaching found it. They followed him about from place to place seeking to help others. In the rainy season when they could not travel, they lived together in a sacred grove, and so evolved the *Sangha* or monastic order which has been the chief institutional feature of southern Buddhism. Eventually a woman's order was founded—*Bhikkhunis* they were called—though not without serious misgivings on the part of Gautama, who seems to have had a deep-seated distrust of women. For forty-five years Buddha went up and down a relatively limited section of north central India, teaching and preaching, then died of food poisoning from a meal prepared by one of his humble followers.

During this long ministry (contrast it with the three years or less of Jesus' ministry) he taught much and said many things many times, and in slightly differing form. Most of his utterances were heard by some one or more of his disciples, who, especially in later years, cherished what he said, and probably remembered a substantial part of it rather correctly. Remember that as yet men were dependent upon oral recall. That writing may have existed, is quite probable. That men trusted, at least in the case of the sacred scriptures, more to oral transmission than to writing is certain. So it may well be supposed that the disciples of Buddha, hearing over and over again his discourses, would be able to remember them fairly well. At all events there is no evidence that at Gautama's death in c. 485 B.C. there was a single written record of anything he ever said or did. Yet a great part of the extensive body of sacred Buddhist literature purports to be the record of what he did and said.

Long before Gautama died he had become a tradition. There are traces of near deification, even before his death, or at least a dependence upon him which ordinarily is reserved for deity. Very quickly after his death the process of apotheosis was accelerated and, in the end, he who discovered the very definitely non-theistic way of salvation, declaring that even if the gods exist they are powerless to help man achieve salvation, became himself essentially a god. He who declared that man could only save himself by his own effort came either directly or indirectly to be regarded as a helper in the process of achieving salvation. Soon his relics were being venerated, stupas being erected around some very insignificant part of his body or something that had belonged to him. One of the greatest pagodas in the Buddhist world enshrines a tooth of the Buddha, another a hair from his head.

Obviously as he assumed more and more this character of divinity (though never so acknowledged even by his followers), his words became of greater and greater significance. There was a definite effort to recall what he said, and many different disciples must have contributed to the growing store of remembered words. Naturally there was not always agreement as to just what he had said. Variant versions of his sayings thus arose, and as these were transmitted orally they must have been added to, or some things may have dropped out. Thus went forward the definite, but for a time wholly informal, process of gathering his sayings and doings which were gradually brought into collections. Tradition has it that this had already been accomplished by the time of his death and that immediately following the death of Gautama, a Council was held attended by five-hundred Arhants, as those were called who had attained to enlightenment. At this First Council, as it is called, Ananda, close follower of Buddha, was requested to recite what are now regarded as the first two parts of the canon, the Suttas and the Vinaya, so that it might be known exactly what they were. The historicity of this Council, or at least of the fact that so much of the canon was already in existence at that time is generally doubted. This seems to scholars hardly to have been possible—certainly not in the form in which we now have it.

About a hundred years after the death of Gautama a second Council was called by the elder Yasa at Vesali. A relaxation of discipline in the Order had developed, which threatened the stability of the brotherhood. The very fact of heresy points at a generally accepted norm from which heresy is a variant, though this need not have been the canon as it now exists. While this particular controversy related only to the Vinaya, or book of discipline, it would not be unnatural that other parts might also be considered. Certainly there is a tradition that the defeated heretical monks held a rival council of ten thousand members, known as the Great Council, and drew up a different recension of the scriptures which among other things, according to the *Dipavamsa*,[1] "broke up the sense and doctrine in the five Nikayas," and "rejecting some portions of the Sutta and the profound Vinaya, they made another counterfeit Sutta and Vinaya."

Not all scholars are agreed as to the historicity of this Second Council, though most of them think there is some historic basis for the tradition. Differences certainly had begun to develop within the Order, and it is from this event that the traditional eighteen schismatic schools are thought to have taken their rise.[2]

But in the reign of the Buddhist emperor, Asoka, in 247 B.C., a third Council was held, convoked by the elder Tissa Mogalliputta, attended by a thousand monks, in the city of Pataliputra. It was called with the purpose of compiling an authoritative set of texts setting forth the true religion. The result of their labor, which continued, according to tradition, for nine months, was the Theravada or "doctrine of the elders," which is held by the Buddhists of Ceylon to be the Pali Canon which is in use there today. They believe that it was brought to Ceylon by one, Mahinda, son of the Emperor Asoka, who, with his sister, introduced Buddhism into Ceylon. Here it was transmitted orally until, during the reign of Vattagamani, 29–17 B.C. it was put in writing. This may not mean that there had been no part of the canon in written form before that time, but there is no certain evidence that earlier written copies existed. It may be significant that Fa-hsien, the Chinese pilgrim, who travelled in north India during the years 399–414 A.D., found no manuscript of the Vinaya, but only oral tradition. In Pataliputra, reputed site

[1] Vs. 32–38.
[2] So Edward J. Thomas, *op. cit.*, p. 170.

of the Third Council, he came upon a written copy of it.[3] If the late writing of this great mass of material is true, we have here another testimony to the remarkable ability of the Indian to transmit an extensive literature *solely* through memory. At the same time this would make it easier to explain the vast accretions of matter which could not possibly have come directly from the lips of Buddha himself.

We turn now to an examination of the content of this Theravada, or Pali Canon. Later we shall have occasion to mention at least some of the major Mahayana variants. It falls into three very distinct parts which are designated as *Pitakas* or "baskets." Thus the whole scripture is called the Tripitaka or the "three baskets." These are:

1. Vinaya-pitaka; 2. Sutta-pitaka; and 3. Abhidhamma-pitaka, or the basket of discipline for the *Sangha* or Order; the basket of the sayings of the Buddha; and "the basket of higher subtleties" as given by Winternitz, or variously as given by others, "the basket of philosophy," or the "basket of apologetic," or defense of the doctrine. The first two may very well contain much that comes from the Buddha himself, though perhaps modified and misinterpreted, but the third, which was not even traditionally supposed to be in existence at the time of the so-called First Council, must certainly have been quite late in taking form.

The Vinaya-pitaka is wholly concerned with the monastic life and, as such, is of little interest to the general reader. Unless he is desirous of knowing what goes on inside a monastery or convent, he is not likely to read far in this part of Buddhist scripture. The heart of it is the discipline practiced by the monks and nuns. Twice every month at the new and full moon the *Upasatha* ceremony took place. This consisted of the reciting of the Patimokkha or set of rules, two hundred and twenty-seven in number, by which the monks were supposed to live. At the conclusion of each of the eight chapters the reciter would ask whether any monk had been guilty

[3] *A Record of Buddhistic Kingdoms*, translated by James Legge, Oxford, 1886. Chapter 36, p. 98.

of the particular sin therein mentioned. If so, he must make confession of his guilt. For each infraction there was a corresponding penalty, for four, expulsion from the order was indicated. These were incontinence, theft, killing or persuading one to suicide, and false boasting of divine powers. The Patimokkha itself is not a part of the canon, but the whole first section of the Vinaya-pitaka, known as the Sutta-Vibhanga, is little more than a commentary upon it. Each separate sutta, or, in this case, each single article of the Patimokkha is explained word by word and the occasion which gave rise to its promulgation by the Buddha is told. There are eight kinds of greater or lesser sins described in the eight chapters, each with its corresponding penalty. Following the rules for monks is a corresponding section which gives rules for the nuns, or Bhikkhunis.

The second part consists of the Mahavagga and Cullavagga or greater and lesser sections, which form a supplement to part I. The Mahavagga itself in ten sections treats of the rules for admission to the order, for the Upasatha ceremony described above, for life during the rainy seasons, and for the celebration at its conclusion; rules for articles of dress and furniture; medicines and food; the annual distribution of robes; materials for robes; regulations for sleeping and for sick monks; legal procedure inside the order; and, finally, procedure in case of schism.

The Cullavagga deals with discipline in case of minor infractions of order, rules for bathing, dress, dwellings, furniture, duties of different classes of monks, teachers, novices, and exclusion from the Upasatha ceremony. In the tenth section are given the corresponding lesser rules for the nuns, and then follow two sections giving the history of the first and second Councils, to which reference was made above.

The third section, the Parivara, is probably a late addition and is of little interest or importance.

A rule book is never a very interesting or inspiring document except for those involved in the game. But happily there is a lighter side to the Vinaya-pitaka which, if it can be found, is not without popular interest. Since, as indicated, in explaining the rules, stories are sometimes told indicating their origin, some quite interesting legends and stories are recounted, which are found nowhere else in Buddhist literature.

One which, whether it ever actually happened or not, throws light upon the character of Buddha as he was remembered by his followers, is, in abridged form, as follows:

Once a certain monk had a serious disturbance of the bowels and lay fallen in his own excrement. The blessed one, or Buddha, and Ananda, found him.

"Have you no one to wait on you," said Buddha.

"No, Lord."

"Why do not the Bhikkhus wait upon you?"

"Because I am of no service to them," he replied.

Then Buddha sent Ananda to bring water and with his help he washed the monk of his filth and carried him to his own bed.

Later Buddha spoke to the assembled monks and asked them:

"Is there a sick monk among you?"

"There is, Lord."

"Is there any one to wait upon him?"

"No, Lord."

"Why do not the monks wait on him?"

"Because he is of no service to the monks, Lord." Then the Buddha said to them:

"You, O Monks, have no father or mother to wait upon you. If you do not wait on each other who is there who will wait upon you? Whosoever, O Monks, would wait upon me, let him wait upon the sick." Is there not a ring here of that saying of Jesus in Matthew 25:40 "Inasmuch as ye have done it unto one of the least of these my brethren, ye have done it unto me"?[4]

Another story, told in connection with the rules on clothing, is that of a famous physician, Jivaka, who treated Buddha in his illnesses and was a good friend of the Order. It throws interesting light on the practice of medicine in that ancient time as well as deep psychological understanding on the part of the doctor. A certain merchant became very ill. None of the other physicians had been able to help him. Jivaka, who was court physician, was given

[4] Mahavagga VIII, 26, *Sacred Books of the East,* Vol. 17, pp. 240 ff.

permission to treat him. After arranging the fee, one hundred thousand florins each for himself and the king, he asks whether the patient thinks he can lie quietly first on one side then the other and finally on his back, seven months in each position. He thinks he can. Whereupon Jivaka ties him down on the bed—probably no anaesthetics—cuts open his scalp, removes two worms, and sews him up once more. But the patient was unable to lie on each side and on his back for seven months. The best he could do was seven days. In three weeks he was well. Jivaka then tells him that if he hadn't agreed to remain quiet for the seven months he wouldn't have been able to hold out for even seven days.[5] Another, not without humor, a very welcome diversion in this otherwise dry rule book, is that of a boy Upali whose parents are concerned with what the boy shall do when he grows up. If he writes, his fingers will get sore, arithmetic may cause pains in his chest (why, one wonders); painting would hurt his eyes; so in the end they decide he shall become a monk, since this is the easiest and most comfortable way to make a living![6]

But if the Vinaya-pitaka holds little general-reader interest, it is fundamental to an understanding of Buddhism, for the very genius of Buddhism, in its original form, was to take man out of the common life of the world and set him apart on the way to enlightenment, which was the end of all his seeking, for this meant escape from the wheel of birth. There were lay followers of course, and their way of life and the way of life of the total community was deeply affected by the teachings of the Buddha and the ministry of the monks, but in the end enlightenment, which was the final goal, was not to be won as long as man was caught up in the ordinary round of daily work of the world. So the rules for the maintenance of discipline among the monks were of very great importance. To the historian of religion they are a priceless source for an understanding of the development of Buddhism. Also they are of interest to any student of monasticism, East or West, for there is much that is common to the monastic way of life, whether in

[5] Mahavagga VIII, 1, 17–20, *Sacred Books of the East*, Vol. 17, pp. 181–184.
[6] Mahavagga I, 49, *Sacred Books of the East*, Vol. 13, pp. 201–202.

Christianity or among the Aztecs of Mexico, or the Buddhists and Taoists of the Far East.

It is in the Sutta-pitaka that the greater part of Buddha's teachings is found. These correspond, in Christianity, with the Gospels. While the Vinaya and Abhidhamma both purport, in the main, to come from the Buddha, it is here, if anywhere, we must look to find what he said and to some extent what he did. The Sutta-pitaka—sutta means sayings—is made up of five major divisions called Nikayas. In outline form it is thus:

I. Sutta-pitaka
   1. Digha Nikaya or Long Discourses.
   2. Majjhima Nikaya or Shorter Discourses.
   3. Samyutta Nikaya or Connected Sayings.
   4. Anguttara Nikaya or Gradual Sayings.
   5. Khuddaka Nikaya or Division of Small Books.

In so brief a chapter on the Buddhist scriptures, only the sketchiest kind of treatment of these various divisions can be given—just enough to suggest their general character. For the Digha Nikaya runs to three volumes and a total of over nine hundred and fifty pages, including some added notes.[7] It consists of thirty-four discourses, roughly grouped in three *vaggas* or sections. The Majjhima contains one hundred and fifty-two discourses grouped in fifteen sections. It fills two volumes, with about seven hundred pages in translation.[8] Here at once appears a great contrast to the Gospels, which in the newest translation occupy two hundred and fifty pages in a fairly large-print edition. But a more notable difference is in the length of the reported sayings. In the Gospels they are brief, many quite epigrammatic. Of sustained discourse there is almost nothing, at least in the Synoptic Gospels, and in John the longest scarcely goes beyond a page or two in length. It is true that in the division of small books we shall find much of this kind of reported

---

[7] *Dialogues of the Buddha*, three vols., translated by T. W. and C. A. F. Davids. Published as Vols. 2–4, in Max Muller, *Sacred Books of the Buddhists*, London, 1899, 1910, 1921.

[8] *Further Dialogues of the Buddha*, two vols., translated by Lord Chalmers. Published as Vols. 5 and 6. *Sacred Books of the Buddhists*, edited by Max Muller, Oxford University Press, London, 1926–1927.

sayings of Buddha too, but here are pages and pages of the most subtle and profound discussions of very difficult subjects. It is true that Buddha refuses to speculate on the idea of God, or many another theme, which seems to him of secondary importance or interest. How shall man achieve Nirvana—or salvation? Anything that seems to distract attention from that, he will not discuss. One may wonder as he reads even the titles of some of these discourses just how important they are to the main drive. Here are only a few of them, to indicate about what he did think it worth while to talk— and at length. Many of them are in dialogue form.

The very first one, "the net of Brahma," gives a list of sixty-two forms of speculations concerning the world and the self as held by other teachers. The second on the "fruits of being an ascetic," presents the advantages of being a Buddhist monk. Another is on the subject of caste, which Buddha repudiated. Still another is on a favorite topic, the nature of a true Brahmin. One is against animal sacrifice, one against self-mortification; one is on the Chain of Causation and the theories of the soul. This latter is of interest because of the peculiar belief of Buddhists concerning the soul. There exist today two beliefs, that of soul and no-soul, both based upon purported sayings of the Buddha. In discourse 20, a god, Sakka, visits Buddha and, asking him a series of ten questions, learns from the Buddha that everything that comes into being is destined to destruction. Discourse 30 discloses the thirty-two marks of a universal king or Buddha. Discourse 31 sets forth the duties of a layman. A few of these long discourses are attributed not to Buddha but to some of his disciples, for example, number 10 is a discourse on training given by Ananda to a pupil not long after the death of Buddha.

Of all the long discourses, Winternitz holds that the Paranib-bana-Sutta, number 16, is in every respect the most important. It is really not a speech or dialogue but a well connected account of the later period of the Buddha's life, his sayings and discourses, and finally his death. He regards it as one of the oldest parts of the whole Tripitaka and the nearest thing to a biographical treatment of the Buddha—and it is only the beginning of one—to be found in the whole Tripitaka. Even here there is a strange intermixture of the early and the later, as exhibited elsewhere in the *Digha,* for, in parts, Buddha is described in wholly human terms, while in the latter part reference is made to the authority of the suttas, miracles of the Buddha, the building of *stupas,* and of Buddha relics, all clear evidences of the long growth of the Buddha tradition.

The Majjhima deals with much the same matters as indicated above, only more briefly. But even some of these shorter ones run to as many as fourteen pages. Some of the topics dealt with here are life in a lonely forest; the things a monk may wish for; on how to meditate so as to get rid of evil doubts; on the danger of gain and honor; on the duties of an ascetic; on the classification of feelings; on falsehood; on qualities that make a person virtuous; on caste; on the theories of the soul; on the good and evil qualities of a monk; on meditation on emptiness; on the six senses; on the middle path. There are here also, as in the longer discourses, accounts of Buddha's former existences, one is of his one-time existence as Jotipala, another as a king, Makhadeva. Here also are a few discourses, attributed not to Buddha, but to some of his disciples. One of these, number 50, is the account of how Mara, the tempter, gets into the stomach of Mogallana who gets rid of him and reminds him that he himself was once a Mara and this Mara his nephew. Another is a dialogue on defilement between Mogallana and Sariputta, two of the most famous of Buddha's disciples. There is more of the legendary and mythological in the Majjhima, some quite interesting stories occurring as, for example, that of the conversion of a terrible bandit who thus attained Arhantship, i.e., who attained to Nirvana in this present existence (number 86). This is partly in verse. There is an intermixture here also of the early and the late as in the Digha. One example of the style of these discourses and also illustrative of the outlook of Buddhists—not to say the Buddha —upon the body and the vanity of caring for it, may be seen in the rather melancholy meditations in a charnel field.

Just as a competent butcher or his apprentice when he has killed a cow, might sit at the cross-roads with the carcase and cut up into joints (sic), even so does the Almsman reflect on this self-same body . . . from the point of view of its elements, as containing within it the four elements.

Again just as if the Almsman were actually looking on a festering corpse after one or two or three days exposure in a charnel-ground, even so does he sum up his self-same body as having these properties and this nature and this future before it . . . again just as if he were looking upon a corpse exposed in the charnel-ground showing as a chain of bones either still with flesh and blood and sinews to bind them together, or with . . . the flesh and blood gone . . . or the sinews gone, and only the bones left scattered around, here a leg, there an arm, . . . even so does he sum up this self-same body . . . and as he dwells thus unflagging and ardent, and purged of self, all worldly thoughts that idly come and go are abandoned, and with their abandonment his heart within grows stablished fast and planted fast, settled and concentrated—in this way an Almsman develops mindfulness of body.[9]

The third section, the Samyutta Nikaya, or Connected Sayings contains, all told, twenty-eight hundred and eighty-nine suttas, or sayings grouped roughly together, either because they treat of some similar topic, or were spoken by or refer to some particular individual or refer to some classes of divinities or demons. It is this grouping, however done, that gives it its name Samyutta Nikaya. There are fifty-six different groups divided into five Vaggas or sections. While there was some poetry found in the longer and shorter discourses, here poetry plays a prominent role as it does in most of the remaining subdivisions of the "Sayings basket." Particularly is this true in the first Vagga which is called the Sagathavagga or section with the song verses.

To mention the content of only a few of the groups: one contains sayings of various deities on a great variety of subjects; two of the most interesting tell stories of how Mara the tempter seeks to get either some monk or some nun to abandon the way of Buddha, and so to lose salvation—but never successfully. One of the stories is as follows, much abbreviated save in the verses: a nun, Kisa-Gotami, or Gotami, the slender, went one day into the dark forest to spend the day. Mara approaching her said:

[9] *Majjhima Nikaya,* translated by Lord Chalmers, CXIX, pp. 205–207, *passim.*

"How now? Dost sit alone with tearful face
  As mother stricken with the loss of child?
  Thou who hast plunged into the woods alone
  Is it a man that thou hast come to seek?"

Who is this who thus speaks to me, thought Gotami. Then it occurs to her, it is Mara the evil one, come to tempt me—so she addresses him thus:

"Past are the days when I was she whose child
  Was lost! Men to that past belong, for me!
  I do not grieve, I am not shedding tears.
  And as for thee, good sir, I fear thee not.
  Lost on all sides is love of worldly joys.
  The gloom of ignorance is rent in twain.
  Defeating all the myrmidons of death,
  Here do I bide (to rest) safe and immune."

Then Mara, knowing that Gotami had recognized him, vanished, unhappy and dejected.[10]

One section the Nidana, in ninety-two sayings, deals with the famous chain of causation, so important in Buddhist thought; another deals with methods of contemplation; still another with the strength and weakness of women and what forms they may take in the birth cycle; and the last group, LVI, deals with the all-important Noble Truths. Here once more is repeated the famous sermon at Benares, perhaps the most basic statement of primitive Buddhist thought.[11]

An interesting riddle, of which not a few are found scattered through these sayings, illustrates the monkish outlook on the common life:

"Hast thou no little hut? Hast thou no rest?
  Hast thou no line stretched out? Art free from ties?"
  "Nay, never hut is mine or any nest
  Nor line stretched out. Yea, I am free from ties."
  "What do I mean who speak to thee of 'hut'

[10] The translation of the poems is that of Mrs. Rhys Davids, *Kindred Sayings*, Vol. 1, pp. 162–163.
[11] Vol. 5, pp. 356–362.

And 'nest' and 'line stretched out,' and 'ties'?"
"*Mother* thou meanest when thou sayest 'hut'
And *wife* thou meanest where thou speakest of 'nest'
And *children* when thou sayest 'line stretched out'
And *men's desires* when thou dost speak of 'ties.' "
"O well is thee for whom no hut doth wait!
O well is thee who hast no nest at night!
Thou hast no line stretched out—O well is thee!
And happy thou from whom all ties art free!"[12]

The fourth of the Nikayas is the Anguttara, which is translated *Gradual Sayings*.[13] It contains a total of twenty three hundred and eight Sayings. The peculiarity of this book is its arrangement. Its eleven sections each treat of things of which there are as many as the number of the section. Thus in the Book of Ones:

"Monks, I know of no other single thing by which a man's heart is so enslaved as by a woman." Other "ones" are "any other single thing so intractable as the uncultivated mind," or "so tractable as the cultivated mind." And, of course, "there is one person whose birth is for the welfare of many folk, who is born out of compassion for the world, for the profit welfare and happiness of the *devas* and mankind, the Buddha, the fully enlightened one."

In the Book of Twos one finds that there are two faults, "What two?" "That which has its results in this very life, and that which has its results in some future life."[14]

There are two fools, "What two?" "He who sees not his fault as such, and he who does not pardon as he should the fault confessed by another."[15]

There are two wise ones. "What two?" "He who sees his faults as such, and he who pardons as he should."

"One can never repay two persons." "What two?" "Father and mother, of course."

[12] *Kindred Sayings*, translated by Mrs. Rhys Davids, I, p. 13.
[13] *The Book of Gradual Sayings*, translated by F. L. Woodward, 5 vols., Pali Text Society, Oxford University Press, London, 1932–1936.
[14] *Op. cit.*, p. 42.
[15] *Id.*, p. 54.

There are two companies, "the shallow, who are empty-headed busy-bodies of harsh speech, loose in talk, lacking concentration, unsteady, not composed, of flighty mind, with senses uncontrolled"; and the deep who are just the opposite.

Other twos are the discordant and the harmonious; the distinguished and the ignoble; the crooked and the straight; the righteous and the unrighteous. There are two pleasures, home and home-leaving (and the latter has precedence); carnal and non-carnal, or bodily and mental—the total list is a long one.

In the Book of the Threes, a fool is known by *three* characteristics, immorality in thought, speech and deed; and a wise man by morality in thought, speech and deed. Three persons are found existing in the world, the tricky-tongued, the fair-spoken and the honey-tongued. Other threes are: the blind, the one-eyed, and the two-eyed; the topsy-turvy brained, the scatter-brained, and the comprehensive brained. There are three kinds of pride, pride of youth, of health, of life; three attainments, faith, virtue, insight.

Each book becomes more complicated, as one would naturally expect, and perhaps it will be enough to cite further examples only from the Book of Fours:

There are four bases of sympathy, charity, kind speech, doing a good turn, and treating all alike.

> Charity, kind words and doing a good turn
> And treating all alike as each deserves
> These bonds of sympathy are in the world
> Just like the linch-pin of a moving car.
> Now if these bonds were lacking, mother who bore
> And father who begat would not receive
> The honor and respect (which are their due)
> But since the wise rightly regard these bonds
> They win to greatness and *are* worthy praise.[16]

There are four kinds of rain clouds:

> The thunderer-not-rainer, rainer-not-thunderer, the
> neither thunderer nor rainer, both thunderer and rainer.

[16] P. 36.

There are four kinds of mice (though just what importance this has for religious faith is not apparent):

> One that digs a hole but doesn't live in it.
> One that lives in a hole it has not dug.
> One that neither digs a hole nor lives in a hole.
> One that both digs a hole and lives in a hole.

There are four kinds of replies (as any teacher can well testify, for he knows them all):

> He who replies to the point not diffusely.
> He who replies diffusely not to the point.
> He who does both.
> He who does neither.[17]

Obviously the purpose here is memory—to make it easy to remember. It is an old teaching device.

One of the chief drawbacks to reading Buddhist sacred literature that has not been edited for the modern reader, is its repetitiousness which we saw to be a characteristic of Hindu literature also, particularly of the Brahmanas. Professor Oldenberg, speaking especially of the longer discourses, has this to say:

> The periods of these addresses, in their motionless and rigid uniformity, on which no lights and shadows fall, are an accurate picture of the world as it represented itself to the eye of that monastic fraternity, the grim world of origination and decease, which goes on like clockwork in an ever uniform course, and behind which rests the still deep of the Nirvana. In the words of this ministry, there is heard no sound of working within, . . . no impassioned entreating of men to come to the faith, no bitterness for the unbelieving who remain afar off. In these addresses, one word, one sentence, lies beside another in stony stillness, whether it expresses the most trivial thing or the most important. As worlds of gods and men are, for the Buddhist, consciousness, ruled by everlasting necessity, so also are the worlds of ideas and of verities: for these, too, there is one, and only one necessary form of knowledge and expression, and the thinker does not make this form but he adopts what is ready to hand . . . and thus those endless repetitions accumulate

[17] P. 38.

which Buddha's disciples were never tired of listening to anew, and always honouring afresh as the necessary garb of holy thought.[18]

Winternitz thinks that the repetitiousness "had the double purpose of impressing the speeches more deeply on the memory and of making them rhetorically more effective. As texts written down and intended for reading, they would probably have been quite as tedious to the Indians as they are to the Westerners. In the recitation the repetitions played a considerable part as parts of a purely musical construction and proved no more tiring to the ears of a Buddhist audience than the repetitions of the motifs in the musical compositions of Bach or Wagner."[19]

But along with the tiresome repetition we find the text now and then lightened up with bits of lively dialogue and a great use of figures of speech and similes, and parables. In this, Buddha was like Jesus. He knew and his disciples knew how to teach by the use of illustrations and stories. This will appear even more strikingly as we turn to the consideration of the fifth section of the Sutta-pitaka, the Khuddaka Nikaya or Division of Small Books.

This section of the canon is quite different in many ways from the four Nikayas already discussed. First of all, it is a sort of miscellany, gathering together the most varied kinds of material. Again, it is almost certainly later in its present form than the other Nikayas, though it contains very ancient sayings. It is not found in the canon of the schools which were translated into the Chinese language.[20] It contains much more in the nature of poetry, songs, proverbs, parables, and fables than the other divisions. The term Division of Small Books is really a misnomer, for some of the fifteen books which make up this section are quite lengthy. Not all the books of the division have as yet been translated into English. Because of limitations of space and the comparative unimportance of a number of them, attention can be given to only a few of the most important collections of the Khuddaka Nikaya.

[18] Coomaraswamy, *Buddha and Gospel of Buddha,* quoting Professor Oldenberg, p. 273.
[19] Vol. II, p. 68.
[20] Edward J. Thomas, *Life of Buddha as Legend and History,* p. 272.

The first Khuddaka-patha or "the reading of small passages," is used chiefly today by Ceylonese Buddhists in a ceremony for the warding off of evil spirits. The Vimana-vatthu or "stories of celestial mansions," contains some eighty-five poems recounting how various beings who have tasted birth in heaven attained this state. The *Peta-vatthu* is the story of ghosts or spirits who have been condemned to this state by their various misdeeds. It is largely modelled on the *Vimana-vatthu*. Another, the *Nidessa*, is a commentary on part of the more important book the Sutta-nipata. Still another, Patisambhida-Magga, "the way of analysis" deals with such concepts as knowledge, heresy, meditation, etc. It is in dialogue form like the Abhidhamma.

The *Apadana* recites in verse the story of the present and former lives of certain monks and nuns. The Buddhavamsa, or "history of the Buddhas" purports to give the story of Gautama's own decision to become a Buddha and a history of twenty-four previous Buddhas who had foretold his coming, and something of his own story. The last of the less important books is the *Cariya-pitaka,* which contains thirty-five stories from the Jataka told in verse and arranged topically to illustrate the ten perfections.

Perhaps best known to the Western world, and most frequently translated is the famous Dhammapada.[21] It is really a Buddhist anthology. If one could read no more than one book, this would give one the best impression of Buddhism, at least in its ethical aspect. It would not be the whole of Buddhism, by any means, of course, but it would give the high lights of that faith.

It consists of four hundred and twenty-three sayings, or verses purporting to come from the Buddha, arranged in a rather loosely conceived topical fashion. In its general make-up, it resembles the Biblical book of Proverbs more closely than anything else. Oldenberg has written concerning it:

[21] There are several English translations besides that of Max Muller quoted here. Two of these easily available are:

The Buddha's Way of Virtue, translated by W. D. C. Wagiswara and Kenneth J. Saunders, Wisdom of the East Series, John Murray, London, 1912.

Hymns of the Faith, translated by Albert J. Edmunds, Open Court Publishing Co., Chicago, 1902.

For the elucidation of Buddhism nothing better could happen than that, at the very outset of Buddhist studies, there should be presented to the student by an auspicious hand the Dhammapada, that most beautiful and richest collection of proverbs, to which anyone who is determined to know Buddhism must over and over again return. This proverbial wisdom gives a true picture of Buddhist thought and feeling, but expressed in terms of emotion and poetry which lend to the themes of transcience and to the formulae of the psychologist a tragic poignancy that is often lacking in the set dialogues.[22]

One can only sample a work such as this. Thus it begins:

1

All that we are is the result of what we have thought: it is founded on our thoughts, it is made up of our thoughts. If a man speaks or acts with an evil thought, pain follows him, as the wheel follows the foot of him who draws the carriage.

2

All that we are is the result of what we have thought: it is founded on our thoughts, it is made up of thoughts. If a man speaks or acts with a pure thought, happiness follows him, like a shadow that never leaves him.[23]

In the three short, pungent statements which follow is set forth a gospel familiar to those acquainted with the Sermon on the Mount.

3

"He abused me, he beat me, he defeated me, he robbed me,"—hatred in those who harbor such thoughts will never cease.

4

"He abused me, he beat me, he defeated me, he robbed me,"—hatred in those who do not harbor such thoughts will cease.

5

For hatred does not cease by hatred at any time; hatred ceases by love; this is an old rule.[24]

[22] Coomaraswamy, *Buddha and Gospel of Buddha*, p. 279.

[23] Max Muller, *Lectures on the Science of Religion;* with a paper on *Buddhist Nihilism,* and a translation of the Dhammapada or "Path of Virtue," p. 193. Also published in *Sacred Books of the East,* Vol. 10, Pt. 1. Oxford, 1881. Page references here are to the former.

[24] Max Muller, *op. cit.,* p. 194.

Note that Buddha says it is an old rule. But how difficult of acceptance, as the recurring wars, growing out of persistent hate in our present age, so thoroughly prove. When will mankind learn? Or were Buddha and Jesus wrong? Similar statements appear again and again.

223

Let a man overcome anger by love, let him overcome evil by good, let him overcome the greedy by liberality, the liar by truth!

224

Speak the truth, do not yield to anger; give, if thou art asked, from the little thou hast; by those steps thou wilt go near the gods.

234

The wise who control their body, who control their tongue, the wise who control their mind, are indeed well controlled.[25]

Good psychologist that Buddha was, he over and over again emphasized the importance of thought.

35

It is good to tame the mind, which is difficult to hold in and flighty, rushing wherever it listeth; a tamed mind brings happiness.

36

Let the wise man guard his thoughts, for they are difficult to perceive, very artful, and they rush wherever they list; thoughts well guarded bring happiness.

37

Those who bridle their mind which travels far, moves about alone, is without a body, and hides in the chamber (of the heart), will be free from the bonds of Mara (the tempter).[26]

Self-conquest, is the greatest conquest of all:

[25] *Id.*, pp. 256, 258.
[26] *Id.*, p. 203.

103

If one man conquer in battle a thousand times a thousand men, and if another conquer himself, he is the greatest conqueror.

111

And he who lives a hundred years, ignorant and unrestrained, a life of one day is better, if a man is wise and reflecting.[27]

Concerning the evil and the good he has much to say:

117

If a man commits a sin, let him not do it again; let him not delight in sin; pain is the outcome of evil.

118

If a man does what is good, let him do it again; let him delight in it; happiness is the outcome of good.

121

Let no man think lightly of evil, saying in his heart, it will not come near unto me. Even by the falling of waterdrops a water-pot is filled; the fool becomes full of evil, even if he gathers it little by little.

124

He who has no wound on his hand, may touch poison with his hand; poison does not affect one who has no wound; nor is there evil for one who does not commit evil.

127

Not in the sky, not in the midst of the sea, not if we enter into the clefts of the mountains, is there known a spot in the whole world where a man might be freed from an evil deed.[28]

By oneself the evil is done, by oneself one suffers; by oneself evil is left undone, by oneself one is purified. Purity and impurity belong to oneself, no one can purify another.[29]

[27] Max Muller, *op. cit.*, pp. 223, 225.
[28] *Ibid.*, pp. 227, 228, 229.
[29] Max Muller, *op. cit.*, pp. 238, 239.

The characteristic outlook of Buddhism on detachment and desirelessness appears again and again:

210

Let no man ever look for what is pleasant, or what is unpleasant. Not to see what is pleasant is pain, and it is pain to see what is unpleasant.

211

Let, therefore, no man love anything; loss of the beloved is evil. Those who love nothing, and hate nothing, have no fetters.

212

From pleasure comes grief, from pleasure comes fear; he who is free from pleasure knows neither grief nor fear.

213

From affection comes grief, from affection comes fear; he who is free from affection knows neither grief nor fear.[30]

The five universal commandments of Buddhism appear in these sayings:

246

He who destroys life, who speaks untruth, who takes in this world what is not given him, who takes another man's wife;

247

And the man who gives himself to drinking intoxicating liquors, he, even in this world, digs up his own root.[31]

He recurs in the following utterances to a familiar theme: What constitutes a real Brahmin? For him birth has no place in its determination, for:

393

A man does not become a Brahmana by his plaited hair, by his family, or by both; in whom there is truth and righteousness, he is blessed, he is a Brahmana.

[30] *Ibid.,* p. 253.
[31] *Ibid.,* p. 261.

394

What is the use of plaited hair, O fool! what of the raiment of goat-skins? Within thee there is ravening, but the outside thou makest clean.

400

He who is free from anger, dutiful, virtuous, without weakness, and subdued, who has received his last body, him I call indeed a Brahmana.[32]

Well over half of the verses in the Dhammapada are found in other books of the canon, and were probably culled from these books with a definite purpose, by the compiler. The sources of the rest, it is difficult to determine. All purport to come from Buddha himself, but Winternitz insists that some of the sayings are not really Buddhist at all. They were drawn from old Indian sources from which they also found their way into other non-Buddhist, Hindu and Jain writings. It does not seem at all impossible that Buddha himself might have drawn from this common ancient source without being conscious of it, and so the sayings, while not originally his, may actually have come through him. At all events it is a most valuable compendium of Buddhist ethical teaching— not unlike the Sermon on the Mount of Jesus.

The Dhammapada is unique among the "small books" in being only a collection of sayings, without the addition of narratives and commentary which are found in the others. The *Udana* or "pithy sayings" is a collection consisting of eight sections of ten sayings each. Each saying is preceded by a narrative out of which the saying more or less appropriately grows. A stereotyped phrase usually introduces the "pithy saying": "Now when the Lord had gained knowledge of this matter he uttered the following pithy saying." The sayings are of many kinds, dealing with typical Buddhist concepts, the bliss of Nirvana, detachment, meditation, etc. Some of the sayings do not seem to grow at all naturally out of the narrative, but seem forced. It is in one of the narratives that the famous parable of the elephant is found. Told in abbreviated form and without the repetitiousness of the original it is as follows:

[32] Max Muller, *op. cit.*, pp. 295, 296.

Some Brahmins and ascetics fell to quarreling over doctrinal matters, whether or not the world is eternal, whether body and soul are separate. Informed by the monks of this quarrel Buddha told them the parable: A king had a company of blind men brought together. Then he commanded that an elephant be shown them. So one was brought. One blind man felt his head, another the trunk, another the tusk, another a leg, still another the tail.

Then asked the king, "How does an elephant look?" Those who had touched the head said, "Like a pot," those who had touched the ear said, "Like a winnowing basket," those who had touched the tusk said: "Like a plowshare"; those who had touched the trunk said: "Like the pole of a plough"; those who had touched the tail said: "Like a broom." A tumult arose. An elephant is like this, he is like that, until at last they fell to fighting, to the great amusement of the king.

Even so, said the Buddha, is the case of the ascetics and the Brahmins, each of whom sees only a part of the truth, and who claims "This is true, not that; or that is true, not this."

This is a familiar parable used often by Hindus and Jains also. This does not mean that Buddha may not himself have used it, but the likelihood is that it was adopted by later Buddhist teachers, as they did so much other material, for their own purposes, particularly in the Jatakas, as will shortly appear.

The Iti-Vuttaka, or "Thus spake Buddha, saying," (since every paragraph begins with the formula, "This was said by the Lord,") is a collection of one hundred and twelve prose and poetry sayings attributed to the Buddha, most of them rather brief. Usually the prose is not, as in other collections, in the nature of a narrative or an introduction. In almost half the sayings the poetry simply repeats in metrical form what the prose has already stated. Sometimes the prose statement has a corresponding poetic form, with additional verses going beyond the prose idea. Sometimes prose and poetry alternate in full expression of an idea. Two brief examples will suffice to reveal the nature of this work.

1. This verily was said by the Blessed One, said by the Sanctified One, so I have heard.

"One of the Laws, O monks, ye do forsake. I am your surety, in that I have entered the path from which there is no return." "Which one of the Laws?" "Ye forsake, O monks, the law against Desire (lobha-). I am your surety in that I have entered the path from which there is no return."

To this effect spake the Blessed One, and hereupon said the following:

> "Through their proper knowledge
> Creatures of Discernment forsake that Desire
> Through which lustful creatures
> Go to misfortune.
> When they have forsaken it
> They never return to this world."

Exactly to that effect was it spoken by the Blessed One, so I have heard.[33]

17. This verily was said by the Blessed One, said by the Sanctified One, so I have heard.

"For a novitiate-monk who hath not yet attained supreme Security, but who is striving for it, and who liveth with the idea that what is external is a qualification, I see no other single qualification, O monks, so exceeding helpful as the quality of having goodness as a friend. A (novitiate) monk, then, O monks, who hath goodness as his friend, renounceth that which is evil, and obtaineth that which is good."

To this effect spake the Blessed One, and hereupon said the following:

> "The monk that hath goodness as friend,
> Who is obedient and respectful,
> Doing the behest of his friends,
> Mindful and thoughtful,
> May attain in due course
> The destruction of all the Fetters."

Exactly to that effect was it spoken by the Blessed One, so I have heard.[34]

[33] *Iti-Vuttaka,* translated by Justin Harley Moore, p. 21.
[34] *Ibid.,* pp. 30–31.

The Sutta-Nipata or "collection of suttas" is chiefly made up of poetry, much of it quite ancient, in five sections. The last was probably at one time an independent collection. It is quite a long poem divided into sixteen parts. Commentaries, on two of the five parts, form the Nidessa, one of the divisions of small books. Not a few of the sayings throughout can be found in modified form in other parts of the canon. Perhaps, next to the Dhammapada, the sayings from this book are found more frequently quoted than from any other of the canonical books. Its poetry is of higher rank than that of most other collections.

The sayings deal with many subjects of interest to Buddhists. The true Brahmin is described in sixty-three verses in one section, each verse ending with the refrain "Him do I call a true Brahmin." One of the poems contrasts the joy of the Buddha who is homeless, but free, with the comfort and prosperity of a rich owner of herds, to the advantage, of course, of the former.

Typical of the book is the following poem on true friendship:

1. He who transgresses and despises modesty, who says, "I am a friend," but does not undertake any work that can be done, know (about) him: "he is not my (friend)."

2. Whosoever uses pleasing words to friends without effect, him the wise know as one that (only) talks, but does not do anything.

3. He is not a friend who always eagerly suspects a breach and looks out for faults; but he with whom he dwells as a son at the breast (of his mother), he is indeed a friend that cannot be severed (from him) by others.

4. He who hopes for fruit, cultivates the energy that produces joy and the pleasure that brings praise, (while) carrying the human yoke.

5. Having tasted the sweetness of seclusion and tranquillity one becomes free from fear and free from sin, drinking in the sweetness of the Dhamma.[35]

Or this poem of advice against luke-warmness and slothfulness:

1. Rise, sit up, what is the use of your sleeping; to those who are sick, pierced by the arrow (of pain), and suffering, what sleep is there?

[35] *Sacred Books of the East*, Sutta-Nipata, translated by V. Fausboll (part II), pp. 42–43.

2. Rise, sit up, learn steadfastly for the sake of peace, let not the king of death, knowing you to be indolent (pamatta), befool you and lead you into his power.

3. Conquer this desire which gods and men stand wishing for and are dependent upon, let not the (right) moment pass by you; for those who have let the (right) moment pass, will grieve when they have been consigned to hell.

4. Indolence (pamada) is defilement, continued indolence is defilement; by earnestness (appamada) and knowledge let one pull out his arrow.[36]

One more illustration must suffice, a warning against sinful pleasures—a constant note in Buddhist teaching:

1. If he who desires sensual pleasure is successful, he certainly becomes glad-minded, having obtained what a mortal wishes for.

2. But if those sensual pleasures fail the person who desires and wishes (for them), he will suffer, pierced by the arrow (of pain).

3. He who avoids sensual pleasures as (he would avoid treading upon) the head of a snake with his foot, such a one, being thoughtful (sato), will conquer this desire.

4. He who covets extensively (such) pleasures (as these), fields, goods, or gold, cows and horses, servants, women, relations,

5. Sins will overpower him, dangers will crush him, and pain will follow him as water (pours into) a broken ship.

6. Therefore let one always be thoughtful, and avoid pleasures; having abandoned them, let him cross the stream, after bailing out the ship, and go to the other shore.[37]

Not only didactic material but some narrative is included among the sayings, sometimes in ballad form. One deals with happenings just after the birth of the Buddha, another with his renunciation of home and his princely birthright, and his experiences as a mendicant. Still another recounts the attempts of Mara to turn him back to his worldly life, and the abandonment of his search for enlightenment. The first and third of these have been thought to be

[36] *Ibid.,* p. 55.
[37] *Sacred Books of the East,* Sutta-Nipata—translation by Fausboll, Parts II, IV. Atthakavagga I. Kamasutta, p. 146.

parallels to gospel stories of Simeon in St. Luke 2:25 ff. and the temptation stories in the life of Jesus.

From the standpoint of sheer literary beauty and charm nothing in the canon equals the collection of poems known in translation as the Psalms of the Brethren and Psalms of the Sisters.[38] Of the former there are two hundred and sixty-four and of the latter seventy-three. These purport to be, and probably are, poems written by early Buddhist monks and nuns expressive of some deep personal experience or insight which came to them either as motivation to entrance into the order or some new attainment of spiritual excellence, including that final achievement of all, enlightenment, or Arhantship, which meant that at the close of their present mortal life span there would be no recurrence of birth. They were free from the wheel. This collection like the Vinaya-pitaka is definitely monastic in character and outlook. Here, however, it is not the rules and regulations, but the spirit found within those dedicated to the life apart from the world, the inner experiences which came to them, often seen in contrast to the life of the everyday world to which they once belonged. One catches here, as no rule book can possibly portray it, the inner heart of the "religious." Take for example the poem in which a monk sees in his wife and child approaching, a veritable snare of the tempter, Mara:

> In golden gear bedecked, a troop of maids
> Attending in her train, bearing the babe
> Upon her hip, my wife drew near to me.
> I marked her coming, mother of my child,
> In brave array, like snare of Mara laid.
> Thereat arose in me the deeper thought:
> Attention to the fact and to the cause.
> The misery of it all was manifest;
> Distaste, indifference, the mind possessed;
> And so my heart was set at liberty.
> O see the seemly order of the Norm!

[38] Translated by Mrs. C. A. F. Davids, *Psalms of the Early Buddhists*, Vol. 1, *Psalms of the Sisters*, Oxford University Press, London, 1909; Vol. 2, *Psalms of the Brethren*, 1913.

> The Threefold Wisdom have I made my own,
> And all the Buddha bids me do is done.[39]

These poems, were, many of them, quite early, no doubt. The collection was put in writing, says Mrs. Davids, about 30 B.C. As time passed legends grew up about the putative authors of the verses. In the sixth century A.D. Dhammapala wrote down the previously unwritten introduction to the poems, usually relating some story about the former lives of the author, the birth in the Buddha age, the family or class from which he came, and quite frequently the experience or experiences which led the person to leave the world for the cloister. Then follows the poem. How much of all this represents fact, and how much legend is not for our purposes of any importance. These introductions are fascinating reading, often more interesting than the poems themselves. Sometimes the poem is little more than a poetic rendering of the story already told in prose.

One of the most poignant of all the stories is that of Kisa-Gotami, Gotami the lean. Born in the Buddha era of poor parents, she was married, but badly treated until she bore a son, when she was treated with honor. When the child was old enough to run about it died. Fearful that she would again be mistreated, as having no son, she carried the dead child about upon her hip from house to house, crying, "Give me medicine for my baby." But the people, looking at her with contempt, said, "Medicine! Of what use?" One wise person, seeing that she was crazed with grief for her child, sent her to the Buddha to ask medicine. So she went to the Master and made her plea. He replied, seeing in her real promise, "My child, go, enter the town and at any house where yet no man hath died, thence bring me a little mustard seed."

So she went to a house asking for a little mustard seed, if in that house none had died. But death had entered there. She went to another. Death had preceded her; and to another, and another, but nowhere could she find a house death had not entered. By night her tortured mind felt relief, and she thought, this is the way everywhere.

"The Exalted one foresaw this out of his pity for my good." Thus comforted, she took her child to the charnel field, saying:

> "No village law is this, no city law
> No law for this clan or for that alone,
> For the whole world—ay, and the gods in heaven—
> This is the law: All is impermanent."

Then she returned to the Master. He said: "Have you brought me the mustard, Gotami?" She replied, "Wrought is the work, lord, of the little mustard. Give me thou confirmation." Whereupon the Master spoke a verse (not given here) and she was received into the order. Later she attained Arhantship and wrote her poem, ending thus:

> "Lo! I have gone
> Upon the Ariyan, on the Eightfold Path
> That goeth to the state ambrosial.
> Nibbana have I realized, and gazed
> Into the mirror of the holy Norm.
> I, even I, am healed of my hurt,
> Low is my burden laid, my task is done,
> My heart is wholly set at liberty."[40]

Typical of the motives that led women to enter the order is that expressed by Ubbiri in Ps. 33. Well born, according to Dhammapala's commentary, she gave birth to a lovely daughter. But soon the child died. Daily the mother went weeping to the cemetery. Once there she was accosted by the Master who revealed himself and asked her: "Why do you weep?" "I weep because of my daughter."

But replied the Buddha, "Burnt in this cemetery are some eighty-four thousand of thy daughters. For which of them dost thou weep?" Pointing to this grave and that he said,

---

[40] Mrs. Rhys Davids, *Psalms of the Early Buddhists,* Vol. 1, pp. 109–110. Edwin Arnold tells the story in verse in the fifth book of *Light of Asia,* Roberts Brothers, Boston, 1880, pp. 124–128.

"O Ubbiri, who wailest in the wood,
Crying, 'O Jiva! O my daughter dear!'
Come to thyself! Lo, in this burying-ground
Are burnt full many a thousand daughters dear,
And all of them were named like unto her.
Now which of all those Jivas dost thou mourn?"[41]

Pondering this, and being won by his teaching she fulfilled the requirements and attained Arhantship. Then she spoke the second half of the Psalm:

"O woman, well set free! how free am I,
How thoroughly free from kitchen drudgery!
Me stained and squalid 'mong my cooking-pots
My brutal husband ranked as even less
Than the sunshades he sits and weaves alway.

"Purged now of all my former lust and hate,
I dwell, musing at ease beneath the shade
Of spreading boughs—O, but 'tis well with me!"[42]

Another, Mutta, daughter of a poor Brahmin, was given in marriage to a hunchbacked Brahmin; but she told him that she could not continue in the life of the household and asked his consent to her leaving the world. He consented. She practiced self-control, and at last won Arhantship. Exulting, she cried:

"O free, indeed! O gloriously free
Am I in freedom from three crooked things:—
From quern, from mortar, from my crookback'd
    lord!
Ay, but I'm free from rebirth and from death,
And all that dragged me back is hurled away."[43]

These men and women came from many different backgrounds. The *Sangha* was a great leveller. Though the Indian world was now divided into rigid castes, Buddha would have none of it in his order, and continually rebuked the pretension to superiority on the

[41] Mrs. Rhys Davids, *Psalms of the Early Buddhists,* Vol. 1, p. 39.
[42] *Ibid.,* p. 25.
[43] *Ibid.,* p. 15.

grounds of birth rather than excellence of character. We have seen examples of such sayings in different sections of the canon. Among the Brethren the greater number were of Brahmin families, one hundred and thirteen, with sixty from the warrior ruler caste, the rest presumably from the other lower castes. We know that fifty were merchants and ten were laborers and seven were land tenants. The women came from royal families of great wealth, and from families of the poor—as Kisa-Gotami. At least one was daughter of a slave. Several had been prostitutes or were daughters of "fallen women." It was a motley company. But they all had something in common—they were seeking or had found the goal of all seeking, Arhantship, which meant the deeply coveted end of rebirth.

The arrangement of the poems in each collection is by length—first those of one stanza, then of two, etc., until in the *Psalms of the Sisters* the latter poems run to forty verses or more. Our quotations, naturally, are taken chiefly from the shorter ones, though some of the longer are beautiful and deeply revealing, not alone of the monastic life, but often also of the common life of the people of the day, from which the sisters have escaped. Some of them relate experiences of temptation that came to them after adopting the cloistered life. One records the temptation which came one day to one of the sisters, Subha, in a sacred grove:

Now one day a certain libertine of Rajagaha, in the prime of youth, was standing in the Jivaka Mango-grove, and saw her going to siesta; and feeling enamored, he barred her way, soliciting her to sensuous pleasures. She declared to him the bane of sensuous pleasures and her own choice of renunciation, teaching him the Norm. Even then he was not cured, but persisted. The Theri, not stopping short at her own words, and seeing his passion for the beauty of her eyes, extracted one of them, and handed it to him saying: "Come, then! here is the offending eye of her!" Thereat the man was horrified and appalled and, his lust all gone, asked her forgiveness. The Theri went to the Master's presence, and there, at sight of Him, her eye became as it was before. Thereat she stood vibrating with unceasing joy at the Buddha. The Master, knowing the state of her mind, taught her, and showed her exercise for reaching the highest. Repressing her joy, she developed insight, and attained Arhantship, together with thorough grasp of the Norm in form and meaning. Thereafter, abiding in the bliss and fruition of Nibbana, she, reflecting on what she had won, uttered her dialogue with the libertine in these verses: [44]

There follows then a lengthy poem too long to quote simply describing in beautiful poetic language what has here been narrated. The eye episode is couched thus:

> What is this eye but a little ball lodged in the
> fork of a hollow tree,
> Bubble of film anointed with tear brine, exuding
> shine drops,
> Compact wrought in the shape of an eye of manifold
> aspects?
> Forthwith the maiden so lovely tore out her eye and
> gave to him.

Quite the longest of the collection is the story of Sumedha, daughter of a king, whose parents desired her to marry a prince. But she had already had contact with the Bhikkhunis and had resolved to leave the world. When her parents came to give her away, she refused, crying: "Or let me leave the world or let me die." Then she burst into a tirade of denunciation of the body which was so typical of the Buddhist monastic outlook that it is given here in part:

> "What is it worth—this body foul, unclean,
> Emitting odours, source of fears, a bag
> Of skin with carrion filled, oozing impure
> The while? What is it worth to me who know—
> Repulsive carcass, plastered o'er with flesh
> And blood, the haunt of worms, dinner of birds—
> To whom shall such a thing as this be given?
> Borne in a little while to charnel-field,
> There is this body thrown, when mind hath sped,
> Like useless log, from which e'en kinsfolk turn.
> Throwing the thing that they have bathed to be

---

[44] Mrs. Rhys Davids, *Psalms of the Early Buddhists*, Vol. 1, pp. 148–149.

The food of alien things, whereat recoil
The very parents, let alone their kin.
They have a fondness for this soulless frame,
That's knit of bones and sinews, body foul,
Filled full of exudations manifold.
Were one the body to dissect, and turn
The inside outermost, the smell would prove
Too much for e'en one's mother to endure,
The factors of my being, organs, elements,
All are a transient compound, rooted deep
In birth, are ill, and first and last the thing
I would not. Whom, then, could I choose to wed?"[45]

Though in the order some measure of peace and calm was found, by no means all ever claimed to have attained Arhantship. Long was it sought—and in vain for most. But when found, what joy, what peace! Sama, who, according to the introduction, was once born as a fairy, was born in the Buddha age in a clansman's family, and became a friend of a famous teacher, Samavati. Grieved at the death of Samavati, she entered the order, but for long could not obtain self-mastery.

At last it came and she sang her song:

"Full five-and-twenty years since I came forth!
But in my troubled heart in no way yet
Could I discern the calm of victory.
The peace of mind, the governance of thoughts
Long sought, I found not; and with anguish thrilled
I dwelt in memory on the Conqueror's word.
To free my path from all that breedeth ill
I strove with passionate ardour, and I won!
Craving is dead, and the Lord's will is done.
Today is now the seventh day since first
Was withered up within that ancient Thirst."[46]

It is a temptation to multiply examples of these poems. The reader who wishes to read more will have to seek out sources in

[45] Mrs. Rhys Davids, *Psalms of the Early Buddhists,* Vol. 1, pp. 168–169.
[46] *Ibid.,* Vol. 1, pp. 34–35.

which they may be found. Unfortunately, in the anthologies only the verses are usually given, which robs the reader of half the joy of reading the poems, for they take on greater meaning as the background out of which they arose is known. Available sources are listed at the end of the section.

Quite the most readable and entertaining, and therefore, perhaps, the most popular of the Buddhist scriptures are the Jataka Tales, for this is the great Buddhist story-book, and who does not like stories? For Western readers, it requires a deal of editing, the elimination of the repetitious element, and some clarification of proper names and of some peculiarly oriental customs and ideas, but when this is done it is among the great story books of the world. It deserves to be better known in the West than it is.

Buddha was himself a master story-teller, as most great teachers are. His disciples, recognizing this, undertook to use this method for the propagation of their faith. Buddha had given utterance to many wise observations, on all sorts of subjects, practical, moral, spiritual, or if he did not say all that is reported of him, and in the form in which they are now given, they were in his spirit, and the problem was how to get a hearing for them. What better way than to put them into a story? That is essentially what the Jataka Tales do. There is a central core in each story, purportedly, directly from the lips of the master. Indeed, that is all that is really canonical. But, for all practical purposes, all the story material and commentary which have since been added by nameless teachers and commentators have become a very influential body of sacred material widely used in the training of Buddhist children as well as of older folk. Many of the stories are familiar to all India, whether Hindu, Buddhist, or any other faith, but here they have been adapted to Buddhist purposes.

Each Jataka or tale contains four elements. First there is the time setting, something like the "Once upon a time" with which so many of our own stories begin. A favorite and oft-repeated beginning is, "When Brahmadatta was reigning in Benares, the Bodhisatta was born as—" Then the story is told, leading in the end to the moral which is usually in verse, this is the original canonical feature. Finally comes the identification of the character through which the verse teaching is given, the Buddha, of course. The story itself is usually that of something that occurred in some one of the unnumbered births of the Buddha before he was born as Gautama, the historic Buddha. Sometimes the story is short, sometimes it is quite long. Sometimes it is very simple; sometimes it is highly complicated. Sometimes it is very picturesque and interesting. Sometimes it is inordinately dull, for there are good stories and stories not so good, here as in most collections. All told, there are over five hundred Jatakas. Cowell in his six-volume translation gives five hundred and fifty. Thomas says there are five hundred and forty-seven. That many of the Jatakas are quite ancient is evidenced by the fact that archaeological remains, dating well back into the third century, picture some of the tales—even some of the prose portions, though this is generally regarded as later than the *gathas* or verses.

Since the idea of rebirth was generally accepted by Buddhists as well as by all other people in India, and since birth was not limited to the human level, it was possible to have Buddha born to fit any ancient tale of India, whether of beast or people—and this was actually done. India had a vast folklore. There are at least three great collections which, overlapping and duplicating each other greatly, furnish a vast reservoir of story from which the Buddhists were able to draw for the Jatakas. In Hinduism these have played an important role in the teaching of the virtues and vices, and in inculcating the accepted moral ideals in the children of successive generations. But in Hinduism they never became scripture. It is recommended that the reader look into these ancient Hindu story-books, the Panchatantra, the Book of Good Counsels —or Hitopadesa and the Ocean of Story. Here he will find many a story familiar to himself. For not a few of them probably go back to an ancient Aryan or Indo-European source which underlies Western as well as Indian and Persian culture. Only in Buddhism did they actually attain to the status of scripture, but in all lands they have been an important factor in the moral instruction of the young.

Many of the stories are nothing but old beast fables adapted to

Buddhist purposes simply by having the Buddha in a former birth take the form of one of the beasts of the fable. Such a story is that of the wolf that fasted. (It is told in western style rather than in literal translation.)

On one occasion while making a tour of inspection in a monastery Buddha discovered ragged beggar garments which some of the monks had discarded after but a short period of the practice of poverty, for more comfortable and respectable clothing.

"Ah," said the Master, "the practice undertaken by the brethren has not long endured, like the wolf's sabbath fast." Then he told the following story.

A wolf once lived on the banks of the sacred river Ganges. A flood came while he slept one day and left him on a rock without food, or any means of securing it. As the water continued rising the wolf said to himself, "Here I am caught with nothing to eat and nothing to do. I might as well keep a sabbath fast." So he solemnly resolved to perform his religious duties.

But the king of the gods, perceiving the weakness of his resolve, said to himself, "I'll test his resolution," so, taking the form of a mountain goat, he came and stood near so the wolf could see him.

"Ah," thought the wolf, "I'll keep this fast another day," and forthwith leaped to catch the goat. But the goat was too quick for him and jumped about so that the wolf was unable to come near him. Seeing that it was impossible to catch the goat, he came at length to a halt, then lay down again as before saying to himself, "Well, after all, I have not broken the fast." But the king of the gods, quickly changing his form again, floated above him in the air, rebuked him for his insincerity in failing to keep his resolution, and returned to the abode of the gods.[47]

Another beast fable is found in the story Penny Wise—Pound Foolish which, freely told, runs as follows:

A king of a great country was informed of an uprising in a distant section of his kingdom. Although it was in the midst of the rainy season, an army was mobilized and made ready to hasten and put down the revolt.

[47] *Jataka Tales*, Vol. 2, pp. 307–308.

The future Buddha came and stood in the presence of the king. Just at that time the people had cooked some peas for the horses and had poured them into a trough. A hungry monkey, watching from a nearby tree, hurried down, filled his fist with peas and climbed back up and, sitting on a limb, began to eat. As he was eating one pea fell from his hand to the ground. Letting go all the others, down he scrambled from the tree to hunt the lost pea but, unable to find it, he climbed back up again and sat disconsolately on his limb, looking like one who had lost a fortune.

The king saw what the monkey did. Turning to the future Buddha he said, "What do you make of that?" The Buddha replied, "O King, that is what fools are always doing. They spend a pound to win a penny."

Thereupon the king gave up his expedition, fearing to lose his own kingdom. Meanwhile those making the trouble, hearing that the king was coming, fled quickly out of the country.[48]

With what do the stories deal? An analysis of the first two volumes of Cowell's translation reveals in part the following: ten tales against greediness; nine deal with friendship; five are on the wickedness of women; four on unthankfulness; three against the use of sacrifice; three on the folly of ignorance; three on the follies of passion; three against self-will; two on the use of riches; two on doing harm to others; two against the use of trickery. Other single Jatakas deal with immodesty, head-strongness, corruption of manners, cheating, envy, on accepting the advice of others, etc. etc.

Illustrating the folly of ignorance was the story of the monkeys, left to water new plants, who pulled the plants up to see how much water to give them. On envy, an ox who is dissatisfied with his food envies a pig; on greediness a greedy bird eating on a road is crushed by a vehicle, and they did not have cars in those days either.

The arrangement of the Jatakas within the twenty-two sections of which it is made up is the familiar one according to the number of verses or *gathas* in the story. For example section one has one hundred and fifty stories with but one verse, section two one hundred stories of two verses—the number of stories in each suc-

[48] *Jataka Tales*, Vol. 2, pp. 51–52.

ceeding decreasing as the number of gathas increases, until later sections contain not more than two stories.

In the collection there is found included a great variety of literary forms, prose narratives, fables, fairy tales, much poetry of various sorts, a good deal of ballad form, reported sayings on many subjects, and fragments of epics. Some of the longer stories are really novels of a sort, or long romances, with little or nothing Buddhistic about them except that the Bodhisatta is the hero. There are many pious legends not only of Buddhist origin but many from the great general body of Indian ascetic lore. Winternitz, indeed, says, "We can scarcely be mistaken in saying that far more than one half of all the Jatakas, if we omit the commentary, is not of Buddhist origin."[49] He explains it by the fact that the monks were recruited from all classes of people and that they were acquainted with a wide range of story material, folklore, legend, etc., which they sought when converted to Buddhism to make use of for Buddhist purposes. This constitutes a work of great value, therefore, not only to an understanding of Buddhism, but to the study of the history of Indian literature.

Because of space limitation more extended examples of the Jatakas cannot be given here. Below are suggested easily available sources in which further reading can be done.[50]

The remaining *Pitaka* or basket, the Abhidhamma-pitaka, adds little that is new to the canon, and contains little of general reader interest. The term itself means "higher religion" or "the higher subtleties of religion."[51] The chief difference between it and the Sutta-pitaka is not one of the substance, but method of treatment. Even in the *Digha* and *Majjhima* the Western reader is impressed by the dry, the long drawn-out repetitious discussions. Here it is

[49] II, p. 125.
[50] E. B. Cowell, Editor, *The Jataka*. 6 Volumes, Cambridge, 1885–1913. H. T. Francis and Ed. J. Thomas, Editors, *The Jataka Tales*, Cambridge, 1916. Davids, T. W. Rhys, Editor, *Buddhist Birth Stories*, George H. Routledge and Sons, London, 1925. Mrs. C. A. F. Davids, *Stories of the Buddha*, Frederick A. Stokes, N. Y., 1929. *Twenty Jataka Tales*, retold by Noor Inayat, David McKay, Philadelphia, 1939. Margaret Aspinwall, *Jataka Tales Out of Old India*, G. P. Putnam's Sons, N. Y., 1927.
[51] Winternitz II, p. 167.

even drier, more repetitious, more scholastic. The peculiarity of the Abhidhamma in general is the question-answer or catechetical method of treating its subject matter. Much attention is given to detailed definitions, and there is endless classification, often to the point of weariness.

It is divided into seven sections of which only the barest suggestions of general content may be here given. Mrs. Rhys Davids translates section one as *A Buddhist Manual of Psychological Ethics.*[52]

It is a sort of text for the use of monks who already have an intimate knowledge of the Dhamma, rather than being an exposition of Ethics itself.[53]

Book II merely continues the first book; Book III is a "discourse on the elements" in fourteen brief chapters. The fourth book, called a description of individuals, is closer in form and content to the Suttas than any other sections of the Abhidhamma, though, in general, most of the life has been squeezed out of it. An example will suffice:

What sort of a person is shameless? What then is shamelessness? That which is the not being ashamed where one should be ashamed, the not being ashamed of acquiring sinful and immoral qualities, that is said to be shamelessness. A person who is possessed of this shamelessness is said to be a shameless person.[54]

The fifth book, which purports to have been written by Tissa Mogalliputa, president of the Third Council, in connection with the meeting of that Council is called the Kathavatthu, or Subjects of Discourse, and is the most important portion of the whole for the history of Buddhism. If, indeed, parts of it were actually written at the time of said Council, other parts certainly were not, for they bear on their face evidence of later composition. In general it consists of the statement of the greatest varieties of false views

[52] London, 1900.
[53] So Winternitz II, 167.
[54] *Designation of Human Types,* translated by B. C. Law, Pali Text Society, London, 1923, p. 30.

which, in question and answer form, are duly refuted. Mrs. Davids translates it under the title *Points of Controversy*.[55]

Is there an intermediate state of existence (VIII, 2)? Are death and decay a result of Karma (VII, 7)? Is virtue automatic (X, 7, 8)? How do Buddhas differ mutually (XX, 1, 5)? Was everything about the Buddha fragrant (XVIII, 4), even the excreta, as certain sectarians out of affection for the Buddha, affirm? Did the Buddha feel pity? Is spiritual emancipation a gradual process of liberation (III, 4)? etc. Material for supporting or refuting ideas advanced is taken from the Sutta-pitaka and the Vinaya-pitaka, evidence of the relatively later appearances of at least this portion of the 3rd *pitaka*. The sixth book is a very obscure one, "The Book of Double Questions," and the seventh, "The Book of Causal Relationships," deals with the twenty-four kinds of relationships which are supposed to exist between the body and mind, or the corporeal and psychical.

Generally regarded as the latest of the three *pitakas* it is impossible to say just how early it appeared. If credence is given to the claim that the Katthavattu or fifth book was actually written in connection with the Third Council, then the scholastic development of Buddhism must go well back into early Buddhist times, because this book makes reference to at least two other parts of the *pitaka*. That a great deal of it is quite late is generally believed by Buddhist scholars. It is not universally accepted by all Buddhist sects as canonical. Those who do so hold it, esteem it highly. But for Western general readers it will hold less of interest than any other portion of the canon.

This brings us to the end of the discussion of the Pali canon. But this is only one of several, if it is, indeed, the one most sharply drawn of all. There is a vast literature which is acknowledged as sacred by other sects of Buddhism.

The Pali canon represents best southern Buddhism or Hinayana. But there is another school, the Mahayana, found chiefly in Tibet, China, and Japan which cherishes other works as basic to their form of faith. We can here mention, and that but briefly, only a few of such works.

[55] Pali Text Society, Humphrey Milford, London, 1915.

For those not familiar with the distinction between the two great schools of Buddhism, a very brief characterization of the difference in outlook will be helpful to an appreciation of the literature of the Mahayana to which we now turn. Hinayana may be said to be fairly close to the original teaching of Buddha, as represented in the Pali canon which we have just surveyed. In general it is a system whereby the individual, by his own unaided efforts and following the middle path taught by the Buddha in his first Sermon at Benares and expressed variously in other discourses, attains to Nirvana or the end of the rebirth cycle in which man finds himself. This involves leading the common life and becoming a monk. There is little or no chance of becoming an Arhant, that is one who has attained enlightenment, and at the end of his present life will enter Nirvana, without first becoming a monk. A layman benefits from Buddhist teaching, of course, and in another life he may hope to become a monk, if not in this, and so attain birthlessness; but the scheme narrows greatly the opportunity to attain salvation. This is one of the reasons given for calling this teaching the Hinayana, or the little vehicle, since only a few find their way to Nirvana thereby.

The Mahayana, on the other hand, particularly in the great popular sects, opens the doors of salvation to everyman, and without the long exacting discipline required by the Hinayana, because in Mahayana, man is not left without helpers. The ideal shifts from that of attaining Nirvana to that of achieving Buddhahood. Any man may aspire to this, and become a Bodhisattva, i.e., one who is on the way to becoming a Buddha. Millions of Bodhisattvas there are, many of whom are cosmic helpers who lend their aid to the humble men and women who call upon them for help, who do good works, or who worship the Buddhas.

This seems a far cry from non-theistic primitive Buddhism, but there is a natural line of development from Buddha's original teaching and the regard had for him by his followers, to the extravagant multiplication of Buddhas and Bodhisattvas which are found in fully developed Mahayana. A chief influence was the old polytheistic medium of Hinduism in which Buddhism arose, against which it reacted so vigorously, but to which it was gradually reassimilated with the passing of the centuries, until it practically disappeared from India, probably because there was no longer anything very distinctive about it. Clearly, the Bodhisattvas and the unnumbered Buddhas, and the dependence for salvation upon Buddhas or Bodhisattvas—toward whom the characteristic *Bhakti* or love, or service or faith is directed in the popular sects—all find their roots in the contemporary Hinduism of the years when Mahayana was developing. This phase of Buddhism found its continuing life not in India itself but in Tibet, China, Korea, and Japan. Indeed, it is only because many of their scriptures were translated into the Tibetan or the Chinese that they were preserved, for the Sanskrit originals or even copies are no longer extant. Most of the Mahayana texts were written either in Sanskrit or Mixed Sanskrit.

There was probably at one time a Sanskrit canon. Some remnants seem to point in that direction, but there is today no specific Mahayana canon. Different sects usually make primary use of some particular book or books. The Tripitaka is known in China, though it is substantially different from that of the Pali. There are some books still extant which represent a stage in the development toward the Mahayana which are yet of Hinayana, though not a part of the Pali canon, for this was but the canon of a particular Hinayana sect. There were other sectarian canons which, while substantially like the Pali or Theravadin canon, nevertheless admitted other books and excluded some of the Pali canonical books.

Most interesting of such books and of no slight importance was the Mahavastu, because it is the source of many wonder stories in connection with the life of Buddha, not found elsewhere. It differs from the canonical Pali books chiefly in a greater extravagance in this respect—a tendency very marked in the Mahayana. It was a part of the Vinaya-pitaka according to one of the Buddhist sects (the Lakottaravadins—subsect of the Mahasanghikas, one of the early schismatic groups). The peculiarity of this sect was their doctrine of the Buddhas, already plural, which exalted them above the world. The Mahavastu, which is essentially a biography of Buddha, is written definitely in this strain, which is Mahayanist in tendency.

It begins Buddha's life story with some of his existences in the time of other former Buddhas. He is then born into the Tusita heaven of the gods and there determines to be reborn as a human to Queen Maya. Then follows the story of his miraculous conception and birth, his life as prince, his renunciation, the conflicts with Mara the tempter, and his enlightenment. The tale is replete with miracles and wonder stories. The latter part of the book tells the story of the early conversions and the founding of the order.

It is not a very systematic treatment. Repetition of stories is frequent. There are a great many Jataka tales included, sometimes duplicated, a number of them *not* found in the Pali canon; and there is an intermixture of prose and poetry. But it is important in that it preserves some very ancient material concerning the Buddha, though dating in its present form from the fourth century A.D. or later.[56]

An outright Mahayana biography of the Buddha is the *Lalita-Vistara*, though based, thinks Winternitz, on a Hinayana original of the Saravastivada school, but expanded and modified in accord with the Mahayana spirit.[57] The very title reveals an outlook foreign to Hinayana. *Lalita* means "sport." The whole earthly life of the Buddha is thus told as the "sport" of a highly exalted divine being.

In the prologue, in contrast to the setting so frequently given for the utterance of some of the Suttas in the Pali canon, where the Buddha is represented as surrounded by a few disciples, he is here surrounded by twelve thousand monks and some thirty-two thousand Bodhisattvas. While sitting in meditation, a powerful ray of light bursts from his head, penetrates the heavens and arouses the gods, who immediately burst into songs of praise in his honor. Isvara and others appear and beseech him for the blessing and salvation of the world to reveal the Lalita-Vistara which they praise in most extravagant terms. Buddha consents, by remaining silent—and the real story begins. Here again the utmost extravagance is employed in detailing the scene. He decides after much consultation to be born to the wonderful Queen Maya, who is the most beautiful and most pure and virtuous of all women. In her is the strength of ten

[56] So Winternitz, II, p. 247.
[57] II, p. 252.

thousand elephants. The conception takes place with the aid of the gods, and he enters her womb in the shape of an elephant. A jewelled palace is created in her womb for his dwelling, whence he radiates beauty and light for miles around. The sick are healed when she lays hands upon them, and the Buddha, yet unborn, preaches piously from her womb.

The birth in the Lumbini gardens is accompanied by many marvelous miracles and signs, and he is born, not as a mortal of ordinary sort, but as a mighty spirit, omniscient and exalted. This is the Mahayana touch. This story is fittingly enough followed by a dialogue between Ananda, a disciple, and the Buddha, in which the belief in the miraculous birth is taught as necessary. Oddly enough the rest of the Buddha story is very much like that related in the Pali canon, and in some parts seems to be even older than the corresponding sections of the Pali. There are some episodes not found in the Hinayana story. In one, when the Buddha as a boy is taken to the temple, all the images of the gods fall down at his feet. In another his first day at school is described. It makes interesting reading. He is accompanied, not by a mother, who is half in tears at the thought that her little boy is growing up and a separation between them is imminent, but by ten thousand boys, and all the gods, and eight thousand divine maidens strewing his path with flowers. It really impressed the teacher. Indeed, he fell to the ground before the glow of the Bodhisattva. Of course the Buddha was omniscient and had no need to learn anything. When the teacher undertook to teach him the alphabet, the young Bodhisattva uttered a wise saying beginning with each letter. When the same material found in the Pali narrative is included, it is distinguished chiefly by exaggeration and accentuation of the wonder element. The book closes with a glorification of the book itself, and the advantages to be gained by honoring and propagating it.

The delightfully written book by F. Herold, *The Buddha*,[58] follows essentially the text of the Lalita-Vistara.

When it was finally put in its present form, it is impossible to say. It contains some very old material and other that is late. Sub-

[58] Albert and Charles Boni, New York, 1927.

stantial parts of it were certainly in existence in the second century of the Christian era.[59]

The Buddha-Carita of Asvaghosa is the great Buddhist epic, "an actual epic created by a real poet, who, filled with intense love and reverence for the exalted figure of the Buddha, and deeply imbued with the truth of the Buddha doctrine, was able to present the life and doctrine of the Master in noble and artistic, but not artificial language."[60] It was written in Sanskrit and translated into Chinese and the Tibetan. The available English translation was made from the Chinese.[61] It was upon this work that Edwin Arnold based his famous *Light of Asia*.[62] Two of the Mahayana-Sutras which have great popular appeal in China and Japan are the Saddharma-Pundarika, or Lotus Gospel and the Sukhavati-Vyuha.

The Lotus Gospel is perhaps the most important of all the Mahayana Sutras. It is the favorite scripture of a number of Mahayana sects, and is the best introduction to the Mahayana for the general reader. There is not much in it that sounds like the Buddhism of the Pali canon.

There is little of the historic Buddha, Gautama, in it. Here he is the god above all gods, eternally existent. He calls himself "the father of the world, the self-existent, the physician and protector of all creatures."[63] His entrance into Nirvana, i.e., his ceasing to exist, is not real, but pretended because he knows how perverse and deluded men are. It is only out of pity for them that he pretends to have entered Nirvana. He returns thence again and again to preach. And when he does preach it is not simply to a small group of followers, but to untold numbers of monks and nuns as well as Buddhas, Bodhisattvas and gods. When he goes abroad he is accompanied by a retinue of incalculable numbers of Buddhas and Bodhisattvas and gods, as numerous as the sands of the Ganges River. Numbers mean

[59] So Winternitz, II, p. 225.
[60] Winternitz, II, p. 260.
[61] Samuel Beal, *The Buddha-Carita*.
[62] H. H. Gowen, *A History of Indian Literature*, D. Appleton, N. Y., 1931, p. 328.
[63] Gatha 21, Section 15.

nothing in this book, for example, the religion of one Buddha has lasted hundreds of thousands of myriads of tens of millions of ages of the world, as many as these are specks of dust in four continents, a very long time. The book praises itself extravagantly again and again. It is "like a tank for the thirsty, like a fire for those who suffer from cold, like a garment for the naked...like a mother for her children...like a torch for dispelling of darkness."

The rewards of those who hear it are great. A woman who hears it has lived as a female for the last time! One of the notable passages is the parable of the prodigal son, so-called. Its difference from that of the gospel of Luke is more noteworthy than its similarity. The prodigal is the only son of a rich man who wanders for fifty years through strange lands becoming steadily poorer as his father's wealth increases. At last, a beggar, he returns home where his father, yearning for his return, awaits. But the son does not recognize the father in the rich and powerful figure he has become, and in fear runs away. The father sends his servants to bring the son into the house, but he falls into a faint from fear—and his father commands that he be released. He goes away to the poor district of the town. The father has him hired to perform humble tasks about the house, sometimes talks with him, and finally, after twenty years, and only at the hour of death, does he reveal himself as the man's father, and make him his heir. Of course Buddha is the rich man, and the world of human beings is represented in the son. These the Buddha draws to himself and makes his heirs.[64]

One entire chapter, 24, glorifies the Bodhisattva Avalokitesvara, or the Lord of Mercy, as a savior. Whosoever calls upon him is saved, fetters are loosened; he rescues the shipwrecked; protects from highwaymen; gives progeny to women who pray to him. This, as indeed the attitude toward the Buddha throughout the Sutra, is that of Bhakti-loving faith or devotion, much as is found in the Gita,

[64] *Sacred Books of the East,* Vol. 21, Chapter IV, pp. 98 ff. Translated by H. Kern, Oxford, 1894. A much more readable translation is that of W. E. Soothill, *The Lotus of the Wonderful Law,* Clarendon Press, Oxford, 1930. It eliminates much of the repetitious material and includes numerous excerpts from the verse version.

for Krishna, and in the Bhakti cult generally. This is Buddhism as *Bhakti*. The book is relatively late, having been written after the rise of the Mahayana. It was translated into the Chinese in 223 A.D.

It is in the other remaining Sutra, the Sukhavati-Vyuha,[65] that the most popular of the Savior Buddhas appears, honored and worshipped in all the "Pure land," or "Paradise" sects of Buddhism. He is Amitabha, known as Omito-fu in China and Amida in Japan. He was once a monk who entered upon the way of a Bodhisattva. When he had, after long discipline and many lives, arrived at the point of actually taking the last step into Buddhahood—there are ten stages one must pass through—he made a vow that he would not enter upon that final blissful state until he was assured that all who called upon his name would be saved. Salvation is to his paradise, called, usually, the Western Paradise, or the Pure Land, and the Sutra describes this in the most extravagant terms. This is not the sensationless peace of utter quietude, but here there is a beauty and richness, symbolized by jewel trees, singing waters, brilliant color, wonderful lotus blossoms, no day and night, no distinction between gods and men, it is an ideal existence figured forth in material fashion. Amitabha is continually praised. Here is perfect beauty, happiness, calm, wisdom and sinlessness. To this Pure Land come those who in loving trust pray reverently to be reborn into Amitabha's heaven. In some sects, so powerful is the name—now grown magical —thought to be, that he who only once pronounces it is reborn in the Western Paradise. This seems strangely different from the stern, ethically conditioned price which the original Buddha held up before men as a prerequisite to salvation. This Sutra was translated into the Chinese before the end of the second century A.D. Just when it originated is not certainly known. It appears in a longer and a shorter form.

Probably more Buddhists of China and Japan cherish these latter two Sutras than any other. They are the most popular scriptures of the most popular forms of Buddhism in those countries today. One

[65] *Sacred Books of the East*, Vol. 49, translated by F. Max Muller, Oxford, 1894.

writer has compared the Lotus Gospel to the Bhagavad Gita in Hinduism, and the gospel of St. John in Christianity. They do breathe something of the same spirit.[66]

But not all of Mahayana Buddhism is of this popular type. Some sects are deeply mystical, others profoundly philosophical, and these too have their special Sutras. Space does not permit any adequate characterization of such books as the Lankavatara, the Surangama or a dozen other Sutras, yet they record some of the profoundest and most fully developed insights to be found in any scriptures. In the aggregate there are more than one hundred such Sutras. Such a work as the so-called Diamond Sutra, is almost a household classic in China and Japan, despite the fact that it is a more or less repetitious exposition of the abstruse philosophical doctrine of the Void.[67] One who has followed through this brief sketch of Buddhist sacred literature will surely have been impressed by its extent, the varied nature of its content, the high ethical character of much of it, and the extreme development that has occurred in it to carry it from the sublime and relatively austere self-salvation system that is represented in the Pali canon, to the extravagant, popular devotional faith, dependent upon the aid of the Buddha, that appears in its later Mahayana popular forms.

Buddhism is by no means a dead religion. Westerners will perforce have more contacts with it as our world gets smaller and smaller, and it is altogether likely that it will exercise no small influence upon our Western ways of thought and life in the years that lie ahead.

[66] Kenneth J. Saunders, *The Gospel for Asia,* Macmillan, N. Y., 1928.

[67] A brief characterization of a number of the more important Mahayana Sutras is given by Sir Charles Eliot, in his *Hinduism and Buddhism,* 2 vols., Edward Arnold Co., London, 1921, Ch. 20. A complete listing of the Mahayana books is to be found in Bunyiu Nanjio's catalogue of the Translations in the Chinese Buddhist Tripitaka. See also Winternitz, *History of Indian Literature,* Vol. 2, pp. 312 ff.

THE SACRED LITERATURE OF BUDDHISM
Sources for Further Reading

Publications of the Pali Text Society—A number of particular volumes are indicated in footnotes throughout the chapter.

Sacred Books of the Buddhist, translated and edited by Max Muller, Mrs. Rhys Davids and other scholars, and issued by various publishers. Vol. 12 appeared in 1949.

Sacred Books of the East, Volumes 10, 11, 13, 17, 20, 21, 35, 36, 49.

Sacred Books and Literature of the East, Volume 10.

Wisdom of the East Series

W. D. C. Wagiswara and Kenneth J. Saunders, *The Buddha's Way of Virtue,* London, 1927.

Kenneth J. Saunders, *Lotuses of the Mahayana,* London, 1924.

Henry C. Warren, *Buddhism in Translation,* Harvard Oriental Series, Volume 3.

Paul Carus, *The Gospel of Buddha,* Open Court, Chicago, 1921.

F. L. Woodward, *Some Sayings of the Buddha,* Oxford University Press, 1925.

IN THE ANTHOLOGIES:

Bible of the World, pp. 181–376.

Bible of Mankind, pp. 143–179.

Lin Yutang, *The Wisdom of China and India,* pp. 321–356.

The Tree of Life, pp. 115–156.

The World's Great Scriptures, pp. 133–206.

Tongues of Fire, pp. 167–243.

Sacred Writings of the World's Great Religions, pp. 133–151.

Harvard Classics, Vol. 45, pp. 587–798.

CHAPTER VII

The Sacred Literature of the Jains

Perhaps of least interest to general readers, of all the scriptures treated in this volume, are those of the Jain faith, simply because they are so monastic in character. Jainism is a religion of India, considered sometimes by scholars as only a sect of Hinduism, but the Jains themselves will not agree to this. To be sure, it developed out of Hinduism, as Christianity did out of Judaism, but just as Christians do not regard themselves as a sect of Judaism, so Jains are not content to be considered a sectarian branch of Hinduism. They are listed in the Indian census as a separate faith with a total of 1,449,286 adherents, according to the most recent census report.

Jainism is a very old religion. Some Jains, indeed, regard Hinduism as only a degenerate form of it. While Mahavira, an older contemporary of Buddha, is usually thought of as its founder, it is probable that it was much older, and that Mahavira only gave it organized form, so that thenceforth it stood apart from the Hindu medium in which it existed, created a literature which became a sacred scripture, and so perpetuated the ancient faith to our own times.

Like Buddhism it found no help in the multitude of India's gods and made man's salvation wholly dependent on his own self-effort.

Mahavira's classic phrase: "Man thou art thine own friend, why wishest thou for a friend beyond thyself?"[1] sets forth this self-dependence, which marks it off from the theistic Hinduism of his day. It stresses, more than either Buddhism or Hinduism, ascetic practice as a way to salvation, and its insistence on the principle of non-injury, *Ahimsa*, is more absolute and far-reaching than that of any segment of Hinduism or Buddhism which also hold it. The three jewels, right faith, right knowledge, and right conduct, afford the clue to the attainment of *moksha*, or salvation, which to the Jain, as to the Buddhist, meant release from the wheel of birth, on which one is held by the law of Karma. Long before Mahavira, there had been a succession of Jinas or Tirthankaras as they were called, ford-finders, who had attained *moksha*, and so became a guarantee to all mankind that they too might attain it. These Tirthankaras, twenty-four of them, of which Mahavira was the last, are much celebrated in the literature of Jainism, both the canonical and non-canonical, and their statues are set up in Jain temples, not to be prayed to for help, for none can help a man save himself, but as a source of assurance and encouragement to those who seek to find the release which these have already found.

Unlike Buddhism, the Jain faith has remained at home in India, so scholars say; but apparently this view is not held by the Jains. Recent correspondence with a Jain leader reveals a contrary view. "I have reason," he writes, "to believe that it was once a prevailing religion of Central Asia, Java, and Malaya, and other countries. . . . Jain narrative literature is full of instances of Jain existence in foreign countries." He expects to publish a book on the subject within the next few years.[2]

Like Buddhism, its so-called founder was from the Kshatriya or warrior, ruler caste, rather than from the Brahmin or priestly group. Mahavira, like Buddha, was son of a rajah and, like him, abandoned that status in the quest for release. At a number of points there are clear parallels between the two faiths. Many think that when Gautama forsook his princely estate and became for several years a

---

[1] Akaranga Sutra, I, 3, 4, *Sacred Books of the East*, Vol. 22, p. 33.
[2] K. Jain, Hon'y Editor: *The Jain Antiquary*, in a personal letter June 17, 1950

wandering ascetic, he really became a follower of the Jain way of asceticism. Later he abandoned it and found enlightenment through meditation under the sacred Bo tree.

As in the case of the Buddhist scriptures, much of the content purports to be reported sayings of the founder. But not all of it. There are some books assigned definitely to authors other than Mahavira. The growth of the literature probably followed much the same pattern as that of Buddhism, but it was much longer in reaching anything like official canonical form. According to their own tradition, the canon, as we know it today, was agreed upon almost a thousand years after the death of Mahavira, in the late fifth or early sixth century of the Christian era at a Council held at Vallabhi in Gujarat, presided over by the famous monk, Devarddhi Ksamasramana, called for the specific purpose of collecting and putting the sacred texts into written form. Long before this at another Council at Pataliputra, the exact date of which is unknown, because it was feared that the knowledge of the sacred text was being lost, an effort was made to collect them. Tradition says that the original teachings of Mahavira were contained in fourteen Purvas, or "old Texts," handed down orally through his disciples for six generations. A famine caused the migration of a substantial portion of the Jain community to the south, led by the great Bhadrabahu. There remained behind in Magadha only one person who knew the sacred text. Learning the loss of these texts the Council was called and it compiled the eleven angas which form the first division of the canon, and put together as many as remained of the fourteen purvas to form the twelfth anga.

Meanwhile a difference arose between those who had migrated and those who remained at home. Apparently the original Jains were forbidden to wear clothing. Those who had migrated persisted in this custom, while those who remained at home adopted the custom of wearing a white garment. They were therefore called the Svetambaras, or "White Clad," while the other group were called the Digambaras, or "Sky Clad." This distinction still prevails even today. When the Sky Clad folk returned they refused to accept the canon as formulated at Pataliputra, and have their own which, while agreeing substantially in content, at least as to the names of the books included, nevertheless omits some, includes others, and within the texts bearing the same name differs at significant points. Svetambara Jains believe that the canon as adopted at Vallabhi is based squarely upon the old texts compiled at the earlier Council at Pataliputra, and that this goes directly back to Mahavira, and his early disciples.

How dependable the Jain tradition is, it is not possible to assert with certainty. Scholars differ in their judgments in the matter. Jacobi thinks the writing of the Jain works might go back as far as 300 B.C.[3] Bhandarkar thinks none of the works were written before the second or third century A.D. Certainly the canon, as we have it, is the end result of a long process which undoubtedly began with the formation of the order and culminated in the work of Devarddhi. There are clearly earlier and later strata to be discovered in it, which need much more attention from the specialists.

The general make-up of the canon is in outline as follows. It is divided into six sections and contains either forty-five or forty-six books.

I. The twelve *Angas* or limbs. Actually only eleven Angas exist, the twelfth having been lost, although at Pataliputra it had been constituted by the collection of such remnants of the fourteen Purvas as could then be recalled.
II. The twelve *Upangas,* or secondary limbs
III. The ten *Painnas,* or "Scattered pieces"
IV. The six *Cheya-Suttas*
V. Individual texts (two)
VI. The four *Mula-Suttas*

Since only a very few of these have been translated and are therefore available for reading by the general reader, the names of the individual books which constitute each division are not given here.[4] Only a few can be mentioned, and that but briefly, only enough to

---

[3] *Sacred Books of the East,* Vol. 22, p. xliii.
[4] For the complete list, with some description of each see Winternitz, *History of Indian Literature,* Vol. II, pp. 435 ff. J. N. Farquhar, *Outline of the Religious Literature of India,* names them and indicates translations and scholarly treatments of various parts of the canon.

reveal the general nature of the literature. The first Anga, for example, treats of the life of the monks, in a mixture of verse and prose. Mostly it is made up of sermons on various themes of importance to the Jains. *Ahimsa* is a central feature, and often stressed.

All breathing, existing, living sentient creatures should not be slain, nor treated with violence, nor abused, nor tormented nor driven away. This is the pure unchangeable, eternal law which the clever ones who understand the world have declared.[5]

Here is found also much having to do with ascetic practice, which may end in suicide by starving, if, after twelve years of penance and extreme periods of fasting, one is permitted by his *Guru* to do so.[6]

A long narrative poem appears here describing in some detail the ascetic practices of the Master Mahavira himself. He wandered about, homeless and naked. He was persecuted, beaten with sticks, attacked by crawling or flying animals. Often he was without food or shelter. "Moist or dry or cold food, old beans, or bad grain, whether he did or did not get such food, he was rich in control, meditating on things above, free from sin and desire, he was finally freed from delusion and liberated."[7]

Included also is a long section of nearly a hundred pages containing rules for begging which are of some interest. One section on begging for food requires thirty pages. Rules regulating the begging for a couch occupy fifteen pages, for clothes, nine pages, and at least two pages are used to indicate places where the monk or nun "should not ease nature."[8]

This Anga also contains material for the life story of Mahavira, which will be seen to have been used in a later book, the Kalpa-Sutra.

The second Anga deals with the religious life of the monks and devotes much of its attention to refuting heresies which might lead young monks into error. There are all sorts of warnings against the

[5] *Sacred Books of the East,* Vol. 22, I, 4: 1, 2, p. 36.
[6] *Ibid.,* Vol. 22, I, 7–8, pp. 72–78.
[7] *Ibid.,* Vol. 22, pp. 79–87, *passim.*
[8] *Ibid.,* Vol. 22, pp. 88–178.

dangers and temptations to which the monk is exposed. Not the least of the dangers is women. The chapter dealing with this particular danger is well worth quoting in part. Mahavira, like Buddha, and indeed all the believers in the monastic way of life, does not think too well of women. It is not lacking in humor, and it is quite revealing as to the nature of the feminine toilette in that remote period. There is in it a touch of modernity, that makes it of interest to twentieth century men and women. Better it is to let women alone, for when they by their wiles succeed in catching a man he is completely under their control.

Then they make him do what they like. . . . As an antelope caught in a snare, so does he not get out of it, however he struggles. . . .

A worthy monk should have no intercourse with women. . . . When a monk breaks the law, dotes on a woman and is absorbed by that passion, she afterwards scolds him, lifts her foot, and tramples on his head . . . they send him on all sorts of errands: "Fetch some nice fruit . . . bring wood to cook the vegetables . . . paint my feet, come and meanwhile rub my back . . . reach me the lip-salve, fetch the umbrella, and slippers, the knife to cut the string; have my robe dyed bluish! . . . fetch me the pincers, the comb, the ribbon to bind up my hair, reach me the looking-glass, put the toothbrush near me. . . .

. . . pregnant women order their husbands about like slaves to fulfil their craving.

When a son is born the mother bids the father to hold the baby, or to give it to her. Thus some supporters of their sons have to carry burdens like camels.

Getting up at night, they lull the baby asleep like nurses, and though they are ashamed of themselves they wash the clothes like washer-women.[9]

A good description of the Jain idea of hell is found here, as frequently in others of their books.

Another of the Angas, the third, is much like the Gradual Sayings of the Buddhist canon, dealing in ten sections with things of which there are one, two to ten.

The fifth Anga sets forth Jain dogma largely in the form of answers by Mahavira to questions asked by one of the chief of his

[9] *Sacred Books of the East*, Vol. 45, pp. 272–275, *passim* (I, 4, 1.)

disciples, but it also gives perhaps the most vivid picture of Maha-vira himself and his relationship to his contemporaries to be found in any of the books. There are also legends of some of the earlier Jain ascetics.

In the sixth Anga are to be found a series of narratives or parables spun out to form a more or less lengthy narrative. One of these parables bears some resemblance to the parable of the talents in the Christian gospels. Here however, it is the story of a man who has four daughters-in-law. In order to test them he gives each five grains of rice. One throws them away thinking to herself that there are plenty of grains of rice in the larder and that she can easily replace them with five other grains. The second thinks more or less the same, only she eats her five grains. The third puts them care-fully away in her jewel box. But the fourth plants them, harvests and replants again and again for a period of five years when she has accumulated a large store of rice. On the return of the merchant he punishes the first two by requiring that they perform the most menial tasks about the house. To the third he entrusts the guarding of the entire property, but to the fourth he gives the management of the entire household. These daughters-in-law represent the monks, some of whom do not keep their vows at all, others neglect them, the better ones keep them joyfully, while the best not only keep but propagate them.[10]

There are other stories of travellers, adventurers, robbers, some approaching the novel type—all with a moral conveniently attached. One of these stories concerns one Malli—the only female among the twenty-four Tirthankaras.

She was the daughter of a noted king and beautiful beyond words. Six princes learn of her and seek to woo her, one of them having seen only her great toe in a portrait of the lady. She will accept none of them. They are outraged and make war on her father's kingdom. He is helpless. Then she tells her father to invite one after another of the princes into the city offering to give him his daughter. Meanwhile she had constructed a "puzzle house" in which by some peculiar arrangement the six princes from different

[10] Told in abbreviated form as found more fully in Winternitz, II. p. 446.

vantage points could see a figure of herself at one point. Then she
made a figure resembling her exactly. She filled the head with a
most unsavory mixture of left-overs from her meals, carefully covering the opening with lotus blossoms.

While the princes, having been admitted, admire the beautiful
figure of the supposed princess she herself appears, opens the figure's head so that it gives off a terrible stench. The princes cover
their faces and turn away, but she moralizes upon the fact that
within her beautiful body there is that that is even more loathsome
than the inside of the artificial figure, and they should therefore not
cherish any more the thought of the enjoyment of love. Telling the
story of her former births, she announces that she intends to become
a nun. Thereupon the princes also renounce the world.[11]

The seventh book treats of the duties of lay adherents of the
movement in the form of legends of pious laymen, mostly merchants who practiced certain forms of asceticism appropriate to laymen, of whom by no means so rigorous a pattern of behavior is
required. As stated in a modern Jain tract, while *absolute* avoidance
of non-injury is required of a monk, the vows of a layman require only
the avoidance of *gross* injury to living things. Writes a modern Jain
correspondent, the layman "should adopt asceticism as much as his
physical strength permits." . . . One should proceed onward according to one's spiritual advancement. Hence even a pariah who hunts
and eats flesh can be a believer in Jainism."[12]

The ninth Anga consists largely of accounts of how faithful
monks have starved themselves to death. Jainism is the one faith
with which the author is acquainted which not only condones but
lauds suicide, only, however, by the method of slow starvation. It
seems not a little strange that the faith which is most insistent upon
the principle of *Ahimsa* and will not take the life of the most humble living thing, makes a definite place for putting an end to one's
own life. No translation is available but it may be of interest to
quote a quite modern Jain tract which tells the story of the fasting
of various saints, some of them unto death.

[11] Abbreviated from Winternitz summary, II, pp. 447–448.
[12] Personal letter, K. Jain, June 17, 1950.

One, it is claimed, fasted not less than 40 days any year from 1873 to 1883. In 5 of the 11 years he fasted more than 100 days, and in 1883 reached the extreme period of 186 days. Another is reported to have fasted a total of about 8,000 days in 35 years. Still another endured 2,975 one-day fasts, 37 of 2 days, 10 of 5 days, one of 15, 17 of 31 days, one of 101 days, one of 186 days and one of 47 days. He passed away as a result of the last one.[13]

The eleventh Anga is filled with legends of the retribution which various people have suffered or enjoyed as a result of the working of the principle of Dharma not only in this but in preceding successive births. These stories are purportedly told by Mahavira who is asked by a disciple why a certain person is suffering some particular disability in this life.

There is an Upanga for each of the Angas. They are of varied content, mainly dogmatic and mythological. In the first there is a description of the state of the soul that has acquired perfect knowledge.

Neither among human beings nor among all the gods is there such illimitable bliss as has begun for the enlightened one. The bliss of the gods multiplied in duration to eternity, even though it were endlessly augmented in its fulness, is not so great as the blissfulness of liberation. . . . As a savage, who becomes acquainted with the manifold beauties of a city, cannot describe them, because he lacks something with which to compare them, so too, the blissfulness of the enlightened ones is incomparable—there is no comparison.[14]

Two of the Upangas give in question-and-answer form detailed classifications of living beings and a description of the world in considerable detail, oceans, islands, the palaces of the gods, as well as a classification of races and their habitations. Three others are "scientific" treatments of geography, astronomy, and cosmology including a discussion of time. Its astronomy is interesting, particularly its treatment of the sun and moon. Five of the Upangas are

---

[13] Chagmal Chophra, *A Short History of the Terepanthi Sect of the Sevetambar Jains and Its Tenets,* fourth edition, 201 Harrison Road, Calcutta, pp. 28–33. The pamphlet is undated, but a letter dated 1946 is quoted in it.

[14] Quoted by Winternitz, II, p. 455.

definitely legendary in character, dealing mainly with the life beyond, one especially with the various hells, one with the birth of
ten different princes into a different heaven. One relates the past
births of ten gods and goddesses who paid homage to Mahavira,
and one narrates the conversion of twelve princes by a famous Jain
teacher.

The Painnas or Scattered Pieces are really a miscellany dealing
with almost every topic of interest to Jains, in both prose and verse.
One gives in forty-eight verses the names of Mahavira, another is
astrological, one is a dialogue on physiology and anatomy between
Mahavira and a disciple, some deal with voluntary death by starvation, one gives in three hundred verses a classification of the kings,
of the gods, etc. etc. It will be seen that there is here no definite
principle of organization, and it is also evident that much of it is
later in origin. In this particular section there is some disagreement
as to just what are the ten pieces. As many as twenty different texts
appear in Jain literature as forming a part of this division of the
canon.

The fourth division of the canon corresponds roughly with the
Vinaya-pitaka of the Pali Buddhist canon, and probably contains a
great deal of quite ancient material. Most representative of this section is the Kalpa-Sutra which is supposed to have been written by
the great Jain Bhadrabahu, sixth head of the movement after Mahavira, though parts of it could not possibly have come from his hand
since they list heads of schools which existed long after the period
of his life.

The Kalpa-Sutra is in three sections, the first of which contains
the biographies of some of the Tirthankaras or Jinas, giving major
attention to Mahavira, last of the line.

It treats of Mahavira very much as the Lalita-Vistara does of the
Buddha. Devananda, a Brahman woman, one night had a succession
of fourteen marvelous dreams in which appeared an elephant, a
bull, a lion...the moon, the sun...a heap of jewels and a flame.
Wakening she told her husband who interpreted the dream to mean
that they would have a son who would be of wonderful beauty and
strength and great wisdom. She conceived a son and was surpass-

ingly happy. But the king of the gods transferred the embryo from the womb of Devananda to that of Trisala, a Kshatriya, wife of King Siddartha (cf. the story of Krishna's birth), who also had the fourteen wonderful dreams. On the night of the birth of Mahavira, a divine light overspread the earth, occasioned by the ascending and descending gods and goddesses, and the spirits rained down upon the palace a great shower of silver and gold and jewels, clothes, ornaments, and riches. But like Buddha, Mahavira renounced wealth, comfort, and ease and set out on a life of discipline. He entered the state of homelessness, walked about naked, neglected his body, but in the thirteenth year, being engaged in deep meditation he "reached the highest knowledge and intuition, called Kevala, which is infinite, supreme, unobstructed, unimpeded, complete and full."[15] When after some thirty years as Kevalin, at the age of about seventy-two he died, it was as he sat alone "reciting the fifty-five lectures which detail the result of Karman, etc. free from all pains."[16] It is because Mahavira and the other Tirthankaras, or ford-finders, finally attained the sought-for release, that men continue to hope and seek for that same release for themselves.

Section two is an enumeration of the various schools and their branches, and of the heads of each. The first section contains rules for the monks and nuns which read very much like those of the Buddhists.

Of the *Mula-Sutras*, the first the *Uttaradhyana-Sutra* is best known in the West, and is one of the most valuable books in the whole canon, for an understanding of Jainism. It in some ways resembles the *Sutta-Nipata* of Buddhism. It is partly poetic, partly prose. It contains sermons, proverbs, advice to students, counsel to monks and nuns, parables, dialogues and ballads. In places it reads like the *Dhammapada*.

Another parable somewhat like the parable of the talents appears here:

Three merchants set out on their travels, each with his capital. One

[15] *Sacred Books of the East*, Vol. 22, p. 263.
[16] *Id.*, p. 269.

of them gained much; the second returned with his capital; the third merchant came home having lost his capital. This parable is taken from common life; Learn (to apply it) to the Law. The capital is human life, the gain is heaven; through the loss of that capital man must be born as a denizen of hell or a brute animal.[17]

One of the old ballads which, incidentally, is of interest because it involves a number of persons who appear in the legends of Krishna, runs thus in summary:

There lived in a certain city two great princes. One of them, Vasudeva, had two wives—Rohini and Devaki—each of whom bore him a son, Rama and Kesava. The second had an elder son Rathanemi, who became an ascetic, and a younger, Aristanenis. Kesava sought Ragimati, daughter of a powerful king, as wife for Aristanenis and it was granted. When Aristanenis set forth with ceremony to get his bride, he saw on his way a great many animals in cages, and learned that they were to be killed for his marriage-feast. Deeply shocked at this, he took the vow of an ascetic. The expectant bride, hearing of this, wept loudly, but she too decided to become a nun. Caught in the rain one day while wandering as a nun, she took refuge in a cave and, believing herself alone, took off her garments to dry them. But the ascetic brother of Aristanenis, Rathanemi, had also taken refuge in the cave, and seeing the nun in her nude loveliness made passionate advances to her. However, she reproved him, admonishing him not to wish to "drink that which another has spat out." Brought to his senses by her forcible rebuke he "returned to religion like an elephant spurred on by the goad."[18]

The two individual texts, sometimes mentioned before, sometimes after the Mula-Sutras, are sometimes listed as among the scattered pieces. They are not primarily religious in content though they do deal in part with religious subjects. They may be characterized rather as encyclopedias "dealing with everything that should be known by a Jain monk."[19]

[17] VII, 14–16. Translated by Jacobi in *Sacred Books of the East*, XIV, p. 29.
[18] Abbreviated from summary as given by Winternitz, II, p. 470.
[19] Winternitz, II, p. 472.

Very little of Jain literature has gotten into the anthologies. What is available for further reading appears below.

THE SACRED LITERATURE OF THE JAINS
Sources for Further Reading

Sacred Books of the East, Vols. 22 and 45.

S. E. Frost, *The Sacred Writings of the World's Great Religions,* pp. 119–132.

CHAPTER VIII

The Sacred Literature of the Sikhs

Sikhism is an offshoot of Hinduism. Regarded by many scholars as only a reformed Hindu sect, it is considered by its own followers as a separate faith. The British Indian census has recognized it as such and each decade numbered the Sikhs apart from the Hindus. The most recent census revealed a total of 5,691,447 followers of the faith. A comparative study of population growth and the growth of the Sikh movement over the last four decades indicates a steady growth, substantially exceeding the percentage increase of the total population.

The scriptures of the Sikhs are almost wholly unknown to the western world. Though there are now a goodly number of anthologies containing selections from most of the sacred books of the world, so far only one that has come to the attention of the writer contains anything from the *Granth,* the Sikh Bible, and that only a very limited selection. Why should this be so? One answer is that, while considered by themselves a separate religion, they are not so regarded by many scholars, and as a mere part of Hinduism, their writings are overshadowed by the much more important writings of that mother faith. Perhaps the real reason is that the literature itself

216

is of a character which is lacking, at least, in popular interest. Another factor in the situation may be that it has not been translated frequently, and that the literary quality of the translations does not commend it to the anthologists.

As a matter of fact the entire work has never been translated into the English language. After having spent seven years in working on his translation of the four principals Rags[1] or sections of it, Ernest Trumpp, the translator, wrote:

> The Sikh Granth is a very big volume, but . . . incoherent and shallow in the extreme, and couched at the same time in dark and perplexing language, in order to cover these defects. It is for us Occidentals a most painful and almost stupefying task, to read only a single *Rag*, and I doubt if any ordinary reader will have the patience to proceed to the second *Rag*, after he shall have perused the first. It would therefore be a mere waste of paper to add also the minor *Rags* which only repeat, in endless variations, what has already been said in the great *Rags* over and over again, without adding the least to our knowledge.[2]

On the other hand, Max Arthur Macauliffe, who was for many years a judge in India, resigned at the request of representative Sikh societies, and undertook the translation of the book. This he felt impelled to do because he felt that Trumpp's translation was "highly inaccurate and unidiomatic, and furthermore gave mortal offense to the Sikhs by the *odium theologicum* introduced into it. Whenever he saw an opportunity of defaming the *Gurus*, the sacred book and the religion of the Sikhs, he eagerly availed himself of it."[3] He hoped by his own work to make some reparation to the Sikhs for the insults which Trumpp offered to their *Gurus*[4] and their religion. He wrote an extensive life of each of the *Gurus*, and translated most, though not all, of the *Rags*. The unfortunate feature of his book is that the translated portions are given without exact designation of

---

[1] *Rag* really means a musical measure, but all those hymns to be sung to a given measure are gathered together in one section. See, further, pp. 221 f.

[2] Ernest Trumpp, *The Adi Granth*, London, 1877, preface, p. vii.

[3] *The Sikh Religion*, Vol. 1, p. vii.

[4] In India generally the term *guru* means teacher. The student learned the Vedas from his *guru*. It means also spiritual guide. In the Sikh faith it has special reference to the founder, Nanak, and his nine successors as heads of the movement. But it not infrequently in the Granth refers to God.

just whence they are taken, so that they cannot be easily compared with any other translation. Trumpp does this. Nevertheless, the Macauliffe translation is much the more readable. Since he secured the approval of the best Sikh scholars before publication, it may be safely assumed that the translation is more nearly accurate than that of Trumpp.

Perhaps the editors of the anthologies read only Trumpp's preface and became discouraged about finding suitable material for their collections. But really, it is not so hopeless. If, indeed, the collection is long and repetitious it is not without its high spots as well as low. Indeed, there are some passages of genuine poetic worth, expressive of very deep religious aspirations and devotion, some of which will be included in this chapter. But first a few facts about the movement and the type of religious faith which gave rise to the book.

It is true that the Sikh movement was a reform movement in Hinduism. There have been many such in the past, and there will continue to be new ones. The distinctive feature of this particular movement is that it represents the result of the impact of the Moslem faith on Hinduism. When religions meet and live side by side there is always a give and take, each influencing the other in some respects, despite efforts usually made to avoid just that. This is what is called a process of syncretism. Usually it is unconscious but sometimes quite deliberate. Often, however, syncretism takes the form of a new synthesis of some elements from each, to form a new faith which is in some respects similar to but different from either of the contributing faiths. The Sikh movement is such a synthesis of Hindu and Moslem elements.

But Hinduism is a very complex faith, and Islam too has its differing varieties of outlook, organization, and practice. If one were to try to say which of the variant Hindu strands were combined with varying Moslem strands, he would be most nearly correct, in the author's opinion, in saying that Sikhism represents a flowing together of the *bhakti* Hindu faith of Ramanuja and Ramanda, and Islamic mysticism represented by Sufism.

Bhakti Hinduism is devotional Hinduism which finds salvation, not through works, as in the Vedas, not through knowledge, as in philosophic Hinduism, but in faith, love, loyalty or devotion to a personal divinity. A classic illustration of this was noted in the Bhagavad Gita, where Krishna is the object of devotion. Ramanuja was the great medieval exponent of this type of faith, as over against the famous philosopher and teacher, Shankara, whose commentary on the Vedanta-Sutras set forth the bases of the Vedanta. Ramananda, who lived in the fourteenth century, was a disciple of Ramanuja. He travelled widely in India preaching the faith of his Master, and became the founder of a sect emphasizing the way of devotion to Rama, an incarnation of Vishnu, as the way of salvation. His movement opened the way to all men of whatever caste as indicated in the famous saying: "Let no one ask a man's caste or with whom he eats. If a man shows love to Hari (God), he is Hari's own."

The poet Kabir was a disciple of Ramananda, and founder of a still existing sect, the Kabirpanth. He in turn greatly influenced Nanak, founder of the Sikh faith. Thus there is a clear line of connection between Sikhism and devotional Hinduism. But Kabir was probably of Moslem origin. As a matter of fact each faith claims him as its own. The Moslem influence is clear in the poetry of the Granth and in the organizational form the movement took. If not, like Islam, completely monotheistic in its conception of God—it looks definitely in that direction. Sat Nam, or True Name, the most frequently used divine name, seems clearly to be the Supreme Being. Late Sikh thought frankly admitted the worship of other beings, for example, the tenth Guru certainly was a devotee also of Durga.

But since Sikhism is a syncretism, it is not unnatural that the concept of God should be near monotheistic, but with overtones of Hindu pantheism. Professor Archer says of Nanak that he was not a pantheist or a polytheist, nor yet quite a monotheist,[5] which makes one wonder where to classify him. Perhaps the difficulty may be resolved by noting that he is sometimes one, sometimes another. This is not at all strange. One finds in many persons an alternation of attitudes toward God. Christian Science is a good example. On

[5] John C. Archer, *The Sikhs*, Princeton University Press, 1946, p. 116.

one page one may think himself in an atmosphere of pantheism—on another God is described or approached in warmly personal fashion. Certainly God is called by many names in the Granth, now Hari, now Ram, now Brahma, or again Allah. One gets the impression, however, that these are but variant names of the one Supreme.

In the first of the thirty-eight Psalms of Nanak that stand at the beginning of the Granth, as a kind of introduction to the whole, Nanak sings thus of God:

> Thinking comprehendeth him not, although there be thoughts
>   by the thousands,
> Silence discovers him not, though it be continuous silence,
> Man is persistently hungry, though he eats of tasty abundance;
> Not one of a hundred thousand artful devices avails him!
> How may the truth be attained, the bonds of falsehood be
>   broken?
> By obeying the will of God as surely recorded, saith Nanak.[6]

As a matter of fact the important thing to Nanak and to his followers is not the correct comprehension of the nature of the ultimate but their attitude of obedience and devotion to God. In another Psalm, he sings:

> Forms have come out of his order, but his order goes
>   undetected.
> Life has come by his will, through which comes life's exaltation,
> High and low are his will, and joy and sorrow his pleasure;
> In his will alone is he blessed who runs the round of his
>   nature
> All are subject to him, not one beyond his jurisdiction
> If any perceives his will, he humbles himself, saith Nanak.[7]

For salvation lies in devotion to the True Name:

> The Lord is true, plainly known, his loving kindness infinite;
> To those who crave and seek he gives, gives with full abandon.
> What indeed must he be offered to throw his court wide open?
> What words must lips be uttering to make his love responsive?

---

[6] From *The Japuji*, A Book of Psalms of Guru Nanak Nirankari, J. C. Archer, *The Sikhs*, p. 120.
[7] *Ibid.*

At deathless dawn give Sat Nam thought and glory,
Put on the garb of deeds—and salvation's way is open!
Be sure that he himself is fully true, saith Nanak.[8]

The non-idolatrous worship of God is likewise a truly Mohammedan principle—Hindu worship was generally not only polytheistic but idolatrous. Idolatry is ridiculed in the Granth, for example
by Kabir:

> Kabir says: a stone is made the Lord, the
>   whole world worships it
> Who remains in reliance upon this is
>   drowned in the black stream.[9]

And later Sikhism developed much of the militant spirit of Islam,
seeking at one time the political domination of India. It became an
effective theocracy just as Islam had been.

The entire Granth is a very substantial body of poetry, consisting mainly of the writings of Guru Nanak and his first four successors, to which were added poems of a dozen or more, one-time
famous saints, or bhagats, including Ramananda, Kabir and the
well-known Maratha poet, Namdev.

The general plan of the book is as follows:

There is first the Japji, or as Archer calls it, the Book of Psalms
of Guru Nanak, thirty-eight in number, a total of about four hundred lines, forming a kind of introduction to the whole collection.
Following this come three collections of extracts from later portions
of the book, designed for devotional use by Sikhs, particularly for
evening prayer and before retiring for the night. The greater part
of the remainder of the book is made up of collections of hymns to
be sung to thirty-one different Rags or musical measures, each of
which bears a specific name. They vary greatly in length but are
themselves collections of verse from various poets.

The general plan seems to be to include, first, a collection of
verses by Guru Nanak, followed successively by verses composed

[8] *Op. cit.,* p. 121.
[9] Trumpp, *The Adi Granth,* p. 678.

by the other Gurus. The poetic meter varies, something like a dozen different meters being employed. Where within the same Rag, the *Gurus* use differing meters, all those of identical meter are grouped together, the work of each Guru appearing in the order in which the *Gurus* came chronologically. Thus for example *Rag Siri Rag* has a collection of *sabds*, a term which may include three differing meters,[10] another of *astpadas* or Chants, and of Vars, which, because of limitation of space, and, perhaps also of popular interest, we cannot describe in detail. Under each of these there may be verses from some or all of the Gurus. These are then followed by verses from various *bhagats* or saints. Following the Rags is a section known as the *Bhog*, or conclusion, consisting mostly of miscellaneous *sloks* including some from the last two of the Gurus. There seems to be little or no logical connection between the verses from any of the varied sources, either within the collection of their own verse or with that collected from other Gurus or saints. Indeed, the whole thing seems to be a miscellaneous collection of poetry arranged in an artificial, rather than logical fashion. The translation of only the four Rags, by Trumpp, requires almost seven hundred pages. Together with Nanak's *Japji* and the ritual sections the whole translated work of Trumpp requires seven hundred and eight large pages. And this omits twenty-seven other Rags of whose total bulk the writer has seen no estimate.

The original poems were written in a dozen or more different languages, or dialects, so that almost no one can read the entire book. Eventually the tenth Guru, or successor of Nanak, the religious and political head of the Sikhs, decreed that there should be no human successor as Guru, but that the Granth Sahib should thenceforth be Guru. And so it has been. Now at the beautiful, principal Sikh temple at Amritsar, a copy of the Granth is the central object of reverence, if not worship. Daily it is brought out from its overnight depository with considerable ceremony, properly adorned and vested, and placed on a dais where the faithful may see and pay homage to it. At evening time it is, with equal ceremony, locked away for the night in a specially prepared vault for

[10] Trumpp, p. 21.

safekeeping.[11] It is not a little strange that a faith which rules out idolatry should have come, in the end, very near, if not quite, to making their sacred book an object of worship.

The Granth, it will have been noted, is not like most other sacred books in that it is exclusively in poetry. The Tao Te Ching, it is true, is wholly poetic, but it does not constitute the whole of Taoist sacred writ. Again, there is here no connected history or story of the beginning of the world, or the people, or any story of the founder, or of the beginnings of the faith. There is current to be sure, a life of Nanak, and some account of each of the *Gurus,* which abound in wonder stories, as do so many such accounts of other founders of religions. Trumpp happily includes translations of both in the introduction to the book. They are both interesting and instructive if not accurately historical. But these are not a part of the sacred scriptures.

The book is interesting as a scripture of a particular religion, in that it includes so much material from poets who were never associated with the movement, though some of them deeply influenced Nanak.

Namdev, earliest of the great Maratha poets, is noted for his devotional verse. He was a contemporary of Kabir, living toward the latter part of the fifteenth century A.D. Several of his poems are translated in *Psalms of the Maratha Saints* by Nicol MacNicol.

---

[11] This ceremony first reported by Monier-Williams, *Brahmanism and Hinduism,* page 177, and given wide circulation through repetition in various popular books on the History of Religions, has been questioned by J. C. Archer, who states that during a lengthy stay among Sikhs he never observed it. (Personal letter, 2–14–51.) Dr. Archer does, however, in an article in *The Review of Religion,* January 1949, pp. 118, 119, describe the ceremony with which the reputed original copy or first edition of the book was shown to him together with some friends at a special *darshan.* It was taken from a safe, placed upon an altar while the *gyani,* or reader, in charge of it, uttered certain prescribed prayers. The successive seven wrappings were then removed and the book finally exposed. Afterward it was carefully re-wrapped and put away. Such exhibitions generally occur each night when the moon is full. This was, however, not at Amritsar, but at Kartarpur in the Hall of Mirrors on an upper floor of the palace fort built by Guru Arjun. This hall serves as a place of worship. In the Golden Temple at Amritsar, says Archer, a canopy on the altar hangs above the two copies of the book and royal peacock feathers are waved over it, both indicative of the royalty assigned to it. He says also that some signs of bibliolatry toward the Granth are to be found among the people (p. 122).

> As chiming anklets sweet ring
>   So rings Thy name abroad;
> To human spirits hungering
>   Thou givest peace with God.
>
> Thou on Thy shoulders carrying
>   All the world's load of care,
> To thee 'tis such a little thing
>   My trouble, too, to bear![12]

NAMDEV

In it one catches something of the spirit of the poet, and his warmly personal dependence upon God. The two poems of Namdev contained in the Granth are not the equal of some found elsewhere, or else the translation is not so well done. These lines are typical of his thought.

> Day and night I utter the name of Ram.
> With dye-stuff I color, a seam I sew.
> Without the name of Ram I do not live twenty-four minutes.[13]

Kabir, as already indicated, was a major influence upon Nanak, the founder. He was a weaver by trade, but a most prolific poet. One who wishes to appreciate Kabir would do well to read from Tagore's beautiful translation of one hundred of his poems in *One Hundred Poems of Kabir*.[14] Reading the Tagore version, over against the translation of Kabir's poetry included in the Granth (by Trumpp), one is constrained to wonder whether there is not more of Tagore than Kabir in the former's renderings. Tagore was, of course, one of the greatest of all the writers of poetry in English—winner of the Nobel Prize in 1913, though himself one of the most illustrious of India's sons. Here is just a sample of one of his songs according to Tagore:

[12] Association Press, Calcutta, 1919, p. 43. This and several others are included in the delightful anthology of Indian verse, much of it of a devotional nature, *Temple Bells*, edited by M. A. Appasamy, Association Press, Calcutta, 1930.

[13] Trumpp, *op. cit.*, p. 666.

[14] Macmillan and Co., London, 1923.

LXIII

Why so impatient, my heart?
He who watches over birds and beasts
    and insects,
He who cared for you while you were yet
    in your mother's womb,
Shall He not care for you now that you are
    come forth?

O my heart, how could you turn from
The smile of your Lord and wander
    so far from Him?
You have left your Beloved and are
    thinking of others: and this is
    Why all your work is in vain.[15]

But even in the plodding translation of Trumpp one finds beautiful bits of verse expressive of profound religious devotion.

"O Madhava, (my) thirst for water does not cease!
(In drinking) the water the fire increases still more.
(1). Thou art the ocean, I am the fish of the water.
I dwell in the water, without the water I am done for.
(2). Thou art the cage, I am thy parrot.
Yama, the cat, what can he do unto me?
(3). Thou art the tree, I am the bird.
The unlucky one does not get thy sight.
(4). Thou art the Guru, I am thy new disciple (= apprentice).
Kabir says: join me at the time of the end!"[16]

XIX

(1). For gold he is not obtained.
Ram is obtained for the price of the heart.

Now that Ram is considered by me as my own,
My heart is comforted with natural ease.

[15] *Op. cit.,* p. 66.
[16] Trumpp, *Adi Granth,* Ragu Gauri, The Sayings of the Devotees, p. 458.

(2). Brahma, though always speaking (of him), did not get his end.
(But) Ram comes to the house of his devotee, who is sitting
(there in rest).
(3). Kabir says: I have given up my fickle mind.
Devotion to Ram alone is my lot.[17]

XL

Now that King Ram has become my helper:
Birth and death are cut off, I have obtained final emancipation.
(1). I have been joined to the society of the pious.
I have been rescued from the five attackers.
The nectar-name I mutter (now) with (my) tongue.
I have been made his own slave with a price (being paid for me).
(2). The true Guru has afforded (me) assistance.
I have been drawn out from the way of the world.
Love to the lotus-feet has sprung up (in me).
Govind dwells continually in my mind.
(3). The burning coals of the Maya are extinguished.
In (my) heart is contentment, the name (is my) support.
In water and on land the Lord is omnipresent.
Wherever I see, there he is near and dear.
(4). His own worship is established by himself.
What is written before, that is obtained, O my brother!
On whom he bestows mercy, his accoutrement is complete.
The Lord of Kabir is cherishing the poor.[18]

(1). Dwelling in heaven should not be desired nor should dwelling
in hell be dreaded.
What is to be, that will be, no desire should be made in the
heart.

The excellences of the sweetheart should be sung,
From whom the highest treasure is obtained.
(2). What is muttering, what austerity and control of the
passions, what vows, what ablutions,
As long as the right, loving worship of the Lord is not known?

[17] *Adi Granth,* p. 464.
[18] *Ibid.,* p. 470.

(3). Seeing prosperity, one should not be joyful, seeing
  misfortune, one should not weep.
As prosperity is, so is misfortune; what is arranged by destiny,
  that happens.
(4). Those worshippers are excellent (by their) worship,
  in whose heart the enemy of Mura dwells.[19]

Now and then Kabir gives evidence of a sense of humor as well
as of understanding of the true nature of God and salvation. He
has evidently observed people bathing in the holy Ganges or elsewhere, believing that thus salvation might be attained. But he
cries:

> "Adore Ram, the one God
> The service of God is true bathing.
> If by immersion in the water salvation be
>   obtained, the frogs bathe continually.
> As the frogs, so are those men."[20]

Just what is the meaning of the following verse is not clear but
surely it could have been meant humorously:

> Hear one wonderful thing, O brother!
> I see that the lion is pasturing the cows.
> The fish of the water is delivered of young on a tree.
> I see that the cat has carried off the dog.
> Below is the Rebarsa (a tree), above its root.
> To the stem of that stick fruits and blossoms.
> Mounting a horse the buffalo goes out to pasture cattle.
> Without the bullock the sack has come to the house.
> Kabir says; who comprehends this verse:
> To him uttering Ram, all is manifest.[21]

Altogether a surprising amount of Kabir's verse appears in the
Granth. If to what is actually of his own composition be added all
that has the flavor of his religious ideas and attitudes, those who
are quoted by Archer as asserting that the Kabir portions of the

[19] *Adi Granth*, p. 478.
[20] Trumpp, p. 664.
[21] *Ibid.*, p. 660.

Granth Sahib make up in reality "two thirds of the Granth," may not be far wrong in their estimate.[22]

There are even bits by a Moslem, Shekh Farid—a Sufi, and a contemporary of Nanak, who seems to have had rather a close association with him. In all there are one hundred and thirty verses, called *Sloks*. They are quite disconnected for the most part, and the reason for their inclusion does not seem clear. One reads:

"O Farid, if thou art clever in understanding, do not write an account of the evil deeds of others.

Lowering thy head look into thine own collar, that is, look into thine own heart."

Another rather surprisingly reads:

"O Farid, who beat thee with their fists, do not beat them again!

Go to thine own house, having kissed their feet."[23]

Sikhs have not been known for turning the other cheek. Rather, many, though not all, have been much given to fighting. For a long time they have been regarded as the best soldier material in all of India. But, in all fairness, it must be said that they were not given to military activity in the earlier phase of the movement.

On the whole the good Shekh's *sloks* give rather a gloomy view of life and its sufferings.

"O Farid, he who is bound by death appears like one who
        is thrown into the river.

In the other world the hell is heated, a howl is heard
        and a scream rises.

Some have become very prudent, some wander about careless.

The works that are done in the world, are witnesses at the
        court of god."[24]

The assembling of all but a small portion of the Granth was done by the Fifth Guru, Arjun (1581–1606). According to legend, a group of disciples came to him one day saying that they were greatly

[22] *The Sikhs,* p. 53.

[23] Trumpp. *Op. cit.,* p. 686. His spelling frequently differs from that of other authorities, e.g., Shekh is spelled Shaikh by others.

[24] *Ibid.,* pp. 691–692.

benefited and inspired by the true songs of Nanak, but that other verses, falsely attributed to Nanak, were the occasion of the growth of pride and worldly wisdom in men's hearts. Could there not be some way of indicating which were the genuine words of Guru Nanak? Acting on the suggestion, Arjun set about collecting the authentic hymns of Nanak, as well as those of his successors, including his own, and to these added many hymns from the Indian Saints which were not in disagreement with the thought of Nanak. Thus was the Granth formed. To this were later added short selections from Teg Bahadur, the ninth Guru, and the Gobind Singh, the tenth and the last of the *Gurus*.

It is called the *Adi* or original *Granth,* and is accepted by all Sikhs of whatever sect. There is another, the *Daswan Granth* which contains a substantial number of hymns from Gobind Singh, last of the Gurus, and some of his father, Teg Bahadur. It is not accepted by all Sikhs, but it is especially honored by the Akali sect of Sikhism.

The line of living Gurus ended with Gobind Singh who ordered that, thenceforth, the Granth should be as a living Guru to them. Macauliffe asserted that eventually the Sikhs came to believe in the Gurus as but one, each succeeding one being but a new embodiment of the soul of the preceding Guru, and that now this has passed into the Granth.[25] However, J. C. Archer declares categorically that the Sikhs do not believe that each succeeding Guru was the reincarnation of his predecessor.[26]

It is fitting that, at least, a brief bit from each of the Gurus be included though it is impossible to judge any one of them by a single brief song. We have already included several hymns by Nanak but here are two further brief selections.

The first is but one of many, expressive of his relationship to God, the center of his life and thought:

I have no friend like God
Who gave me soul and body, and infused into me understanding.

[25] Macauliffe, XVI, Vol. I.
[26] Personal letter, 2–14–51.

He cherisheth and watcheth over all creatures; He is wise and knoweth
    the secrets of hearts.
The *Guru* is like a lake; we are his beloved swans;
In the water are many jewels and rubies.
God's praises are pearls, gems, and diamonds; singing them maketh soul
    and body happy.[27]

It is in God that his hope of salvation rests:

My soul is in fear; to whom shall I complain?
I have served Him who causeth us to forget our sorrows; He is ever
and ever the Giver.
My Lord is ever young; He is ever and ever the Giver.
Night and day serve the Lord, and in the end He will deliver thee.
Hark, hark, my friend, thus shalt thou cross over.
O Merciful One, by Thy name shall I cross over; I am ever a sacrifice
unto Thee.[28]

The second Guru, Angad, did not contribute much to the Granth,
only a few *sloks*. One, expressive of the typical mystic thought of
God, is this:

They who possess the greatness of Thy name, O God,
    are happy at heart.
Nanak, there is only one nectar; there is none other;
Nanak, that nectar is in the heart, but it is only
    obtained by the favor of the *Guru;*
They who were so destined from the beginning
    quaff it with delight.[29]

The note of predestination found in the last line is common in
the Granth. It is a part of their Moslem heritage.

Superior to any of his verse found in the Granth is a poem that
has been preserved in manuscript form.

O Thou who art perfect, light of the Soul, the Supreme
    God, my beloved, my soul and body.
Bewitcher, Thou hast bewitched my heart; I have

---

[27] *Op. cit.,* Vol. 1, p. 362.
[28] Macauliffe, Vol. I, p. 336.
[29] *Op. cit.,* Vol. II, p. 57.

obtained understanding by pondering on Thy Word.
I am the handmaiden of my Lord. . . .

Since I began to love the joyous God, my mind hath
 been consoled by repeating His name. . . .

O my Beloved, Support of my soul, there has been none
 like unto Thee in the past,
There shall be none like Thee in the future. . . .
Thy name is my refuge.[30]

From Amar Das, let two poems suffice, one on the evil of pride:

Nanak, the gate of salvation is very narrow; only the lowly can pass
through.
How can he whose mind is inflated with pride enter therein?
When one meeteth the true Guru, pride departeth and every thing is
illumined.
The soul is emancipated for ever, and becometh easily absorbed in
God.

and one on the condition of the holy:

By serving the true *Guru* happiness and the true Name of the Lord of
excellences are obtained.
By the *Guru's* instruction man knoweth himself, and God's name is
manifested to him.
He who is true acteth truly, and obtaineth greatness near the great
One:
He praiseth and supplicateth God to whom belong body and soul.
They who praise the true Word, dwell in supreme happiness.
Though man may have practised devotion, penance, and self-restraint,
yet without the Name in his heart accursed is his life.
The Name is obtained by the Guru's instruction; the perverse perish
through worldly love.
Preserve me, O God, according to Thy will; Nanak is Thy slave.[31]

The Sikhs are true to Hinduism in their belief both in Karma
and in rebirth. Guru Amar Das sings of it thus:

[30] Macauliffe, Vol. II, p. 201, *passim*.
[31] *Op. cit.*, Vol. II, 164–165.

Through how many ages hath this soul wandered! it abideth not permanently but cometh and goeth.

When God pleaseth, He causeth it to wonder; He produceth this play of illusion.

If God be gracious, the *Guru* shall be found, the soul shall be fixed, and become absorbed *in its Creator.*

Nanak, when man's mind believeth through the mind *of the Guru,* he neither dieth nor is born again.[32]

A song from the fourth Guru, Ram Das, is reminiscent of some of the great penitential psalms.

> O God, I a sinner have taken refuge at Thy gate . . .
> O God, my demerits are great, and could never be
>   numbered.
> It is Thou who possessest merits; it is Thou who
>   art compassionate:
> It is Thou who pardonest when Thou pleasest.
> I am a sinner but thou hast saved me by
>   association with the *Guru,* who, by teaching me God's name
>   hath delivered me.
> Can any one else preserve a sinner like me—
> Thou, O *Guru,* art my father, Thou art my mother,
> Thou art my relations and companions . . .[33]

If it is through the *Guru* that one attains to salvation, then what can be the fate of those who deny the *Guru?* Ram Das expresses it thus:

> They who leave the *Guru,* who is present *with them,* shall find no entrance into God's court.
>
> Let any one go and meet those slanderers, *and he will see* their faces pale and spat upon.
>
> They who are accursed of the *Guru* are accursed of the whole world, and shall ever be vagrants.
>
> They who deny their *Guru* shall wander about groaning.
>
> Their hunger shall never depart; they shall ever shriek from its pangs.
> No one heareth what they say; they are ever dying of fear.

[32] *Op. cit.,* Vol. II, p. 207.
[33] *Op. cit.,* Vol. II, p. 294.

They cannot bear the true *Guru's* greatness; they cannot find room in this world or the next.[34]

The fifth Guru, Arjun, who collected the Granth, was himself a prolific writer. He was a profound mystic—a lover of God. He expresses his love in many ways:

> Thou art, O God, an ocean of water; I am thy fish. . . .
> In Thee is my hope, for Thee I thirst, my heart is
>   absorbed in Thee
> As a child is satisfied by drinking milk,
> As a poor man is happy on finding wealth,
> As a thirsty man is refreshed by drinking water, so
>   is my soul happy with God. . . .
> God is mine; I am His slave—[35]

For him God was everything,

> Thou art my father, Thou art my mother,
> Thou art my kinsman, Thou art my brother,
> Thou art everywhere my protector; then why should
>   I feel fear and anxiety? . . .
> Thou art my shelter, Thou art mine honour. . . .
> My heart is refreshed by singing Thy praises.[36]

After he had collected the Granth, charges were made that he had blasphemed against the religion of the Hindus and Moslems. Made a prisoner by the Emperor, he was ordered, on pain of death, to remove the supposedly objectionable passages from the Granth and to include praises of Mohammad and the Hindu gods. This he refused to do, saying, "The Granth Sahib hath been compiled to confer on men happiness and not misery in this world and the next. It is impossible to write it anew and make the omissions and insertions you require." He was submitted to the cruelest kind of torture, but remained unmoved. In the very midst of excruciating torture he is said to have exclaimed:

[34] Macauliffe, Vol. II, p. 305.
[35] *Ibid.*, Vol. III, p. 114.
[36] *Ibid.*, Vol. III, p. 118.

When very great troubles befall, and nobody
    receiveth one;
When enemies pursue and relatives flee away,
When all from whom man looked for assistance have
    fled and all succor is at an end,
If he then remember God, no hot wind shall strike him.
God is the strength of the strengthless.
He neither cometh nor goeth; He is permanent ever;
    by the *Guru's* instruction know Him as the True One.[37]

When the torture was momentarily discontinued and he was
given a chance to recant, he is said to have cried: "O fools, I shall
never fear this treatment of yours. It is all according to God's will;
wherefore the torture only affordeth me pleasure." He further repeated, in part, the following:

The egg of superstition hath burst; the mind is illumined;
The *Guru* hath cut the fetters off the feet and freed the
    captive.
My transmigration is at an end.
The heated caldron hath become cold; the *Guru*
    hath given the cooling Name. . . .
The load of my karma is removed; I am freed therefrom.
From the sea I have reached the shore.[38]

He died June, 1606, and was succeeded by his son, Har Gobind
the sixth Guru. But the Granth was complete, save for brief bits
from the ninth and the tenth Gurus.

[37] Macauliffe, *op. cit.,* p. 95.
[38] *Ibid.,* p. 93.

THE SACRED LITERATURE OF THE SIKHS
Sources for Further Reading

THE ADI GRANTH

There is no complete translation, but the following contain substantial sections of the work:

The Holy Scriptures of the Sikhs, translated by Ernest Trumpp, London, 1877, contains only four of thirty-one *Rags*. It is said not to be a very good translation, and the general tone of the work not sympathetic to the faith. It contains a substantial amount of introductory material.

Max Arthur Macauliffe. *The Sikh Religion,* its Gurus, sacred writing and authors. Six volumes, Oxford, Clarendon Press, 1909. Contains the greater part of the Granth in a translation approved by Sikh scholars. It is a highly sympathetic study of the religion in all its aspects. The translation in general is more readable than that of Trumpp. Unfortunately the translated material does not appear in the same order as in the original collection. All the poems of Nanak, e.g., are assembled together in one place—and so in the case of the other Gurus. The hymns are quite lacking in notations as to the particular sections of the Granth from which they were drawn.

John C. Archer, *The Sikhs,* Princeton University Press, 1946, has only the translation of the Japuji, or Psalms of Nanak, and a few scattered verses. A good study of the religion of the Sikhs.

Among the anthologies, there is only a very limited selection in S. E. Frost, *Sacred Writings of the World's Great Religions,* pp. 356–365.

CHAPTER IX

The Sacred Literature of the Chinese

CONFUCIANISM

In the strict sense of the word there is no *sacred* literature of Confucianism. There is no belief that the books associated with the Sage were in any sense inspired by God, and yet in every other respect they may well be considered alongside the other sacred literatures. There is a definite canon, made up of the five canonical books and four classics, often collectively called the Chinese Classics. They are the authoritative basis of religious and moral teaching for what has in the West been called Confucianism, and have actually been quite as influential on the religious and moral life of the Chinese people as has any other sacred collection upon the people for whom it is divinely inspired literature.

Much of the content of the collection has little or nothing to do with religion at all and popular religion may not have looked to it as the final authority, but higher religion in China has found in it a secure foundation, and morally it has been the predominant influence upon the Chinese people for more than two thousand years. Its ethical precepts have been the basis of moral education of most of the Chinese people for a period longer than the entire Christian era. And while the impact of the modern world has brought many changes in Chinese outlook and the Confucian books have lost their place of preëminence in the Chinese educational system, they have by no means ceased to exert a tremendous influence upon the Chinese people. What will be their fate under the Communist regime it is too early to predict with any assurance, but it is likely that Communism will be quite as much modified by Confucian ideas as will the age-old traditions based upon these ancient classics, by modern Communism.

The religion known as Confucianism is not a product of Confucius and the books attributed to him. The religion associated with his name is far older than the sixth century B.C. which saw the birth of the Sage. He was no religious prophet or innovator. It is probable rather that these books only gathered up and channeled one aspect of Chinese religion present in Confucius' day, that which has usually had official sanction; and thereby gave it a definiteness of form which enabled it to exert its influence more effectively than would otherwise have been possible.

Confucius stands in sharp contrast to Zoroaster, Buddha, Jesus, and Mohammed, indeed, to most of the great founders of religion, in that he represents no sharp break with the past. Jesus pointedly says: "Ye have heard that it was said of old time . . . but I say unto you." Confucius on the other hand remarks, "How I love the old things!" And he finds the basis for his moral teachings in what the ancients did, constantly citing the sayings and acts of certain paragons of virtue, either legendary or real, in the remote past. He took their ideas, their moral values, their religious teachings and practices, and gave them a permanent form in which they have been transmitted for centuries,[1] and been the effective moral basis, at least, of Chinese culture as a whole. Whatever China may be religiously, and sometimes she is Buddhist, sometimes Taoist, sometimes animist, or Moslem, or Christian, or all of them together, morally she has been dominantly Confucian, thanks largely to the literature

[1] Modern Chinese scholarship tends to credit Confucius with having been not merely a transmitter, but also a transformer of the ideas he inherited from the past; indeed some make him a thoroughgoing reformer, notably H. G. Creel in *Confucius, the Man and the Myth*. Others think he is at least partly correct.

which in one way or another is associated with Confucius, the Sage.

Some even regard Confucianism as not properly a religion at all, but an ethical philosophy, and there is something to be said for this point of view. In the end, however, as we shall presently see, there is, underlying Confucian ethics, as found in the classics, a profound religious basis, which justifies calling Confucianism a religion. Whether this basis was put there by Confucius himself, or has been imported into them by a later hand, it is definitely a part of the so-called Confucian classics, as they have been transmitted to the present day. We now know that there has been a great deal of editing and re-editing of these books, until it is not now always possible to say with certainty what is early and what is late.

The scholars of recent years have been applying to the Confucian classics the same rigorous, scientific, historico-literary study that the Bible has undergone, and with comparable results. Furthermore archaeological work has had at least a beginning in China, though rudely interrupted by war, and valuable finds have been made which tend to modify the conclusions of older scholars, who had only literary sources upon which to base their inquiries. Some of these results will be pointed out as we discuss the various books.

The books that have for more than a thousand years formed the fixed and unvariable canon are in outline:

    I. The Five Canonical Books
      1. The *Shu Ching,* or Book of History
      2. The *Shih Ching,* or Book of Poetry, or Odes
      3. The *I Ching,* or Book of Changes
      4. The *Li Chi,* or Book of Rites
      5. The *Ch'un Chi'iu,* or Spring and Autumn
    II. The Four Classics
      1. The *Lun Yu,* or Analects
      2. *Ta Hsueh,* or Great Learning
      3. *Chung Yung,* or Doctrine of the Mean
      4. *Meng Tzu,* or the Teaching of Mencius

The Shu Ching, or Book of History, is one of the most valuable of the Chinese classics for an understanding of the Chinese people and Confucianism. Lin Yutang says, "It is to Confucianism as the Upanishads are to Hinduism."[2] That is, it is much more than just history. It is important as revealing also the character of the people, of government to some extent, of their ancient religion, and very revealing indeed as to their moral ideals. It was held for a long time to have been the work of Confucius, then that at least Confucius edited it; but later scholars will grant little more than that Confucius knew it and used it, so that it finally became connected with his name. This fact was a powerful factor in its preservation. For when, in 213 B.C., the first Ch'in emperor, Shih Huang, burned the Confucian books, there were scholars who had committed them to memory and were able to reproduce them in writing. It is possible they did not remember all, or that they did not remember them exactly, but what they did recall, they wrote down in the newer script, known as the "Modern Script," that had been introduced during the Ch'in regime. Nor did they agree exactly among themselves in every detail. Later, manuscripts were found that had been hidden away, written in the "ancient script," one in Confucius' own house, where it had been concealed in a wall. The text of these differs from that of the Modern Script, and each includes material not found in the other. Scholars are in disagreement as to the true text. By some modern scholars the ancient script is regarded as forgery. On the other hand, there are quotations from the Book of History found in writings that recognizably go back of the time of the destruction of the books, which give support to the belief that the "Ancient Script" is reliable, or that at least it contains genuine early material. The controversy cannot be resolved here, nor for our purposes does it greatly matter whether it is all authentic. It has entered into the stream of Confucian history as it is and had its influence, rightly or wrongly, in making Confucianism what it is.[3]

The Chinese, earlier than most people, came to have an interest in history. The Tai Shih or Great Historian was recognized, to the extent of being a Minister of State, from a very early period. The

---

[2] *Wisdom of China and India*, Random House, N. Y., 1942, p. 698.
[3] The merits of the case are discussed by Lin Yutang in *The Wisdom of China and India*, pp. 700 ff.

fact that the historian of one period not infrequently quotes the records of his predecessors is clear evidence that there were written records, probably preserved in the state archives. Thus, whoever put the Book of History together as we have it, had access to sources going far back of his own time. Recent scholars are disposed to find more of legendary material in the narrative than older scholars, and are more critical in evaluating the ancient sources, basing their conclusions upon wide comparative study of the ancient literature of China. To these scholars some of the ancient emperors are only legendary, but again, for our present purposes, this is not of great concern. It may be of academic interest to know whether the virtues attributed to the redoubtable Yu can be traced so far back into history as the ancient narrative seems to carry them, but there can be no doubt that from the time of Confucius these were the virtues approved and exalted by him, and as such have played a highly significant role in Chinese life.

The Book of History is not just history in the limited sense of being a chronicle of events. It is history with a purpose, very much like that of the historical sections of the Bible, where the interest is not so much in what happened, but in the relationship of what happened to the central interest of the writers, which was definitely religious. The judgments and the character of God are revealed in Hebrew history. In the Book of History one gets the impression that the interest is primarily moral. Moral interest seems to determine to a considerable degree the selection of material included in the book. Some of the narratives do seem casual, and circumstantial, but by far the greater part can be seen to be concerned in one way or another with moral purpose. A few brief examples will reveal this.

Examining into antiquity (we find that) the Ti Yao was styled Fanghsiin. He was reverential, intelligent, accomplished, and thoughtful,—naturally and without effort. He was sincerely courteous and capable of (all) complaisance. The bright (influence of the qualities) was felt through the four quarters (of the land), and reached to (heaven) above and (earth) beneath.

He made the able and virtuous distinguished, and thence proceeded to the love of (all in) the nine classes of his kindred, who (thus) be came harmonious. He (also) regulated and polished the people (of his domain), who all became brightly intelligent. (Finally), he united and harmonized the myriad states; and so the black-haired people were transformed. The result was (universal) concord.[4]

When he sought for some one whom he could employ for a certain task his own son was suggested as highly intelligent. Emperor Yao said, "Alas! he is insincere and quarrelsome! Can he do?"

He sought someone to control the floods which in that early day (traditionally dated as in the twenty-third century B.C.) he said, "embrace the hills and overtop great heights, threatening the heavens with their flood so that the lower people groan and murmur." Kun was suggested. "Alas, how perverse he is," said the Emperor. "He is disobedient to orders, and tries to injure his peer." Nevertheless, he was tried and after nine years did not succeed.

When he sought a successor saying, "Show me someone among the illustrious, or set forth one from among the poor and the mean," they all said, "There is Shun of Yu. He is the son of a blind man. His father was obstinately unprincipled, his (step-) mother was insincere; his half brother, Hsiang, was arrogant. He has been able (however) by his filial piety to live in harmony with them, and to lead them gradually to self-government, so that they no longer proceed to great wickedness."

Said Emperor Yao, "I will try him." So he gave him two of his daughters to wife, saying to them, "Be reverent."[5]

Shun became emperor and chose his ministers wisely. Floods plagued the land. Said Shun, "Find me the man who shall cause the rivers to flow in their appointed channels and abate these floods which devastate my people's country." At once they suggested Lord Yu and he was appointed Surveyor General. His industry and attention to his task were notable.

He went forth upon his marriage morn, nor tarried in dalliance, but having received the commands of his emperor he straightway sought to fulfill them. He divided the country into nine provinces, partitioning the land and fixing the boundaries by the high hills and great rivers.

[4] *Sacred Books of the East,* Vol. III, p. 32. Translation of James Legge.
[5] *Sacred Books of the East,* Vol. 3, pp. 34–36, *passim.*

Ascending the hills he filled the timber; and making dams, bridges and pontoons, he widened and deepened the canals and drained off the marshes into the rivers, conducting them into the Yang-tze and the Ho. Three times in the course of his survey he passed the door of his own dwelling and heard the voice of his bride and the prattle of his infant son, but yet he did not enter. Thus after eight years he completed his task, and presented his staff to the emperor.[6]

Shun, like his predecessors, sought as his successor not one of his own family but the ablest man in his realm. He approached Yu thus: "Come, you Yu. I have occupied my place for thirty and three years. I am between ninety and a hundred years old, and the laborious duties weary me. Do you, eschewing all indolence, take the leading of my people." Yu replied, "My virtue is not equal (to the position) and the people will not repose in me, (but there is) Kao-yao with vigorous activity, sowing abroad his virtue, which has descended on the black-haired people, till they cherish him in their heart. O, Ti, think of him."

But Shun persisted, "You are without any prideful assumption, but no one under heaven can contest with you the palm of ability; you make no boasting, but no one under heaven can contest with you the palm of merit. I see how great is your virtue, how admirable your vast achievements. The determinate appointment of Heaven rests on your person; you must eventually ascend the throne of the great sovereign."[7] At last Yu accepted and became emperor. With him the succession became hereditary.

There are many speeches and counsels recorded as given by kings to ministers and people and by counsellors to kings. One of the kings charged his prime minister as follows:

"Morning and evening present your instructions to aid my virtue. Suppose me a weapon of steel, I will use you for a whetstone. Suppose me crossing a great stream; I will use you for a boat with its oars. Suppose me in a year of great drought; I will use you as a copious rain. Open your mind and enrich my mind. (Be you) like medicine, which must distress the patient in order to cure his sick-

[6] *Book of History*, p. 27, translation of W. Gorn Old, Wisdom of East Series.
[7] *Sacred Books of the East*, Vol. 3, pp. 48–49, *passim*.

ness. Think me as one walking barefoot, whose feet are sure to be wounded if he do not see the ground."[8]

Part of an announcement of T'ang on his return from conquering the last of the Hsia dynasty sets forth the idea that he rules by mandate from Heaven.

The way of Heaven is to bless the good and make the bad miserable. It sent down calamities on the (House of) Hsia to make manifest its guilt. Therefore I, the little child, charged with the decree of Heaven and its bright terrors, did not dare to forgive the criminal . . . and the criminal has been degraded and subjected. What Heaven appoints is without error. . . .

It is given to me the One man to secure the harmony and tranquillity of your states and clans . . . do not, ye princes, follow lawless ways; make no approach to insolence and dissoluteness; let every one be careful to keep his statutes; so that we may receive the favor of Heaven. The good in you I will not dare to keep concealed; and for the evil in me I will not dare to forgive myself. I will examine these things in harmony with the mind of God. When guilt is found anywhere in you who occupy the myriad regions, let it rest on me, the One man. When guilt is found in me, the One man; it shall not attach to you who occupy the myriad regions. Oh! let us attain to be sincere in these things, and so we shall likewise have a (happy) consummation.[9]

Not a few of the selected pieces are for the purpose of illustrating the folly of evil practices and the certainty of retribution upon evildoers. There was, for example, Wu-Yih, who was unprincipled and profane.

"He made images of the gods and caused the people to play at chess with them. He also made trial of his powers therein, and when he lost the game, he forthwith abused the gods for their incompetence. Moreover he made bladders to be filled with blood and used them for flying targets which sport he denominated 'shooting the heavens.'

"For this cause he was smitten from Heaven while hunting in the Valley of Wei."

[8] *Sacred Books of the East*, Vol. 3, p. 114.
[9] *Id.*, pp. 90–91, *passim.*

Also there was Chow-Sin, King of Yiu. He was a "man of great strength and ungodly nature. Those who reproved him he slew without remorse, and those who flattered him he advanced. He gave himself over to luxury and extravagance and his patronage to women without virtue. . . . He became tyrannical and despotic, regarding himself in all respects as a god.

"When he first made chop-sticks of ivory, the wise Ki-tze rebuked him saying: 'Now that you make chop-sticks of ivory you will shortly be making crystal cups. Then you will be eating the paws of bears and the wombs of leopards. These and other things in like measure you will want in great abundance. Surely the country will soon become impoverished.'"

He took a wife, Ta-ki, who exercised great influence upon him. "Whomsoever she favored, him did the emperor advance, and whomsoever she hated, him did the emperor slay. . . . For her delight he built a gallery . . . with chambers and doors of precious stones . . . a thousand cubits high and half a *li* in length (about seven hundred feet long). Seven years of heavy taxation and oppression were endured by the people during the building . . . so that it might be filled with gold and grain.

"And the black-haired people trembled with rage and vexation.

"Then Ta-ki said, 'Lord, the executions are too rare, the punishments are too simple. The throne is thereby endangered.'

"She therefore invented the trial by fire, the hot brazen pillar or climbing pole, and the punishment of the roasting pit. And the people repined with shuddering."

When reproved for his tyranny he only slew his accusers. One reproved him thus: "The people have withdrawn their favor and Heaven hath turned its face away because of your transgressions. Amend your ways before you become the ruin of your country, or in the days to come the people will only mention your name to pronounce an anathema."

But retribution only delayed. In the end he was undone by one of the men he had thrown in prison. By a bit of clever strategy the prisoner secured his release, and being Duke of Chow, he governed his realm so wisely that his fame spread abroad and forty-two states accepted his government. He himself died leaving to his son, Fa, this wise counsel: "My son, look for that which is good and be not slow to practice it. When opportunity serves, do not hesitate. Exterminate evil, and let it not abide. In these three points do virtue and goodness consist." To the son, Fa, "was given the decree of Heaven to cut off and destroy the tyrant emperor, who upon being defeated in the desert was bereft of his senses and fled to Lu-tai (the Stag Gallery) where he adorned himself in jewels and precious stones and burned himself to death."

So evil destroys itself.[10]

The Shih Ching, or Book of Odes or the Book of Poetry, was for a long time thought to be an anthology of old Chinese poetry compiled by Confucius. But even James Legge, one of the older Chinese scholars, believed that Confucius' contribution to the Odes lay only in the reformation in the music by which each ode was accompanied. All that is completely certain is that Confucius knew the Odes; that he esteemed them highly, and made them a definite object of study. It was his approval of them, and the subsequent linking of them with his name which assured their survival. There is no doubt that he was fond of poetry, and that he referred to this particular collection many times in his reported sayings. A disciple once remarked to Confucius' son that he must surely have heard from his father things not disclosed to the others. But the son replied, "No, once when he was standing in the courtyard alone and I passed by he suddenly asked, 'Have you studied the Songs?' I

[10] From the translation of W. Gorn Old, *The Book of History,* Wisdom of the East Series, John Murray, London, 1918, pp. 55–63, *passim.*

The entire text of the Book of History is printed and translated in James Legge, *Chinese Classics,* Vol. III. It is also to be found entire in *The Sacred Books of the East,* Vol. III.

Lin Yutang, *Wisdom of China and India,* has a good selection of what he chooses to call *Documents of Chinese Democracy,* pp. 707–742, and a good introduction.

W. Gorn Old, *Book of History,* Wisdom of the East Series, has a brief introduction and a selection of about fifty pages which disclose the nature of the book.

Lewis Browne, *The World's Great Scriptures,* pp. 211–222, has a very brief selection.

replied that I had not. Then said he, 'If you do not study the Odes you will not be fit to converse with.' "[11] On another occasion the Sage likened a man who did not know the first two books of the Odes to one who had his face pressed against a wall.[12]

The book consists of a total of three hundred and five poems of which only forty are distinctly religious, being chiefly odes for the temple and the altar. Thirty-one are laudatory poems for use at court and feudal festivals, seventy-four are festive songs of many kinds, and the remainder, more than half, are what may be called songs of the people. There is in the book the greatest variety of poetic forms, ballads, hymns, narrative poems, dirges, prayers, odes, lyrics; and the range of subjects is wide. There are poems of home, of love, of loneliness, political, festive, martial, ethical, didactic, ritual. Some are melancholy, some serious and profound, but some are distinctly humorous. A great variety of moods is evoked by them: patriotism, parental love, romantic love, a deep sense of responsibility, humility, pride, courage, determination. In short, they pretty well run the gamut of human interest. It is for this reason doubtless that the book lives, for even the great name of the Sage could hardly have kept it alive for so many centuries, had it not made a genuine appeal to human interest and expressed much of what humanity longs to express but cannot do unaided.

The poetry of the Odes differs greatly from the modern Chinese poetry in form. It is rhymed verse and generally the line contains four characters. Obviously it must be read in translation by people of the West, and Chinese verse is exceedingly difficult to translate. It is interesting to read the same poem translated by different persons. Since the Chinese language is very different from our European speech, has no auxiliary verbs and is not inflected, much has to be supplied by the translator which is not explicitly to be found in the original. Hence the surprising differences in what comes out in English. An example of this will be illuminating, four translations of the same identical stanza:

[11] *Analects*, 16:13.
[12] 17:10.

I

Kwan kwan go the ospreys
On the islet in the river
The modest, retiring, virtuous young lady
For our prince a good mate she.[13]

II

As the ospreys woo
On the river ait (island)
So the graceful lass
Has her manly mate.[14]

III

They sent me to gather the cresses which lie
And sway on the stream as it glances by,
That a fitting welcome we might provide,
For our prince's modest and virtuous bride.[15]

IV

Hark from the islet in the stream the voice
Of the fish hawks that o'er their nests rejoice
From them our thoughts to that young lady go
Modest and virtuous, loth herself to show.
Where could be found to share our prince's state
So fair, so virtuous, and so fit a mate?[16]

Whether the poem has suffered or been made better by the translator, who can tell—if he knows no Chinese? Some of the English titles are interesting. "O fell not that sweet pear tree," "O Sweet Maiden, so fair and retiring," "Behold, a rat," "My worthy Ching, I pray," "The widow," "Anxiety of a young lady to get married,"

[13] J. Legge translator, *Chinese Classics*, Vol. 4, Pt. 1, p. 1, 5 vols., Oxford University Press.
[14] *Sacred Books and Literature of the East*, Vol. 11, p. 124, no indication of translator.
[15] C. Allen.
[16] J. Legge, *The She King* or *The Book of Ancient Poetry*, Truebner and Co., London, 1876, p. 59. For still another translation see Arthur Waley, *The Book of Songs*, Allen and Unwin, London, 1937.

etc. Only a very few poems can be included here. "The Pear Tree" has something of a familiar ring about it. We give only the first stanza.

> The Pear tree, woodman spare,
> Touch not a single bough,
> Shao's chief once rested there
> Leave it uninjured now.[17]

Or in another translation:

> This shade bestowing pear tree thou
> Hurt not, nor lay its leafage low:
> Beneath it slept the Duke of Shaou.[18]

A brief poem on Clothes or Robes carries a philosophy that might well commend itself to Western peoples who are much troubled about matters of dress:

> I have no clothes at all, you declare!
> You are wrong: I have plenty, you see,
> They may not be so rich or so rare
> As your own, but they're excellent wear,
> And warm, and do nicely for me.[19]

A romantic bit celebrates the young lady who kept her young man waiting—again we give but the first stanza:

> O sweet maiden, so fair and retiring,
> At the corner I'm waiting for you
> And I'm scratching my head, and inquiring
> What on earth it were best I should do.

The young lady for whom time is passing all too rapidly and who is threatened with being left an old maid voices her anxiety thus:

> The plums are ripening quickly;
> Nay, some are falling too,
> 'Tis surely time for suitors
> To come to me and woo.

[17] *Sacred Books and Literature of the East*, Vol. 11, p. 136.
[18] L. Cranmer-Byng, *Confucius—The Odes*, p. 34.
[19] *Sacred Books and Literature of the East*, Vol. 11, p. 146.

> See, more and more are falling
> From off the parent tree
> Why don't the men come forward
> To win a maid like me?
>
> At length upon the plum tree
> No fruit can be espied
> Yet no one comes to woo me
> Or bid me be his bride.[20]

A frequent note in Chinese poetry, ancient and modern, is the loneliness of the wife whose husband is absent on some distant duty of war, or peace.

1

> My noble husband has gone away
>   To fight for his king, and the country's weal.
> No moment he snatches to rest or stay,
>   No toil nor danger can quench his zeal.

2

> I list to the distant thunder's roar
>   To the south of the mountains across the plain;
> And wish that my husband may come once more
>   To gladden his home and his wife again.[21]

Also the plaintive note of the widow in her loneliness is heard:

THE WIDOW

1

> The trailing creepers shroud the thorns in gloom,
>   The wild vines spreading o'er the wasted plains
> But mock my sorrow, for they hide the tomb
>   Which holds my lord's remains.

2

> My husband, oh, the night when first we met,
>   My head lay on the pillow at his side.

[20] *Sacred Books and Literature of the East,* Vol. 11, pp. 138–139.
[21] *Sacred Books and Literature of the East,* Vol. 11, p. 138.

They threw the splendid broidered coverlet
O'er bridegroom and his bride.

3

By me must now long days of summer heat,
    Long winter nights, in loneliness be passed
But though I live a hundred years, we'll meet
    Within the grave at last.[22]

The myriad flies buzzing about lead the poet to reflect on other pests of a political sort.

THE FLIES

1

The blue flies float on the summer air,
They are humming and buzzing everywhere
They pollute each fence, and our trees infest,
Till no spot is clear of this noisome pest.

2

Some men I know like these loathsome flies,
Who infest the realm with their slanderous lies.
Their hatred and spite they will not restrain,
So confusion, malice, and mischief reign.

3

Ah, be not careless, dear Lord, be wise,
And crush these men, as we crush the flies;
Lest the friendship between old friends should fail,
And contentious strife in its stead prevail.[23]

Typical of a number of poems descriptive of the common work-a-day life of the Chinese farmer is this. One gets a pretty good idea from it of a number of aspects of the farmer's life, how he works, what he eats, what he wears, etc.

[22] *Sacred Books and Literature of the East*, Vol. 11, p. 147.
[23] *Ibid.*, p. 174–175.

THE LËANG SZE

With sharp and well-shaped glittering share,
The toilers turn, with patient care,
The southern acres to prepare.

The different kinds of grain they sow.
Each seed, though hid the earth below,
Its form of life will quickly show.

Behold their wives and children there!
These the cooked millet to them bear,
Carried in baskets round and square.

In light splint hats their hoes they speed,
Clearing the ground for fruitful seed,
And rooting out the noisome weed.

The weeds, uprooted, die away,
And feed the ground by their decay.
The millets grow from day to day.

And now the golden stalks and tall
Before the reapers, rustling, fall.
Straightway they're built up like a wall.

High as a wall the sheaves are placed,
Like comb-teeth close, and interlaced.
Anon the grain is stored in haste.

Hundreds of houses hold the store;
The wives and children fret no more;
The labours of the year are o'er.

This black-lipped tawny bull we slay,
Whose horns the well-known curve display,
The rites of husbandry to pay.

> Thus to the future hand we down
> These rites long held in high renown,
> Glad the ancestral ways to own.[24]

Among the religious poems is an ode of Thanksgiving for a plentiful year.

THE FUNG NËEN

> The plenteous ear has given us large supply
> Of rice and millet, and our granaries high
> Hardly suffice the produce to contain,—
> Millions of measures of the garnered grain!
> From this distilled, shall spirits, strong and sweet,
> Our sires and mothers with their fragrance greet,
> When to their shrines each season we repair;
> And in all other rites their part shall bear.
> Blessings of every kind our land shall crown;—
> And all the Spirits our devotion own![25]

And finally, for space is all too limited, here is the prayer of an emperor, which certainly strikes an authentic note of humility as he faces the responsibilities of empire.

THE PRAYER OF THE EMPEROR CHING—I

> Let me be reverent, be reverent,
> Even as the way of Heaven is evident,
> And its appointment easy is to mar.
>
> Let me not say, "It is too high above,"
> Above us and below us doth it move,
> And daily watches wheresoe'er we are.
>
> It is but as a little child I ask,
> Without intelligence to do my task,
> Yet learning, month by month, and day by day,
>
> I will hold fast some gleams of knowledge bright.
> Help me to bear my heavy burden right,
> And show me how to walk in wisdom's way.[26]

---

[24] James Legge, *The She King* or *The Book of Ancient Poetry*, p. 369.
[25] *Ibid.*, pp. 358–359.
[26] L. Cranmer-Byng, *Confucius—The Odes*, J. Murray, London, 1927, p. 25.

THE PRAYER OF THE EMPEROR CHING—II

Even as a little helpless child am I,
On whom hath fallen the perplexed affairs
Of this unsettled state. High loneliness
And sorrow are my portion. Thou great Father,
Thou kingly pattern of parental awe,
Whose mind for ever in the courts beheld,
Roaming, the royal image of thy sire,
Night long and day long, I—the little child—
Will so be reverent.

    O ye great kings!
Your crowned successor crowns you in his heart.
Live unforgotten. Here, upon the verge
Of the momentous years, I pause and trace
The shining footsteps of my forefathers,
And the far distant goal that drew them on—
Too distant for my range. Howe'er resolved
I may go forward. Lo! a thousand tracks
Cause me to swerve aside. A little child—
Only a little child—I am too frail
To cope with the anxieties of state
And cares of king-craft. Yet I will ascend
Into my Father's room, and through the courts
Below, for ever seeking, I will pass,
To brush the skirts of inspiration
And touch the sleeves of memory.

    O great
And gracious Father, hear and condescend
To guard, to cherish, to enlighten me.[27]

The I Ching, or Book of Changes is a curious book. It is a book of divination and quite unintelligible to people who do not take stock in the occult. One is amazed to read that Confucius once said that if he had fifty more years to live he would give half of it to the

[27] *Ibid.,* pp. 26–27.

study of the I Ching. Yet the book has been the object of intense interest to many of the Chinese sages.

The legendary story of its origin is that one of the emperors on an occasion was down by the river. There he saw a tortoise with some curious markings on his back. Having them copied he found that they formed eight trigrams or various arrangements of three broken and unbroken lines, thus three unbroken lines⸺⸺; the two top lines unbroken, the lowest broken, and so on. There are eight possible combinations. To each of these he gave a name, making it the symbol of some natural object and some moral quality consistent with that natural object. And these became means of divination. Later the trigrams became hexagrams of which sixty-four exist, and to each was given a name and qualities.

These mysterious signs, open to an infinite number of interpretations, have been of perennial interest to the type of mind that revels in obscure symbolism. Only in recent years a book was published in America in which the authors claim that they have discovered the key to its interpretation and that they have found a degree of correlation with the Bible. They declare: "assuredly in the fulness of time, it, the I Ching, will take its rightful place as a World Scripture, a presentment of vital and undying truth."[28] As an example of the kind of a book it is we include here what is said about the first, called the Ch'ien Hexagram. It is made up of six unbroken lines:

I. The Ch'ien Hexagram

Explanation of the entire figure by King Wan. *Ch'ien* represents what is great and originating, penetrating, advantageous, correct and firm.

Explanation of the separate lines by the Duke of Chou:

1. In the first or (lowest line) undivided, we see its subject as the dragon lying hid (in the deep). It is not the time for active doing.

[28] G. Mears and L. E. Mears, *Creative Energy*, E. P. Dutton and Co., N. Y., 1932.

2. In the second line, undivided, (we see its subject as) the dragon appearing in the field. It will be advantageous to meet with the great man.

3. In the third line, undivided, we see its subject as the superior man active and vigilant all the day, and in the evening still careful, and apprehensive. (The position) is dangerous but there will be no mistake.

4. In the fourth line, undivided, (we see its subject) as the dragon looking) as if he were leaping up, but still in the deep. There will be no mistake.

5. In the fifth line, undivided, (we see its subject as) the dragon on the wing in the sky. It will be advantageous to meet the great man.

6. In the sixth or topmost line, undivided, (we see its subject as) the dragon exceeding the proper limits. There will be occasion for repentance.

7. The lines of this hexagram are all strong and undivided, as appears from) the use of the number nine. If the host of dragons thus appearing were to divest themselves of their heads, there would be good fortune.[29]

The Li Chi, or Book of Rites, is called by James Legge, the translator, "a collection of treatises on the rules of propriety or ceremonial usages." It is made up of forty-six books. Something of the nature of the collection may be seen in the titles of some of the books. The first is a "Summary of the Rules of Propriety."

It is by no means a summary of all the rules of propriety, for that would be a summary of the entire book. It does, however, deal with important aspects of *propriety,* a word which probably more than any other lies at the center of Confucian teaching. "A life ordered in harmony with it would realize the highest Chinese ideal, and surely a very high ideal, of human character," writes James Legge.[30] It is one of four primary human qualities which belong as naturally to men as do their limbs according to Mencius. The others are benevolence (jen), righteousness (i), and understanding (Chih). To do the proper thing on the proper occasion is the mark of the "superior man," or as both Arthur Waley and Lin Yutang translate it, the gentleman.

Other books are: T'an Kung, which deals in three parts chiefly

[29] *Sacred Books of the East,* Vol. 16, pp. 57–58.
[30] *Sacred Books of the East,* Vol. 27, p. 10.

with Mourning Rites. It contains also a number of historical incidents which involve Confucius and so throw additional light upon
the master, though most scholars hold that they are only legendary.
Book III deals with "Royal Regulations," which purport to be a
report of regulations of early kings for the behavior of feudal nobles,
other officers, their slaves, their sacrifices, and their care for the
aged. Book IV is called the "Proceedings of Government in the
Different Months"; Book X, "The Pattern of the Family"; Book
XIV, "The Great Treatise"; treating of the greatest sacrifice, the
greatest instance of filial piety, the greatest principle of regulation of
the family, etc.; Book XVI, "Record of Studies," dealing with education; Book XVII, "Record of Music"; Book XX, "Laws or Rules of
Sacrifice." In Book X, "Pattern of the Family," there are directions
as to food which reveal the variety available, presumably to the
well-to-do:

21. Of grain food, there was millet, the glutinous rice, rice, maize, the
white millet, and the yellow maize, cut when ripe, or when green.

Of prepared meats, there were beef soup, mutton soup, pork soup,
and roast beef; pickle slices of beef, pickle and minced beef; roast mutton, slices of mutton, pickle, and roast pork; pickle, slices of pork,
mustard sauce, and minced fish; pheasant, hare, quail, and partridge.

23. For relishes, snail-juice, and a condiment of the broad-leaved
water-squash were used with pheasant soup, a condiment of wheat with
soups and dried slices of fowl; broken glutinous rice with dog soup and
hare soup; the rice-balls mixed with these soups had no smart-weed in
them.

A suckling-pig was stewed, wrapped up in sonchus leaves and stuffed
with smart-weed; a fowl, with the same stuffing, and along with pickle
sauce; a fish, with the same stuffing and egg sauce; a tortoise, with the
same stuffing and pickle sauce.

For meat spiced and dried they placed the brine of ants; for soup
made of sliced meat, that of hare; for a ragout of elk, that of fish; for
minced fish, mustard sauce; for raw elk flesh, pickle sauce; for preserved
peaches and plums, egg-like suet.

24. . . . In all attempering ingredients, sour predominated in the
spring; bitter, in the summer; acrid, in the autumn; and salt, in the
winter:—with the due proportioning of the unctuous and sweet.[31]

[31] *Sacred Books of the East,* Vol. XXVII, Book X, pp. 459–461.

Some interesting directions as to filial piety, the duties of sons to parents are also included in the tenth book:

Sons, in serving their parents, on the first crowing of the cock, should all wash their hands and rinse their mouths, comb their hair, draw over it the covering of silk, fix this with the hair-pin, bind the hair at the roots with the fillet, brush the dust from that which is left free, and then put on their caps, leaving the ends of the strings hanging down. They should then put on their squarely made black jackets, knee-covers, and girdles, fixing in the last their tablets. From the left and right of the girdle they should hang their articles for use:—on the left side, the duster and hand-kerchief, the knife and whetstone, the small spike, and the metal speculum for getting fire from the sun; on the right, the archer's thimble for the thumb and the armlet, the tube for writing instruments, the knife-case, the larger spike, and the borer for getting fire from wood. They should put on their leggings, and adjust their shoe-strings.[32]

4. Thus dressed, they should go to their parents and parents-in-law. On getting to where they are, with bated breath and gentle voice, they should ask if their clothes are (too) warm or (too) cold, whether they are ill or pained, or uncomfortable in any part; and if they be so, they should proceed reverently to stroke and scratch the place. They should in the same way, going before or following after, help and support their parents in quitting or entering (the apartment). In bringing in the basin for them to wash, the younger will carry the stand and the elder the water; they will beg to be allowed to pour out the water, and when the washing is concluded, they will hand the towel. They will ask whether they want anything, and then respectfully bring it. All this they will do with an appearance of pleasure to make their parents feel at ease. (They should bring) gruel, thick or thin, spirits or must, soup with vege-tables, beans, wheat, spinach, rice millet, maize, and glutinous millet,—whatever they wish, in fact; with dates, chestnuts, sugar and honey, to sweeten their dishes; with the ordinary or the large-leaved violets, leaves of elm-trees, fresh or dry, and the most soothing rice-water to lubricate them; and with fat and oil to enrich them. The parents will be sure to taste them, and when they have done so, the young people should with-draw.[33]

11. When with their parents, (sons and their wives), when ordered to do anything, should immediately respond and reverently proceed to

[32] *Sacred Books of the East,* Book X, Sec. 1, 2, p. 449.
[33] *Sacred Books of the East,* Vol. XXVII, Book X, Sec. 14, pp. 450–451.

do it. In going forwards or backwards, or turning round, they should be careful and grave; while going out or coming in, while bowing or walking, they should not presume to eructate, sneeze, or cough, to yawn or stretch themselves, to stand on one foot, or to lean against anything or to look askance. They should not dare to spit or snivel, nor, if it be cold, to put on more clothes, nor, if they itch anywhere, to scratch themselves.[34]

Book XXVIII, sometimes translated as the Doctrine of the Mean, which Legge says "gives the best account of the Confucian philosophy and morals," and Book XXXIX, the "Great Learning," are now usually published as separate books and considered as among the "Four Books" which, in addition to the "Five Classics," constitute the generally accepted Confucian canon. These will be discussed later.

The Book of Rites is not the work of Confucius, at least as we have it today. The very fact that it is called a *Chi* or "record" rather than a *Ching* or "text" is evidence that the orthodox do not regard it as of Confucian origin, for they reserve that term only for books which they believe were by Confucius. It is rather a compilation from documents purporting to come from Confucius and his followers, made late in the pre-Christian era, and edited and re-edited until it reached its present form near the end of the second century A.D. But it has all the force of Confucius' teaching, since it is believed to derive ultimately from him, and has been authoritative for the regulation of many phases of Chinese life down to the modern period. Under the stress of modern life, and the influx of foreign influences it has lost much of its former compelling influence over the lives of the Chinese people.

Two other similar works, the Chan Li, and the I Li, have also been important in controlling Chinese practices. The Chou Li, said to be older than the Li Ki, was regarded as a sixth classic, until the Ming dynasty in the fourteenth century. It dealt more specifically with political matters. The I Li has to do with the conduct of everyday life. It is of more recent origin than the other two and has not been as authoritative as either of the other two.

Spring and Autumn, the last of the "Five Classics," is the only

[34] *Op. cit.*, pp. 449–454, *passim.*

book of the five which may confidently be assigned to the authorship of Confucius. And it turns out to be quite the least important
of the lot. The title itself is deceptive, and one wonders as he reads
why it was chosen. Probably its only significance is that it was the
annals of the state of Lu of the four seasons, and came to be called
Spring and Autumn for short. There are numerous references to
nothing more than the change of season, thus "It was autumn, the
seventh month." "It was winter, the tenth month." Later when the
book had come to be thought of as of great moral significance, probably just because it was the work of Confucius, some said that it
was so called because "its commendations are like life-giving spring
and its censures are withering like the autumn."[35]

Confucius is reported to have said of the book that it was the
work by which men would remember and commend him. Mencius
rated it very highly. Said he: "Confucius completed the Spring
and Autumn and rebellious ministers and bad sons were struck with
terror." On reading it one wonders why, for it seems on the surface
to be nothing more nor less than a bare catalogue of events which
occurred in Confucius' native state of Lu, compiled by the Master from the State Annals. It covers the period 722–484 B.C., or from
more or less the end of the Book of History to nearly the end of
Confucius' own lifetime. It follows through the period of rule of
the successive dukes who headed the state and gives by years, within
each administration, the list of events which were considered of
sufficient importance to note. Here, for example, is the record of the
thirteenth year of Duke Hwan.

1. In his thirteenth year in spring in the second month the duke had
a meeting with the marquis of Ke and the earl of Ch'ing; and on Ke-sze
they fought with the marquis of Tse, the duke of Sung, the marquis of
Wei, and an officer of Yen, . . .
2. In the third month there was the burial of duke Seuen of Wei.
3. In summer there were great floods.
4. It was autumn, the seventh month.
5. It was winter, the tenth month.[36]

[35] Legge, *Chinese Classics*, V, Part 2, p. 7.
[36] *Op. cit.*, V, Part 1, p. 60.

It is neither inspired nor inspiring writing. But in time, as Confucius acquired prestige and authority, it must have been assumed that there was more to it than met the eye. So commentators began to find in the barren record profound meanings. If this seems strange let Western readers reflect on what commentators on the Bible have found in some similar barren passages, or what preachers have been able to get out of a simple historical statement like "and Jesus went up to Jerusalem."

It is the commentators who have given life to the annals; taking the bare statements of fact, they have woven about them a mass of detailed exposition, including history, legend, and homily, which is not without interest or significance. The great commentary, that of Tso, known as the Tso Chuen, is by no means uninteresting, and its value as an aid to the study of Chinese history is great. Often moral discourses are included which are of the Confucian order, so that the book seems to have importance in the teaching of morals as well as history. For example, Book I, IV, has this item:

The Duke of Sung, the marquis of Ch'in, an army of Ts'ae and an army of Wei invaded Ch'ing.

As part of the lengthy comment on the verse this homily on the use of violence appears:

Your servant has heard that the people may be made well affected by virtue: I have not heard that they may be made so by violence. To use violence with that in view, is like trying to put silk in order and only ravelling it. Chow-yu relies on his military force and can do cruel things, for his military likings the multitude will not cleave to him; and for his cruelties his relatives will not. With the multitude rebellious and his friends leaving him, it will be difficult for him to be successful. Military weapons are like fire; if you don't lay the fire aside it will burn yourself. Chow-yu murdered his prince, and he uses his people oppressively, thus not making excellent virtue his pursuit; he will certainly not escape calamity.[37]

Or again the occurrence of a great drought furnished the occasion of a condemnation of witch-burning. In Book V, year XXI it is said:

[37] Legge, *Chinese Classics*, Vol. V, Part 1, pp. 15, 16.

"In summer, there was great drought." The Tso-Chuen comments thus. The duke wished in consequence of the drought to burn a witch, and a person much emaciated, Ts'ang Wau-Chung said to him, "That is not proper preparation in a time of drought. Put in good repair your walls, the inner and the outer; lessen your food; be sparing in all your expenditures. Be in earnest to be economical and encourage people to help one another; this is the most important preparation. What have the witch and the emaciated person to do with the matter? If Heaven wish to put them to death, it had better not have given them life. If they can really produce drought, to burn them will increase the calamity." The duke followed his advice and that year the scarcity was not very great.[38]

The mention of the flood in the 13th year of Duke Hwan, given above, is commented upon by another commentator, Wang Paou, thus:

Nine times is the calamity of floods recorded in the Ch'un Ch'iu; twice in the time of Hwan, and thrice in the time of Chwang. Of the nine calamities five of them occurred in the days of the father and his son. May we conclude that they were in retribution to the father for his wickedness accumulated and unrepented of, and to the son for allowing his father's wrong to go unavenged? So speculate Chinese scholars.[39]

The fact that the *Spring and Autumn* falls so far short of what might be expected from Confucius' own estimate of the work, and that of Mencius, has led some to the belief that the book, now known under that name, is not at all the book to which Confucius or Mencius referred. If it is not, where is the book? The answer given is that it was really destroyed by Emperor Shih Hwang in 213 B.C., in the general attempt to destroy the Confucian books, and that the book of annals which was somehow preserved came to bear the name of the real document, *Spring and Autumn*. This seems not to be a wholly unplausible conjecture, but we shall probably never know certainly.

The Lun Yu, variously translated, the Analects, or the sayings, or Aphorisms of Confucius, were not of course written or collected by the sage himself. It rather consists, chiefly, of the sayings of the

[38] *Id.*, pp. 179–180.
[39] Legge, *op. cit.*, Vol. 5, Part 1, p. 61.

Master which his disciples remembered, and some description of him and his characteristic behavior. The book thus resembles the Gospels of the New Testament. More is to be learned directly concerning Confucius from this source than from any other. But it is in no sense a biography of Confucius, much less so indeed than the gospels are of Jesus. Most of the sayings, as recorded, are isolated utterances, with little or no indication as to whom spoken, or under what circumstances, though in some cases both the persons and the situation under which the words were uttered are given. They are grouped into twenty books, but the books are seldom a unit, rather each is a collection of miscellaneous sayings of the Sage. Lin Yutang wonders that no Chinese writer has undertaken to regroup the related sayings in some more or less topical fashion. This he himself has done in his *Wisdom of Confucius* under such headings as "Description of Confucius by Himself and Others," "The Emotional and Artistic Life of Confucius," "The Conversational Style"; "Wit and Wisdom," "The Superior Man and the Inferior Man" etc. But he adds to the sayings taken from the *Analects* others taken from certain chapters of the Li Chi, which differ but little from the *Analects,* unfortunately, without indicating which ones. Also he includes not more than a fourth of the whole collection.

Modern scholars differ considerably in their estimate of the authenticity of these sayings. Arthur Waley says, "I think we are justified in supposing that the book does not contain many authentic sayings, and possibly none at all."[40] Creel, on the other hand, says that while all scholars agree that some parts of the book are open to question, they nevertheless agree that "the book in general is our best single source for Confucius."[41] He regards it as an early book, on the basis of internal evidence; Confucius has not yet become the legendary figure of later Chinese thought. He is still a man of doubts and weaknesses as well as struggle. Also it contains statements about the Sage which Confucius might have preferred not to have mentioned. These would seem to be out of place in an un-

---

[40] *The Analects of Confucius,* p. 25.
[41] H. G. Creel, *Confucius, the Man and the Myth,* John Day Co., N. Y., 1949.

doubtedly Confucian book, if there were no basis in fact for them. It was probably not the collection of his immediate disciples, but of a generation farther removed from his own time, made perhaps by disciples of some Confucian followers. Legge thinks it may have appeared near the end of the fifth or the beginning of the fourth century B.C. Both Creel and Waley agree that the oldest stratum is to be found within the first nine books. Book X, which many regard as descriptive of Confucius and so the most revealing of all the Confucian literature as to his personal characteristics, is held by Waley to be a compilation of old maxims on ritual. The last five books seem to have been the latest additions to the collection, but, even so, may contain genuine early material. Some of the sayings herein included are really hostile to Confucian ideas as set forth in other portions of the book.

But whether early or late, authentic or not, traditionally, it has come to be accepted as the most basic of the Confucian books, and the Confucius recognized by the greater number of the Chinese is precisely the Confucius of the *Analects*.

It is not a book to sit down and read from cover to cover, any more than is the Book of Proverbs. Lin Yutang compares it to *Bartlett's Quotations*. He quotes the great Chinese philosopher, Chu Hsi, on the way to read the *Analects*. "Just take one or two sections a day. Never mind whether the passage is difficult or easy to understand, or whether it is a profound passage or not. Just read on from the beginning of the section, and if you don't get the meaning by thinking, then read again. Turn it back and forth and try to get the flavor. Thus, after a long while you will understand what is in it."[42]

A few examples, chosen more or less at random will give something of the flavor of the book.

At fifteen I had my mind bent on learning. At thirty, I stood firm. At forty I had no doubts. At fifty, I knew the decrees of Heaven. At sixty, my ear was an obedient organ for the reception of truth. At seventy I could follow what my heart desired (II, 4).

[42] *The Wisdom of Confucius*, p. 157.

Tsze Kung asked what constituted the superior man. The Master said, "He acts before he speaks, and afterwards speaks according to his actions" (II, 13).

The Master said, "If the will be set on virtue, there will be no practice of wickedness" (IV, 4).

The mind of the superior man is conversant with righteousness; the mind of the mean man is conversant with gain (IV, 16).

The cautious seldom err (IV, 23).

The superior man wishes to be slow in his speech and earnest in his conduct (IV, 24).

Tsze Kung said, "What I do not wish men to do to me, I also wish not to do to men." The Master said, "Tsze, you have not attained to that" (V, 11).

The Master said, "In a hamlet of ten families there may be found one honorable and sincere as I am, but not so fond of learning" (V, 27).

When a prince's personal conduct is correct, his government is effective without issuing of orders. If his personal conduct is not correct, he may issue orders but they will not be followed (XIII, 6).

The superior man is modest in his speech but exceeds in actions (XIV, 29).

If a man take no thought about what is distant he will find sorrow near at hand (XV, 11).

When a man at forty is the object of dislike he will always continue what he is (XVII, 26).[43]

[43] Translation of James Legge.

NOTE: The *Analects* may be read entire in the translation of James Legge in Chinese Classics, Vol. 1, pp. 137–354, where the text and copious scholarly notes accompany it. Legge's translation is used in a number of anthologies which include parts or all of the collection. See also Wm. Jennings, *The Confucian Analects*, Routledge, London, 1895, Lionel Giles, *The Sayings of Confucius*, E. P. Dutton, N. Y., 1932. Still a later translation taking into account a great deal of critical work on the text is that of Arthur Waley, *The Analects of Confucius*, Macmillan Company, N. Y., 1938. Selections from the *Analects* may be found in Lin Yutang, *The Wisdom of Confucius*, The Modern Library, N. Y., 1938, chapter 5, and in *The Wisdom of China and India*, Random House, N. Y., 1942, in his own translation, pp. 814–842.

The Bible of the World, pp. 398–419.

The Bible of Mankind, pp. 183–280.

Lewis Browne, *The World's Great Scriptures*, Macmillan, N. Y., 1946, pp. 229–244.

Harvard Classics, Vol. 43, pp. 1–69.

Ruth Smith, *The Tree of Life*, pp. 174–180.

S. E. Frost, *Sacred Writings of the World's Great Religions*, pp. 103–108.

James Mare, *The Best of Confucius*, Garden City, Halcyon House, 1950.

If, indeed, the tenth book is a description of Confucius, as traditionally held, and not the book of ritual maxims Waley considers it to be, the sage is seen to be a very precise person, extremely meticulous in his observance of the amenities of life.

He did not eat meat which was not cut properly, nor what was served without its proper sauce (VIII, 3).

He did not eat much. When eating he did not converse. When in bed he did not speak. If his mat was not straight, he did not sit on it. He required his sleeping dress to be half as long again as his body (VIII, 7, 9, IX, VI, 6).

Although his food might be coarse rice and vegetable soup, he would offer a little of it in sacrifice with a grave respectful air (VIII, 10).

When he saw anyone in a mourning dress though it might be an acquaintance, he would change countenance, when he saw anyone wearing the cap of full dress, or a blind person, though he might be in his undress, he would salute him in a ceremonious manner (XVI, 2).[44]

The Chung Yung, translated variously as the "Doctrine of the Mean," or the "Golden Mean," is traditionally thought to have been the work of a grandson of Confucius, Tsu Ssu, who had been a disciple of Tseng Tzu, one of Confucius' outstanding followers, himself the teacher of Mencius, whose work constitutes one of the "Four Books." It consists, in part, of reported sayings of the Sage, and in part of the sayings of Tsu Ssu himself. It has generally been regarded as the best statement of Confucius' philosophy and ethics. It forms a part of the Li Chi and is, therefore, probably a much later work than the other Confucian books. This may account for the religious development evident in it.

An ancient Chinese sage enthusiastically says of it, "Unroll it, and it fills the universe; roll it up and it retires and lies hid in mysteriousness. The relish of it is inexhaustible. The whole of it is solid learning. When the skilled leader has explored it, he may carry it into practice all his life, and will find that it cannot be exhausted."[45] The modern writer, Lin Yutang, thinks that it gives the best approach to Confucian philosophy.[46]

[44] *Op. cit.*, Legge translation, pp. 232–236, *passim.*
[45] Quoted in Ku Hung Ming, *The Conduct of Life,* Wisdom of the East Series, London, 1920, p. 8.
[46] *Wisdom of Confucius*, p. 101.

It has been the custom to minimize the religious basis of Confucian ethics, and to regard the system as purely humanistic. But on the basis of this book it is difficult to see how one could arrive at such a conception. For here, in crystal clear form, is a statement of the moral nature of the universe itself.

The ordinance of God is what we call the law of our being. To fulfil the law of our being is what we call the moral law. The moral law when reduced to a system is what we call religion.

The moral law is a law from whose operation we cannot for one instant in our existence escape. A law from which we may escape is not the moral law. Therefore it is that the moral man watches diligently over what his eyes cannot see and is in fear and awe of what his ears cannot hear.

There is nothing more evident than that which cannot be seen by the eyes and nothing more palpable than that which cannot be perceived by the senses. Wherefore the moral man watches diligently over his secret thoughts.

When the passions such as joy, anger, grief, and pleasure, have not awakened, that is our true self, or moral being. When these passions awaken and each and all attain due measure and degree that is the moral order. Our true self or moral being is the great reality (lit. great root) of existence, and moral order is the universal law in the world.

When true moral being and moral order are realized, the universe then becomes a cosmos and all things attain their full growth and development.[47]

Nor is this the only such statement. The book is full of it.

There is no place in the highest heavens above nor in the deepest waters below where the moral law does not reign. The moral law takes its rise in the relation between man and woman; but in the utmost reaches it reigns supreme over heaven and earth (Sec. 12).[48]

In considering the nature and organization of human society it is necessary for him to understand the laws of God.

Truth is the law of God. Acquired truth is the law of man.

Confucius remarked, "The power of spiritual forces in the Universe—how active it is everywhere! Invisible to the eyes, and unpalpable to the

[47] *The Conduct of Life,* Wisdom of the East Series, p. 14.
[48] *Id.,* p. 24.

senses, it is inherent in all things and nothing can escape its operation.
. . . Like the rush of mighty waters the presence of unseen Powers is
felt: sometimes above us, sometimes around us . . . such is the evidence
of things invisible that it is impossible to doubt the spiritual nature of
man.

Oh, how great is the divine moral law in man! Vast and illimitable, it
gives birth and life to all created things. . . . All the institutions of
human society and civilization—laws, customs, usages—have their origin
there. . . . Unless there be highest moral power, the highest moral law
cannot be realized.

There moral laws form one system with the laws by which Heaven
and Earth support and contain; overshadow and canopy all things. . . .
It is this—one system running through all—that makes the Universe so
impressively great.[49]

This book is undoubtedly more religious in its emphasis than the
others, but all through the *Book of History* and the *Odes* and the
Analects (less here perhaps than elsewhere) is evidence that while
Confucius was eminently practical and commonsense in his ethical
outlook, he was also a deeply religious man who believed that there
was a power beyond man whereon he was dependent. And he was
apparently most scrupulous in the performance of the rituals, both
religious and social, which were proper to his time and station.

This book, if more philosophical than the others, is nevertheless
also packed with moral counsel as are the other books. One example
must suffice:

The moral man conforms himself to his life circumstances; he does not
desire anything outside of his position.

Finding himself in a position of wealth and honor he lives as becomes
one living in a position of poverty and humble circumstances. Finding
himself in uncivilized countries, he lives as becomes one living in uncivilized countries. Finding himself in circumstances of danger and difficulty, he acts according to what is required of a man under such
circumstances. In one word, the moral man can find himself in no situation in life in which he is not master of himself.

In a high position he does not domineer over his subordinates. In a
subordinate position he does not court the favours of his superiors. He

[49] *Conduct of Life*, pp. 31, 37, 43–44, 49–50, 53.

puts in order his own personal conduct and seeks nothing from others; hence he has no complaint to make. He complains not against God nor rails against men.

Thus it is that the moral man lives out the even tenor of his life, calmly waiting for the appointment of God, whereas the vulgar person takes to dangerous courses, expecting the uncertain changes of luck.

Confucius remarked: "In the practice of archery we have something resembling the principle in a moral man's life. When the archer misses the centre of the target he turns around and seeks the cause for his failure within himself."[50]

The Ta Hsueh or Great Learning, better translated, thinks Ku Hung Ming, as "Higher Education,"[51] is also to be found as Chapter 39 of the Li Chi. It was the twelfth-century philosopher, Chu Hsi, who lifted this book and the Chung Yung out of the Li Chi and, joining them with the *Analects* and the works of Mencius, formed the Four Books, thus giving them a greater importance than they had, tucked away in the Book of Rites. The Ta Hsueh may have been written primarily as the basis of an education for princes, but it has for centuries been studied by all who have aspired to any important place in government.

It consists chiefly of an introductory statement of principle, when it is then commented upon and expounded in considerable detail. Its method of statement is the familiar regressus which we saw used in the Upanishads. There is an orderliness about things, one thing resting back upon another, and true education seems to arise from an appreciation of this fact and a willingness to take the necessary and logical steps, in order.

The principles of higher education consist in preserving man's clear character, in giving new life to the people, and in dwelling (or resting) in perfection, or the ultimate good.

But how does one arrive at these desirable ends?

Only after knowing the goal of perfection where one should dwell, can one have a definite purpose in life. Only after having a definite purpose in life can one achieve calmness of mind. Only after having

[50] Quoted in *The Conduct of Life*, Wisdom of the East Series, pp. 27–28.
[51] *Conduct of Life*, p. 8.

achieved a calmness of mind can one have peaceful repose. Only after having peaceful repose can one begin to think. Only after one has learned to think, can one achieve knowledge. There are a foundation and a superstructure in the constitution of things, and a beginning and an end in the course of events. Therefore to know the proper sequence or relative order of things is the beginning of wisdom.

Then follows what is the real heart of Confucian ethics and of Confucian education. Knowledge is the basic requisite for moral ends and knowledge depends upon the investigation of things. This is strikingly similar to the modern empirical emphasis.

The ancients who wished to illustrate illustrious virtue throughout the kingdom first ordered well their own states. Wishing to order well their own states, they first regulated their families. Wishing to regulate their families, they first cultivated their persons. Wishing to cultivate their persons, they first rectified their hearts. Wishing to rectify their hearts, they first sought to be sincere in their thoughts. Wishing to be sincere in their thoughts, they first extended to the utmost their knowledge. Such extension of knowledge lay in the investigation of things.

Things being investigated, knowledge became complete. Their knowledge being complete, their thoughts were sincere. Their thoughts being sincere, their hearts were thus rectified. Their hearts being rectified, their persons were cultivated. Their persons being cultivated, their families were regulated. Their families being regulated, their states were rightly governed. Their states being rightly governed, the whole kingdom was made tranquil and happy.[52]

The remainder of the document is chiefly commentary upon the foregoing.

Longest section of the commentary is the one explaining the saying "the restoration of peace in the world depends on ordering the material life"; quite in keeping with Confucius' well-known preoccupation with questions of a political nature. Sentences taken at random from this part are:

Those who have the people with them can keep their rule over a country, and those who have forfeited the following of their people thereby forfeit their rule over the country.

[52] *The Chinese Classics,* James Legge translation, Vol. I, pp. 357–359.

The mandate of Heaven is not fixed and unchangeable. The good rulers get it and the bad rulers forfeit it.

The material prosperity of a nation does not consist in its material prosperity but in righteousness.[53]

The last of the "Four Books" does not purport to come from Confucius at all. It was the work of Mencius, a man who lived about a century later, who drank deeply at the fountain of Confucian wisdom, as it had been transmitted to his times, and who became the foremost Confucian teacher of antiquity, or perhaps of all time. He has often been likened to St. Paul, not of course because of any similarity that exists between the teachings of the two, but because of the relative position he occupies in relation to the founder of the faith of which he was a major apostle. In many respects his life was parallel to that of his Master. He was of humble birth; he became a scholar and a teacher. He also held public office, and like Confucius seemed more interested in political matters than religious. He, too, lost his government employment, and for years sought, wandering from state to state, some ruler who would allow him to test out his theory of government in actual practice, but found no one willing to give him the chance.

Confucian thought had, with the passage of time, been variously interpreted and there came to be various schools. Mencius stands in the orthodox line, and in it was preëminent. He took some of the Confucian ideas, developed them, and gave them well defined and systematic form, particularly his ideas of government. He was an excellent speaker and writer, good at debate and at detailed exposition of his thought. Where we have only brief sayings of Confucius, the work of Mencius contains fairly long and well-reasoned discourses. The seven books of Mencius represent in bulk about a third more than the *Analects*, and are said to be written in much better Chinese prose. He was a pupil of Tsu Ssu to whom the Chung Yung is attributed, who was in turn a disciple of Tseng Tzu or Master Tseng, whose name figures so often in the *Analects*. Lin Yutang quotes a Chinese scholar, Han Yu, as saying: "In order to understand the Sage one must begin with Mencius," and also,

[53] Lin Yutang, *Wisdom of Confucius*, pp. 149–151, *passim*.

"Mencius was the purest of the pure in the interpretation of Confucius."[54]

One of the teachings for which Mencius is noted is his doctrine of the goodness of human nature.

The philosopher Kaou said, "Man's Nature is like water whirling round in a corner. Open a passage for it to the east, and it will flow to the east; open a passage for it to the west and it will flow to the west. Man's nature is indifferent to good and evil, just as the water is indifferent to the east and west."

Mencius replied, "Water indeed will flow indifferently to the east or west, but will it flow indifferently up or down? The tendency of man's nature to good is like the tendency of water to flow downwards. There are none but have this tendency to good, just as all water flows downwards."[55]

This single quotation states the doctrine, but it is defended at length against the objections of the philosopher, Kao Tzu, in what might be entitled an essay on the goodness of human nature.[56]

In respect to government, Mencius states not only general principles as in the case of most of Confucian sayings on the subject, but goes into specific detail as to what should or should not be done, for example the following bit as to husbandry and conservation:

If the seasons of husbandry be not interfered with, the grain will be more than can be eaten. If close nets are not allowed to enter the pools and ponds, the fishes and turtles will be more than can be consumed. If the axes and bills enter the hills and forests only at the proper time, the wood will be more than can be used. When the grain and fish and turtles are more than can be eaten, and there is more wood than can be used, this enables the people to nourish their living and bury their dead, without any feeling against any. The condition, in which the people nourish their living and bury their dead without any feeling against any, is the first step of royal government.

Let mulberry trees be planted about the homesteads with their five *mow*, and persons of fifty years may be clothed with silk. In keeping

[54] *Wisdom of Confucius*, p. 274.

[55] James Legge, *The Works of Mencius*, Chinese Classics, Vol. II, pp. 395–396; Vol. VI, I; 2–3.

[56] See *Wisdom of Confucius*, pp. 276–282.

fowls, pigs, dogs, and swine, let not their times of breeding be neglected, and persons of seventy years may eat flesh. Let there not be taken away the time that is proper for the cultivation of the farm with its hundred *mow,* and the family of several mouths that is supported by it shall not suffer from hunger. Let careful attention be paid to education in schools, inculcating in it especially the filial and fraternal duties, and grey-haired men will not be seen upon the roads, carrying burdens on their backs or on their heads. It never has been that the ruler of a state where such results were seen,—persons of seventy wearing silk and eating flesh and the black-haired people suffering neither from hunger nor cold—did not attain to the imperial dignity.

Your dogs and swine eat the food of men, and you do not know to make any restrictive arrangements. There are people dying from famine on the roads, and you do not know to issue the stores of your granaries for them. When people die, you say, "It is not owing to me; it is owing to the year." In what does this differ from stabbing a man and killing him, and then saying, "It was not I; it was the weapon?" Let your Majesty cease to lay the blame on the year, and instantly from all the empire the people will come to you.

King Hui of Liang said, "I wish quietly to receive your instruction!" Mencius replied, "Is there any difference between killing a man with a stick and with a sword?" The king said, "There is no difference." "Is there any difference between doing it with a sword and with the style of government?" "There is no difference," was the reply.[57]

Mencius, like Confucius, was a man of strong character and with a passion for righteousness. It is the most important thing in the world, more important than life itself.

Mencius said, "I like fish and I also like bear's paws. If I cannot have the two together, I will let the fish go, and take the bear's paws. So, I like life, and I also like righteousness. If I cannot keep the two together, I will let life go and choose righteousness.

"I like life indeed, but there is that which I like more than life, and therefore, I will not seek to possess it by any improper ways. I dislike death indeed, but there is that which I dislike more than death, and therefore there are occasions when I will not avoid danger."[58]

[57] *Works of Mencius;* Book I, Part 1, Chapter III, 3; Chapter IV, 2. Translation of James Legge. *Chinese Classics,* Vol. II, pp. 130–133.
[58] *Works of Mencius,* Bk. VI, Part 1, Chapter 10. Legge translation. *Op. cit.* Vol. 2, pp. 411–412.

Probably it was to Mencius, more than any other of his disciples, that Confucius owes his great influence, for Mencius served to popularize and give currency to the teachings of the sage. The fact that the work came, in the end, to rank as one of the "Four Books," is an indication of the high esteem in which he came to be held by the Chinese, and of the faithfulness with which he interpreted and developed the teachings of the Master.

Eventually, these Confucian books, which we have passed so rapidly in review, became the basis of Chinese education, particularly the education of those who aspired to rule the people. For centuries scholars studied them, learned them by rote and sought to understand them and expound their meaning. The examinations, held annually, brought great numbers to the capital city of the reigning dynasty. In Nanking, or the Southern capital, halls are said to stand even yet, where candidates spent days in what was probably as formidable a set of examinations as students anywhere have had to pass. They have not been used since the coming of the revolution.

And even now, when the Confucian books are no longer a required study, they still continue to exercise a great influence, for even with the changes the modern world and modern war have brought to China, the major institutions of Chinese life are still largely determined by the age-old traditions of China, which were and still are largely in accord with patterns laid down in this literature. What will be the effect of Communism on these traditions? China is an anvil that has worn out many hammers. It is likely that in the end Communism will be affected by it, as much as or more than it will affect Chinese culture.

TAOISM

There are two native religions of China. Confucianism, which, until the twentieth century revolution, was for centuries the State religion, has been the dominant faith, and has been most influential in shaping the patterns of the religious and moral life of the people. But there has always been a minority group which held quite a different view of religion and life from that of the Confucian majority. This was true long before the time either of Confucius or Lao Tzu, the so-called founders of the two faiths. For Confucius and Lao Tzu were founders only in the sense of channelling and giving definite form to attitudes and outlooks already present in China long before they came along. In general, Confucianism represents the more humanistic outlook, the common-sense, down-to-earth attitude, while Taoism represents the more mystical, other-worldly point of view. Since in China there is no such sharp separation into religious groups as in the West, it may be said that most Chinese have in them something of both tendencies, and feel perfectly free to express themselves at one time through one, at another time through the other. Someone has truly said that these two so-called faiths represent simply different moods of the Chinese people.

But in time separate organizations and institutions did emerge, and have existed side by side for over two thousand years, generally at peace one with another, though Taoism has suffered persecution, at times, at the hands of the State religion.

It was perhaps the emergence of a literature in both cases which had the effect of crystallizing them into institutions. Confucianism grew up around the books attributed directly or indirectly to Confucius, as we have seen. Taoism in a somewhat less definitely traceable fashion was the outgrowth of writings attributed to Lao Tzu, and one of his great disciples Chuang Tzu. Taoism flourished as a philosophy long before it became the popular religion known as Taoism today. The philosophy dates from the time of Lao Tzu, formerly thought to be a slightly older contemporary of Confucius: but recent scholars are inclined to date Lao Tzu some two or three centuries later than the traditionally accepted date. Taoism as a distinct religion is thought to have arisen in the second century A.D., founded by one Chang Tao Ling. But in any event the sacred writings are the same—the little classic attributed to Lao Tzu, and the writings of Chuang Tzu.

There is a legend to account for the Tao-Te-Ching, the supposed work of Lao Tzu. He was a scholar, keeper of the archives of his native state. He was a gentle soul, much troubled by the unsettled times in which he lived, and about which nobody seemed to be doing anything very effective. Perhaps he did see one attempt after another to improve the situation, but without success. Pondering deeply upon the problems, he came to the conclusion that there was really only one solution to the whole sorry situation, and that was to give up active striving and to leave it all to the Tao, or the Way, the very nature of things. Accordingly, he resolved to abandon the world, and so set out one day to leave it all behind. World flight was the logical result of this thinking.

Legend has it that when he was about to pass through the gate, bound for an unknown destination, the gatekeeper recognized him and besought him that, before leaving, he set down his thought for other men to read and profit by. He consented, and before going out, sat down and wrote quickly the five thousand characters which constitute what is at once the most delightful, and perhaps also the most baffling of all the sacred books.[59] It is translated variously into English as *The Canon of Reason and Virtue, The Way and Its Power,* and otherwise, but when one compares the translations, they differ greatly one from the other, probably reflecting therein the religious biases of the several translators. By one, a Buddhist, it has become almost entirely a Buddhist document. No one who is not himself acquainted with the Chinese language can say whether it is well translated by one or another of the translators, and even Chinese differ among themselves as to its meaning. But, curiously enough, whether one understands it completely or not, it makes interesting reading. The difficulty is that it deals with concepts so vague and so intangible, that precise meanings are difficult to make clear to the reader.

The central concept of the document is the Tao, or the Way. It is described in a dozen different ways, and yet when all of them have been carefully read and considered, one is not yet certain that he has captured its meaning. It is like trying to grasp a handful of air or of fog. It is elusive.

Take for example the first section as translated by Lin Yutang:

[59] It need hardly be said that the legend is not generally credited as true by scholars.

> The Tao that can be told of
> Is not the absolute Tao
> The names that can be given
> Are not absolute names.[60]

Earlier translators gave an English translation of the word Tao. G. G. Alexander translates the same passage thus:

> God (the great everlasting infinite First Cause from whom all things in heaven and earth proceed) can neither be defined nor named. For the God which can be defined or named is but the Creator, the Great Mother of all those things of which our sense have cognizance.[61]

Since the term *God* conveys such a definitely personal meaning to Western readers, it is much better to use the Chinese term, Tao, and let the document itself reveal what it may as to the nature of the Tao, as conceived by Lao Tzu.

But if the Tao is essentially indescribable, Lao Tzu does not fail to characterize it in a variety of ways.

> Tao is all-pervading
>> And its use is inexhaustible,
> Fathomless!
>> Like the fountain head of all things
>> Its sharp edges rounded off.
>> Its tangles untied,
>> Its light tempered,
>> Its turmoil submerged.
> Yet crystal clear like water it seems to remain.
>> I do not know whose son it is,
>> An image which existed before God.[62]
> The thing called Tao is elusive
>> Is elusive, evasive,
> Evasive, elusive,

[60] *Wisdom of China and India,* Section IV, p. 585.
[61] *Sacred Books and Literature of the East,* Vol. 12, p. 15.
[62] *Wisdom of China and India,* p. 585, Section IV, copyright 1942 by Random House, Inc., New York. This and subsequent quotations from this source reprinted by permission of Random House.

> Yet latent in it are forms,
> Elusive, evasive,
> Yet latent in it are objects.
> Dark and dim,
> Yet latent in it is the life-force.
> The life-force being very true,
> Latent in it are evidences. . . .[63]

Once again:

> But Tao is mild to the taste.
> Looked at it cannot be seen;
> Listened to it cannot be heard;
> Applied, its supply never fails.[64]

Though difficult to grasp, there is nothing to compare with the Tao in the effectiveness of its operation. Paradoxically, says Lao Tzu:

> The Tao never does,
> Yet through it everything is done.[65]

There are many paradoxes in the work of Lao Tzu. Section XXXVI, which Lin Yutang entitles "The Rhythm of Life," is a series of paradoxes.

> He who is to be made to dwindle (in power)
> Must first be caused to expand.
> He who is to be weakened
> Must first be made strong.
> He who is to be laid low
> Must first be exalted to power.
> He who is to be taken away from
> Must first be given.
>
> This is the subtle light
> Gentleness overcomes strength. . . .[66]

---

[63] *Wisdom of China and India,* Sec. XXI, p. 594.
[64] *Id.,* Sec. XXXV, p. 603.
[65] *Id.,* Sec. XXXVII, p. 603.
[66] *Id.,* p. 603.

Other striking paradoxes are found in section XXII.

> To yield is to be preserved whole,
> To become bent is to become straight.
> To be hollow is to be filled,
> To be tattered is to be renewed.
> To be in want is to possess,
> To have plenty is to be confused.
>
> Therefore the Sage embraces the One
> And becomes the model of the world.
> He does not reveal himself
> And is therefore luminous.
> He does not justify himself
>   And is therefore far-famed.
> He does not boast himself
>   And therefore people give him credit.
> He does not pride himself
>   And is therefore the ruler among men.
>
> It is because he does not contend
> That no one in the world can contend against him.[67]

Lao Tzu comes close to the New Testament in many of his utterances for example in section VII.

> The universe is everlasting.
> The reason that the universe is everlasting
> Is that it does not live for Self.
> Therefore it can long endure.
>
> Therefore the Sage puts himself last
>   And finds himself in a foremost place;
> Regards his body as accidental
>   And his body is thereby preserved.
> Is it not because he does not live for Self.
>   That his Self achieves perfection?[68]

[67] Lin Yutang, *op. cit.*, pp. 594–595.
[68] Lin Yutang, *op. cit.*, p. 586.

He advocates returning good for evil as do Buddha and Jesus. "To the good I do good," he said, "and to the evil I also do good." This is in contrast to Confucius who said in effect "Requite good with good, but requite evil with justice."

Perhaps his most outstanding emphasis was upon the principle of *wu wei*. This has been translated variously as "harmlessness," "non-action," and even as *laissez-faire*.

> The softest substance of the world
> Goes through the hardest.
> That which is without form penetrates that
> which has no crevice;
> Through this I know the benefit of taking no action
> The teaching without words,
> And the benefit of taking no action
> Are without compare in the universe.[69]

The most famous statement of it is that which inquires how one goes about making muddy water clear. The answer is, of course, by doing precisely nothing. Let it alone and it will clear itself.

> By doing nothing everything is done.
> He who conquers the world often does so by doing nothing.
> Where one is compelled to do something,
> The world is already beyond his conquering.[70]

Naturally, violent action would be excluded by this principle, so he is not only a passivist but a pacifist.

> Of all things, soldiers are instruments of evil
> Hated by men.
> Therefore the religious man possessed of Tao avoids them.[71]

> Others have taught this maxim
> Which I preach also:
> The violent man shall die a violent death
> This I shall regard as my spiritual teacher.[72]

[69] Lin Yutang, *op. cit.*, Sec. XLIII, p. 607.
[70] Lin Yutang, *op. cit.*, Sec. XLVIII, p. 608.
[71] Lin Yutang, *op. cit.*, Sec. XXXI, p. 600.
[72] Lin Yutang, *op. cit.*, p. 607.

Although passages occur which may be interpreted as permitting force where it cannot be helped, it is likely that this persistent emphasis of Lao Tzu may have contributed much to the generally pacific nature of Chinese culture, and in particular to the low esteem in which, until very recently, the military also has been held.

His prescription for world peace will make little appeal to a hyper-activist generation, but maybe he had something after all. Activism and aggressiveness do not seem to be doing too well at attaining it.

> If kings and barons can keep the Tao,
> The world will of its own accord be reformed. . . .
> Let it be restrained by the Nameless pristine simplicity,
> The Nameless pristine simplicity
> Is stripped of desire (for contention).
> By stripping of desire quiescence is achieved
> And the world arrives at peace of its own accord.[73]

The Tao-Te-Ching, perhaps because of its rather vague, elusive character, has not become so widely known as the more practical, common-sense, far more easily understood Confucian books. But mystics have always prized it highly, both in China and elsewhere. Aldous Huxley quotes it again and again in the *Perennial Philosophy* which he describes as "the metaphysic that recognizes a divine Reality, substantial to the world of things and lives and minds; the psychology that finds in the soul something similar to, or even identical with final Reality; the ethic that places man's final end in the knowledge of the immanent and transcendent Ground of all being."[74]

Lin Yutang, the very modern Chinese writer, says of it:

If there is one book in the whole of Oriental literature which one should read above all others, it is, in my opinion, Lao Tzu's Book of Tao. It teaches the wisdom of appearing foolish, the success of appearing to

[73] *Id.,* p. 603.
[74] P. vii, Harper and Brothers, New York, 1944.

fail, the strength of weakness and the advantage of lying low, the benefit of yielding to your adversary and the futility of contention for power
. . . if there is one book advising against the multifarious activities and
futile busy-ness of the modern man . . . it is the Book of Tao. It is one of
the profoundest books in the world's philosophy.[75]

The Tao-Te-Ching is a book not to be read through at a sitting
but to be read a little at a time and pondered. It is a book which
grows on one as he reads.

CHUANG TZU

Chuang Tzu stands in relation to Lao Tzu somewhat as does
Paul to Jesus, and Mencius to Confucius. He was a contemporary of Mencius. On the basis of the older chronology he lived some
two centuries after his Master. But, if the suggestions of later
scholars that Lao Tzu belonged to the fourth century is accepted,
the interval between the two men is greatly lessened. Certainty at
this point is not at present possible.

Little is known of his life. He held an inconspicuous govern-
mental position in a small provincial city. Once he tells us that he
was asked to assume a position of greater importance as Prince
Minister in the Ch'u state. But he declined. Public office of high
degree was not for him. He was essentially a poet and a dreamer,
to whom the responsibilities of high office would have been irk-
some. But his writings brought him into contact with many of the
great scholars of his time.

He was a profound disciple of Lao Tzu. Confucianism he deeply
disliked, and attacked with great vigor. This brought down upon
him the enmity of the exponents of the popular and dominant Confucian teaching, which precisely during his own time was being
expounded by the great Mencius. It is rather curious that the two
men never met, and that there is no reference in the writings of
either one to the other.

Lao Tzu's teaching, never highly popular, was being rapidly
eclipsed by the revival of Confucianism, due to Mencius and others.

---

[75] Lin Yutang, *Wisdom of China and India*, p. 579.

There was an increasing emphasis upon the Confucian controls upon the whole of life, against which the teachings of Lao Tzu stood in such extreme contrast. Confucius was essentially an activist. Lao Tzu was a passivist. His great principle of non-action (*wu-wei*) was diametrically opposed to the regimented activism of Confucius and his school. Chuang Tzu came boldly to the defense of his master's teaching and lent it much needed support. He gave it a currency it might never have gained otherwise, and he modified it in some respects.

For Chuang Tzu was no mere slavish follower of Lao Tzu. Some phases of his teaching he ignores, or passes over very lightly. Others he extends possibly far beyond what Lao Tzu would have been willing to do. But the central core of his teaching is unmistakably faithful to the Master.

Perhaps the greatest contribution he made was to give Taoism a literary expression which would carry it far beyond where the Tao-Te-Ching would reach. He is rated as one of China's greatest literary figures. Lionel Giles writes almost lyrically in his praise:

> He of all ancients wielded the most perfect mastery over Chinese prose style, and was the first to show to what heights of eloquence and beauty his native language could attain. And in these respects, great as the achievements are of which later Chinese literature can boast, he has never been surpassed. Indeed, his master-hand sounded chords that have vibrated to no other touch.[76]

Lin Yutang calls him the greatest prose writer of the Chou dynasty because of "the brilliance of his style and the depth of his thought." Despite his marked antagonism to Confucius and Confucian ideas, his opponents were obliged to admire his writing, even when disagreeing with his ideas.[77]

But Lin Yutang does go on to say that no pure-blooded Chinese could ever quite disagree with Chuang Tzu's ideas, since: "Taoism is not a school of thought in China, it is a deep, fundamental trait

[76] *Musings of a Chinese Mystic,* John Murray, London, 1927, p. 36.
[77] Lin Yutang, *Wisdom of China and India,* p. 625.

of Chinese thinking, and of the Chinese attitude toward life and toward society. It has depth, while Confucianism has only a practical sense of proportion; it enriches Chinese poetry and imagination in an immeasurable manner, and it gives a philosophic sanction to whatever is in the idle, freedom-loving, poetic, vagabond Chinese soul. It provides the only safe, romantic release from the severe Confucian classic restraint and humanizes the very humanists themselves."[78]

Not only is Chuang Tzu a philosopher, he is also a humorist. No more delightfully humorous writing is to be found anywhere than in some of the whimsical anecdotes found in his book. One is tempted to present a number of such examples as a relief from the more or less solemn material which has perforce been drawn from most of the books discussed here.

(3) Chuang Tzu was fishing in the P'u when the prince of Ch'u sent two high officials to ask him to take charge of the administration of the Ch'u State.

Chuang Tzu went on fishing, and without turning his head said, "I have heard that in Ch'u there is a sacred tortoise which has been dead now some three thousand years. And that the prince keeps this tortoise carefully enclosed in a chest on the altar of his ancestral temple. Now would this tortoise rather be dead, and have its remains venerated, or be alive and wagging its tail in the mud?"

"It would rather be alive," replied the two officials, "and wagging its tail in the mud."

"Begone!" cried Chuang Tzu. "I, too, will wag my tail in the mud!"[79]

Another reads:

(5) The Grand Augur, in his ceremonial robes, approached the shambles and thus addressed the pigs:—

"How can you object to die? I shall fatten you for three months. I shall discipline myself for ten days and fast for three. I shall strew fine grass, and place you bodily upon a carved sacrificial dish. Does this not satisfy you?"

[78] Lin Yutang, *op. cit.*, pp. 625–626.
[79] H. A. Giles, *History of Chinese Literature*, p. 66.

Then, speaking from the pigs' point of view, he continued, "It is better perhaps after all to live on bran and escape the shambles." . . .

"But then," added he, speaking from his own point of view, "to enjoy honour when alive, one would readily die on a war-shield or in the headsman's basket."

So he rejected the pigs' point of view and adopted his own point of view. In what sense then was he different from the pigs?[80]

He is a master of the use of figures of speech. He draws his numerous illustrations from the common things of everyday life, the river, the spring, the horse, the frog, the pigs, the market, the fish, the fisherman, the seasons. And they are very telling. "The life of man passes by like a galloping horse" (p. 100). "A man does not seek to see himself in running water, but in still water" (p. 94). "The life of a man is but as a stoppage at an inn" (p. 103). "A dog is not considered a good dog because he is a good barker" (p. 105).[81]

Could anything be more graphic, or delightful than his story of the well frog and the sea turtle?

(2) Have you never heard of the frog in the old well? The frog said to the turtle of the eastern seas, "Happy indeed am I! I hop on the rail around the well. I rest in the hollow of some broken brick. Swimming, I gather the water under my arms and shut my mouth. I plunge into the mud, burying my feet and toes; and not one of the cockles, crabs, or tadpoles I see around me are my match. (Fancy pitting the happiness of an old well, ejaculates Chuang Tzu, against all the water of ocean!) Why do you not come, sir, and pay me a visit!"

Now the turtle of the eastern sea had not got its left leg down ere its right had already stuck fast, so it shrank back and begged to be excused. It then described the sea, saying, "A thousand *li* would not measure its breadth, nor a thousand fathoms its depth. In the days of the Great Yu, there were nine years of flood out of ten; and this did not add to its bulk. In the days of T'ang, there were seven years out of eight of drought, but this did not narrow its span. Not to be affected by duration of time, not to be affected by volume of water, such is the great happiness of the eastern sea."

[80] Giles, *op. cit.,* p. 67.
[81] Page references are to *Musings of a Chinese Mystic,* John Murray, London, 1927. Translation of Herbert A. Giles.

At this the well frog was considerably astonished, and knew not what to say next. And for one whose knowledge does not reach to the positive-negative domain, to attempt to understand me, Chuang Tzu, is like a mosquito trying to carry a mountain, or an ant to swim a river, . . . they cannot succeed.[82]

His chapter on "Autumn Floods" from which the story of the well frog is taken, and incidentally also the quotation preceding that, begins with the following story:

(1) It was the time of autumn floods. Every stream poured into the river, which swelled in its turbid course. The banks receded so far from one another that it was impossible to tell a cow from a horse.

Then the Spirit of the River laughed for joy that all the beauty of the earth was gathered to himself. Down with the stream he journeyed east, until he reached the ocean. There, looking eastwards and seeing no limit to its waves, his countenance changed. And as he gazed over the expanse, he sighed and said to the Spirit of the Ocean, "A vulgar proverb says, that he who has heard but part of the truth thinks no one equal to himself. And such a one am I.

"When formerly I heard people detracting from the learning of Confucius, or underrating the heroism of Po I, I did not believe. But now that I have looked upon your inexhaustibility, alas for me had I not reached your abode, I should have been for ever a laughing stock to those of comprehensive enlightenment."

To which the Spirit of the Ocean replied, "You cannot speak of ocean to a well frog,—the creature of a narrower sphere. You cannot speak of ice to a summer-insect,—the creature of a season. You cannot speak of Tao to a pedagogue: his scope is too restricted. But now that you have emerged from your narrow sphere and have seen the great ocean, you know your own insignificance, and I can speak to you of great principles."[83]

The whole chapter seems, to some extent, to be a discussion of relativity: "If we look at the great from the standpoint of the small—we cannot reach its limit; and if we look at the small from the standpoint of the great it eludes our sight." Different things are differently applied. A battering ram can knock down a wall, but it

---

[82] Herbert A. Giles, *op. cit.*, p. 65.
[83] H. A. Giles, *History of Chinese Literature*, pp. 64–65.

cannot repair a break. An owl can catch fleas at night and see the tip of a hair, but if it comes out in the daytime it can open its eyes and yet fail to see a mountain. Different creatures are differently constituted.

From all this he draws the conclusion: "Thus, those who say they would have right without its correlate wrong; or good government without its correlate, misrule, do not apprehend the great principles of the universe, nor the nature of creation. One might as well talk of the existence of Heaven without that of Earth, or of the negative principles without the positives which is clearly impossible. Yet people keep on discussing it without stop; such people must be either fools or knaves."[84]

While Chuang Tzu writes with a light touch, he does not fail to discuss most abstruse matters, for example:

There is nothing which is not objective, there is nothing which is not subjective. But it is impossible to start from the objective. Only from subjective knowledge is it possible to proceed to objective knowledge. When subjective and objective are both without their correlates that is the very axis of Tao. And when that axis passes through the center at which all infinities emerge, positive and negative alike blend into an infinite One.

Therefore it is that viewed from the standpoint of Tao, a beam and a pillar are identical. So are ugliness and beauty, greatness, wickedness, perverseness and strangeness. Separation is the same as construction; construction is the same as destruction; nothing is subject either to construction or to destruction, for these conditions are brought together into One.[85]

Like his great master, Chuang Tzu was a firm believer in *wu wei.*

"Repose, tranquillity, stillness, inaction,—these were the levels of the universe, the ultimate perfection of Tao. Therefore wise rulers and sages rest therein . . . from repose comes inaction, and from inaction comes potentiality of action. And inaction is happiness: and where there is happiness no cares abide, and life is long. . . . Ap-

[84] Lin Yutang, *op. cit.*, pp. 685–686.
[85] Ballou, *Bible of the World*, p. 507.

peal to arms is the lowest form of virtue. Rewards and punishments are the lowest form of education. Ceremonies and laws are the lowest form of government. Music and fine clothes are the lowest form of happiness. Weeping and mourning are the lowest form of grief. These five should follow the movement of the mind."[86]

Space does not permit a discussion of all Chuang Tzu's ideas, nor even of the manner in which he deviates from Lao Tzu. Here it was only our purpose to show the general nature of his writing which will be found to be among the most unique and readable of all the scriptures here examined. His was a unique personality. He has made a deep impression upon Chinese life and thought. During a portion of China's long history his works, like those of Confucius, were required to be studied by persons seeking high political posts. These final selections must suffice, two of which, rather, oddly, show his attitude toward death.

When his wife died one of his followers went to express his sympathy. He found Chuang Tzu "sitting on the ground, singing, with his legs spread out at a right angle and beating time on a bowl."

"To live with your wife," exclaimed Hui Tzu "and see your oldest son grow up to be a man, and then not to shed a tear over her corpse,—this would be bad enough. But to drum on a bowl, and sing; surely this is going too far."

"Not at all," replied Chuang Tzu. "When she died, I could not help being affected by her death. Soon, however, I remembered that she had already existed in a previous state before birth, without form, or even substance; that while in that unconditional condition substance was added to spirit; that this substance then assumed form; and that the next stage was birth. And now, by virtue of a further change, she is dead, passing from one phase to another, like the sequence of spring, summer, autumn, and winter. And while she is lying thus asleep in eternity, for me to go about weeping and wailing would be to proclaim myself ignorant of these natural laws. Therefore, I refrain."[87]

[86] *Musings of a Chinese Mystic,* John Murray, London, 1927, pp. 98–99.
[87] *Musings of a Chinese Mystic,* p. 111. Translation of Herbert A. Giles.

When he himself was about to die his disciples wished to give him a splendid funeral. Characteristically, Chuang Tzu said:

"With Heaven and Earth for my coffin and shell; with the sun, moon, and stars, as my burial regalia; and with all creation to escort me to my grave, are not my funeral paraphernalia ready to hand?"

"We fear," argued his disciples, "lest the carrion kite should eat the body of our Master." To which Chuang Tzu replied: "Above ground I shall be food for kites; below I shall be food for moles, crickets, and ants. Why rob one to feed the other?"[88]

By reason of one of his stories he came to be known as "butterfly Chuang." Said he, on one occasion:

How then do I know but that the dead repent of having previously clung to life?

Those who dream of the banquet, wake to lamentation and sorrow, wake to join the hunt. While they dream, they do not know what they dream. Some will even interpret the very dream they are dreaming; and only when they awake do they know it was a dream. By and by comes the Great Awakening, and then we find out that this life is really a great dream. Fools think they are awake now, and flatter themselves they know if they are really princes or peasants. Confucius and you are both dreams; and I who say you are dreams,—I am but a dream myself.

Once upon a time, I, Chuang Tzu, dreamt I was a butterfly, fluttering hither and thither, to all intents and purposes a butterfly. I was conscious only of following my fancies as a butterfly, and was unconscious of my individuality as a man. Suddenly, I awakened, and there I lay, myself again. Now I do not know whether I was then a man dreaming I was a butterfly, or whether I am now a butterfly dreaming I am a man.[89]

[88] *Id.*, p. 112.
[89] H. A. Giles, *History of Chinese Literature*, p. 63.

CONFUCIAN LITERATURE
Sources for Further Reading

GENERAL SOURCES

James Legge, *The Chinese Classics*, 5 Vols., Oxford University Press.
Sacred Books of the East.
Sacred Books and Literature of the East.
Lin Yutang, *The Wisdom of Confucius*, Modern Library, N. Y., 1938.
For sources in which separate books may be found, see footnotes, *ad loc.*

IN THE ANTHOLOGIES

Harvard Classics, Vol. 43, pp. 5–72.
Bible of the World, pp. 379–470.
Bible of Mankind, pp. 183–280.
The Wisdom of China and India, Lin Yutang, pp. 695–862.
The World's Great Scriptures, pp. 209–280.
Tongues of Fire, pp. 121–156.
The Tree of Life, pp. 157–187.
Sacred Writings of the World's Great Religions, pp. 91–118.

TAOIST LITERATURE
Sources for Further Reading

ON THE TAO-TE-CHING

Sacred Books and Literature of the East, Vol. 12, pp. 15–74. Translation of G. G. Alexander.
Sacred Books of the East, Vol. 19. Translation by James Legge.
Paul Carus, *The Canon of Reason and Virtue*, Open Court Publishing Co., Chicago, 1927.
Arthur Waley, *The Way and Its Power*, G. Allen and Unwin, London, 1934. Excellent introduction.

IN THE ANTHOLOGIES

Lin Yutang, *The Wisdom of China and India*, excellent introduction, pp. 579–582 and translation by Lin Yutang, pp. 583–624.
Robert Ballou, *The Bible of the World*. Translation by Chu Ta Kao, pp. 471–505.
Lewis Browne, *World's Great Scriptures*, pp. 297–327. Selections only. Translation of Lin Yutang.
Ruth Smith, *The Tree of Life*, pp. 193–198. Selections only.
Lionel Giles, *Sayings of Lao Tzu*, Wisdom of the East Series. The arrangement is topical, and in prose form.
S. E. Frost, *Sacred Writings of the World's Religions*, pp. 81–86.
Grace Turnbull, *Tongues of Fire*, pp. 159–164. Selected sentences only, prose translation.
M. A. Sohrab, *The Bible of Mankind*, pp. 289–348.

ON THE WRITINGS OF CHUANG TZU

Sacred Books of the East, Volume 39. Translation by James Legge.

Sacred Books and Literature of the East, Vol. 12, pp. 75–197. A good selection, translation of James Legge.

Lin Yutang, *Wisdom of China and India,* pp. 629–691. Translation of Lin Yutang. Some good longer selections, good introduction.

The Bible of the World, pp. 505–558. Translation of Herbert A. Giles. Good selection, generally of short pieces.

Lewis Browne, *The World's Great Scriptures,* pp. 328–358. Translation of H. A. Giles.

Ruth Smith, *The Tree of Life,* pp. 203–212.

S. E. Frost, *The Sacred Writings of the World's Great Religions,* pp. 87–90.

Grace Turnbull, *Tongues of Fire,* pp. 164–166. Only scattered sentences.

M. A. Sohrab, *The Bible of Mankind,* pp. 281–350.

Lionel Giles, *Musings of a Chinese Mystic,* Wisdom of the East Series, pp. 37–112. Excellent introduction, pp. 11–36, good selection, arranged topically.

CHAPTER X

The Sacred Literature of the Japanese

The native religion of the Japanese people is called Shinto. The word Shinto itself tells something about the history of Japanese culture. For, strangely enough, they have borrowed the very name of their religion from China. Shinto means literally the "way of the gods," from the two Chinese words Shen—gods, and Tao—way.

Japanese culture is much more recent in its origin than that of the Chinese. If the traditional beginning of the Japanese Kingdom, some twenty-six hundred years ago, be accepted as true, that would mean that it came into being about the time of Confucius, and Chinese culture stretches many many centuries back of Confucius' time. Indeed, in his time there was a very highly developed civilization in China, a rich art, many books, and a very complex system of government.

Japan's culture owes much to that of China. First definitely mentioned in the fifth century A.D., it is quite certain that elements of Chinese culture had begun to flow into Japan well before that time. This flow was greatly accelerated by the incoming of Buddhism, which came first from Korea, but mainly from China proper. With it came many things Chinese, beside Buddhism itself.

Japan has from her earliest history been an avid borrower. The modern world is well aware of the rapid borrowing of occidental culture by the Japanese after the opening of Japan to world commerce by Commodore Perry in the middle of the nineteenth century. Japan's meteoric rise from an isolated, little-known power to the proud position of one of the five great powers in the twentieth century, was accomplished in less than seventy-five years. It was possible chiefly because of her borrowing from the West. But Japan was only exhibiting a characteristic feature of her culture in her rapid appropriation of Western ideas. At an early period, from the fifth to the eighth century A.D. particularly, she had done almost exactly the same thing, only at that time the source of her borrowing was China.

She took over much of Chinese art and religion. Her language was deeply affected by the Chinese language. Indeed, there was scarcely an important feature of Chinese culture that she did not borrow. Anthropologists have discovered two things which Japan did not borrow and are at a loss to explain this omission. Japan did not take over the use of brick in building, as commonly practiced in China, and she did not take over the use of pork as an article of diet. Perhaps the most striking illustration of her borrowing tendency is the fact that one of her two sacred books is written wholly in Chinese, and the other in a queer mixture of Japanese and Chinese. The reason for this seems clear. Japanese culture had not as yet evolved a language adequate to the expression of the religious ideas which, by this time, she had adopted.

Yet, it must be said that with all her borrowing, Japan has never been slavish in the matter. She has had extraordinary ability to adapt, and make her own, that which has come to her from abroad. Probably no nation in the world has excelled her in this ability to borrow and adapt. It seems to be her peculiar genius to do things that way.

In a real sense Japan has no sacred books, that is, books that are the equivalent of the Bible, or, say, of the Buddhist Canon. But she does have three books which serve some of the purposes which sacred books generally serve, and, particularly in recent times, an attitude has been taken toward their critical study, similar to that manifested when the early higher critical work began to be done on the Bible. For upon these books had been erected a set of dogmas which it was to the interest of certain elements in Japan to protect at all costs. Specifically, the dogmas of the superhuman founding of the state and of its indestructible character, as well as that of the divine ancestry of the Emperor depend upon them. All of these, but especially the last named, were doctrines of paramount importance during the half century preceding the fall of Japan, at the end of World War II.[1] But of that we shall speak at greater length presently. The two books that are most basic are the *Kojiki,* or Records of Ancient Matters, and the *Nihongi,* or Chronicles of Japan. The third book is the *Yengishiki.* Its importance lies in the ancient Shinto rituals which it contains. These three we shall undertake to discuss briefly in order.

RECORDS OF ANCIENT MATTERS

In the preface to the *Kojiki,* Yasumaro, the reputed author, after a brief résumé of the earlier part of the book, tells us that in the year 673 A.D. the Heavenly Sovereign, Emperor Temmu, laid the basis for its writing. Said the emperor, "I hear that the chronicles of the emperors, and likewise the original words in possession of the various families, deviate from the exact truth, and are mostly amplified by empty falsehoods." He rightly recognized that unless these were corrected, great evil could befall the monarchy, so he ordered that "the chronicles of the emperors be selected and recorded, errors and falsehoods eliminated, and the truth determined and written down for transmission to later ages."

Now there was a young man at court, Hiyeda no Are, who had a great gift of memory so that "he could repeat with his mouth whatever met his eyes, and record in his heart whatever struck his ears." He was, therefore, commanded "to learn by heart the genealogies of the emperors, and likewise the words of former ages."

---

[1] During World War II, according to Dr. Holtom, Shinto nationalists frequently declared that the most sacred of all their texts was the "divine" edict pronounced by Amaterasu-Omi-Kami when she sent her grandson down from Takama-ga-Hara to establish the state. This they called the most sacred absolute of Japanese nationalism.

But this was not done at once. At least nothing was put in writing. The emperor died and it fell to the lot of the empress, Gemmiyo, to see that the work was brought to completion.

In 711 A.D. she commanded Yasumaro "to select and record the old words, learnt by heart by Hiyeda no Are, according to the Imperial Decree, and to lift them up to Her." This Yasumaro proceeded to do, and on the 10th of March, 712 A.D., he presented it in three volumes to her majesty, the empress.[2]

Thus, the book purports to have been written down by Yasumaro, but from the memory of Hiyeda no Are. Where did the latter get the material, which, for a period of some twenty-five years, he had preserved in his memory? For this question the preface provides no answer. Mr. Ernest Satow, a distinguished early student of Shinto, is quoted by Chamberlain as saying that the Emperor Temmu "took pains to instruct this person in the genuine traditions and old language of former ages, and to make him repeat them until he had the whole by heart." Did the emperor himself draw from other sources? Of this there is no indication. One earlier historical book is mentioned as having been compiled in 620 A.D. but destroyed in a fire in 645. The exact nature of its content is not certainly known. *The Records of Ancient Matters* is then the oldest extant book of the Japanese people—indeed, according to W. G. Aston, it is the first book written in any Turanian tongue.[3] Chamberlain regards it as the most important book in all the mass of Japanese literature. "It is the most important because it has preserved for us more faithfully than any other book the mythology, manners, language, and the traditional history of Ancient Japan."[4] Soon after its appearance the influx of Chinese language, ideas, and

---

[2] The *Kojiki*, Vol. 1, pp. 3–13, *passim*. Translated by Basil Hall Chamberlain, it was published as a supplement to Vol. 10 of *Transactions of the Asiatic Society of Japan*, 1882. It was reprinted again in 1906 and republished in 1920. This and all subsequent volume, section, and page references are to this latter edition which will be referred to simply as *Kojiki*. It was again published in 1932 by J. L. Thompson, Kobe, and Kegan Paul, London, with valuable critical notes by W. G. Aston, and a bibliography of books in Japanese on the *Kojiki*, written since 1883.

[3] *Literature of Japan*, pp. 18–19.

[4] *Op. cit.*, pp. i and ii.

other culture traits pretty well obscured the chief features of native Japanese culture.

When a modern historian sets about writing the history of the United States he feels it necessary of course to go back to the period of discovery and colonization; and to give some account of the European people, chiefly the English who colonized and came to rule the Continent.

When the Japanese historian undertook to write the history of his people, like the Hebrews, he went back to the very beginning of the world. "In the beginning God," wrote the Hebrews. The Japanese historian takes us back to the birth of the gods themselves. He begins thus: "The names of the deities that were born in the Plain of High Heaven, when the Heaven and the Earth began, were the Deity Master-of-the-August-Center-of-Heaven, next the High-August-Producing-Wondrous-Deity, next the Divine-Producing-Wondrous-Deity. These three Deities were all Deities born alone, and hid their persons."

These long and largely honorific names are the literal translation of what is written in the Japanese. Thus the first was *Ame-no-mi-naka-nushi-no-kami*.[5] The frequent repetition of the names of the numerous gods gives to the text a stilted character. We are not accustomed to piling up honorific titles referring to deity. But if one desires to read the *Kojiki* he must get used to it. Section one accounts for the birth of five such Divinities. It continues: "The names of the Deities that were born next from a thing that sprouted up like unto a reed-shoot when the earth, young and like unto floating oil, drifted about medusa-like, were the Pleasant-Reed-Shoot-Prince-Elder-Deity, next the Heavenly-Eternally-Standing-Deity. These two Deities were likewise born alone and hid their persons."[6] The five deities in the above list are separate heavenly deities.

In the second section, gods continue to be born, among them, Earthly-Eternally-Standing-Deity, Mud-Earth-Lord and Mud-

---

[5] This deity and two others associated with him in the opening section, says Dr. Holtom, furnish the basis of a claim by some nineteenth and twentieth century Shinto scholars that Shinto believes in a trinitarian monotheism.

[6] *Op. cit.*, p. 15.

Earth-Lady, Germ-Integrating-Deity, Elder-Lady-the-Great-Place and Deity Oh-Awful-Lady, seven generations, none of them gods important in cult. Then appear a divine pair, Izanagi and Izanami, or the Male-Who-Invites and the Female-Who-Invites, from whom are born most of the gods who figure in present-day Japanese religion.[7]

Now begins the creation proper. Izanagi and Izanami are ordered by the heavenly deities to "make, consolidate and give birth to this drifting land." Standing on the Floating Bridge of Heaven, Izanagi toys in the water with a jewelled spear which had been given him. Lifting it from the water the foam which dripped back into the ocean coagulated and became an island, one of the Japanese group called Onogoro.

Izanagi and Izanami descend to the island and there takes place an interesting courtship. A pillar is planted in the middle of the island. They walk about it in opposite directions. Meeting, the Female-Who-Invites, says, "Ah, I have met a fine gentleman," to which the Male-Who-Invites replies gallantly, "Ah, I have met a fine maiden." They are wed and of the union a child is born, but it is misshapen. Something was evidently wrong. The heavenly deities whom they had informed of the mischance said it was because the lady had spoken first. So they went through the ceremony once again, but this time the Male-Who-Invites spoke first. Born of the union, thus properly attained, were first, a number of the Japanese islands, then a number of the gods which now figure in the Shinto cult.

On giving birth to the fire god Izanami was badly burned and died. Izanagi was overwhelmed with sorrow. In anger he slew one of his sons, the deity Shining-Elder, and from his blood and various parts were born many deities. Izanagi then sought to follow his wife into the underworld. Forbidden to look upon her, he nevertheless lighted the tooth of a comb for a torch and saw her, now a mass of corruption. Horrified he fled, and she, put to shame by being seen, sent an ugly goddess to pursue him. Removing his helmet he threw it down and it turned to grapes, which the goddess

[7] *Op. cit.*, p. 17.

stopped to pick up and eat. But she still pursued him. Then he threw down his many-toothed comb and it turned to bamboo sprouts, which she pulled up and ate.

Thereupon, Izanami sent eight thunder deities with a thousand five hundred warriors to pursue him. On reaching the base of the "Even Pass of Hades" he found three peaches growing. He plucked them and hurling them at the oncoming host drove them back. Whereupon he gave to the peaches the name, "Their Augustness-Great-Divine-Fruit." Izanami herself also pursued him, but with a great rock he blocked the "Even Pass of Hades," so she could not reach him. There they exchanged farewells. Said she: "My lovely elder brother, thine Augustness! If thou do like this I will in one day strangle a thousand of folks of your land." Izanagi replied, "My lovely younger sister, thine Augustness! If *thou* do this, *I* will in one day set up a thousand and five hundred parturition houses. In this manner each day a thousand people would surely be born."[8]

Because of all this Izanami came to be called the Great Deity of Hades.

Having become unclean by his experiences in the underworld Izanagi felt it necessary to purify himself. From the staff he threw down was born a deity, from the girdle another, from each of his garments still others—from his trousers, was the Road-Fork-Deity! Altogether twelve of them. From the bath were born a further number. "The name of the Deity that was born as he thereupon washed his left august eye was the Heaven-Shining-Great-August-Deity," Amaterasu-Omikami, the sun goddess, the head of the Japanese pantheon as today held. From the washing of the right eye came the Moon Deity, and from the washing of his nose came His-Brace-Swift-Impetuous-Male-Augustness, Susa-no-Wo or, to give him his full Japanese name, Take-haya-susa-no-Wo-no-Mikoto, often given, for short, in the English translation as "the impetuous male."

To the latter three deities Izanagi gives the rule respectively of the Plain of High Heaven, the night, and the Sea Plain. Eventually Susa-no-Wo becomes the god of storm.

We cannot here follow in detail the further unfolding of the

[8] Vol. 1, Sec. 7–9, *passim.*

creative process. But it is all there in the *Kojiki*, in the greatest detail.

It is not too easy to discern just where the history of the creation of the gods ends and that of men begins. Most of the first volume is concerned with the gods. In Section 33, Ninigi-no-Mikoto, grandson of the sun goddess, is sent down from heaven to found the state. Volume II begins with the rule of Kamu-Yamato-ibare-iko-no-Mikoto, known to history as Jim-mu Tenno, the first emperor of Japan, from whom all subsequent emperors, including the contemporary Hirohito, are believed to be descended in an unbroken line. Jim-mu was himself a direct descendant of Amaterasu, the sun goddess, five generations removed, according to the official genealogy. This is the basis for the belief, held in Japan for centuries, that the emperor was divine, a belief repudiated for the first time by Hirohito, in a radio broadcast after the surrender of Japan, at the end of World War II. Although held in theory over a long period, the belief was accentuated during the latter part of the nineteenth century and since, and became finally a basic dogma underlying the Japanese Imperial thrust, which is often regarded as the beginning of World War II.[9] The idea was taught in the schools, in the army, and resulted finally in a fanatical religious, as well as patriotic, devotion to the emperor, without which, it seems to the writer, it is impossible to explain the daring attack of the island empire of Japan upon the richest and most powerful nation in the world, the United States. It is still not surely known whether the emperor himself was guilty of the aggression or whether he was only a tool in the hands of an unscrupulous and power-mad military group in Japan who used him for their own ends. It still remains one of the anomalies of the modern age that a belief in the divinity of the emperor with the natural corollaries that flow from such a concept could have been developed within a people. It only goes to show that people can be made to believe almost anything and led almost anywhere the leaders wish, if they begin early enough and work assiduously enough at the task of indoctrination.

[9] See D. C. Holtom, *Modern Japan and Shinto Nationalism*, University of Chicago Press, Rev. Ed., 1947.

The remainder of the book is an account, largely legendary, of the rule of various emperors, down to the year 628 B.C. It is believed by scholars that the historical authenticity of the record increases as it approaches the close of the period. But in no case is it anything like a carefully written or complete history of the Japanese people or state. In the latter part there are many ancient songs, and all through the book there are numerous genealogies. Of most of the emperors included it is told how long each lived and where he was buried. Some of these statements resemble the early Biblical stories of longevity. One lived 106 years, another 168 years.

A few factual statements appear. For example, in Volume II, Section 96, the possession of Korea is promised and succeeding sections tell of the preparation for and finally the conquest of Korea under the Empress Jin-go. In Section 110, it is mentioned that Korea, in sending tribute, included the Confucian *Analects* and another book. Occasionally there is a story to account for something of common use among the people. The orange is thus explained:

The emperor sent one of his chiefs to the "Eternal Land" to bring back the fruit of the "everlasting fragrant tree." Meanwhile the emperor died. Returning, the faithful chief made an offering at the tomb of his sovereign and wailed and wept saying: "Bringing the fruit of the everlasting fragrant tree from the Eternal Land, I have come to serve thee," and at last he wailed and wept himself to death. "This fruit of the everlasting fragrant tree is now called the orange."[10]

It is obvious, from the reading of the book, that the age of which it tells was a crude age. Chamberlain calls attention to the fact that they had no tea—imagine Japan without tea!—no fans, porcelain, lacquer, no vehicles of any kind, no way of computing time, no money, very little knowledge of medicine, and there is no mention of writing. The mention of the *Analects* and one other book occurs in the period near the end of the third century A.D.[11] There is in the book a great deal of what the West regards as obscenity. Cham-

[10] *Op. cit.*, Vol. II, Section 74, pp. 245–246.
[11] *Op. cit.*, Introduction, pp. lvi-lvii, *passim.*

berlain puts into Latin the sections which he regards as offensive to Western readers, and he uses not a little Latin. While remarking that of course a barbarous age is not expected to hold to modern standards of decency, Chamberlain writes: "At the same time the whole range of literature might be ransacked in vain for a parallel to the naïve filthiness of the passage forming Section IV, or to the extraordinary topic which the hero Yamato-take and his mistress Miyazu are made to select as the theme of their repartee."

An interesting bit of magic is indicated in Section 116. A mother took a basket of jointed bamboo in which there were eight holes. Into this she placed stones wrapped in bamboo leaves, then she caused this curse to be spoken: "Like unto the becoming green of these bamboo leaves do thou become green and wither. . . . Again like unto the sinking of these stones do thou sink and be prostrate."[12] She then placed the basket over smoke. Whereupon the elder brother dried up, withered, sickened, and lay prostrate for the period of eight years. Upon his earnest pleading, she reversed the process and his body became sound again.

THE NIHONGI

The other book, important as a source for early Japanese religious beliefs, is the *Nihongi* which was written only eight years later than the *Kojiki*, in 720 A.D. Alike in many respects and dealing with almost identical matters, there are also many differences between them. The *Nihongi* is about twice the volume of the *Kojiki*. The *Kojiki* dates nothing. On the other hand, the *Nihongi* gives an exact date, often to the very month and day of many of the events and chronicles. This is not to say that the dates are correctly given. Indeed, save for those in the later years of the Chronicles these dates are obviously not exact. As in the case of the *Kojiki* the later accounts are much more trustworthy historically than the earlier. The *Kojiki* brings the story down to 628, the *Nihongi* to 697. The *Nihongi* is written wholly in Chinese, and much of the manner of treatment of the events narrated betrays definite Chinese influence. Another difference to be noted is that the *Nihongi*, in the account

[12] *Op. cit.*, Vol. II, Sec. 116, p. 327.

of the earlier mythologies, gives not a single story of a particular incident, but two or more—sometimes several. This is evidence of a different attitude toward sources than that of the authors of the *Kojiki.* Aston, who translates the document, believes they had access to written sources. He regards the history written in 620, which we mentioned above, as having been burnt. He evidently believes that at least a part, if not all, of it was preserved in what is known today as the *Kiujiki.*

The *Nihongi* is supposedly the work of two men, one of them the same Yasumaro who wrote the *Kojiki.* The other was one, Prince Toneri, according to the testimony of an early commentary written 810–824 A.D. There is no direct mention of the *Kojiki* in the *Nihongi,* though it appears that some use may have been made of it.

The first part of the book is, like the *Kojiki,* the story of the birth of the gods and is wholly legendary. It disagrees at a number of points with the story as told in the *Kojiki,* or, at least, some of the variant stories of the *Nihongi* do. For example the birth of the three divinities, Amaterasu, or the sun goddess; Tsuki-yomi-no-Mikoto, the moon-god; and Susa-no-Wo-no Mikoto, the Impetuous Male was, in one of the stories, simply the result of an agreement between Izanagi and Izanami. "We have now produced the Great Island Country, etc. Why should we not now produce some one who shall rule the universe?" To be sure other accounts are given paralleling that of the *Kojiki.*

The *Nihongi* begins its account in true Chinese fashion:

Of old, Heaven and Earth were not yet separated, and the In and Yo not yet divided, i.e., the Chinese Yin and Yang. They formed a chaotic mass like an egg, which was of obscurely defined limits and contained germs.

The purer and clearer part was thinly drawn out, and formed Heaven, while the heavier, grosser element settled down and became Earth.

The finer element easily became a united body, but the consolidation of the heavy and gross element was accomplished with difficulty.

Heaven was therefore formed first, and earth was established subsequently.

Thereafter Divine Beings were produced between them. . . .[13]

Thenceforward, the book follows much the same plan as the *Kojiki.*

Generally speaking the *Nihongi* has been held in much higher esteem than the *Kojiki.* Until fairly recently its superiority as a source of information concerning ancient Japan has been unquestioned. Now it begins to be seen that the *Nihongi,* under Chinese influence, has obscured much that was native Japanese. If the *Kojiki* is not completely dependable as to specific historical facts, it probably preserves more accurately the flavor of the Japanese culture which antedated the invasion of Chinese culture in the fifth century.

THE NORITO OR SHINTO RITUALS

In some ways the *Norito,* or Shinto rituals, correspond more closely to the Western conception of sacred scripture than any other Shinto writings. The ancient *Norito* are collected in a work known as the *Yengishiki,* or Institutes of Yengi (901–923 A.D.). Here seventy-five of them are enumerated and the text of twenty-seven of the most important ones is given. The *Norito,* literally "words spoken to the kami," or divinity, are largely ritualistic prayers containing stanzas of praise and thanksgiving to the gods, and special petitions suited to the particular occasion for which they are being employed. In addition to those found in the *Yengishiki,* new *Norito* have been prepared from time to time as changing circumstances required. The new ones are modeled carefully upon the old, using much the same archaic style and imagery. New *Norito* were issued in 1875. These were revised in 1914 and again in 1927. Forty-two Norito were published in the 1914 edition together with a number of short sentence rituals.

The *Norito* provide an excellent index as to the desires of worshippers in Shinto. They vary from prayers for good crops to prosperity, national prestige, long life and a glorious reign for the emperor, etc. The *Norito* for use in celebrating the emperor's

---

[13] Book I, Pt. I, 1, pp. 1–2.

birthday includes a prayer for his long life, a prosperous reign, that the imperial glory shine ever more widely and that his Imperial Benevolence be revered forever. Unfortunately the modern *Norito* have not been translated in full, but excerpts from them have been published by Dr. D. C. Holtom.[14]

Dr. Holtom reports that after the disestablishment of State Shinto following the fall of Japan in 1945, the *Norito* were revised and the old nationalistic elements eliminated. Each shrine was left free to formulate its own *Norito*. Soon, however, a non-government Shrine Association was formed to exercise some oversight of the shrines, and this organization published a book of rituals in 1948 which contains thirty-three *Norito*. Here may be given only a part of the ritual of the great purification service—most notable of them all. It bears some resemblance to Yom Kippur of the Hebrews (Lev. 16).

It begins with a call to the Imperial Princes, Ministers of State, and high officials, to give ear to the great purification by which "are purged and washed away all sins which have been committed by Imperial officials and attendants," men or women, civil or military. It recites the founding of their empire by the gods. Then it lists the offenses, heavenly and earthly, which the people commit. It is an interesting list:

Heavenly offenses are the breaking down of divisions between rice fields, filling up water courses, removing water-pipes, flaying alive backwards, spreading excrement over the doors. . . . Earthly offenses are the cutting of living bodies, the cutting of dead bodies, leprosy, incest, calamities from creeping things, from the high gods and from high birds, killing of cattle, bewitchment.

When these offenses are committed then certain offerings must be made and the great liturgy recited:

When they do so, the gods of heaven, thrusting open the adamantine doors of heaven and cleaving the many-piled clouds of heaven with an awful way—cleaving, will approach and lend ear. The gods of earth,

[14] *Political Philosophy of Modern Shinto*, pp. 286–292. The *Yengishiki* has been translated in part by Ernest Satow, in *Transactions of the Asiatic Society of Japan*, Vols. 7 and 9, and by a German scholar, Karl Florens in Vol. 27, part 4.

ascending to the tops of the high mountains and the tops of the low mountains, sweeping aside the mists of the high mountains and mists of the low mountains, will approach and lend ear.

Then shall no offences remain unpurged, from the court of the august child of the gods even to the remotest ends of the realm. As the many-piled clouds of heaven are scattered at the breath of the Wind Gods; as the morning breezes disperse the morning vapours and the evening vapours; as a huge ship casting off its bow moorings, drives forth into the vast ocean; as yonder thick brushwood is smitten and cleared away by the sharp sickle forged in the fire—so shall all offences be swept utterly away. . . .

They are now destroyed, and all, from the servants of the Imperial court down to the people in the four quarters of the realm, are from this day forth void of offence.

Attend, all of you, with ears pricked up to the plain of heaven, to this great purification by which, on this interlune of the sixth month as the sun goes down, your offences are purged and purified.[15]

If there is any one other document which might properly be included in a discussion of the Sacred Literature of Japan it would be the Imperial Rescript on Education. Given by the Emperor Meiji, it has been perhaps as influential as any one other single utterance upon the life of Japan, particularly in the field of moral education. It is interesting to note in the rescript the confirmation of the divine descent of the emperor, in the use of the phrase, "our imperial throne, coeval with heaven and earth."

Know ye, our subjects:

Our imperial ancestors have founded our Empire on a basis broad and everlasting and have deeply and firmly implanted virtue; our subjects, ever united in loyalty and filial piety, have from generation to generation illustrated the beauty thereof. This is the glory and the fundamental character of our Empire, and herein also lies the source of our education. Ye, our subjects, be filial to your parents, affectionate to your brothers and sisters; as husbands and wives be harmonious; as friends true; bear yourselves in modesty and moderation; extend your benevolence to all; pursue learning and cultivate arts, and thereby develop intellectual facul-

[15] W. G. Aston, *A History of Japanese Literature*, D. Appleton and Co., N. Y., 1916, pp. 11–13.

ties and perfect moral powers; furthermore, advance public good and promote common interests; always respect the Constitution and observe the laws; should emergency arise, offer yourselves courageously to the state; and thus guard and maintain the prosperity of our imperial throne coeval with heaven and earth. So shall ye not only be our good and faithful subjects, but render illustrious the best traditions of your forefathers.

The way here set forth is indeed the teaching bequeathed by our imperial ancestors, to be observed alike by their descendants and the subjects, infallible for all ages and true in all places. It is our wish to lay it to heart in all reverence, in common with you, our subjects, that we may all thus attain to the same virtue.

The 30th day of the 19th month of the 23rd year of Meiji (1890).

Some of the Shinto sects, of which there were thirteen officially recognized by government before World War II, have special scriptures of their own which cannot be discussed here. Two of these are briefly described in the last chapter of the book as examples of Modern Sacred Books.

SACRED LITERATURE OF THE JAPANESE
Sources for Further Reading

The Kojiki, Records of Ancient Matters, translated by Basil Hall Chamberlain. Transactions of the Asiatic Society of Japan, Supplement to Vol. X. Reprinted 1920, Tokyo. Again published by J. L. Thompson, Kobe, and Kegan Paul, London, 1932.

The Nihongi, Chronicles of Japan from earliest times to A.D. 697. Translated by W. G. Aston. Original edition published for the Japan Society by Kegan Paul, Trench, Truebner and Company, 1896, in 2 Vol. Reissued in 1 Volume, Kegan Paul, Trench, Truebner and Company, London, 1924.

The Yengishiki, Transactions of the Asiatic Society of Japan, Vols. 7 and 9, and Vol. 27, Part 1.

Sacred Books and Literature of the Early East. Vol. 13.
    Pp. 1–51, selections from the *Kojiki.*
    Pp. 63–147, selections from the *Nihongi.*
    Pp. 161–174, selections from the *Yengishiki.*

Frost, S. E., *Sacred Writings of the World's Great Religions,* pp. 347–354.

CHAPTER XI

The Sacred Literature of the Persians—Zoroastrianism

The sacred book of Zoroastrianism is the Avesta, though often, but improperly, it is called the Zend-Avesta. It is comparatively little known in the Western world, probably because Zoroastrianism as a living faith no longer occupies a place of great importance. At one time one of the great missionary faiths of the world, it has declined under persecution, or pressure from without, until there remain only a little more than a hundred thousand Zoroastrians in the whole world. Most of these are not to be found in the land in which the faith began. There is in Persia, or Iran, a small remnant of probably less than thirty thousand followers of the prophet, Zoroaster. The larger group is a remnant of the company of Zoroastrians, now known as Parsis, who migrated to India many centuries ago, in search of freedom to worship according to their own beliefs, for freedom was denied them by their Mohammedan conquerors at home.

Nevertheless, the faith of Zoroastrianism has been of very great influence upon three of the great religions of the world, Judaism, Christianity, and Islam, and therefore deserves to be better known.

The extant Zoroastrian writings are probably only a small part of what once constituted a very extensive collection of sacred writ. It is mentioned by Pliny the Elder that some two million verses were composed by the prophet, Zoroaster. There is also a reference in late sources to twenty-one Nasks, or books originally, of which there remain little more than a half-dozen today. In fact, we are told the very content of each of the books. The collection as a whole covers a very wide range of material—historical, religious, cultural—indeed, it is almost encyclopedic in character.

The invasion of Alexander was the occasion for the destruction of a considerable part of the book, and in the years following little attempt was made to restore what had been destroyed, or to preserve what remained. It appears that some time in the third or fourth century of the Christian era an effort was made to bring together all the writings that remained, and to put into written form such oral traditions as were still retained concerning the lost parts of the book. This work was brought to completion perhaps in the fourth century, revised and finally declared canonical. It is this which remains and constitutes the Avesta today. However, even this has undergone change, because to the original Avestan text has been added a commentary, or paraphrase, to some of the material, and this material has also come to be regarded as sacred.

In its present form there are seven divisions in the Avesta: the Yasna, the Gathas, the Visparad, the Yashts, certain minor texts, the Vendidad, and a group of fragments.

The *Gathas*, which are today found interspersed throughout the *Yasna*,[1] constitute the oldest as well as the most important part of scripture, for here are preserved, more than anywhere, the authentic words of the prophet himself, Zoroaster. On linguistic grounds, it is adjudged much older than the other parts of the book, and may well go back to the time of Zoroaster himself, some scholars think. There is in these songs more of spontaneity and depth of religious insight than is found in the other parts of the book. Here apparently religion was simpler and less complicated. It is in these verses that

---

[1] They are to be found as Chapters 28–34; 43–51; 53, of the Yasna, *Sacred Books of the East*, Vol. 31, pp. 1–194.

one discovers the apparent monotheistic belief of Zoroaster who seems to have reacted vigorously against the polytheism of his day. But if there is monotheism here, it is not to be found elsewhere in the scriptures, which are full of reference to, and praises of, numerous other gods, angels, and spirits. Apparently the vigorous reform of Zoroaster himself had failed to sustain itself after his death, and the whole pantheon crowded back into the picture.

In the *Gathas* is told the story of the call of Zoroaster. The "Soul of the Kine," representative of the economic base of the Iranian people, addresses Ahura, the divinity raised to the place of Supreme God by Zoroaster's reform, inquiring why she was ever created since suffering and afflictions are her lot, and beseeching the Divine Order to instruct her in the benefits of agriculture, and serve as her protector. In response Ahura names Zarathustra (Zoroaster) who, inspired by Good Mind—an attribute of Ahura himself—will serve the Iranian people. They object at first, but he is confirmed in the appointment, and accepts it, only praying: "Do ye, O Ahura, and thou, O righteousness, grant gladness unto these our disciples. . . . And when shall the (Divine) Righteousness, the good Mind (of the Lord and His) Sovereign Power (come) hastening to me (to give me strength for my task and mission) O Great Creator, the Living Lord? (For without this I cannot advance or undertake my toil). Do ye now therefore assign unto us your aid and in abundance for our great cause. May we be partakers of the bountiful grace of these your equals."[2]

Following his call, under a sense of his own inadequacy he prays earnestly for the necessary gifts and knowledge to perform his task effectively: "That best of gifts therefore do I beseech of Thee, O Thou best (of beings) Ahura! Who art one in will with (Thy Divine) Righteousness . . . do Thou teach me from Thyself, yea, from Thine own mouth of spirit, that I may declare it forth to (these Thy waiting people) by what (powers and according to what laws) the primeval world arose."[3]

Again and again he inquires about the origin of things: "Tell me

[2] *Sacred Books of the East,* Vol. 31, pp. 1–13, *passim.*
[3] Yasna, 38:9, 12. *Sacred Books of the East,* Vol. 31, pp. 22–24.

I ask thee, O Ahura! Tell me aright, Who by generation was the first father of the Righteous Order (within the world)? Who gave the sun and stars their (undeviating) way? Who established that whereby the moon waxes and whereby she wanes, save Thee? . . . Who from beneath hath sustained the earth and the clouds above that they do not fall? Who made the waters and the plants? Who to the wind has yoked the storm clouds? . . . Who . . . is the inspirer of the good thoughts?"[4] "Who is the righteous one . . . and who is evil? . . . How shall I banish this Demon-of-the-Lie from us hence . . . and deliver him into the two hands of Thine Order to cast her down to death . . . and send mighty destruction among her believers, to keep those deceitful and harsh oppressors from reaching their (fell) aims?"[5]

He had strong opposition to his preaching and, for a long time, won no converts to the cause. He cries out: "To what land to turn; aye, whither turning shall I go?" Neither kinsmen nor princes will aid him. "How then shall I establish well the faith, and thus conciliate Thy (grace), O Lord?"[6]

Judgment shall fall upon those of evil deeds "and when they approach there where the Judge's Bridge (extends, unlike the believing ones of God, who go so firmly forth with me as a guide and helper, these shall miss their path and fall), and in the Lie's abode forever shall their habitation be. But for the penitent there is yet hope."[7]

Here is prophetic judgment of an ethical God upon those who sin. It is reminiscent of some of the utterances of the prophets of Israel. The whole scheme of salvation was to be developed into a highly elaborate and eschatological scheme in late Zoroastrianism, which undoubtedly had its influence upon Judaism and through it upon Christianity. It was an ethically conditioned immortality which Zoroaster taught.

These *Gathas* are not easy reading. They lack the grace and charm that one finds in an Isaiah or a Jeremiah. Part of the difficulty

[4] Yasna XLIV, 2–4, *passim. Sacred Books of the East*, Vol. 31, pp. 112–113.
[5] *Ibid.,* 12, 13, 14, *passim.*
[6] XLVI, 1, pp. 134–135.
[7] *Op. cit.,* XLVI, 11–12, pp. 140–141.

lies in the fact that the text is often corrupt, and the language obscure to modern scholars. But there is a strength and forthrightness about the Gathas which sets them apart from the later scriptures, which preserve chiefly the rituals of the faith of a later day.

Zoroastrianism is strongly dualistic in its developed form. Over against Ahura-Mazda, or Ormuzd, the good Lord and his holy attributes, the Amesha Spentas, there stands in increasing conflict Angra-Mainyu, or Ahriman, the evil one and his unholy attributes, corresponding to the Amesha Spentas. But the basis of this is clearly laid in the Gathas themselves, though not so fully or explicitly spelled out. In *Yasna* XXX the concept is set forth for the first time. "Thus there are the primeval spirits who as a pair (combining their opposite strivings) and (yet each) independent in his action, have been famed (of old). They are a better thing, they two, and a worse as to thought, as to word, and as to deed. And between these two let the wisely acting choose aright. (Choose ye) not (as) evil doers!"[8]

These two came together and created each his separate realm, quaintly expressed as "making life and life's absence," determined how the world should be ordered at the last for the good and for the wicked. Thus the good Ahura was not to be held responsible for the creation of the evil in the world. Says L. S. Mills: "The swallowing up of sin and sorrow in ultimate happiness belongs to a later period. It is not Gathic Zarathustrianism. Evil was the work of an independent being."[9] Yet, in a later verse of the same Gatha, mention is made of the final attainment of perfection, when "the blow of destruction shall fall upon the Demon of falsehood, and her adherents shall perish with her."[10] Surely this foreshadows the scenes of final judgment of later Zoroastrianism, when all the evil shall be destroyed and only the good remain.

The *Yasna* is a liturgical book. It is used in connection with the *Yasna* ceremony which is very much like the Vedic ceremony of preparation of the *soma* for ritual use in sacrifice. The *soma* of the Vedas becomes *Haoma* in the *Avesta* but the ceremony is strikingly

---

[8] *Sacred Books of the East*, Vol. 31, p. 291.
[9] *Op. cit.*, Vol. 31, p. 26.
[10] *Id.*, p. 34.

similar in both cases, due no doubt to the fact that it was an old custom common to the Indo-Iranian Aryans for a long time before they became separated into their Persian and Indian branches. The ceremony here is too long to repeat but a few verses will be included:

Thereupon spake Zarathustra: Praise to H(a)oma. Good is H(a)oma, and the well-endowed, exact and righteous in its nature, and good inherently, and healing, beautiful of form, and good in deed, and most successful in its working, goldenhued, with bending sprouts. As it is the best for drinking, so (through its sacred stimulus) is it the most nutritious for the soul.

This first blessing I beseech of thee, O H(a)oma, thou that drivest death afar! I beseech of thee for (heaven), the best life of the saints, the radiant, all-glorious.

This second blessing I beseech of thee, O H(a)oma, thou that drivest death afar! this body's health (before that blest life is attained.)

This third blessing I beseech of thee, O H(a)oma, thou that drivest death afar! that I may stand victorious on earth, conquering in battles, overwhelming the assaults of hate, and conquering the lie. . . .

This sixth blessing I ask of thee, O H(a)oma, thou that drivest death afar! that we may get good warning of the thief, good warning of the murderer, see first the bludgeon-bearer, get first sight of the world. May no one whichsoever get first sight of us. In the strife with each, may we be they who get the first alarm!

Hail to thee, O H(a)oma, who hast power as thou wilt, by thine inborn strength! Hail to thee, thou art well-versed in many sayings, and true and holy words. Hail to thee for thou dost ask no wily questions, but questionest direct.

O H(a)oma, thou house-Lord, and thou clan-Lord, thou tribe-Lord, and chieftain of the land, and thou successful learned teacher, for aggressive strength I speak to thee, for that which smites with victory, and for my body's saving, for manifold delight!

Bear off from us the torment and the malice of the hateful. Divert the angry foe's intent!

What man soever in this house is violent and wicked, what man soever in this village, or this tribe, or province, seize thou away the fleetness from his feet; throw thou a veil of darkness o'er his mind; make thou his intellect (at once) a wreck!

Let not the man who harms us, mind or body, have power to go forth on both his legs, or hold with both his hands, or see with both his eyes, not the land (beneath his feet), or the herd before his face.

H(a)oma grows while he is praised, and the man who praises him is therewith more victorious. The lightest pressure of thee, H(a)oma, thy feeblest praise, the slightest tasting of thy juice, avails to the thousand-smiting of the D(a)evas.

Wasting doth vanish from that house, and with it foulness, whither in verity they bear thee, and where thy praise in truth is sung, the drink of H(a)oma, famed, health-bringing (as thou art). [(Pazand) to his village and abode they bear him.]

All other toxicants go hand in hand with Rapine of the bloody spear, but H(a)oma's stirring power goes hand in hand with friendship. [Light is the drunkenness of H(a)oma (Pazand).]

Who as a tender son caresses H(a)oma, forth to the bodies of such persons H(a)oma comes to heal.

Of all the healing virtues, H(a)oma, whereby thou art a healer, grant me some. Of all the victorious powers, whereby thou art a victor, grant me some. A faithful praiser will I be to thee, O H(a)oma, and a faithful praiser (is) a better (thing) than Righteousness the Best; so hath the Lord, declaring (it), decreed.[11]

A collection of twenty-one hymns of various angels and heroes of ancient Persia, legendary and probably pre-Zoroastrian, make up the *Yashts*. They contain little of interest to a modern reader, as indeed do few of the Zoroastrian texts apart from the *Gathas*. The *Vendidad* resembles very much the book of Leviticus in the Bible, for it is a priestly book, largely concerned with ritual purity. This has led to innumerable taboos, and ceremonies which are incumbent upon those who would cleanse themselves of the defilement which comes from violating taboos.

Thus is to be accounted for, for example, the odd custom of the Parsis in the disposal of their dead. In order not to bury them, an act which would pollute the earth, the body is exposed in an elevated tower (Tower of Silence), for the vultures to consume. Anyone who is in contact with the dead becomes defiled and must be purified.

If a man bury the body of a dog or a man in the earth and not

[11] *Sacred Books of the East*, Vol. 31, pp. 235–241, *passim*.

disinter it for half a year, he shall be beaten with five hundred stripes with a goad. If he leave the body in the ground a full year a thousand stripes is the penalty. If it be left for two years it is a deed which nothing can pay, a trespass for which there is not atonement even possible.[12]

Land upon which a man or a dog died must lie fallow for a year before it can be used for agricultural purposes.[13]

Ground in which a body has been buried is not purified for use until fifty years have passed.[14]

One may not dispose lightly of such things as parings of the nails or hair that has been cut off from the head. The improper disposition of them constitutes "a deadly deed whereby a man increases the strength of the Daevas" (or evil spirits). They must be taken away ten paces from the faithful, twenty paces from fire, thirty paces from water and fifty paces from certain consecrated articles. A hole of prescribed depth must be dug, the hair or nails deposited, with certain "fiend smiting words," then furrows must be drawn with a metal knife around the hole, to the accompaniment of appropriate chanting.[15]

There is a good deal of medical lore in the book just as there is in the Book of Leviticus.

There are also regulations concerning those who would practice surgery. One must not practice upon worshippers of Mazda until he has successfully practiced upon three worshippers of the Daevas. If unsuccessful there, he may never practice on the faithful.

There are even rules regulating the fees physicians may charge. The charge is proportional to the importance of the patient. A priest he shall heal for a blessing, a master of a house he shall heal for the value of a not too good ox; the lord of a town must pay the value of a very valuable ox; and the lord of a province the value of a chariot and four.[16]

Included also within the *Vendidad* there are occasional stories,

---

[12] Vendidad, III, 36–39, *Sacred Books of the East,* Vol. 4, p. 3.
[13] *Id.,* VI, 1, p. 66.
[14] *Id.,* VII, 45, p. 86.
[15] *Id.,* XVII, *passim,* pp. 186–189.
[16] *Vendidad,* VII, *Sacred Books of the East,* Vol. 4, p. 87.

for example, concerning the temptation of Zoroaster, also stories concerning the destiny of the soul after death. Probably the book as a whole, if one skips the repetitions which run throughout, is as interesting reading as anything to be found in Zoroastrian scriptures.

But the *Vendidad* is not solely concerned with ritual. There is at least one section (IV) which deals with contracts—six different kinds—and various kinds of outrages, that is to say it is in some senses a book of law. Each kind of contract is specifically defined and an appropriate penalty assessed for violation. For example, if one breaks a word contract, that is, one made simply by word of mouth, he shall be beaten with six hundred stripes and his next of kin is answerable for his atonement. More serious contracts carry correspondingly higher penalties if broken. So for outrages such as assaults, blows, wounds, broken bones, manslaughter.

The *Yashts* and minor texts combined, as they often are, form a kind of abridged *Avesta* or smaller *Avesta,* called the *Khordah Avesta* which serves as a book of prayers for laymen.

In addition to the *Avesta,* as above described, there are late Pahlavi works which are much used by Zoroastrians of the later periods. Chief of these are the *Bundahish* and the *Dinkard.* The former is concerned chiefly with eschatology, that is the end of the world, and the final judgment. It presents the most elaborate eschatological scheme the world has yet seen. Much of it sounds familiar to those acquainted with the more extreme millenarian beliefs held by some Christian groups. While this book itself is too late in origin to have affected Christian thought since it comes from perhaps the ninth century A.D., it is probably true that Zoroastrian beliefs concerning eschatology, here carried to such an extreme, did materially affect late Hebrew and early Christian ideas of the ending of the world and the final judgment. Indeed, not a little of the content of the book may have been taken from now lost earlier Avestan sources.

The *Dinkard,* longest of the Pahlavi works, consisted at one time of nine books, though two of them have been lost. It is a sort of miscellaneous collection of material on a great variety of subjects, literary, social, scientific, and religious, for instance one book discusses astrology, another miracles that have occurred, another morality and custom. While not canonical in the sense that the Avestan books are, both are of great importance in late Zoroastrian belief and practice. There is now a movement among young modern Zoroastrians to go back to the earlier purer form of their faith, not unlike movements that have occurred within Hinduism and Christianity under such names as "Back to the Vedas," or "Back to Christ," or "Back to the gospels," in an attempt to throw off the accretions of the years which are felt to have obscured the original teachings of those faiths.

ZOROASTRIANISM

Sources for Further Reading

Sacred Books of the East. Vol. IV. *The Vendidad.* Vol. XXXI. The *Gathas,* the *Yasnas,* the *Visparad* and some fragments.
Sacred Books and Literature of the East, Vol. 7. The *Gathas,* pp. 14–58, *Vendidad,* pp. 59–162; *Bundahish,* pp. 179–184.

IN THE ANTHOLOGIES

Bible of the World, pp. 561–639. The *Gathas,* pp. 561–570.
World's Great Scriptures, pp. 361–374. The *Gathas, Vendidad, Yasna.*
Tree of Life, pp. 307–334.
Tongues of Fire, pp. 103–120.
Scriptures of the World's Great Religions (Frost), pp. 67–78.

CHAPTER XII

Hebreo-Christian Sacred Literature

The Bible belongs both to Jews and Christians. It would not, therefore, be correct to call the Old Testament simply the sacred literature of the Jews. It seemed wise, therefore, to divide this chapter into three parts: Part I, the Old Testament with brief mention of the Talmud, the Shulhan Aruch and the Responsa; Part II, the New Testament; Part III, the versions of both Old and New Testaments.

PART I: THE OLD TESTAMENT

In any survey of sacred literatures of the world's religions written primarily for occidental readers, the writer is always somewhat at a loss as to how to deal with the Bible. He may assume safely that the great majority of his readers will know little or nothing about the Bibles of other cultures. He knows, therefore, that he must provide a good deal of detailed background material, both historical and religious, in order to make them intelligible. But the Bible is an integral part of Western culture. It is wrought into the very fabric of the life and literature of Western peoples. A substantial percentage of his readers will have had some opportunity in Sunday School or in church to have acquainted themselves with at least portions of the Bible, the religion out of which it grew and which it so largely expresses. Will he not be carrying coals to Newcastle if he repeats here the supposedly familiar facts concerning it?

In a few cases this will undoubtedly be true, but if the general run of readers of the book—and it is not designed for specialists in the field—are anything at all like the students who, across the years, have enrolled in the writer's courses in the Bible, then it is fairly safe to assume that their knowledge of the book is not too extensive or detailed. He recalls the answers given, year after year at the beginning of the course, to ten simple questions which he gave the class—not profound questions as to the hidden meaning of sacred passages, but simple questions of fact about the make-up of the book or about some outstanding character or event recounted in the Bible. When he asked, "Who was Amos, and for what was he noted?" he felt he must request that the answers not be facetious. So very few know the real answer. To the question, "Who was David and for what was he noted?" nine out of ten who evidenced any knowledge about him said that he was the slayer of Goliath, or perhaps more often, "he killed a giant." Goliath seems to have made a deep impression upon the minds of most. One volunteered that he was a good man. Several Jewish students gave no answers at all to the question.

The first time the questions were given, apology was made to the class for possibly insulting their intelligence by asking them to name the four gospels. Some got one, some two, some three, some four, though attributing some of them to apostles not usually known to have left gospels. One stalwart senior, who said afterward that he had earned a series of medals for perfect attendance at Sunday School over a period of several years, remarked, "What were those gospels, prof? I have heard of them, I suppose, but I can't name them."

Where not a little understanding of the general moral and spiritual Biblical values on the part of students was evidenced, there was still quite often an amazing lack of acquaintance with the Bible from which our culture has largely drawn them. Perhaps the fault lies not so much with the students themselves as with the kind of religious education to which they have been subjected. It is noteworthy that, in contradistinction to the older Bible-centered training in the past, most of these students had come up through the modern graded Sunday Schools in which not the Bible but the child has been central; in which the Bible has been brought into the focus of attention only when the situation demanded it.

The older Bible-centered curriculum gave only a very fragmentary view of the book. One learned "verses," portions, chapters— even books—but concerning the Bible as a whole there was little instruction given—almost nothing as to its literary and historical origins and values. One did not see the forest for the trees.

Good books there are which tell the story of the Bible, interestingly and well, but few, comparatively, read them. (A list of some of the better ones appears below in a footnote.) Not so frequently has a writer attempted, in the brief compass of a chapter or two, to give a comprehensive over-view of the whole Bible. Yet that is a thing highly to be desired. What is needed is that people read the Bible—not books about it. Yet, paradoxically enough, unless some understanding of the Biblical books as a whole is had, the Bible does not so readily yield its store of wealth of value to the reader.

The reason for this is not far to seek. For the Bible is a book of an ancient people which has had to be translated into the language of peoples of very different cultures. Even when these translations have been good, and quite intelligible to the people of the period of the translators, with the passage of time these versions have become archaic in language to later generations. But because a certain sacredness attaches to them, people resent newer and more accurate versions couched in the familiar idiom of their own times. An excellent illustration of this is the strong resistance to the superseding of the King James version by other later versions. Although the American Standard Version has now been in existence for roughly a half century it has by no means succeeded in displacing the older authorized version. And now a new version is in the process of preparation and publication. The New Testament appeared in 1946,[1] the Old Testament should appear in 1952. Will it succeed any better than its predecessor in displacing the older authorized version? (If any one is in doubt as to the lack of clarity for modern readers in the King James translation let him read L. A. Weigle, *The English New Testament* (Abingdon-Cokesbury, N. Y., 1946, pp. 149–153) where the author lists nearly two hundred words in the New Testament alone that have changed meaning.)

Let us look, then, at some of the facts about the making and transmission of the Bible to our own times, with the view to seeing out of what it grew; what it meant to the peoples through whom it came to us; and how it has influenced and been esteemed by the people to whom it has been the very revelation of God to man.

To both Christians and Jews the Old Testament is the word of God. Just what does that mean? To the ultra-conservative representative of either faith it means first that it is the infallible, inerrant, very very word of God, *ipsissima verba*, i.e., a verbally inspired record of God's revelation to man. To the modern-minded it may mean only that here in some way, though certainly not infallibly or verbally inspired, the authentic voice of God has spoken to man more clearly than in any other way in history. For both it is a rich repository of faith, to be used possibly in different ways to stimulate and nourish religious faith through the ages. Between the two extremes there is a wide variety of ways in which men conceive of it, and these differing views of the Bible have important consequences for religious faith, and certainly for the ways in which men approach and study the Bible.

The conservative has studied it diligently to discover whatever might be the religious truth hidden within the sacred text. He has been an avid student of the text in the original languages. He has used every device of linguistic inquiry to render its meaning clear. He has carefully collated manuscripts which differed in some respects in their reading and sought to purify the text of errors of copying or transmission. Unable to assert infallibility in any actual

[1] *The Revised Standard Version of the New Testament*, Thomas Nelson & Sons, N. Y., 1946.

existing text, he has sought to push farther and farther back toward the original which he believes to have been quite without error. In this, which is known as textual criticism, he has worked side by side with the liberal scholar, for he knows how easily mistakes can creep in when one copies from another manuscript. Letters somewhat similar in appearance are easily confused, for example, "i" and "e," or "v" and "u," or "l" and "t" when the cross on the letter is omitted, or "m" and "n," or "m" and "w," etc. Most languages have just such similarities. For example, "d" and "r" are very similar in Hebrew, also "n" and "g," and others. Furthermore, in early Hebrew only the consonants were written. The vowels had to be supplied by the reader. Also the words were not separated one from another as in modern languages, and to complicate the matter still more, there were no capital letters and no punctuation. At a comparatively late time these helps were added in the so-called Massoretic text, which has been generally followed since, but what guarantee is there that the Massoretes, who did it several centuries after the last book was originally written, were always correct in their word divisions, supplying vowels and punctuation?

But with the coming of the scientific age, which ventured to raise questions about anything and everything, a new kind of study was applied to the Bible. The new method was primarily inductive. Instead of starting with a preconceived idea of what a thing was, men started with such facts as they were able to discover by thorough investigation and then, on the basis of these facts, made a generalization or an hypothesis which seemed best and most adequately to explain the facts. Could such a method be applied to the Bible? By no means, cried the ultra-conservatives. This is a sacred book—something different, apart—on which violent hands must not be laid. By all means, cried the devotees of the new method. How can it be known whether it is the word of God? Does it make any such claim of itself? Only in a thoroughgoing investigation of the book and the unearthing of all available facts about the book could one base any opinion so far-reaching as the claim that it was in a special way the word of God. Other books were being studied in this way by every possible historico-literary device. Why not the Bible? If it were true, no damage could possibly be done to it. Or if it were false—well, ought not men to know that also? The issue was squarely joined and a century-long battle has been waged by the "ultras" against what they regarded as an attack upon the Bible with the intent to destroy it, but what was from the standpoint of the liberal scholar, his attempt to discover the truth about the Bible, and to preserve it from its friends in an age of almost universal questioning. "If it be of God," he has contended, with the ancient teacher, Gamaliel,[2] it will stand the most searching inquiry.

The methods, the modern scholar used were simply the recognized techniques of the historian, the linguist, and the student of literatures. He laid under tribute every contribution of the archaeologist, the anthropologist, the psychologist, the historian, the sociologist, the literary critic in his attempt to discover the truth about the Bible, and in it. To be sure, there is here the possibility of a greater degree of subjectivity than in the more formal linguistic and textual study, but even there pure objectivity is by no means possible.

As a result of all this, there are today differing schools of thought concerning the Bible. The one here presented chiefly, though sometimes both positions may be indicated, is the so-called modern viewpoint, because that is the author's own point of view, arrived at deliberately after having been in childhood and youth indoctrinated with the older, more orthodox view. In so brief a treatment it is not possible or desirable to document fully all the positions stated but reference will be made to first-rate treatments from both points of view.

It is the belief of "modern" Biblical scholars that the Old Testament was of very slow growth, that parts of it passed through many hands before they reached the form in which they are now found, that it is in no sense chronological in its arrangement, i.e., from the standpoint of the time when its various parts were written; that some portions describing very early events were written quite late; that there seems to have been a great deal of reading back into the

[2] Acts 5:39.

distant past of ideas which came comparatively late upon the scene; that much of what was earlier thought to be the work of some single author was really the result of a long process of growth to which not a few writers or editors contributed to bring it into the form in which we read it today.

Does all this invalidate the Bible as a source of religious truth? Not at all, they say, for when did the truth or falsity of a saying reside in who said it, or when, or where? Truth is truth whether spoken by a Moses, an Isaiah, a Jeremiah, or by a nameless story-teller or editor in either earlier or later Hebrew history. It may come with greater prestige and authority from the lips of one of the great accredited spokesmen of God, but it is not true because of this fact. All truth, say the liberal scholars, is God's truth; there is no other. That so much of what is in the Bible has, in the long experience of men and women, validated itself over and over again as true, constitutes the justification for speaking of it as the Word of God. It would have been true had it been found outside the Bible, or if uttered by those who make no claim of being the spokesmen of the divine. Nor, on the other hand, does the fact that a statement is found within the covers of the Sacred Book guarantee its truth. It is a saying long since become trite but still true of the thought of modern liberal students of the Bible, that the Bible is not in its entirety the word of God, but that the Bible does contain the word of God. That some, indeed much, of its content of truth has been known to people who have never known the Bible at all does not invalidate the statement. The Bible is the book which has been uniquely the revealer of that truth to the peoples who have become Christian or Jewish throughout the world. It is a belief confidently held by liberal Jews and Christians, and stated authoritatively in the very Bible itself, that God "left not himself without witness"[3] among any people. But "peoples of the Book," as Moslems called the Jews and Christians, have found that witness chiefly through the pages of the Bible.

The Old Testament, while a part of the scriptures of the Christians, and wholly that of the Jews, is more than that. It is the entire,

[3] Acts 14:17.

extant, early literature of the Jews as a people. There is in existence little or nothing of a literary character from Hebrew sources, outside their canonical writings, which goes very far back of the Christian era. Yet they had had a national existence of one sort or another of well-authenticated historical character, for at least a thousand years. Only that survived, apparently, which came to be regarded as sacred. But fortunately for us the Hebrew found God in history, in law, in the folk wisdom of the people and in his flights of poetic inspiration, as well as in his profound questionings concerning the meaning of life; so we have actually preserved for us a veritable wealth of literary variety of expression. Here one finds the dull report of the census-taker, the uninspired but minute directions for the performance of the cult, stories of man's beginnings and that of many of the common experiences of his life, such as language, relationship of races, why the rainbow; colorful stories, of the might and prowess of ancient ancestors of the race, riddles, puns, fables, prayers, songs that have become almost the universal songs of the human race, the history of the rise and fall of dynasties, the preaching of reformers and prophets, the questioning of it all by men grown weary of the struggle, proverbial sayings of great wisdom; the dreams of conquest both of earth and heaven.

All this is there and more—for it is the literature of a people, but a literature shot through and through with the consciousness of a guiding presence, that of God, upon whom rests the destiny of man and the nations. It is an amazing literature. Born of a people who never attained greatness as a nation, buffeted by greater and lesser enemies throughout their whole existence, a nation that at its widest period of expansion would have ruled a region scarcely larger than Pennsylvania, this book has mothered three great religions which between them touch very nearly half the entire population of the world.

The Old Testament comprises, in the form used by Protestant Christians and the Palestinian Jews, whom they follow, thirty-nine so-called books. Roman Catholics add to that number a few other books and additions to some of those as held by Protestants who refer to this added material as the Apocrypha. These are very much like canonical books, as any Protestant will readily see if he dips into them without knowing that they are non-canonical. How they came to be regarded as canonical by some and not so by others we shall later see.

Jews generally divide their Bible into three major divisions, these representing three separate stages in the process of canonization. The first is the Torah, or the Law, which is the most sacred of all. Indeed, it is generally held that the later collections are only a further expansion of the Torah, the making explicit of what was only implicit there. It comprises the first five books, Genesis, Exodus, Leviticus, Numbers, and Deuteronomy, the so-called books of Moses.

The second is the Book of the Prophets or the book of the former and the latter prophets. The former prophets comprise the books of Joshua, Judges, I and II Samuel, I and II Kings, while the latter include the writings of the three major prophets, Isaiah, Jeremiah, and Ezekiel, and the book of the twelve, often called the minor prophets; Hosea, Joel, Amos, Obadiah, Jonah, Micah, Nahum, Habakkuk, Zephaniah, Haggai, Zechariah and Malachi.

The third division called the *Hagiographa*, or simply "the writings," is a miscellany comprising the entire remainder of the books. Some of it is historical but from a special viewpoint, such as I and II Chronicles, Ezra, Nehemiah. One of the books, that of Daniel, an apocalypse, traditionally regarded as prophetic by orthodox Christianity, was not so considered by the Jews, or it was written too late to be included in the Book of the Prophets. Much is poetry including Psalms, the Lamentations, Job which is a philosophic drama, the Song of Songs, Proverbs, Ecclesiastes. Two stories, Ruth and Esther, possibly short historical novels each written for a definite purpose, conclude the section.

The Torah had become scripture and thus basically authoritative for Jewish life and religion—for religion and life were very closely intertwined in ancient Hebrew culture—some time in the fifth century B.C. The canonization of the Prophets could hardly have been earlier than about 200 B.C. while the acceptance of the *Hagiographa* as sacred was not complete until about a hundred years after the birth of Jesus when at a council at Jamnia the entire Old Testament, as now held, was officially recognized. It was the book of Esther which was the latest to be admitted to the canon.

Between the Jews of Palestine and those of the great Greek city of Alexandria in Egypt there developed a difference of outlook. The Jews of Palestine became convinced that inspiration came to an end with the period of Ezra and Nehemiah and would accept no book as inspired which they believed originated after that time. On the other hand, Alexandrian Jews set no limit upon inspiration. God might still be active and inspiring men as of old. Thus they were led to accept certain books as equally authoritative, though recognizably late in appearing. The material so accepted, but refused acceptance by the Jews of Palestine, comprised the books I and II of Maccabees, I and II Esdras, Tobit, Judith, the Wisdom of Solomon, Ecclesiasticus, Baruch, the Prayer of Manasses and certain additions to the canonical books of Esther and Daniel. These are accepted by Catholics, but regarded as Apocrypha by Protestants, books to be read with profit for instruction and edification, but not as a basis for religious dogma.

The Torah, as we have already said, is the basic scripture of the Jews. According to traditional belief of both Jews and Christians, it was given by God to Moses, the founder of Hebrew religion, and by Moses given literary form to serve as the foundation of all of Jewish life. According to modern Biblical scholarship it is the product of a great many hands, containing ancient materials, undoubtedly, but having come together in more or less informal fashion —parts of it, at least—then worked over, re-edited perhaps again and again in line with the development of Hebrew thought, until it finally attained its present form.

The Hebrews, like every other people, must early have wondered how things had come to be as they were, and they had built storied explanations of many things long before they had developed their critical faculties to the point where they could really discover, as in our modern scientific age we have done, how the great natural laws operate. They knew nothing of geology, the stratification of the earth's surface, the hidden fires within, the laws of gravitation which held not only the world but the universe itself in leash. Even yet, when we know the laws so well and how they operate, we do not know why they do so. We haven't yet found a better or more satisfying answer than the Hebrews ultimately gave in the magnificent first verse of the first chapter of Genesis. "In the beginning God . . ."

Not that this indeed was their earliest statement of ultimate cause. Modern scholarship considers the creation story, as given in the first chapter, to be decidedly late, when the concept of God had been refined and universalized as it clearly had not been even in the time of David, if the records of Samuel and Kings are trustworthy evidence of what religious belief and practice then were. But there is little doubt that the appeal to deity as final source of the world was early. There are indications here and there that the ancient Babylonian creation myth was known to the Hebrews, as it may very well have been, since Abraham had gone out from Ur of the Chaldees to become the progenitor of the Hebrew people. But what a difference there is in the two stories will be readily seen by reading Genesis I after the account given on pp. 64–66 of this book.

The first chapter is one of the most magnificent stories of creation in all the literature of the world. Its simple picture of the majestic power of the Creator of the universe in action is incomparable. God said, "Let there be light," and the lights of the universe flashed on. "Let the dry land appear," he cried, and up out of the deep came the continents and the islands. "Let vegetation cover the earth," he commanded, and the hills and meadows became green with trees and grass. Six days he wrought, on the sixth bringing man and woman into being, and God saw that it was good. And on the seventh day he rested. Therefore the Jew was to regard the seventh day as holy, and do no work on it. There are those who think that it was to establish the seventh day as holy or, in other words, to account for the Sabbath, that the whole story was told.

If the reader will continue on through the second chapter he will discover that the whole story is told over again. Here the order in which various things appeared is different, and a good deal of detail is given that is lacking in the first chapter. There it was stated

simply that he created man, "male and female created He him."
Here he takes dust of the earth, forms a manlike image, breathes
into its nostrils the breath of life and man becomes a living being.
But there was no female. So he caused a deep sleep to fall upon
the man and out of a rib taken from his side woman was created.
There is a delightful naïveté about this story. Lacking the majestic
quality of Chapter I, the creator is very manlike, or anthropomor-
phic. Adam and Eve hide themselves as he walks through the
Garden of Eden calling them, because they are ashamed. For he had
told them that of all of the trees of the garden they might eat save
one and they had disobeyed him. Having eaten of the tree of
knowledge, they now saw themselves naked, and shrank from exposure to his gaze. The tempter, in the form of a serpent, talking
freely with them had got Eve first to taste from the tree, then she
gave to Adam, "and he did eat." So entered evil into the world
which at creation had been perfect, and man must suffer judgment
for his willful sin.

Woven into the same tragic story which brought sin and judgment into the world are explanations of many things for which
man sought an explanation. Why do women suffer in childbirth?
Why do men have to toil so arduously in order to live? The answers
to all these questions are there—and in successive chapters are
found many such explanations. The whole early part of the book is
precisely a story of the beginnings or genesis, of the world and
many things in it. Why do men speak different languages? The
answer is in the story of the Tower of Babel. How are the varied
races of man to be explained? The story of the flood and its survivors, Noah and his sons, accounts for that. Note that there was no
felt necessity, apparently, for accounting for yellow men and red
men and brown men. Shem, father of the Semitic peoples, Ham
of the Hamitic folk, and Japheth for the rest, were enough to explain all the races with whom these early folk had contact.

It is a fascinating book of origins, but probably not even the
very conservative believers of the Bible would insist today that these
were actually the ways these things began. They were the far-off,
storied attempts of a people of pre-scientific training to explain to

themselves and others how things came to be as they were. In other cultures such stories are usually thought of as myths, but it is an offense to suggest to the pious Christian or Jew of the older school that the Bible is in any sense mythical in character. They are accustomed to think of myth as something false or untrue rather than a poetic, imaginative attempt, through story, to explain things. What these ancient Hebrew stories witness to is a confidence in the creative and providential activity of God in the world and the affairs of men, a faith which may very well be maintained even though recognizing that the factual correctness of the story may be readily called in question.

It was the insistence upon the literal factual nature of the Biblical story of creation which caused such bitter opposition to the earlier scientists, the geologists and the zoologists, whose painstaking attempt to arrive at a scientific concept of the world's beginnings led them to talk in terms not of days, but aeons of time required for the building up of layer after layer of the earth's surface and the development of the complex forms, of life such as now exists from the simpler forms. This controversy and others like it long rocked the world of religious faith and are still being waged in some quarters. Gradually some adjustment has been made to the scientific view of the age of the world. Fundamentalists, even, have come to recognize that the six days of creation were not the twenty-four-hour kind, but might represent ages. Does not the Psalmist cry, "a day in the sight of the Lord is as a thousand years," etc. But there is no truce with the evolutionist on the part of the ultra-conservatives. They still think largely in terms of evolution *or* God. You may believe in one or the other, but not both. On the other hand, vast numbers of Jews and Christians, who may not even be rated as liberal, have made their peace with evolution and find in it only the method which the Creator God used when he set out to create the universe and even man.

To the modern scholar there is here no serious problem. His view of the Bible, even when held still to be the inspired revelation of God to man, does not require literal acceptance of the ancient stories of creation or even of the purported history of the Hebrew people. It is recognized that the Bible is a book which grew, that it represents the folk belief of ancient people which in time, and demonstrably from the record, grew into the complex, highly moral, monotheistic faith of today. Men wrote as they thought and believed in terms that were consonant with their peculiar cultural status at the time, and so the burden of being scientific in a prescientific era may not fairly be laid upon them. This has little or no relation to the depth of their spiritual and moral insight, and these are the values to be primarily sought in the Bible. It is a religious book, preëminently, not a textbook of science or law or history or geography. Once this is recognized and consistently held to, the scientific limitations of the book are of little or no concern.

This view of the Bible was not easily or quickly won. It was a by-product of an age of scientific inquiry, in which no phase of life was exempted from the questioning of the human mind. It set men to seeking all the facts which might have a bearing upon the question as to the nature of the Bible. Was it such a book as tradition held it to be? What facts supported such a theory? Facts were sought in the Bible itself, in history, archaeology, ethnology, astronomy, indeed wherever they might appear. One of the early facts disclosed was that the Bible itself makes no such absolute claims to inspiration and infallibility as are made for it. The only text that really affirmed categorically the inspiration of the Bible was a verse in II Timothy[4] which in the older translations read: "All scripture *is* given by inspiration of God, and is profitable . . . for instruction . . ." But on examining the Greek text it appeared that the "is" of the English translation does not occur at all but is conjecturally supplied to make the sentence meaningful in English. But this can quite as readily be achieved by placing it after the word "God" to read thus: "Every scripture inspired of God is useful," etc., a statement that could hardly be questioned. Such is the reading of the American Standard Version.[5] So absolute a doctrine could hardly be based, surely, upon so equivocal a passage.

---

[4] 3:16, *King James Version.*
[5] The new *Revised Standard Version* reverts to the King James reading with the other as a recognized variant reading.

Among the facts early noted by Old Testament scholars was the twice-repeated story of Creation, but in somewhat different terms. Would one person writing the book of Genesis do such a thing? But there are also duplicate stories of the flood; of the selection of Saul as king, of the choice of David as his successor, and many other Biblical events. How account for these?

In this brief chapter no detailed account of the process can be given, but in the end liberal scholarship, while disagreeing among themselves in many small details, came to the conclusion that the books of the Law, while containing much early material, were late in taking their present form, which shows very definitely the influence of the prophets and priests who lived centuries after Moses ascended Mt. Pisgah, viewed the promised land, and died.

Like every people the Hebrews had poems, stories, and legends which were told and retold generation after generation for many centuries before anyone felt the impulse to write them down. Like other peoples they had their bards or ballad singers who had each his remembered repertoire of songs celebrating the heroes and warriors of the ancient past (Numbers 21:27). Possibly collections of such songs may have been the first Hebrew writings. Two such "books" are definitely quoted from, *The Book of the Wars of Yahweh*, Numbers 21:14 ff., and the *Book of Jashar*, or The Upright. From the latter is taken the fascinating story of Joshua's commanding the sun to stand still during the battle of Gibeon in order to give time to rout the enemy completely.

> "Sun, stand thou still upon Gibeon
> And thou, Moon, in the valley of Aijalon." . . .

> And the sun stood still, and the moon stayed
> Until the nation had avenged themselves of their enemies.[6]

Here, if taken as a sober statement of fact, was a miracle indeed, one which has troubled many people in this scientific age. One of the great services of modern scholarship was to reveal that this was but a quotation from an ancient poem, celebrating a grand victory,

---

[6] Joshua 10:12–13. *American Revised Version.*

and was probably never meant to be taken literally. When was the poet in the throes of patriotic fervor ever to be held to strict statement of fact! Hyperbole is a recognized prerogative of the poet. But literal-minded interpreters of scripture have held that this must be accepted as a plain statement of historic fact. What a rejoicing in the camp of the conservatives there has been over the publication of the recent volume of Velikovsky, *Worlds in Collision,* which asserts that it was a literal statement of fact, attested by the legends of peoples all over the world, to be explained by the birth of the planet Venus. Few books have had greater publicity than this. It has been viewed by scientists as impossible of credulity, and unanswerable questions have been raised by scientific historians and other scholars concerning the hypothesis. But there is little doubt that the book will be cited for many years by those who feel it needful to defend the Biblical story as literal fact.

Another poem from the *Book of Jashar* is the lament of David over the death of Saul and Jonathan, II Samuel 1:19–27.

One of the oldest bits of remembered verse is the fierce, vindictive song of Lamech. It comes undoubtedly from the barbaric early period of Hebrew history. Lamech boasts to his two wives:

> Ye wives of Lamech, hearken unto my speech:
> "Adah and Zillah, hear my voice,
> For I have slain a man for wounding me,
> And a young man for bruising me:
> If Cain shall be avenged seven-fold
> Truly Lamech seventy and seven-fold!"[7]

It is a far cry from this ancient hymn of revenge to the saying of a later Hebrew who adjured one of his disciples to *forgive* one who had sinned against him "until seventy-times seven." But both are in the Bible. Another noted song, which was probably long transmitted orally, was the famous Song of Deborah in Judges 5, which celebrates the victory of Israel over Sisera. It recounts the march of Jahweh from Sinai to battle. Mount Sinai was his ancient home, they believed. Then it tells of the rallying of the tribes,

[7] Gen. 4:23–24. *American Revised Version.*

called by Deborah, six of them, to fight the common enemy, and curses those tribes which failed to answer the summons. Barak is chief general.

> From heaven fought the stars,
> From their courses they fought against Sisera.
> The river Kishon swept them away,
> That ancient river, the river Kishon,
> O, my soul, march on with strength.

The Hebrews won a great victory. The enemy was routed. Sisera, their leader, was in flight. He sought refuge in the tent of Jael. His sad end is dramatically told:

> Blessed above women shall Jael be.
> He asked water and she gave him milk,
> She brought him butter in a lordly dish
> She put her hand to the tent pin,
> And her right hand to the workman's hammer:
> And with the hammer she smote Sisera,
> She smote through his head,
> Yea, she pierced and struck through his temples.
> At her feet he bowed, he fell:
> Where he bowed down, there he fell down dead.

The conclusion of the poem pictures Sisera's mother at the window, wondering why her son delays to come:

> Why is his chariot so long in coming?
> Why tarry the wheels of his chariots?
> Her wise ladies answered her. . . .
> Have they not divided the spoil?
> A damsel or two damsels to every man;
> To Sisera a spoil of dyed garments
> A spoil of dyed garments embroidered, . . .

It ends with the pious prayer:

So let all Thine enemies perish, O Jehovah, but let them that love him be as the son when he goeth forth in his might.[8]

[8] Judges 5, *passim*.

Numerous other ancient poems are found scattered here and there throughout the earlier books. One delightful poem of obvious didactic character takes the form of a fable in which the trees set about to choose from among themselves a king. They first approached the olive tree but it refused.

> "Should I leave my fatness
> Which gods and men prize in me
> And go to sway over the trees?"

They then sought the fig tree, but it replied:

> "Should I leave my sweetness
> And my good fruit
> And go to rule over the trees?"

They came then to the grape-vine, but it cried:

> "Should I leave my wine
> That cheers gods and men
> And go to rule over the trees?"

Whereupon, they betook themselves to the thorn or, as sometimes translated, the bramble, and said:

> "Come thou and reign over us."
> And the thorn said unto the trees,
> "If in truth ye anoint
> me as king over you
> then come, take refuge in my shade,
> But if not, fire shall proceed from the thorns
> and devour the cedars of Lebanon."[9]

Good men and strong will not give themselves to kingship but only the weak and dangerous, seems to be the moral of the story. It may well have reflected the mood of the people of Israel before the introduction of the monarchy.

There are numbers of poems which take the form of prediction though modern scholarship regards them as merely a literary form. Examples are the Blessing of Noah, Genesis 9:25–27, the Blessing

[9] Judges 9:8–15. Bewer's translation in *The Literature of the Old Testament*, Columbia University Press, pp. 10–11.

of Jacob, Genesis 49, and the oracles of Balaam, Numbers 23:7–24:24. One of the most poignant of all is the lament of David over Saul and Jonathan, taken from the *Book of Jashar*.

Thy glory, O Israel is slain on the heights,
    how are the mighty fallen! . . .

Saul and Jonathan, the beloved and dear,
    in their lives and their death not divided!
They were swifter than eagles,
They were stronger than lions! . . .

How are the heroes fallen in the thick of battle!
O Jonathan, slain in thy heights
I am in anguish for thee, O Jonathan my brother!
Very dear hast thou been unto me:
Thy love to me was wonderful
    passing the love of women.
How are the heroes fallen
    and the weapons of war perished.[10]

There were also prose legends and narratives of the ancestral founders and leaders of the tribes, stories of the pioneer Abraham, of Isaac and Jacob, and of Joseph and his brothers too well known to require retelling here. These were told over and over by parents to children. Naturally the stories would vary somewhat in the telling. Particularly there seem to have been differences as they were remembered among the northern tribes from the way southern tribes recalled them. If this seems strange it is only necessary to recall the differences between our Northern and Southern people in their version of past history, especially at points where there was intersectional rivalry or strife. The story of Moses leading the people out of Egypt is told in great detail and of course the stories narrating his providential saving from death by being left in a waterproof basket at the edge of the Nile, to be found by no less a personage than a royal princess herself, who took him and reared him as a prince of the royal house. These were marvellous stories-

<hr>

[10] II Samuel 1:19–27, *passim*. Bewer's Translation, *op. cit.*, pp. 16–17.

they still are—to be told by mothers to children. Then there were the anxious years of wandering in the desert, the conquest of Canaan, led by mighty Joshua, successor to Moses. Local heroes like Samson were centers for the growth of hero stories. Certainly few stories are more calculated to hold the interest of boys and girls than those of this Hebrew strong man who, though singularly lacking in desirable moral and spiritual qualities, is a most excellent example of what not to be—selfish, wilful, lustful, proud, lacking in loyalty, weak in self-control. He could kill a lion with his bare hands, slay a thousand men in battle with the jawbone of an ass, carry off the gates of a city, snap ropes that bound him as if they were thread, and finally bring down a mighty building, killing three thousand people by pushing apart the stone pillars that supported it. What a man, physically!

There were stories of Gideon, of Barak, of Deborah and others of the so-called Judges, who ruled locally in a time of national anarchy when "every man did that which was right in his own eyes." Around Samuel, one of the first great constructive figures in the building of the united nation, there were many stories, and of course there were stories of Saul and particularly of the great David. Bewer thinks that probably "Israel's first great literary production in prose was . . . the Story of the Founding of the Kingdom."[11] Certainly no figure in all Hebrew history contains more of interest than that of David. It was he who completed the task begun by Samuel and Saul of forging out of the disparate and often mutually hostile tribes of Israel a real, united nation; who won victory over foreign enemies and laid the basis for a reign of peace and international influence and power never before, or since, equalled in the life of the Hebrews. Solomon's rule, for the most part peaceful, with wide international connections, great prosperity, a time of building and a beginning of development of the arts and general culture, rests squarely upon the work of mighty King David.

Even today, as throughout past centuries, Jews still dream of the glories of the Davidic kingdom, and pray for its restoration, idealized, no doubt, and moralized, and spiritualized, far beyond

[11] Bewer, *op. cit.*, p. 21.

what it actually was. But that it could even be a symbol of Jewish hopes and aspirations fixes for all time the place of David in Jewish thought. The more tragic then—certainly from the standpoint of Judaism, is the failure of many modern Jewish young people to answer the simple question: "Who was David and for what was he noted?" About David as about others the stories differed. There are two recorded stories recounting his introduction to Saul, whom he succeeded as king. They are found in I Samuel 16:14–23 and in chapter 17. One is an inimitable story, that of a simple shepherd lad, who comes up to bring supplies to his warrior brothers, listens with consternation to the repeated challenge of a boasting Philistine giant who insults the whole Hebrew army, calling them cowards, with no one responding to the challenge; goes out himself with no armor or any other weapon than his trusty sling, chooses round stones from a brook and sends one of them crashing fatally to the temple of the giant Goliath, whose vast spear and sword and shield are helpless against such an attack. Beheading the fallen antagonist, he returns triumphant to Israel's camp, and they, attacking, rout the enemy with great slaughter. It is bloody, to be sure, but perhaps that is just why gentle little Sunday School boys and girls remember it better than almost anything else in the Bible. Their elders buy murder mysteries by the millions for relaxation and escape reading. They could save themselves some money by going back over the Old Testament stories of tribal heroes.

In the other he is a mighty man of valor and a man of war. Because of his skill as a harpist he is brought to the tent of King Saul to dispel the periods of melancholia which come upon him at intervals. Soon David's prowess led to popular adulation. Jealousy was aroused in Saul who attempted to kill him, making it necessary for him to flee the court. He was aided by his friend Jonathan, son of Saul, one of the most delightful stories of human friendship to be found in any literature. For some time he was forced to live as an outlaw with a price upon his head. Eventually, with the death of Saul and Jonathan, he became king, first of the southern tribes, then, later, of the northern tribes; and fixed his capital at the city of Jerusalem, which had been neither northern nor southern—a fine stroke of political strategy. Thus he gave to the Hebrews the city which was to become not only their political capital, but idealized, the very center for the rule of God himself—not finally, or always, on the Palestinian hills, but high and lifted up in the heavens—"Zion, city of our God." Three millennia later Christians on another side of the world were to sing of "Jerusalem the Golden! with milk and honey blest," and others of

> ... marching to Zion,
> Beautiful, beautiful Zion
> Were marching upward to Zion,
> The Beautiful City of God.

From the time of David on there were definitely recorded annals, kept by someone in the court. These no longer exist, but again and again in the historic books of Kings and Chronicles quotations are made from these no longer extant sources.

When people live together it is always necessary to formulate some rules or, in other words, to establish some kind of law. Every people has something of this nature, whether written or unwritten. Gradually, as a result of sheer necessity there arise informal codes of what may or may not be done by members of the society. There are many non-literate peoples in existence today who of course have no written law, but whose lives are closely regulated by a well-recognized set of laws and customs which are taught to children by parents, and are enforced in one way or another by the community.

There is no reason to suppose that in this respect the Hebrews were any different from other peoples. Even if it be true that they attributed them all to Moses, given at the hand of God, it may well be that he, for the first time, only formalized some early code and gave it the religious sanctions which it bears in scripture. But long before Moses, it may be confidently asserted, there were understood limitations upon the matters at least of stealing, killing, and adultery, that is the sacredness of family relationships. There are within the Old Testament five great codes, the decalogue or ten commandments, Exodus 20:1–17, and Deut. 5:7–21; the Covenant Code, Exodus 20:22–23:33 and in shorter form, Exodus 34:17–26; the

Holiness Code, Leviticus 17–26; the Deuteronomic Code, found in the Book of Deuteronomy; and the Priestly Code found scattered through Exodus, Leviticus and Numbers.

Of these the Covenant Code seems clearly to be the oldest. Exodus 20:2–17 includes the ten commandments, several of them with brief bits of commentary. The decalogue is repeated again in Deuteronomy 5:6–21 in the same ten brief words, and again with commentary, which differs somewhat from that in Exodus. Whether this actually goes back to Moses in the form we now have it, is doubted by modern scholarship, though it must be regarded as a possibility, but it may well be believed that from the time of Moses the Hebrew people did regard themselves as worshippers of Yahweh only, and that obedience to his law was mandatory upon them. Some scholars find in Exodus 34 what they think is an older, perhaps original ten commandments, which are quite different from the traditional ten. Whatever may be the facts as to date or authorship, unquestionably it is the ten commandments which represent for the Western world, both Christian and Jew, the very epitome of true religion and morals. Though the Christians, purportedly, base their faith and morals on the New Testament, it is the ten commandments, not the ten beatitudes, which they are most likely to be able to repeat if called upon. Curiously enough, not all are agreed upon just exactly what the commandments are. As given by Jews, most Protestants and the Eastern Orthodox Christians, they are as follows:

1. Thou shalt have no other gods before me.
2. Thou shalt not make unto thee a graven image, nor any likeness of anything that is in heaven above, or that is in the earth beneath, or that is in the water under the earth. Thou shalt not bow down thyself unto them, nor serve them.
3. Thou shalt not take the name of Jehovah thy God in vain.
4. Remember the sabbath day, to keep it holy.
5. Honor thy father and thy mother, that thy days may be long in the land which Jehovah thy God giveth thee.
6. Thou shalt not kill.
7. Thou shalt not commit adultery.

8. Thou shalt not steal.

9. Thou shalt not bear false witness against thy neighbor.

10. Thou shalt not covet thy neighbor's house, thou shalt not covet thy neighbor's wife, nor his man-servant, nor his maid-servant, nor his ox, nor his ass, nor anything that is thy neighbor's.[12]

Roman Catholics and Lutherans omit the commandment "Thou shalt make unto thee no graven images," and divide the commandment against covetousness into two; thou shalt not covet they neighbor's wife, and thou shalt not covet thy neighbor's goods. Thus a reference to a specific commandment by number only, as the fifth or seventh, does not convey the same meaning to Catholics as it does to most Protestants.

The Covenant Code is not just what would be expected of a nomadic people, which is what the Hebrews had been before the conquest—at least part of them. Now settled among a people far more advanced in culture than themselves they took up an agricultural form of life, became to some extent city dwellers and were much influenced by the Canaanites, who had long been under Babylonian influence. That may account for the similarity of many of the laws to those of the great Babylonian code of King Hammurabi, although if Abraham, as is supposed by some schools, was a contemporary of Hammurabi, it is possible that some influence of that great code may have been felt by the very early Hebrews.

The Covenant Code, though comparatively brief, contains laws roughly divided into four sections. (I) Laws concerning persons, including rights of slaves, male and female, laws concerning murder, kidnapping, homicides, assault and battery, accidents and contributory negligence. (II) Laws of property, including one, incidentally, on the seduction of a young virgin. The guilty man shall be required to pay a "dowry for her to be his wife." If the father shall refuse to give him the daughter he shall still "pay money according to the dowry of a virgin." That is, she is damaged property. (III) Social laws which include laws for the honest administration of justice, justice for the stranger, the widows and orphans, for the

[12] Exodus 20:3–17, Deut. 5:7–21. For the sake of brevity the commentary which differs slightly in the two versions is omitted.

debtor, and even for kindness to the animals of enemies. "Thou shalt not see the ass of him that hates thee lying under a burden, and forbear to help him; thou shalt surely help him." (IV) Religious laws, dealing with worship of images, blasphemy, first fruits, sacrifices to alien gods, clean and unclean food, the sabbath and the seventh, or sabbath year, during which the land must lie fallow, "that the poor of thy people may eat; and what they leave the beast of the field may eat. In like manner thou shalt deal with thy vineyard and thy oliveyard." And monolatry, that is the worship of one and only one God Yahweh, is strictly enjoined.

We now have the material for the making of considerable parts of the Bible from Genesis through to Kings. Some of it was in the form of floating legend, story, song; some of it may actually have been in writing. The modern fact-seeker had discovered throughout dual narratives, with alternating divine names. Furthermore he had discovered a number of facts which threw doubt upon the authorship of the whole of the first five books by Moses. First of all the latter part of Deuteronomy told circumstantially of Moses' death. Yet there were no marked differences in style between this section and that which preceded. Occasional remarks are found such as "before there reigned any king over the children of Israel" (Genesis 36:31), which seem to imply that from the standpoint of the writer the monarchy had already been established; and "the Canaanite was then in the land" (Genesis 12:6, 13:7), which implied that it was being written after Hebrew occupation; and finally repeated instances of the use of the phrase "on the other side of the Jordan," in reference to events occurring in the lifetime of Moses, which led scholars to doubt if Moses could have been the author at least of the whole of the Pentateuch. To be sure, if one reads the King James version, he will find the phrase, "on this side of the Jordan," where the Revised version translates it "on the other side." But turning to the Hebrew it appears that exactly the same Hebrew phrase is translated in the older version sometimes "on this side," and sometimes "on the other side," just where such a translation is required to support the Mosaic authorship, which at that time no one doubted.

All these and scores of other facts seem to require some theory of the origin of the Pentateuch and the other early historical books other than that traditionally given. The theory of composite authorship had been held in one form or another for a century and a half or more, by at least some scholars, before Wellhausen, a German scholar, gave it so systematic and convincing a statement that it has since been associated with his name. It is this theory which, with some modifications, is generally held by modern Biblical scholarship today. By careful analysis, using various criteria such as are familiar to students of literature, the different strands were separated out which have been called the "J" or Jahwist, because of the predominance of Jahweh as the divine name; also Judean, since it seems to have come from southern Israel or Judah; "E" for the sections where Elohim as divine name is usual, or Ephraimitic, since it seems to have come from Ephraem or northern Israel; and "P" for priestly, as designating a pronounced priestly or ecclesiastical emphasis. Scholars are not wholly agreed on the detailed analysis of each section, particularly as to the fine points; but in general terms they agree remarkably well. All this is not easy to see as one reads the Bible uncritically, but that there is something to the idea, capable of being apprehended by a non-specialist, is easily evident, even working from the English translation. The writer recalls having had one of his students read the characterization of each of these three sources as given in E. S. Brightman's *Sources of the Hexateuch,*[13] then on the basis of these descriptions to try to separate out the various strands in the first chapters of Genesis. The student, without having consulted any other helps, divided the sources almost exactly as they are divided by modern Biblical specialists. Brightman's book prints the narratives consecutively each dissociated from the other. One who wishes to go further into the matter is advised to read this book.

It is generally believed by scholars who hold to this theory that "J" is the earliest of the three and quite the earliest attempt to write the history of the Hebrew people and their faith. It may have taken form as early as the middle of the ninth century, B.C., that is, about

[13] The Abingdon Press, N. Y., 1918.

a century and a half after the time of David. By whom it was written is not known. He is often called the Yahwist. An excellent characterization of it is offered by Professor Bewer who calls it, "the first comprehensive history that had ever been written; even the Greeks had nothing like it, till centuries later. The history of Israel was set in the framework of the history of the world."[14]

"E" is believed to have been the product of a north Israelite writer of the first half of the eighth century. It does not go back to creation, but only to the time of Abraham; however, it carries the story to a point well down into the period of the monarchy. His work shows a definite advance religiously over that of "J," particularly in his idea of Yahweh. After the fall of northern Israel in 722 B.C. there seems to have been an adaptation of "E" to Judean purposes and it was published in a Judean edition.[15] Later the two were fused into what scholars regard as "JE." Each had some material peculiar to itself which of course was retained. Where they ran parallel, sometimes both accounts were retained with little change but sometimes they were skillfully interwoven, to form a connected whole. If sometimes it is objected that no one would ever do such a thing, he need only be reminded of Tatian's *Diatessaron*, which is just exactly such an interweaving of the gospels to form a complete and very readable account of Jesus' life and teaching. Here is tangible evidence not only that it can be done, but that it actually was done, at a later time. Eventually the combined book displaced the separate books and they disappeared. Of the various strands account will be taken later.

It should be said that there are modern scholars like Pfeiffer who question the exactness of the analysis of the material into the several documents, and there is a tendency in some quarters to push some of the documents back to an earlier date. Also the application of "Form Criticism" to this part of the Bible is undermining somewhat the assurance of scholars in their analysis. But this does not mean a return to the acceptance of the Mosaic authorship. At most it means

[14] *The Literature of the Old Testament*, p. 69.
[15] Bewer, *op. cit.*, p. 85.

only a revision of ideas concerning the way in which the composite authorship came about.

At this point there appears in the history of Israel's literature a new and highly influential factor, the prophetic writings.

There is much misunderstanding of the prophets. Nine people out of ten think of prophecy as simply prediction. To be sure, this is an element of it, an important one. The prophets did foretell, but that was perhaps the least important function they fulfilled. In the main their prophecies, as prediction, were short-term affairs. They were men of deep conviction and principle, convinced that they spoke the divine will. "Thus saith the Lord" was the preface to almost everything they proclaimed. The prediction, generally speaking, was as to what would happen, not in some dim and distant future, but next year, next month, if a certain course, indicated as contrary to the will of God, were not abandoned, or if some particular course which God required of them were not taken. That profound insight as to the moral nature of God and the world have proven valid across the centuries and of universal scope, may well be true. Indeed, it was the prophets more than anyone else in Hebrew history who lifted Hebrew religion from the narrow, tribal, racial faith of a barbaric people to the universal monotheistic faith which it finally became, and from a limited tribal ethic to a universal ethic, embracing not only man but God himself, which it finally came to teach and practice. But the prophets as men were, generally speaking, simply outstanding leaders and reformers. In contrast to the priests who, in general, were conservative and intent on preserving the status quo, they were not to be bound by the past; they were innovators, sometimes revolutionaries, in the best sense of that abused term. They were forward-looking, courageous men who fearlessly championed unpopular causes, took the supposedly wrong side of public questions, and often enough suffered persecution and sometimes death for their trouble. Jesus could say of them later, "They stoned the prophets."

Nor were they interested only in religious affairs. They were frequently concerned with the political situation. Should the country remain neutral or side with Egypt or Babylonia? Isaiah and Jeremiah particularly were interested in questions of public policy. Amos was concerned profoundly with social justice, as we shall see later. What we are trying to say is that they were not primarily foretellers of what was to come in some future age, intent on giving a blueprint for the unfolding centuries but, for the most part, very down-to-earth, practical-minded men, who saw the folly of the selfish, unsocial, and sinful actions of men in private and public life and sought in the name of God to lead them into a better way.

There had been prophets in Israel for a long time before any of the "writing prophets" appeared on the scene. At first prophets were ecstatics. This is clearly seen in the story of Saul meeting a band of prophets. "And the Spirit of God came mightily upon him, and he prophesied among them." Wherefore the people said: "Is Saul also among the prophets?"[16] But this concept of prophecy changed. One of the first individual prophets of whom we have any account was Nathan, and one story preserved concerning him illustrates a new type of function. King David had one day seen a very beautiful woman, Bathsheba, bathing in her courtyard, and David desired her and took her. She conceived, and sent word to David that she was with child. Of course he was already married, but plural marriage was at that time an accepted practice. Unfortunately also, she was married to a general of his army. The situation was met by ordering Uriah, her husband, into the front ranks of a conflict in which he was conveniently slain, and David took his wife, honorably! It was a rude age. Kings were privileged. Perhaps David thought nothing of it. But Nathan the prophet did. He came into the presence of his royal highness and told a story.

A certain man had company and wished to prepare a feast for his guest. Now he was a man of wealth who had many sheep. A neighbor, close by, was poor and had but one sheep. The rich man took the poor man's sheep from him, had it richly prepared, and served to his guest.

David's eyes flashed fire as he heard the ugly tale. He was angry and burst forth in condemnation of so unrighteous a deed. "As

16 See I Sam. 10:1–13.

Jehovah liveth, the man that hath done this is worthy to die," he cried, "and he shall restore the lamb fourfold, because he did this thing and had no pity."

Prophet Nathan pointed his finger straight into the face of the king and said, "Thou art the man."[17]

Then David knew that it was he indeed who had sinned. The editor of the Psalms long after the event thought that Psalm 51, greatest of all the penitential Psalms, was born of his feeling of guilt and contrition.

> Have mercy upon me, O God,
>> according to thy loving kindness.
> According unto the multitude of
>> thy tender mercies blot out my transgressions.
> Wash me thoroughly from mine iniquity
> And cleanse me from my sin,
> For I acknowledge my transgressions;
> And my sin is ever before me. . . .
>
> Create in me a clean heart, O God,
> And renew a right spirit within me. . . .
>
> Restore unto me the joy of thy
>> salvation. . . .
>
> Deliver me from bloodguiltiness,
> O God, thou God of my salvation,
> And my tongue shall sing aloud of thy
>> righteousness. . . .[18]

Here only it is to be noted that the prophet was a fearless accuser, even of a king, of sin against God, in whose name he spoke.

There were others, notably Elijah and Elisha, about whom there is a whole cycle of stories. Elijah was a rugged figure, champion of the faithful worship of Yahweh in a time of corruption and going after foreign gods. Jezebel, wife of Ahab, a foreign woman, in-

[17] II Sam. 11–12.

[18] Liberal scholarship generally assigns the Psalm to a much later time largely on the basis of its developed theology.

sisted as queen on maintaining the worship of her own gods. Her religious establishment consisted of some four hundred and fifty priests of Baal. Elijah inveighed against such inconstancy and ultimately challenged these alien priests to a contest on Mount Carmel, to prove which of the gods was strongest. He proposed that each build an altar, lay upon it wood for the fire, and on that place the victim, then call upon their respective gods to consume the sacrifice by setting the altar fire ablaze. It is the dramatic story told in I Kings 18:20–46.

First to try were the priests of Baal. They gathered about the altar and prayed that their god would kindle it. Nothing happened. They danced in a frenzy about it, calling aloud for their god to hear them. Nothing happened. They slashed themselves with knives till blood flowed in streams. But still nothing happened. All this was not without encouragement from Elijah who shouted: "Call a little louder, perchance your god is on a journey or is asleep and must be wakened." Still the fire burned not, and at last they gave up. Now it was Elijah's turn.

The altar was prepared; the wood placed upon it; then the sacrifice.

"Now," said Elijah, "dig a trench around it.

"Now pour buckets of water over it, more and more until the trenches be filled."

Wonderingly his helpers did as he bade them. Then Elijah prayed.

Suddenly the sodden firewood was ablaze upon the altar. It quickly consumed the sacrifice, and the trenches were dried up. The effect upon the crowd was electric. At the bidding of the prophet the people threw themselves upon the priests of Baal and destroyed them. So was Yahweh vindicated.

It was dramatic. It was brutal. It ill accords with the view of God as kind and loving and forgiving as he appears later. But it represents a stage on the way to the development of the higher concepts of God of the later prophets. Elijah plays a conspicuous role in Hebrew development.

Later when John the Baptist, forerunner of Jesus, appeared, it was said that he was Elias (Elijah), who must first come before the Messiah. And in the transfiguration scene on the Mount, it was Moses and Elias who appeared transfigured to the watching disciples.

The first of the "writing prophets" was Amos who lived near the middle of the eighth century. It is his book which is regarded by modern scholarship as the oldest book in the Bible, that is, in its present form. Goodspeed's *Shorter Bible,* which arranges the books in the approximate chronological order of their appearance, according to modern scholarship, places it first.

Like most of the prophets, Amos was a layman, not a priest. He was a man of the people, a sheep-herder and a trimmer of sycamore trees. He had an active, seeing mind, and time to think, and to ponder. His first public appearance was at a market town, Bethel, which already was a center of wealth, idleness, exploitation and other vices. He spoke not in the church, but in the marketplace where he would be sure to have an audience. More often than not the prophets were outdoor preachers, street-corner agitators, who took their message to the people where they were to be found in numbers.

"Jehovah," cried this countryman, "Jehovah will roar from Zion, and utter his voice from Jerusalem; and the pastures of the shepherds shall mourn, and the top of Mt. Carmel shall wither." At once he had their attention. Then skillfully he began to utter the judgment of Yahweh upon neighboring nations, Damascus, Gaza, Tyre, Edom, Ammon, Moab.

Thus saith Jehovah: "For three transgressions of Moab, yea for four, I will not turn away the punishment thereof. . . . I will send a fire upon Moab and it shall devour the palaces of Kerioth: And Moab will die with tumult, with shouting, and with the sound of the trumpet." It may have sounded strange in the ears of the Israelites that their God should be concerned about the sins of foreign peoples, for this idea was new at the time, but it sounded good to them. These people who had so often been their enemies had this judgment coming to them.

But suddenly the prophet turns judgment upon Judah, "For

three transgressions, yea for four, I will not turn away the punishment thereof; because they have rejected the law of Jehovah and have not kept his statutes, and their lies have caused them to err, after which their fathers did walk. But I will send fire upon Judah, and it shall devour the palaces of Jerusalem."[19]

The prophet was himself a man of Judah, though he was speaking in Bethel, a northern city. The people of northern Israel had often been at enmity with their brothers of the south. Judgment on Judah could well be applauded.

Then he turned his accusing finger at them crying, "For three transgressions of Israel, yea for four, I will not turn away the punishment thereof. Why? Because they have sold the righteous for silver, and the needy for a pair of shoes, they pant after the dust of the earth on the head of the poor, and turn aside the way of the meek; and a man and his father go in to the same maiden, to profane my name; and they lay themselves down beside every altar upon clothes taken in pledge; and in the house of their God they drink the wine of such as have been fined."[20]

"Behold I will press you in your place as a cart presseth that is full of sheaves, and flight shall perish from the swift and the strong shall not strengthen his force, neither shall the mighty deliver himself."[21]

In oracle after oracle Amos proclaims the judgment of God upon his people. Yahweh has chosen them of all the families of earth, brought them up out of bondage, established them in a goodly land, yet have they forsaken his way.

"Hear this word, ye kine of Bashan . . . that oppress the poor, that crush the needy, that say unto their lords, Bring and let us drink. The Lord Jehovah hath sworn by his holiness, that, lo, the days shall come upon you, that they shall take you away with hooks, and your residue with fish hooks."[22]

---

[19] Chapters 1–2, *passim*. Some modern scholars question the authorship of the Judah oracle, 2:4–5, since it is concerned rather with the law than with the brutal inhumanity of the others in the series.

[20] 2:6–8.

[21] 2:13–14.

[22] 4:1–2.

"Woe unto them that are at ease in Zion . . . that lie upon beds of ivory and stretch themselves upon their couches and eat the lambs out of the flock . . . that sing idle songs to the sound of the viol . . . that drink wine in bowls, and anoint themselves with the chief oils, for they are not grieved for the affliction of Joseph."[23]

It will not do simply to bring rich sacrifices. "I hate, I despise your feast, and I will take no delight in your solemn assemblies. Yea though you offer me your burnt offerings and meal-offerings, I will not accept them, neither will I regard the peace-offerings of your fat beasts. Take away from me the noise of thy songs, for I will not hear the melody of thy viols. But let justice roll down as the waters and righteousness as a mighty stream."[24]

Here is the first outburst of many that were to be uttered by the prophets against empty formalism in religion to the neglect of moral issues. Jesus was definitely in the prophetic line when he poured withering contempt upon the religion of those who tithe "mint, anise and cummin, but neglect the weightier matters of the law."

"Seek good and not evil, that ye may live," cried Amos, "and so Jehovah, the God of hosts, will be with you as ye say. Hate the evil and love the good, and establish justice in the gate: it may be that Jehovah, the God of hosts will be gracious unto the remnant of Joseph."[25]

Amos was preëminently the prophet of justice, the moral quality upon which Judaism at its moral best has placed its chief emphasis, and he established this as the major character of Yahweh in his dealings with men.

If Amos was the prophet of justice, then Hosea, also an eighth-century prophet, must be characterized as the prophet of mercy or love. Out of a bitter personal experience of a wife who proved unfaithful, but whom he still continued to love, came the great insight into the nature of God as merciful and loving also.[26]

In a chapter so brief, no adequate impression can be given of any

[23] 6:1–6, *passim.*
[24] 5:21–24.
[25] 5:14–15.
[26] This is but one of the various possible interpretations of the experience of Hosea.

one, to say nothing of all the prophets, Isaiah stands out as one of the greatest and best loved of them. His call is perhaps the most dramatic of all. It is related in the sixth chapter.

"In the year that king Uzziah died, I saw the Lord sitting upon a throne, high and lifted up and his train filled the temple. Above him stood the seraphim . . . and one cried to the other, 'Holy, holy, holy is the Lord of hosts, all the earth is full of his glory.' " How many million times has the Sanctus been sung since then and thrilled the hearts of worshippers! "And the foundations of the threshold shook at the voice of him, and the house was filled with smoke. Then said I, 'Woe is me! for I am undone, because I am a man of unclean lips, and dwell in the midst of a people of unclean lips; for mine eyes have seen the King, Jehovah of hosts.'

"Then flew one of the seraphim unto me, having a live coal in his hand which he had taken from off the altar; and he touched my mouth with it and said: 'Lo, this hath touched thy lips; and thine iniquity is taken away, and thy sin forgiven.' And I heard the voice of the Lord saying, 'Whom shall I send, and who will go for us?' Then said I, 'Here am I, send me.' "[27]

Of all the prophets who felt themselves called to be the spokesmen of God, Isaiah was the only one who seems to have received his call in the church. Most of them came to their call through some phase of their ordinary work-a-day life.

Isaiah lived in a time of turmoil and insecurity. His nation lay as a buffer state between the great rival empires of Egypt and Babylonia and was constantly under pressure to side with one or the other of these great powers. He became a counsellor to the king, and often gave his judgment as to foreign policy.

"Woe to them that go down to Egypt for help," he cries, "and rely on horses, and trust in chariots, because they are many, and in horsemen because they are very strong, but they look not unto the Holy One of Israel, neither seek Jehovah."[28] Reliance is to be placed in Jehovah and in him only. God has become for Isaiah much more than a tribal figure. All the nations of the world sit under his judg-

[27] Isaiah 6:1–8, *passim.*
[28] Isaiah 31:1.

ment and he uses them to effect his purposes. Assyria becomes for him a whip-lash with which to scourge his people, Israel. There are oracles to a number of the surrounding nations, Egypt, Moab, Babylonia, and others.

If you would get a vivid picture of Isaiah at work, read chapters 18 and 19 of Second Kings. Assyria threatened invasion of Judah. King Hezekiah, terrorized at the prospect, called on Isaiah to intercede with Jehovah on behalf of the nation. Isaiah sent his messenger back with a reassuring message that the Assyrian king would return to his own land, and fall by his own hand. But other messengers from the Assyrian king threatening destruction, sent Hezekiah to the temple to pray earnestly to Jehovah. "Save thou us, out of his hands." Then Isaiah sent word to Hezekiah declaring that his plea had been heard and that Jehovah would utterly rout the enemy. "And it came to pass that night that the angel of the Lord went forth and smote in the camp of the Assyrians a hundred and four score and five thousand; and when men arose early in the morning, behold, they were all dead men. So Sennacherib, King of Assyria departed". . . and was killed while worshipping in Nineveh. For a stirring poetic account of this episode read Byron's *The Destruction of Sennacherib.*

Nor does Isaiah overlook the corruption and dissoluteness of his time, "Because the daughters of Zion are haughty, and walk with outstretched necks and wanton eyes, walking and mincing as they go, and making a tinkling with their feet: therefore the Lord will smite with a scab the crown of the heads of the daughters of Zion, and Jehovah will lay bare their secret parts. In that day the Lord will take away the beauty of their anklets, and the cauls and the crescents and the pendants and the bracelets and the mufflers, [etc., etc.] . . . Instead of sweet spices there shall be rottenness; and instead of a girdle a rope; and instead of well-set hair, baldness; and instead of a robe a girding of sack cloth; branding instead of beauty."[29]

He, too, denounces formality in religion to the neglect of righteous living. " 'What unto me is the multitude of your sacrifices?'

[29] Isaiah 3:16–24, *passim.*

saith Jehovah. . . . 'Bring me no more vain oblations, incense is an abomination unto me. . . . Your hands are full of blood. Wash you, make you clean; put away the evil of your doings . . . cease to do evil, learn to do well; seek justice, relieve the oppressed, judge the fatherless, plead for the widow. Come now, let us reason together; though your sins be as scarlet, they shall be as white as snow; though they be red like crimson, they shall be as wool. If ye be willing and obedient ye shall eat of the good of the land, but if ye refuse and rebel, ye shall be destroyed with the sword, for the mouth of Jehovah hath spoken it.' "[30]

Isaiah was dramatic in his utterances and his actions. He even gave his children symbolic names expressive of divine judgment. His sayings are rich in imagery. Perhaps he has been quoted more often than any other prophet.

But if Isaiah pronounces the judgment of God upon Israel, there is throughout a hopeful note that a remnant shall escape destruction and shall restore Israel, and there shall be a happy future for Zion![31] Here and there are found intimations of a Messiah to come to restore the Kingdom of Israel. Christians have seen in these passages a clear prediction of Jesus. For example, "And there shall come forth a shoot out of the stock of Jesse (father of David) and a branch out of his roots shall bear fruit. And the spirit of Jehovah shall rest upon him, and the spirit of wisdom and understanding, the spirit of counsel and might, the spirit of knowledge and the fear of Jehovah . . . with righteousness shall he judge the poor, and decide with equity for the meek of the earth . . . and righteousness shall be the girdle of his waist and faithfulness the girdle of his loins.

"And the wolf shall dwell with the lamb, and the leopard shall lie down with the kid; and the calf and the young lion and the fatling together; and the lion shall eat straw like the ox. And the suckling child shall play on the hole of the asp, and the weaned child shall put his hand in the adder's den. They shall not hurt or

[30] Isaiah 1:11–20, *passim.*
[31] For example, Isaiah 10:20–23, II Kings 19:30–31.

destroy in all my holy mountains, for the earth shall be full of the knowledge of Jehovah, as the waters cover the sea."[32]

The Jew, too, regards the passage as Messianic only he does not find its fulfillment, as Christians do, in the person of Jesus of Nazareth.

Even more cogent to Christians is the utterance in chapter 9. "For unto us a child is born, unto us a son is given, and the government shall be upon his shoulders; and his name shall be called Wonderful, Counsellor, Mighty God, Everlasting Father, Prince of Peace. Of the increase of government there shall be no end, upon the throne of David and upon his kingdom, to establish it and to uphold it with justice and with righteousness, from henceforth even forever."[33] But to the Jew, Jesus does not seem to be the fulfillment.

Isaiah shares with a younger contemporary prophet, Micah, the vision of a peaceful world of the future when "they shall beat their swords into plowshares and their spears into pruning hooks; nation shall not lift up sword against nation; neither shall they learn war any more. But they shall sit every man under his vine and his fig-tree; and none shall make them afraid."[34] A generation that has seen two world wars, and stands in fear of an imminent, and many think an inevitable, third world struggle, with the dread atomic power added to magnify its horror and destructiveness, reads the dream of the ancient prophet and sighs: "How long, O Lord, how long?"

There are many literary problems connected with Isaiah. Modern scholars are sure that it is not a literary unit. Some see as many as three and even five Isaiahs. But all are agreed that certainly from chapter 40 to the end cannot have been written by the eighth-century prophet. It is generally regarded as definitely post-exilic, i.e., after the fall of Jerusalem in 586 B.C., written by some unknown prophet of that period. It seems quite different in tone and in literary style. It is more advanced in its religious concepts. The idea of God has become completely universalized, and out of deep suffering

[32] Isaiah 11:1–9, *passim.*
[33] Isaiah 9:6–7.
[34] Micah 4:3–4; Isaiah 2:4.

have come new insights, particularly that of vicarious suffering which plays so profound a role in Christianity. Under the figure of the suffering servant, Israel appears in a new guise, suffering not alone for her own sins, but redemptively for the salvation of others. The classic statement of it most familiar to Christians, since it is the passage from the Old Testament most frequently read during the advent season, is the fifty-third chapter which can only be given in part here. It seems to Christians clearly to prefigure Jesus.

Who hath believed our report, and to whom hath the arm of the Lord been revealed? For he grew up before him as a tender plant, and as a root out of dry ground: he hath no form nor comeliness, and when we see him there is no beauty that we should desire him. He was despised and rejected of men; a man of sorrows acquainted with grief, and as one from whom men hide their faces; he was despised and we esteemed him not.

Surely he hath borne our griefs and carried our sorrows . . . he was wounded for our transgressions, he was bruised for our iniquities, the chastisement of our peace was upon him; and with his stripes are we healed. All we like sheep have gone astray; we have turned every one to his own way; and Jehovah hath laid on him the iniquity of us all.

He was oppressed, yet when he was afflicted, he opened not his mouth; as a lamb that is led to the slaughter, and as a sheep that is dumb he opened not his mouth . . . they made his grave with the wicked and with a rich man in his death; although he had done no violence, neither was any deceit in his mouth . . . he was numbered with the transgressors; yet he bare the sin of many and made intercession for the transgressors.[35]

Some have regarded this unknown prophet of the exile as the greatest of them all. Certainly he ranks high among them. In sheer beauty of style, and majesty of utterance, particularly in depicting God, he is not surpassed anywhere in literature. Passages too long for inclusion here which should be read to get the full flavor of the book are found in chapter 40, in which he sets forth the matchless power and wisdom of God, now no longer limited to race or territory. Nowhere in the Bible, unless in chapters 38–41 of Job, has it been done with greater skill than here. And it ends with the oft-

[35] Chapter 53, *passim.*

quoted assurance, "But they that wait for Jehovah shall renew their strength, they shall mount up with wings as eagles; they shall run and not be weary; they shall walk and not faint."[36] Read also chapter 41, and the three other great "Servant" passages, 42:1–4; 49: 1–8; 50:4–9.

Jeremiah was a prophet of the seventh century, prophesying just before and through the early period following the fall of Jerusalem in 586 B.C. He is often called the weeping prophet, sometimes the prophet of doom. But he lived in perilous times. Doom of national hopes, even of survival, hung heavily over Judah during his years of active ministry. There was plenty to weep about. There were prophets of the day who were hopeful, optimistic, cheerful. But history has justified Jeremiah rather than they. He refused to cry "peace, peace," when there was no peace. He even dared to predict the destruction of the very temple of God and the destruction of the holy city. Seldom, if ever, had a prophet gone as far as that before. Naturally it brought down upon him the enmity and denunciation of the religious establishment of the time, in which many good solid conservative citizens joined.

It fell to Jeremiah, as to Isaiah, to live in a time of war and confusion. His problem, like that of Isaiah, was the political and international situation of the day. He knew the weakness of Judah and the enormous power of Babylon. He saw the futility of trying to solve Judah's problem by violence and the resort to alliances with other powers against Babylon. Always dramatic, he one day appeared before the King with a wooden yoke about his neck signifying the servitude to which the Judeans would surely be subjected if they undertook rebellion against the Babylonian Empire. He was frequently persecuted. Once he was condemned to death and thrown into a miry dungeon. But he was released and lived to see his prophecy of Jerusalem's utter destruction fulfilled. He was not himself taken to Babylon but, with a company of Israelites, went away into Egypt where he still continued to prophesy, first the destruction of Egypt, then later also that of the remaining Israelites. It is possible that in anger these people finally slew him.

[36] Verse 31.

In him writes Bewer, "all the best in Amos, Hosea and Isaiah were brought to full fruition. He spiritualized religion by separating it from all outward institutions, even the nation. They all perish but religion remains."[37]

He was deeply sensitive to the sin and suffering of his people.

> For the hurt of the daughter of my people am I hurt:
> I mourn; dismay hath taken hold on me.
> Is there no balm in Gilead?
> Is there no physician there?
> Why then is not the health
> Of the daughter of my people recovered?
> Oh, that my head were waters
> And mine eyes a fountain of tears
> That I might weep day and night
> For the slain of the daughter of my people![38]

Sometimes the tragedy of life overwhelmed him and he felt that even Jehovah had deserted him.

> Why is my pain perpetual
>   and my wound incurable
>   which refuseth to be healed?
> Wilt thou be unto me as a deceitful brook
>   as waters that fail?[39]

He even goes beyond that which Job refused to do, and cursed the day of his own birth:

> Cursed be the day wherein I was born.
> Let not the day wherein my mother bare me be blessed.[40]

But even Jeremiah sometimes had visions of a better future for a remnant of Israel.

> Behold the days come, saith Jehovah
> That I will make a new covenant with Israel
>   and with the house of Judah. . . .

[37] *Op. cit.*, p. 166.
[38] 8:21–9:1.
[39] 15:18.
[40] 20:14.

I will put my law in their inward parts
and in their heart will I write it.
And I will be their God
and they shall be my people
And they shall teach no more
every man his neighbor
and every man his brother,
Saying: Know Jehovah.
For they shall all know me
From the least of them unto the greatest. . . .
For I will forgive their iniquity
And their sin will I remember no more.[41]

Passages of beauty and power to read are: 8:4–9:26, 13:15–27, 32, and 51.

Among all of the prophetic books, that of Jonah has been generally least understood. Because of the famous story of Jonah and the whale, it has been the center of not a little controversy. In the debate over whether a man could literally be swallowed by a whale, or a great fish, and live therein for three days, the real significance of the book has often been lost. Actually it represents the farthest reach of the Hebrew mind in the expression of universalism. Other prophets, notably Jeremiah and the second Isaiah, had clearly set forth a universal idea of God, but Jonah went beyond them in pointing out in practical terms the implications of that idea. If God is universal, then he is concerned about Nineveh, "that great city." He sends the prophet to call them to repentance. It is the first manifestation in the Bible of the missionary spirit. To be sure, Isaiah had prophesied that the nations would come up to Jerusalem and there learn of the Lord, but Jonah is commissioned to carry God's message to them in their own country. Judaism herself never for long accepted such a task as its responsibility, but Christianity, growing out of Judaism, has been the most aggressively missionary of all the world faiths. Try reading Jonah again and forget about the whale story. Whether it is literally true, as conservatives believe, or an oriental tale, as modern scholars believe, told for the purpose

[41] 31:31–34.

of conveying an idea, does not really matter much. The idea at the heart of Jonah matters a very great deal.

This must suffice for a glimpse of the prophets, though it omits mention, even, of the great priest-prophet Ezekiel in the exilic period, and of a number of the lesser prophets. Daniel, which was written late, differs sharply from the earlier prophets, in that much of his prophecy was apocalyptic in character. But to this type of writing we will return later. Suggested passages for reading in various of the remaining prophets are indicated below:

> Joel 2:28–32, 3:14–20
> Micah 3:1–12, 4:1–5, 6:1–8
> Nahum 1:2–15
> Habakkuk 2:1–5, 9–20
> Zephaniah 1:2–18
> Zechariah 3:1–10, 8:1–7
> Malachi 2:10–3:12

Under the prophetic influence religion took on a new character which was reflected both in the organized cult and in the formulation of civil as well as moral and cultic laws. These changes are reflected in a document found during the reign of Josiah by workmen who were repairing the temple. It made a deep impression upon the king who ordered a thoroughgoing reform in accord with its principles. The chief change lay in the centralization of the worship in Jerusalem, and the closing down of local shrines, where all sorts of abuses and corruption had crept in. This is thought to have been our book of Deuteronomy, or the Second Law. Later under Ezekiel's influence a new Holiness code was written, which scholars believe is now to be found in Leviticus 17–26.

With the destruction of Jerusalem, Israel as an independent nation, ceased to exist. Even after the return from captivity and the rebuilding of the city of Jerusalem and the temple, they were only a vassal people subject first to Babylonia, then to Persia as she swept westward and took over the empire of Babylon. Later as the Persians gave way to Greek power they were tributary to Greek kings, and finally to Rome, which eventually overcame the Greeks and became a world empire. Save for a brief flash of independence under the courageous Maccabees they were never again to be a free people—at least not until, after nearly two thousand years of dispersion, they established the new state of Israel in 1948. It is too soon to predict how permanent this new state will be—or how free!

Their distinctiveness lay now not so much in their nationhood but in their faith. They were the people of Yahweh. Neither Babylon•nor Persia interfered with their religion. In this direction they must look, therefore, for any independence. As a natural result of this fact the priest became of paramount importance and priestly religion underwent a pronounced development. Judah became essentially a theocracy, and the chief priest the leader of the people. It became of the utmost importance to preserve and elaborate the cultic laws. The result of this, in time, was the preparation of what modern scholarship calls the Priest's code, which was much more than a code of law, a whole rewriting of Hebrew history from the standpoint of priestly interest.

As might be expected it proved to be formal and precise, and altogether schematic. It abounds in lists of periods, and genealogies and stereotyped phrases which make it quite easy to detect. It began with the creation of the world, the first chapter of Genesis. Even there note the precision of the creative activity. It moves by days. Each day accounts for certain creative acts, and is neatly finished off with the phrase "and the morning and the evening were the first, etc., day." At the end, on the seventh day, God rests, and the Sabbath is born—certainly a priestly institution, or at least a day of vast importance to the cult which is the care of the priest. Even so, this particular chapter has a dignity and majesty about it that is unsurpassed anywhere. Certainly there are no equals to it in any of the subsequent priestly writings. The priestly narrative carries the story on down through the conquest of Canaan. At every point the legal, and priestly, cultic interest in the origin of a particular cult practice is evident. The building of the tabernacle is described with a degree of detail that quickly loses the layman's attention. In the elaborate direction for the celebration of feasts and sacrifices it approaches what we have seen in the Brahmanas of India; albeit never quite achieving the utter, utter detail of those priestly directions. Just a brief paragraph from the ritual of the important day of atonement will suffice to give the flavor of it.

And Aaron shall come into the tent of meeting and shall put off the linen garments which he put on when he went into the holy place, and shall leave them there. And he shall bathe his flesh in water in a holy place, and put on his garments and come forth, and offer his burnt-offering and the burnt-offering of the people and make atonement for himself and for the people. And the fat of the sin-offering shall he burn upon the altar. And he that letteth go the goat for Azazel (the scape goat) shall wash his flesh in water, and afterward he shall come into the camp. And the bullock of the sin-offering, and the goat of the sin-offering whose blood was brought in to make atonement in the holy place, shall be carried forth without the camp; and they shall burn in fire their skins, and then their flesh and their dung. And he that burneth them shall wash his clothes and bathe his flesh, and afterward shall come into the camp.[42]

According to the priestly code, usually abbreviated as "P," all law, moral and cultic, had originated with Moses, although much of it is believed by modern scholarship to have been very much later in origin.

Under the leadership of Ezra this Priestly code had been adopted as their basic law. But the law of Deuteronomy was also important and had been combined by some editor with JE. It could not, therefore, be set aside or overlooked. Eventually a fusion of all of them together, with P forming the framework, was effected by some priestly editor, and thus, with some editorial additions, necessary in the process of combining them, was born the Pentateuch, or the Book of the Law, more or less as we have it today. However, editorial modifications continued to be made in it even down until after the time of its translation into the Greek about the middle of the third century B.C. The fusing of the narratives was probably accomplished by the middle of the fourth century and perhaps earlier.

During this period also the books of Samuel and Kings which

[42] Lev. 16:23–28.

had been worked over under Deuteronomic influence were subjected to further editing by priestly redactors. But the really priestly history is found in the books of Chronicles, Ezra, and Nehemiah, which retell the entire history from the creation to the rebuilding of the temple, from the ecclesiastical point of view. One beautiful story, that of Ruth, seems to have been written as a protest against the narrow particularistic view developed in this period, especially in its prohibition of marriages to outsiders. Ruth is the simple story of a foreign marriage from which sprang ultimately the line of King David himself. If even the ancestry of David included a foreign marriage, could it be so bad?

As we saw earlier the very oldest preserved literature of Israel was in poetry, and the Hebrews continued to produce poetry of a high order all during their history. Fortunately several collections were made and included in the canon. Most notable was, of course, the Psalms, which have been read more widely and have been more influential than any collection of poetry in the history of the world. Christians as well as Jews have nourished their religious faith upon them. They are the part of the Old Testament most widely read by Christians. Often they are bound up with the New Testament or sometimes only the Gospels and Psalms make up a published edition. Also they are circulated quite alone in cheap editions for mass distribution. Somehow, although the poetic literature of a particular people, they have a unique ability to "find" people of all races and times. This is of course because they are an authentic expression of the universal religious longings and aspirations of mankind. The Hebrew poets have said so well and so unforgettably just what everyman desires and feels, that they have become the ready vehicle for the expression of his religious faith. That is why the Psalms dominate even the ritual of the Christian churches. Where has thanksgiving been more adequately expressed than in some of Israel's songs?

> Oh give thanks unto Jehovah;
> for he is good
> For his loving kindness endureth forever,

the Psalmist cries in the 136th Psalm. "Thanks to him who by understanding made the heavens, that spread forth the waters, that made great lights, the sun to rule by day, the moon and stars by night." Read the whole of it. It is a beautiful litany recounting the many things for which man should be grateful, ending each separate mention of good things, "For his loving kindness endureth forever."

Or where has praise to God been more enthusiastically sung than here:

> Praise ye Jehovah
> Praise ye Jehovah from the heavens:
> Praise ye him in the heights.
> Praise ye him all his angels:
> Praise ye him all his hosts. . . .
> Praise him all ye stars of light,
> Praise him ye heavens of heavens,
> And ye waters that are above the heavens. . . .
>
> Ye sea-monsters and all depths;
> Fire and hail, snow and vapor;
> Stormy wind, fulfilling his word;
> Mountains and all hills;
> Fruitful trees and all cedars;
> Beasts and all cattle;
> Creeping things and flying birds;
> Kings of the earth and all peoples;
> Princes and all judges of the earth;
> Both young men and virgins;
> Old men and children:
> Let them praise the name of Jehovah;
> For his name alone is exalted;
> His glory is above the earth and the heavens. . . .
> Praise ye Jehovah.[43]

Read also Psalms 149 and 150 which ends:

[43] 148, *passim*. The generation which grew up with the King James version has never become reconciled to the substitution "Jehovah" for "the Lord." It is interesting that the new Revised Standard Version will return to the older usage and will read once again "Praise ye the Lord."

Let everything which hath breath praise Jehovah.
Praise ye Jehovah.

Every mood is expressed in the Psalms—sorrow, anger, hate, love, compassion, patriotic fervor, contrition, fear, trust, despair, hope.

Traditionally spoken of as the work of David, only a comparatively few Psalms are assigned to him in the editorial headings added by people long after the birth of the songs. That some go back to him may very well be true. His reputation as sweet singer of Israel was probably won in part by his poetic ability, and many songs which he did not sing have doubtless been attributed to him.

Some of the Psalms are individual expressions of the human heart. Some are national. It is not always possible to distinguish which is which. Psalm 137 was undoubtedly the expression of the collective soul in exile in Babylon, although only one person may have been moved to express it thus:

> By the rivers of Babylon
> There we sat down. Yea, we wept,
> When we remembered Zion.
> Upon the willows in the midst thereof
> We hanged up our harps.
> For there they that led us captive required of us songs
> And they that wasted us required
>   of us mirth saying,
> Sing us one of the songs of Zion.
> How shall we sing Jehovah's song
> In a foreign land?
> If I forget thee, oh Jerusalem,
> Let my right hand forget her cunning.
> Let my tongue cleave to the roof
>   of my mouth,
> If I remember thee not;
> If I prefer not Jerusalem
> Above my chief joy." . . .

Then the mood of nostalgia suddenly gives way to bitter resentment as he cries:

> Oh daughter of Babylon, that art
>   to be destroyed,
> Happy shall he be, that rewardeth thee
> As thou hast served us.
> Happy shall he be, that taketh
>   and dasheth thy little ones
> Against the rock.

Indeed, the mood of imprecation is not infrequent.

> Let them be put to shame and
>   brought to dishonour that seek after
>   my soul:
> Let them be turned back and confounded
>   that devise my hurt
> Let them be as chaff before the wind. . . .
> Let their way be dark and slippery. . . .
>
> Let destruction come upon him unawares.
> And let his net that he hath hid
>   catch himself;
> With destruction let him fall therein.[44]

See also Psalms 58, 70, and 83. In one the Psalmist cries, "Break their teeth, oh God."[45]

Of lament or complaint there are not a few expressions such as Psalm 60 which begins:

> Oh God, thou hast cast us off,
>   thou hast broken us down
> Thou hast been angry: oh
>   restore us again.

See also Psalms 79, 102, 130. Altogether some thirty-two Psalms contain such expressions.

A great many are didactic in character, sometimes meditations on religious and moral subjects. Best known perhaps is Psalm 1, which serves as a kind of introduction to the whole Psalter:

[44] Psalm 35:4–8, *passim.*
[45] Psalm 58:6.

Blessed is the man that walketh
    not in the counsel of the wicked,
Nor standeth in the way of sinners,
Nor sitteth in the seat of the scoffers,
But his delight is in the law of Jehovah
And on his law doth he meditate day and night.
And he shall be like a tree planted
    by the streams of water,
Whose leaf also doth not wither;
And whatsoever he doeth shall prosper.
The wicked are not so. . . .

The way of the wicked shall perish.

Longest and most formal is the acrostic Psalm—there are several others in the collection—the 119th. This consists of a section for every letter of the Hebrew alphabet, and the first word of each line in that section begins with that same letter. Obviously this is for mnemonic purposes. The entire series is a meditation relating to the Law of the Lord. The first begins:

Blessed are they that are perfect in the way,
Who walk in the law of Jehovah.
Blessed are they that keep his testimonies,
That seek him with the whole heart. (1–2)

The second begins:

Wherewithal shall a young man cleanse his ways?
By taking heed thereto according to thy word.

Psalms of trust in God as refuge are numerous:

God is our refuge and strength,
A very present help in time of trouble.[46]

I will lift up mine eyes unto the hills.
From whence cometh my help?
My help cometh from the Lord
Who made heaven and earth.[47]

[46] Psalm 46:1.
[47] Psalm 121:1–2.

Psalms of penitence and a need for forgiveness abound. We have already mentioned Psalm 51, traditionally attributed to David, but there are others. Psalm 130 voices the cry, not only of the Hebrew Psalmist, but of countless others burdened with a sense of guilt and a yearning for the peace of forgiveness:

> Out of the depths have I cried unto thee, oh Lord,
> Lord, hear my voice;
> Let thine ears be attentive
> To the voice of my supplications.
> If thou, Lord, shouldst mark iniquities,
> O Lord, who could stand?
> But there is forgiveness in thee. . . .
>
> O Israel, hope in God,
> For with the Lord there is loving kindness,
> And with him is plenteous redemption.
> And he will redeem Israel
> From all his iniquities.

Best loved of all, and perhaps the most widely cherished poem of the human race is the 23rd Psalm:

> The Lord is my shepherd,
> I shall not want.
> He maketh me to lie down in green pastures;
> He leadeth me beside still waters;
> He restoreth my soul. . . .
>
> Yea though I walk through the valley
>   of the shadow of death,
> I will fear no evil, for thou art with me,
> Thy rod and thy staff they comfort me. . . .

It is said that when Alexander Woollcott, master story-teller, died, he expressed the wish that there be no religious service held for him. He only wanted that among other things Paul Robeson read the 23rd Psalm. Probably this Psalm has been read more often at the bedside of dying folk than any other poem ever written. It finds a universal acceptance, it seems, among people of every race and land, despite its birth among a simple pastoral people to whom pasturing of sheep and caring for them was an everyday affair.

The Psalms served many purposes. A great many were clearly for ritual use. Many litanies are found among them. They were sung sometimes antiphonally by groups of temple singers, to the accompaniment of musical instruments. Some were sung by pilgrims on their way up to Jerusalem for their temple worship.

The book was of slow growth and bears on the face of it the evidence of having been once five different collections but merged into one. Any revised version will indicate the breaks, the first of which is at the end of Psalm 41, which ends with a benediction.

> Blessed be Jehovah, the God of Israel,
> From everlasting to Everlasting,
> Amen and Amen.

Some of the Psalms are very early. One is attributed, whether rightly or wrongly, to Moses. And some of them, on the basis of internal evidence, are quite late.

The Hebrew people, like most others, have a rich store of proverbial wisdom, mostly expressed in poetic form. Nameless were the authors who first gave them expression. Who, among any people, knows who first uttered some of the pithy, epigrammatic sayings that everybody now knows and uses? Benjamin Franklin has the reputation of a coiner of proverbs among us but mostly he only collected sayings that were the common property of people of the English tongue. Solomon was the reputed author of the Hebrew book of Proverbs. The collection bears his name. But while he may have given expression for the first time to some, or even many, of them, the editorial notes heading the sections and chapters ascribe many of them to other persons. As a matter of fact the book of Proverbs, as we have it, is a combination of several collections which probably existed separately at one time. Eight such collections can be discerned. Three of these are attributed to Solomon, 1–9; 10–22: 16; and 25–29. Others are called Words of the Wise, 22:17–24:22, or Sayings of the Wise, 24:23–34, one is "the words of Agur," not a

Jew but an Arab. Chapter 30–31:9, is designated as the words of Lemuel, the oracle, and chapter 31:10–31 is a remarkable alphabetical poem of unknown authorship, in praise of a worthy wife.

Here is to be found the ripe wisdom of a people, which has parallels among almost every people in the world. In general it is prudential wisdom, the expression of "that common sense and insight which is the basis of happiness and prosperity." There are some extended discourses upon a single theme, particularly in the first section, e.g., on the rewards of wisdom in chapter 3:13–26.

> Happy is the man that findeth wisdom,
> And the man that getteth understanding.
> For the gaining of it is better than the gaining of silver,
> And the profit thereof than of fine gold.
> She is more precious than rubies: . . .
>
> Length of days is in her right hand;
> In her left hand are riches and honor. . . .
>
> Her ways are ways of pleasantness
> And all her paths are peace. . . .[48]

Chapter 5 deals with the perils of unchaste love:

> . . . the lips of a strange woman drop honey,
> And her mouth is smoother than oil:
> But in the end she is bitter as wormwood,
> Sharp as a two-edged sword. . . .
>
> Rejoice in the wife of thy youth.
> As a loving hind and a pleasant doe,
> Let her breasts satisfy thee at all times;
> And be thou ravished always with her love.[49]

Over and over in this section wisdom is exalted. In chapter 8 wisdom herself speaks:

> I, wisdom, have made prudence my dwelling,
> And find out knowledge and discretion (v. 12).

[48] *Passim.*
[49] Vs. 3–19, *passim.*

Counsel is mine and sound knowledge,
I am understanding; I have might (v. 14).

I love them that love me,
And those that seek me diligently shall find me (v. 17).

I was set up from everlasting, from the beginning,
Before the earth was (v. 23).

When he marked out the foundations of earth,
Then was I by him, as a master workman (v. 29).

Now therefore my sons hearken unto me,
For blessed are they that keep my ways (v. 32).

He that sinneth against me wrongeth his own soul;
All they that hate me love death (v. 36).

But the greater part of the book is made up of miscellaneous proverbs, to some degree related topically, as for example chapters 10–15, in general, contrast the upright and the wicked, in one form or another.

A false balance is an abomination to Jehovah
But a just weight is his delight (11:1).

The merciful man doeth good to his own soul,
But he that is cruel troubleth his own flesh (11:17).

The thoughts of the righteous are just,
But the counsels of the wicked are deceit (12:5).

These are good illustrations of one of the several kinds of parallelism which constitute the genius of Hebrew poetry where neither rhyme, nor stress, nor the number of feet in a line is important. These represent antithetical parallelism. Synonymous parallelism is seen in these:

He that is slow to anger is better than the mighty;
And he that ruleth his spirit than he that taketh
            a city (16:32).

A good name is rather to be chosen than great riches,
And loving favor rather than silver or gold (22:1).

Such a book is not meant to be read at a sitting or even consecutively, but in such a reading the average reader will be surprised to find how many of the sayings are familiar to him. He did not know they came from the Bible. Try it and see.

Another great poetic book of the Bible is Job, a dramatic poem of great power and beauty, the theme of which is the problem of suffering and evil. It is a problem with which every people that has advanced to the stage of reflective thinking has had to grapple. It was particularly true in the case of the Hebrew people, who had evolved a concept of a single God who was also good. If God is good, why should the righteous suffer? It was an old and widespread belief that the good prosper. They enjoy long life, prosperity and happiness. But so often fact and theory failed to meet. The Psalmist complains bitterly that the wicked flourish as the bay tree while, by rights, they should not do so, but should wither away. Why?

It is a pity that limitations of space do not permit a more extended treatment of this, one of the world's great dramas. Briefly, Satan, who seems to have been of somewhat different nature than later he came to be, insists that a man will not serve God for nought. But says Jehovah, "Have you considered my servant Job?"

"Yes," replies Satan, "but he's prosperous. Take away his goods, let him suffer, and see what will happen." A pact was therefore made that Job was to lose everything he possessed, and to suffer bodily affliction, short of death, in order to test him. Then, one by one misfortunes fell upon him, loss of property, loss of sons, bodily illness, until he was in a sorry state. But Job was unmoved. His wife even counselled him to curse God and die. But he only replied, "Shall we receive good at the hand of God, and shall we not receive evil?" All this is told in the prose prologue.

Three comforters come, sit in silence looking at him for three days without a word, then begin to talk. Each, in his turn, speaks and is answered by Job. This is repeated thrice. In the course of it all the attempt is made to probe the depths of this perennial problem. Little advance is made over the old theory that suffering is the result of sin, though many changes are rung upon the familiar theme. He suffers; obviously he has sinned. Let him confess it and mayhap God will be merciful, and forgive, and restore him. But Job is stubborn. He has not sinned. He knows he has not. How shall he therefore repent? His misery is deep. There is no light.

Then a fourth speaker is introduced, Elihu, who does little more than repeat the charges of the others, and seems to be getting exactly nowhere. Scholars doubt that his speeches were a part of the original drama. There seems to be no answer to the problem. Then God speaks to Job out of the whirlwind (Chapter 38).

> "Who is this that darkeneth counsel
>   By words without knowledge?
> Gird up now thy loins like a man;
> For I will demand of thee, and
>   declare thou unto me,
> Where wast thou when I laid the foundations
>   of the earth?
> Declare if thou hast understanding.
> Who determined the measures thereof,
>   if thou knowest,
> Or who stretched the line upon it?
> Whereupon were the foundations
>   thereof fastened?
> Or who laid the corner stone thereof,
> When the morning stars sang together
> And all the sons of God shouted for joy?
> Or who shut up the sea with doors? . . .
>
> Hast thou commanded the morning
>   since the days began,
> And caused the dayspring to know its place? . . .
>
> Hast thou entered into the springs of the sea? . . .
>
> Where is the way to the dwelling place of light? . . .

> Canst thou bind the cluster of the Pleiades,
> Or loose the bands of Orion? . . ."

Question after question rolls from the mouth of Jehovah, to which, of course, Job can give no answer. At last he cries out:

> "Behold I am of small account
> What shall I answer thee?
> I lay my hand upon my mouth
> Once have I spoken, and I will
>   not answer." (40:4–5).

But God has not finished. Again out of the whirlwind he speaks and piles question on question to humble Job still further.

> Canst thou draw out Leviathan with a fish hook?
> Or press down his tongue with a cord?

Reference is here made to a mythical dragon of the ancient Babylonians, known also to the Hebrews. The description of his power and ability to destroy is magnificent:

> "He maketh the deep to boil like a pot. . . .
> Upon earth there is not his like,
> That is made without fear."

Job is completely overwhelmed, and answers Jehovah:

> "I know that thou canst do all things,
> And that no purpose of thine can be restrained.
> Who is this that hideth counsel without knowledge?
> Therefore have I uttered that which I understood not,
> Things too wonderful for me which I knew not. . . .
>
> Wherefore I abhor myself
> And repent in dust and ashes."[50]

So the drama ends with no answer, other than that of faith and confidence in God who is too great and too wonderful to understand or comprehend.

Whether Job's statement, "I know that my redeemer lives,"[51] etc.

[50] 42:1–6, *passim.*
[51] 19:25 ff.

was part of the original drama is doubted by scholars. The fact that there is elsewhere no suggestion that in a life hereafter, compensation for what is lacking here may be hoped for, indicates the late development of the concept of personal immortality among the Hebrew people. It probably indicates, therefore, the later addition of the intimation of immortality apparent in this saying.

Held by older scholars to be one of the oldest books of the Bible, modern scholarship places it among the latest.

The other poetic book, The Song of Solomon, or the Song of Songs, seems strangely out of place in the Bible. Save once, the name of God does not appear in the poem. It is on the surface a wholly secular poem of love, very earthy love. Some regard it as an erotic poem. How did it ever get into the Bible? Two answers seem possible. First its attachment to the name of Solomon, whose great prestige made its inclusion possible. But better, perhaps, it furnishes a vehicle for the expression of religious mysticism as no other part of scripture. The mystic finds no language so well suited to express symbolically the relationship of his own soul to that of God as the language of love, and here he finds it superbly used. So both Jewish and Christian mystics have used it across the ages.

For sheer poetic beauty it is not easily equalled. It presents definite literary problems. Some regard it as a drama and have, with some rearrangement of order, published it as such. Others have thought it rather a cycle of songs, sung at wedding time, as is still done in Near Eastern lands. This makes it easier to explain the disconnected character of the book. Whatever its literary origin or purpose, and whatever its literary character, it finally found a place in holy writ, though it was one of the latest to be accorded scriptural standing.

If one wants to read pure love poetry here it is. Regardless of its religious value, it is fine that it has been preserved. It is, at least, evidence of the presence of the romantic interest in ancient Hebrew literature.

Ecclesiastes represents the mood of disillusionment which comes soon or late to most peoples. It is not a dominant note, rather, on the other hand, a minor one. But the fact remains that some Hebrew writer, again supposedly Solomon, son of David, called here the preacher, came to think of life in terms of world weariness. "Vanity of Vanity, all is vanity. What profit hath a man of all his labor wherewith he laboreth under the sun? One generation goeth, another cometh, but the earth abideth forever...there is nothing new under the sun. Is there a thing whereof it may be said, this is new? It hath been long ago in the ages which were before us. . . . I have seen all the works that are done under the sun; and behold all is vanity and a striving after wind. That which is crooked cannot be made straight, and that which is wanting cannot be numbered. . . . In much wisdom is much grief, and he that increaseth knowledge increaseth sorrow. . . . Of the wise man even as of the fool there is no remembrance forever; seeing that in the days to come all will have been long forgotten. And how doth the wise die even as the fool! So I hated life because the work that is wrought under the sun was grievous unto me; for all is vanity and a striving after wind."[52]

Rather gloomy, isn't it! No hope of an after life relieves the darkness. Either personal immortality was not known, or the writer did not believe in it. Nevertheless there are passages of rare beauty in the book and here and there the sun breaks through the clouds. Some scholars believe the more hopeful passages to have been later additions, rather than the work of the original writer, and that the book's acceptance in the canon was largely due to these passages, more expressive of religious faith. That it was associated with Solomon's name gave it added prestige.

Most famous perhaps of all the passages in the book is a part of the twelfth chapter.

"Remember also thy Creator in the days of thy youth before the evil days come, and the years draw nigh when thou shalt say, I have no pleasure in them," etc. Richly figurative is the language and deeply moving:

"...Before the silver cord is loosed, or the golden bowl is broken, or the pitcher is broken at the fountain, or the wheel broken at the cistern, and the dust returneth to the earth as it was and the Spirit

[52] Chapters 1–2, *passim.*

returneth unto God who gave it. Vanity of vanities, all is vanity, saith the Preacher, all is vanity."[53]

As the Jewish people fell more and more under the control of foreign powers their hope of a return to the glories of the Davidic Kingdom became more and more difficult to sustain. Certainly on the basis of merely human endeavor, it seemed an impossible dream. But religious faith was undaunted by this. It turned from self-dependence and began to look to God to bring to pass what man himself seemed incapable of realizing. The dream of an earthly kingdom gave way to an other-worldly kingdom, a Holy City, Jerusalem, in the heavens, which God, if not man, would establish.

This falling back upon the divine, together with the loss of confidence in man himself, was called the apocalyptic hope. God would break into the affairs of man in some cataclysmic fashion and bring to pass that which men yearned for but possessed not the strength, themselves, to achieve.

This note appears late in the Old Testament. There is a bit of it in Joel. But in Daniel the apocalypse is the most significant part. Written quite late, probably not far from the Maccabean period of revolt, it couches its hopes in a queer figurative language which becomes the earmark of apocalyptic writing. In the New Testament the book of Revelation is an example of the general apocalyptic type. Cryptic, hidden in its meaning, it was designed to inspire a faith in people who were in desperate straits, which would enable them to endure. There was a great deal of apocalyptic writing in late Hebrew and early Christian times, a natural outgrowth of a very bad time for both Jews and Christians. But most of it did not find a place in the canon.

Last of all the books to be accepted as canonical was the book of Esther. It is a fascinating book to read. It is an historical novel, excellent in its plot and its delineation of the chief characters, probably written as an explanation of the festival of Purim. Esther, a beautiful daughter of Israel, at the court of the Persian Empire, is enabled, through intrigue, to avert a pogrom which would have destroyed large numbers of her people. Gratitude for this fortunate

[53] 12:6-8.

outcome of a very serious situation, gave rise to the feast of Purim. Incidentally instead of being killed themselves, the Jews were permitted to slaughter a large number who were involved in the plot against them. It is a fiercely nationalistic book, quite out of keeping with the nobler ethical universalism of the greater prophets, but eventually it came to be included as canonical.

The growth of the canon we have already traced. It was a slow process. Books were not suddenly admitted or excluded. It was finally those which, in one way or another, received the consensus of approval of the group which were made canonical and so survived. Most of that which failed to get in the canon was lost until well down into the last centuries before the birth of Jesus.

The Apocrypha we have spoken of. These books survived chiefly because at least a part of the Jews regarded them as scriptural.

There was another group of writings which never did become canonical but played a very important role in late Judaism and early Christianity, for they were an integral part of the thought and outlook of the Jewish people which provided the background for the development of Christianity. These books, because they were usually attributed to some ancient worthy, who could not possibly have written them, came to be designated as the false writings or *Pseudepigrapha*. They richly repay the study of those who would understand late Judaism and early Christianity.

This brings to an end the discussion of the Old Testament which is the whole scripture of the Jew. There is no other sacred literature for him. The Christian has also the New Testament. But if there is no other really sacred, inspired scripture for the Jew, there is, nevertheless, a mass of writings which is supplementary to the scripture. This, the Talmud, has played an enormously important role in Jewish life.

We have already indicated that the Torah or the Pentateuch is the most basic of all scripture, and that it has become a dogma, that all the rest of the scripture is but an explanation of it. Obviously the law had to be explained. But also the later scriptures which ostensibly explained it, came in turn to require explanation. At first this explanation was informal in nature; but in the course of time it came to be stereotyped and formal. Early in the third century Rabbi Judah and his disciples put into written form much of this material, known as the Mishnah. It was divided into six main sections, dealing with agriculture; with prayer; with the Sabbath festivals, fasts, and holidays; with phases of family life such as marriage, divorce, children, etc.; with civil and criminal law; and with matters of ritual cleanliness or purity.

But in time and with changing circumstances, these rather brief statements came to require still further explication and adaptation to new situations, so the Gemara came into being, at first orally transmitted; but during the fifth century put into written form, in two different recensions, first by the Palestinian Jews, and later by Jewish scholars in Babylon. So there now exist a Palestinian and a Babylonian Talmud; but the latter is the more widely used in the present day. It is almost three times as long as that of Palestine. It contains a vast amount not only of legal material, but also, folklore, history, religion, medical lore, etc.

The Talmud represents the growing edge of Judaism, its thought and practice, through the early centuries of its dispersion among the nations of the world. It became the basis for Jewish life everywhere. Rabbis studied it probably more than they did the Bible itself, and today even in the liberal Jewish theological schools it is much studied by students preparing for the rabbinate. In medieval times, it was almost the sole basis of Jewish education, and it continued to be so down into the modern period, wherever Jews were confined to the ghettos of Europe and denied access to public educational institutions.

In the course of time, because of its great bulk, the essential requirements of Jewish life were separated out and written into a code known as the Shulhan Aruch, which is still observed by orthodox Jewish communities. Rabbis still study the Torah and the Talmud assiduously in the effort to find the answers to problems which the modern age thrusts upon them. Famous rabbis during the centuries have carefully considered questions, and formulated answers. These are known as Responsa. They have served and continue to serve the very useful function of enabling the Jewish community to make its adjustment to the changing demands of the world about them. These Responsa, never regarded as inspired or authoritative in any official sense, have nevertheless been an influential factor in enabling the Jew to come to terms with a world of change and at the same time to maintain a feeling of continuity with the past of his people. Unfortunately there is no body of the Responsa material available for reading in English.

What a story it is, that of the Old Testament! It is the history of a people, a history of the growth of a people's ideas, particularly with reference to religion. It took almost a thousand years in the writing. It brought together not only history, but law, poetry, legend, story, proverb, drama, a strange collection in some respects. But somehow the conviction grew that behind all this, expressing himself through history, particularly that of the Jewish people, was the very God of the universe, and that he was the Lord of history; that he ruled the universe and man through laws, and that only through obedience to these laws could man live. The elaborate rituals and sacrifices, the detailed codes, were only means whereby man sought to set himself right in the eyes of God and so to achieve salvation. Some of it now seems to the modern mind to be outmoded, clearly dated, limited to a given time and place. But along with the non-essential and accidental elements, there is that which is timeless, and knows no limitation to any particular place or people. It speaks to the universal heart and so continues generation after generation to validate itself in the experience not of one man but the many. This is what makes it scripture and causes men to continue to read it and to say to themselves, this is the very word of God.

PART II: THE NEW TESTAMENT

The New Testament is peculiarly the sacred literature of the Christians. To be sure they regard the Old Testament also as theirs, and find in it the inspired word of God. Ultra-conservative Christians are likely to consider any word found in it equally as valid as any word from the New, for it is all God's word. But even these make the distinction that it is the *Old* Testament; that it refers to a "dispensation" now past; that Christians live under the "New Dispensation" ushered in by the coming of Jesus, the Messiah, who is the fulfillment of the hopes and prophecies of the older dispensation.

Liberal Christians value the Old Testament highly. It provides a background for an understanding of the New. It is of enormous importance as disclosing the long slow process of development that went on in the religious life of the Hebrews. Liberals are particularly appreciative of the profound insights that appear, especially in the prophets, and in some of the great Psalms; insights that are truly universal and timeless, and, therefore as valid today as the day they were uttered. They recognize that Jesus' teaching assumed familiarity with the religious tradition of the nation. But they regard the *New*, not the *Old* Testament as the true expression of the Christian faith, and they feel obliged to test whatever religious or moral teaching is found in the Old Testament by the standards of the New Testament. They do not feel obliged to find in the Old Testament a foreshadowing of everything Jesus was and taught. The Old Testament has its own independent value without relation to the New, but it is not that of a final authority in matters religious and moral. The New Testament is in itself all that is necessary as a basis for Christian faith, but much light is thrown upon God's dealings with man in the story of Israel's halting and gradual discovery of the true nature of God as universal, not national; as law-abiding, not capricious; as a God of peace, not war; as a God of justice, love and mercy rather than of wrath, and vengeance. It proves an inexhaustible storehouse of story, song, proverb, sermon, expressive of the experiences of men from childhood to maturity, which makes it a valuable help in guiding people of our own day in the gradual maturing of their own religious faith. The Old Testament is not lightly to be set aside, nor is it likely to be. But it must always take a subordinate place alongside the Christian's own book, the New.

Some understanding of this point of view may be derived from current assertions of converts recently brought into the Christian faith from other world religions such as Hinduism. Not a few important leaders among these relatively new Christians fail to see why they should take over the Old Testament which was the way by which early Jewish Christians came to the New. Some are asking why they might not regard the sacred books of their own cultures as their Old Testament rather than the Jewish sacred book. At this late date in history, after belonging for nearly two thousand years to the Christian Bible—for the Old Testament was of course the Christians' only scriptures in the time of Jesus—it is not likely that it will ever be set aside. Rather it will come to be thought of and appraised more properly in the light of the New, and continue indefinitely to make its contribution to the building of a world on the pattern disclosed in the New Testament. So believe so-called liberal Christians, at any rate.

The New Testament, as we have it, is a collection of twenty-seven "books." Actually two of these "books" can be typed each on a single sheet of paper. The Sunday edition of almost any of the great metropolitan daily newspapers contains a great many more words than the whole twenty-seven books put together. Catholics and Protestants differ in their canon of the Old Testament, but in the case of the New they are in agreement. Here they only differ in their translations.

The period of the growth of the Old Testament was perhaps a thousand years. The New Testament books were all written in something less than a century, though their canonization, as now determined, took a much longer time. The Old Testament is much richer in its variety of literary forms than the New. Nearly a half of the New is made up of letters, a form hardly to be found at all in the Old Testament. There is poetry in the New Testament, but no poetical book. There is dramatic material aplenty, but no drama. There are brief pithy sayings, many of them, but no book of proverbs. Strictly speaking there are but four main literary types, historical, biographical, epistolary, and apocalyptic.

The New Testament was written almost wholly in Greek. There is a difference of opinion among scholars as to whether the gospels may not have been first written in Aramaic, the language which

Jesus and his disciples and the people of Palestine at that time generally spoke as their native tongue. But if there were Aramaic originals they have long since disappeared. The only ancient manuscripts we have are in Greek. But the Greek of the New Testament was not the Greek of the great classics—far from it. For a long time it was simply thought to be Greek badly written, perhaps by people to whom it was an acquired tongue rather than their native speech. Greek was the *lingua franca* of the world of Jesus' day, and was probably not spoken too well by the relatively poorly educated, early followers of Jesus. But Paul was a highly educated man and had grown up speaking Greek as easily as Hebrew. Later discoveries of all sorts of Greek material current in that day reveal that it was simply the vernacular tongue of the Hellenistic world, a new Greek that was being spoken in contrast to the older classic forms, for Greek was a living language and living languages are constantly subject to change. This Greek is now called the *koine* or Common Greek and there are special grammars and dictionaries of *koine* Greek as well as classic. The discovery of these new facts has thrown a great deal of light on the meaning of New Testament words and phrases that formerly were obscure or unintelligible, from the standpoint of classic Attic Greek. A writer in a current magazine article calls attention to the wide difference between our own contemporary spoken and written language. He calls the former "shirt-sleeve English." Most writers do not express themselves in writing as they do in speech. Less educated writers are more likely to do so. It appears that the New Testament writers wrote the language they spoke rather than writing in the more formal manner affected by the cultured writers of the day.

Why should they have done so? Probably because they were writing for a very definite purpose, to get a message across to people, most of whom were not the highly educated or the cultured folk of the time, but ordinary people who would understand it thus as they would not a more elevated style of writing. It has often been pointed out that most of the so-called books of the New Testament were not carefully wrought literary works, but something more in the nature of tracts, written to meet a special situation or a particular need. This would be particularly true of the letters, not only Paul's, but most of the others, and certainly it would be true of the book of Revelation. To a somewhat lesser extent it would be true also of the gospels which were written not to delight the literary fancy of their readers, but each one to make known to some particular segment or other of the total population one who held for all mankind the very way of life itself, one whose coming was indeed good news to the world.

This does not mean that it was not good literature—nor indeed great literature. Recall what was said concerning great literature in the opening chapters of this book. It may not be polished literature, it may not be learned writing, but judged by its power over the minds and hearts of successive generations of men and women of many races, it would be difficult to give it a lower classification. Much of it is simple, straightforward, direct, without adornment. Now and then Paul's thought in the heat of creativity, runs ahead of his pen, and results in incomplete statements or leaps in thought, but he usually makes himself intelligible and, what is more, succeeds in communicating to understanding readers something of his own great spirit. Sometimes, too, in the very midst of his counselling of followers, he falls quite unpremeditatedly into the most elevated type of poetic discourse, as we shall see later.

The growth of the New Testament was gradual. It is not at all likely that even the finished writings, as we have them, are exactly the same as the original writers wrote long before. They underwent, in early years, no little modification at the hands of editors and copyists who did not hesitate to write into the text minor corrections or even comments, which later came to be incorporated into the writings, and indistinguishable, save to highly specialized scholarship, from the original. This was particularly true in the earlier day before the different books had come to be regarded as sacred, and therefore not to be changed in the slightest degree.

Certain it is that the writers of the books had no idea at the time of writing that they were producing scriptures that would be read for centuries and come to be regarded as the very word of God in every respect. Not that they did not believe in what they were writing and, to some extent even, that they were writing under divine direction or influence, but that the exact verbal form was literally directed by divinity would be very hard indeed to prove.

The final selection of just what books should be canonical and what should be discarded delayed long in coming. Different lists, accepted in one section or another of the church, but not in others, indicate that unanimity of choice was not easily reached. In the end the matter was determined by the consensus of opinion of the church as a whole. It is interesting that the Christian church as a whole was able to come to agreement in the end, as the Jewish church had not, so that there is but one canon of the New Testament, universally accepted. Differences within the church on the canon of scripture are on what shall constitute the Old, not the New Testament.

Differences between Catholics and Protestants in respect to the New Testament have to do rather with the approved text from which translations are made, and of course there are verbal differences in the authorized translations. The two great rival English translations are the nearly contemporaneous King James, or Authorized version, accepted by Protestants, and the Rheims, or Douay version of the Catholics, both now over three hundred years old. In the fourth century St. Jerome translated the entire Bible into Latin, which was then the Vulgate or common language of the western world.[54] This served the church for centuries and at the Council of Trent was decreed to be the official version of the scriptures for the Roman Catholic Church. It was superseded in 1592 by a new edition prepared by order of Clement VIII which became the official Bible.

Meanwhile the Renaissance had turned attention once again to Greek culture and there was a revival of interest in the Greek language and literature. The great humanist scholar, contemporary of Martin Luther, Erasmus, made a study of extant Greek manuscripts of the New Testament and issued a reconstructed Greek text which Luther used as the basis of his great translation into

---

[54] He made a fresh translation of the Old Testament from the Hebrew, but only revised an already existent Latin version of the New Testament.

German. Since that time Protestant scholars have not ceased to search for other ancient Greek manuscripts, to collate them, and to revise the text in accord with the findings of scholars in contributing fields. The result has been a constant revision of the Greek text, which has, in turn, been reflected in the successive versions that have appeared. Unembarrassed by any official fixing of the text by their churches, Protestant scholarship is free to take every advantage of new discoveries in the field of textual study, and to issue new translations whenever they seem to be called for.

The New Testament came into being as the result of the coming of Jesus and the tremendous impact which his life and teaching made upon those who came under his influence. Quite appropriately, therefore, the gospels which tell the story of his life and teachings stand first in the New Testament. But they were not the first books to be written, at least in their present form. It was the letters of Paul, the first great missionary of the new faith, that were first penned. The earliest was the first letter to the Thessalonians, according to most modern scholars, coming very near the middle of the first century. Chronologies differ slightly among scholars, some putting it as early as 44 A.D., others in the early fifties. Paul died, it is agreed rather generally, about 64 A.D., so all of his letters had been written some time before the earliest of our gospels was produced, namely the gospel of Mark, at a time not far from the destruction of Jerusalem in 70 A.D. The others followed by an interval of several years, the Fourth Gospel probably coming down into the early part of the second century. To what extent Paul's letters had been in circulation before the gospels appeared, scholars are not agreed.

But if the gospels, as we have them, came into being later than the Pauline letters, that does not mean that nothing had been written about Jesus until after Paul's death. On the contrary they were on the way to being produced, and probably a good deal of the content of the gospels was circulating among the churches in written form long before the writers of our first three gospels, Matthew, Mark and Luke, gave them their present form. Only a superficial comparison of the four gospels reveals that the gospel of John

stands alone as over against the other three. The latter can easily
be put into a parallel arrangement, or harmony form, as it has come
to be called. When this is done, as it has been many times,[55] much
material will be found in almost identical form in all three, a good
deal more will be found common to two of them, and of course
there is material peculiar to each of the three. John simply does
not fit easily into such a scheme, since the amount of material
found in it and in any one of the other three is so little, save in the
story of the last week, that it is not worthwhile having a fourth
column in the harmony. Because the three run so close together
and "see together" the life of Jesus, they have been called the
Synoptic Gospels. It is generally recognized by both modern and
conservative scholarship that the Synoptics represent the earlier
account of Jesus and his teachings.

How does it happen that we have three separate biographies
of Jesus, agreeing even to the point of verbal identity at many
points, yet differing in no small degree, one from the other? Were
they written quite independently? Verbal identity would seem to
preclude that possibility. If they were not, did one copy from the
others or did they use the same source or sources? This is known
to Biblical scholars as the "Synoptic Problem," and a vast deal of
scholarly work has been done in an attempt to solve it. Needless to
say no unanimous agreement has been reached as yet, nor does it
appear likely that on every point it ever will be. The main lines of
the solution are fairly well agreed upon by modern scholarship,
but it must be said that conservative scholarship differs at many
significant points in its view of the matter.

It is agreed by everyone that when Jesus died, there was no
written record of anything he said or did. He himself wrote nothing
of which we have record save in the story of the woman taken in
adultery, reported only in the gospel of John, and this is not found

---

[55] See Burton and Goodspeed, *A Harmony of the Synoptic Gospels*, Charles
Scribner's Sons, N. Y., 1917; Finney, Ross L., *Huck's Synopsis of the First Three
Gospels*, Methodist Book Concern, N. Y., several editions. *Gospel Parallels, A
Synopsis of the First Three Gospels*, arranged according to the Huck-Leitzman
Synopsis, 1936, Thomas Nelson and Sons, N. Y., 1949, uses the text of the *Re-
vised Standard Version*, 1946.

in all the older manuscripts. There it is said that he stooped down and wrote in the sand, while the woman's accusers slipped away, one by one, after Jesus' remark, "Let him who is without sin cast the first stone." What he wrote, if anything, is unknown. At the first sweeping of the floor it disappeared. Nor had any disciple written down anything, so far as we know. In the first place few of them were men of education, accustomed to write. Furthermore, Jesus' career had hardly begun before it was ended. He was young. It had not occurred to any of them that Jesus would so soon be taken from them. There was as yet no impulse to write down his sayings. So he died leaving no written records of anything he had said or done in the brief years of his public ministry. It all had to be recovered from the memories of those who saw and heard him. In this he was like all the other founders of religions with whom we have thus far dealt. How then can we be sure that what is reported of him is a true and an accurate account? Particularly, when such enormous importance is given to his words for doctrinal purposes, how can we have any certainty that the record is exactly correct?

Well, in all candor, we cannot be absolutely sure. But as to the main lines of his teaching and the effect it produced upon his contemporaries we can be certain enough for all practical purposes. The differing reports as to just what was written on the cross may leave us in justifiable doubt as to which, if either, report is exact, but the crucifixion itself is not thereby brought into question. As a matter of fact it really does not matter what the exact words were. The crucifixion itself is of paramount importance and there is complete agreement as to its having actually occurred.

In our modern day we depend so much upon note-books and written records that it is hard for us to see how people who did not have such helps could have preserved so much by memory and so accurately. But just the fact that we have these mechanical helps for recording everything, deprives us of the necessity of cultivating our memories, and so we do not easily remember. But this was not true of the disciples of Jesus, or Buddha, or Confucius. They were used to having to remember—and so they remembered, and with a remarkable degree of accuracy, those things they had seen and heard.

There are a number of reasons for believing that the disciples of Jesus, and, for that matter, of Buddha, and Confucius, and Mohammed, remembered with substantial accuracy the more important things their Masters said and did. In Jesus' case, note at least three considerations. In the first place the disciples of Jesus were with him for a period of from a year and a half to three years of his itinerant ministry. Jesus probably repeated some of his sayings over and over again as he talked to different groups of people. The writer recalls travelling as one of a group of speakers from place to place and of having to hear substantially the same speeches over and over again. Within a comparatively short time almost any of us could have given the others' speeches almost verbatim. Repetition, then, played its role in the impressing on the minds of his loyal friends the important teachings of Jesus.

Second, note how considerable a part of Jesus' teaching is couched in story form—or in parables. Now a well-told and interesting story is very easily remembered, particularly if it is told repeatedly. Very quickly the story comes to be told in exactly the same words, and very quickly the hearers come to repeat it in almost the identical words. Have you ever told stories to small children, and then tried telling them in different language? The child will almost invariably correct one as to the exact language used in former tellings. Not everyone can remember even a good story, but if they can remember anything, they can remember a story better than almost anything else.

One day in a class I deliberately started out by telling a story. I purposely chose it from an area unfamiliar to most of my students so that the vocabulary and general setting would be outside of their ordinary experience. I did not tell them why I told it, made no reference to ever expecting them to remember it at all. Then I deliberately made a careful statement in clear logical fashion, using language, not beyond them, but somewhat formal, again without giving them any particular reasons for their remembering what I had said.

Several days later, I suddenly asked the class to tell the story I had told that morning. No one remembered the whole exactly as I had told it, but one helping or correcting another, they recalled the story in almost the exact words I had used in telling it. Then I asked them to tell me what I had said following the story—and there was no memory of it at all. At least that class got the point of what I am saying. Stories are easily remembered, especially when they are as well told as the parables of Jesus, who was a master story-teller.

Who could easily forget the story of the woman who had lost a highly prized coin, who sought it in every corner of the house before she found it, and the joy she felt, leading her to call in her neighbors to celebrate the finding? Or the matchless story of the lost son, the prodigal son? You remember how he asked of his father that the estate be divided, took his share and went into a far country where he wasted it in riotous living and was reduced to the extreme—he, a good Jew—of feeding hogs. He came to himself saying, "I will arise and go to my father—and ask to be taken on as a hired servant." But when he was yet afar off, his father saw him and ran to meet him; embraced him tenderly, and said, "Bring hither a ring for his finger and kill the fatted calf, and make a great feast for him, for this my son that was lost is found."

How easy to recall the Good Samaritan! A certain man went down from Jerusalem to Jericho, fell among thieves who wounded him and left him for dead. A priest came by, and a Levite, but neither stopped. Then came a Samaritan, a man of a despised race, and he had compassion upon the wounded man. He bound up his wounds, took him on his own beast to a town, left him at a hospice, paid for his lodging and went his way. Who then proved himself neighbor to the man who was robbed?

Such graphic stories are not hard to remember, and Jesus made much use of this device in teaching. Maybe the reason we have so much in story form and so little in the form of lengthy sermons or discussions is just because these were the things they could remember best.

Again, aside from the parables, there is a great wealth of two types of discourse which are especially easy to recall, the use of figurative language and the use of the aphorism or short sententious utterances which, heard but once, are easily remembered. First the use of figures of speech. Similes or metaphors are to be found on almost every page: "I am the vine, ye are the branches." "I am the good shepherd." "Consider the lilies of the field, they toil not, neither do they spin, yet I say unto you, Solomon in all his glory was not arrayed like one of these." "Like a thief in the night." "A city, set on a hill." "A whited sepulchre." "The blind leading the blind." "The salt of the earth." The list could be lengthened indefinitely. Jesus knew how to make his thought clear and easily rememberable by using in figures of speech the common homely things of the everyday life of the people to whom he was talking. To the fisherman the Kingdom of God was like a "net cast into the sea"; to a farmer it was like the "sower who went forth to sow"; to the housewife like a bit of leaven or yeast; to the merchant like a "pearl of great price"; to the builder like "a house builded upon the rock," etc.

Like so many great teachers, Jesus had the knack of putting things in unforgettable, aphoristic form which, hearing only once, one could easily remember. The beatitudes are examples of this: "Blessed are the pure in heart, for they shall see God." "Blessed are the peacemakers." "Blessed are they that mourn, for they shall be comforted." The whole so-called Sermon on the Mount is a collection of such sayings, with sometimes a bit of further commentary. It has sometimes been conjectured that, so far from being in itself a sermon, it is a collection of pithy sayings perhaps used by Jesus from time to time as texts for longer discourses to his followers. The only point here is how easily they may be recalled. "If a man smite thee on the one cheek, turn to him also the other." "Love your enemies." "Pray for those that persecute you." "By their fruits ye shall know them." "A house divided against itself cannot stand." "Ask and it shall be given you; seek and ye shall find; knock and it shall be opened unto you." "Judge not that ye be not judged." "Do men gather grapes of thorns or figs of thistles?" And throughout the entire gospel record these brief, cogent, utterances are to be found. "Ye cannot serve two masters." "A city set on a hill cannot be hid." "Whatsoever ye would that men should do unto you, do ye even so unto them."

Surely, enough has been said to indicate that much of what is found in the gospels is of a sort that would require no unusual feats of memory on the part of followers, who by their very habits, were accustomed to rely heavily upon their verbal memory of what was told them. And in the early conversations they must have held concerning him whom they had loved so deeply and sincerely, but who was now gone from them, is it not likely that there would have been a tendency to correct a wrongly reported utterance, or an incorrect description of some of his activities, by others who were also privileged to have been present on the same occasion?

We must certainly assume that, for a time at least after Jesus' death, there was only an oral tradition as to what he said and did. It was at first quite informal, and may have differed in some degree as it was told by different members of the original company of those who had known Jesus. But as it was repeated over and over again by those who had now become active witnesses of the new gospel, and were seeking to propagate it, it would have tended to fall into a more or less stereotyped form. Peter would probably have related much the same stories of his thrilling intimate contact with Jesus, and repeated, in nearly identical form, the sayings of Jesus as he remembered them.

It is almost impossible to avoid this even if its avoidance were desirable. We are creatures of habit. Let one who is accustomed to say grace at table reflect on how seldom he varies much the form of his blessing. Let any salesman reflect upon how quickly he falls into an almost unvariable "line," which he uses in trying to sell his article. It would seem most reasonable to suppose that each of the original disciples would formulate a fairly definite way of reporting Jesus' sayings and doings. This might very well have been affected by the predominant influence of some of the more outstanding members of the group, like Peter for example. As new converts were brought into the nascent Christian group they would be obliged to accept the testimony of these disciples, never having known Jesus in person.

So there undoubtedly developed an oral tradition as an original basis for the formation of the gospels. How long before it came to be written down? That is a question impossible to answer. Some scholars of an earlier day thought that the gospels, as we have them, were simply the crystallization, in written form, of the oral tradition as handed down in the church. The differences in the three Synoptics were explained as being due to the possible variations in the tradition and to the personal factor involved in its being written by a particular person who had his own predilections and would choose out of the total mass what especially appealed to himself as most worthy of permanent record.

This might well enough explain the variations but could hardly account for certain observable facts about the three gospels. Verbal identity would not so likely be found if only taken from an oral source, yet there is a remarkable amount of verbal identity to be found. Also the fact of the peculiar order of the gospels which in general follow that of Mark, would not be so likely to occur. In this brief study there is not room to detail all the various theories or the arguments alleged in their favor or against them, put forward as solutions to the Synoptic Problem. The writer can only state rather dogmatically what seems to him the most likely steps in the process of making the gospels as we have them.

Oral tradition might have served quite well for the original disciples, for they had their own vivid memories of the few short months they had spent with Jesus. But after Pentecost the new movement became very active in preaching the good news. This led to persecution which, in time, led to the dispersal of the earlier followers into distant places. Soon there were converts to the gospel who felt themselves impelled to propagate the new faith. But they had never seen or heard Jesus. They had no memory of the forcefulness of his personality or the winsomeness of his appeal. They had only the oral traditions, as gotten from the disciples who had been instrumental in their conversion. And they were also perse-

cuted and forced to separate themselves from the support and confirmation in the tradition, of those who actually knew Jesus. Thus
it seems there would have been a comparatively early demand for
some kind of a written source to which they could appeal. This
demand probably gave rise to the first attempt at a written record.
And there may have been not one such attempt, but several.

There is evidence in the gospel of Luke that this was actually
so. Luke was not himself an original disciple of Jesus, but a convert of St. Paul, and one who accompanied him on at least some of
his missionary tours. In the dedication of his gospel to Theophilus
he takes occasion to say: "Forasmuch as many have taken in hand
to draw up a narrative concerning those matters which have been
fulfilled among us, even as they delivered them unto us who were
from the beginning eye-witnesses and ministers of the word, it
seemed good to me also, having traced the course of all things accurately from the first, to write unto thee in order, most excellent
Theophilus: that thou mightest know the certainty concerning the
things wherein thou wast instructed" (1:1–3). E. F. Scott translates the phrase "in order" as "consecutively."[56] Here Luke is saying
simply that others, *many* of them, had written accounts of what
Jesus said and did. Even if Luke were the latest of the four gospels,
many would seem to be an exaggerated statement if he alluded
only to these gospels as we have them, for that would be but *three*.
But it is held generally that John is later, so there would be but
two, Matthew and Mark, unless he had in mind other writings of
which we have no record. Scott points out that Luke regards these
former accounts as already second-hand reports of things transmitted to them by the first-hand witnesses. He, Luke, himself, has
examined a variety of sources and proposes to write consecutively
of the life and teachings of Jesus, a more complete and adequate
account than that of earlier writers.

If there were any such writings, they have long since vanished,
but modern scholars, painstakingly comparing the three gospels,
have come to the conclusion that there must have been a primary

[56] *Literature of the New Testament,* Columbia University Press, N. Y., 1932.
p. 31.

source from which the various authors of our present Synoptic gospels have drawn. This, it is believed, consisted mainly of sayings of Jesus rather than an extended and orderly account of his life. When one stops to think about it, that would be the natural thing to expect. Events are much more easily recalled than utterances. Besides, the utterances do not depend for their value or validity on a knowledge of the exact occasion on which they are spoken. Matthew and Luke recount many of the same sayings, but in quite different settings, showing either that they depended upon sources which differed, or that they were relatively indifferent to the time, the place, and the occasion on which the utterances were given, and so felt free to group them together topically as seems to have been Matthew's scheme, or to fit them into another and different appropriate setting, as in Luke. Then, too, we must recognize that the gospel material was adapted to the new interests and functions of the early church.

Accordingly, this source has been variously named the Logia or Sayings, but rather more generally, simply, and perhaps more appropriately, since its exact content is not known, as the Q source, after the German word, "Quelle," which means source. But was "Q" the only such source? Not necessarily at all. There is no reason why there may not have been several other like documents in Luke's time. Where, for example, did Luke get most of his material for his magnificent chapters 10–15 which contains some of the most highly regarded teachings of Jesus not found in the other gospels? Here one finds the parable of the Good Samaritan; here also one finds the parable of the Prodigal Son. Why would Matthew or Mark have omitted such a rich vein of material if they had known about it?

It seems evident that there were other sources. Whence Luke's incomparable early story of the annunciation and the Magnificat, found only here—quite different from the Matthew account of the birth and infancy of Jesus. It has been suggested that "Q" may have existed in various forms in different sections of the early church. This does not seem at all an unreasonable suggestion, for the whole Christian gospel must have been in a fluid state for years before it took the form in which it has come down to us. But there is no reason to suppose that even if this were true of "Q" there may not have been other written sources as well. A saying of Papias, an early church father, about the middle of the second century, has it that "Matthew composed the Discourses in the Hebrew language and each one interpreted them as he was able." This was formerly thought to apply to the gospel of Matthew as we have it, but is probably a better description of some such sayings source as our "Q," which Matthew may well have been the first to write down. He was a tax-gatherer and would probably have had more education, and a more ready disposition to write than most of the other humble folk, fishermen, and artisans who composed the twelve.

At all events, whether rightly or wrongly, modern New Testament scholarship has almost unanimously agreed on the existence of at least one "Q" and perhaps others as well, upon which the gospel writers drew for much of the material of the gospels.

For Matthew and Luke the gospel of Mark seems clearly to have been a major source. It is estimated that fifteen-sixteenths of it is found in one or the other or both of the other Synoptics. Furthermore, it is generally agreed by modern scholars that Mark provides the framework for the other two. It is in general the order of Mark that the others follow. There is much digression in both. That is to say, a great deal of new material is introduced into the narrative by both Matthew and Luke, but at the end of a lengthy section of new material the story usually is taken up again where it was left off, and follows the Marcan order. Scott points out that, in the use of Mark, Matthew breaks it up into five sections, and between each inserts a body of Jesus' sayings, while Luke follows Mark closely up to 9:50, then in the nine succeeding chapters introduces material unknown to Mark.[57] Following this he returns to Mark's order, taking up at the point where he had left off. Also when Matthew and Luke agree, they are usually found to agree with Mark, and where they differ, as they do to a considerable degree, either one or the other agrees with Mark.

In summary, then, it may be said that our gospels, appearing

[57] *Op. cit.*, pp. 35–36.

more than a generation after the death of Jesus, do not represent merely the hazy memory of aged men writing down what they remembered of a distant past, or merely the floating legends of a dead hero, but rest back upon written documents which gathered up from many sources the sayings and doings of Jesus as remembered and told by many different people who had seen and known him. It is not a complete picture of Jesus, nor a complete transcript of all he said, but that it is a measurably accurate account of some of the things he did say and do, there can be no reasonable doubt. The modern critical study of the gospels has made the historic Jesus no mere figment of the pious imagination, but a living figure who, at an historic moment in time, appeared in Palestine, lived his brief but tremendously significant life, and gave rise to a vigorous new religious movement that has in time become the most widespread of all the religions of the world.

With this general overall picture of the process which produced the gospels we may look briefly at each of them in turn.

Concerning the gospel of Mark there is a very old tradition that Mark, not himself one of the twelve, but a young man who saw Jesus often in his mother's home, and must have been a follower; who later was for a time a companion of Paul and Barnabas; and still later became the interpreter of Peter; wrote down at last what he had so often heard Peter say about Jesus. It was Papias, already quoted concerning Matthew, who wrote, about 140 A.D., reporting the statement of an elder who had told him many things about the early church:

"Mark, who had become the interpreter of Peter, wrote accurately, but not in order, all that he remembered concerning the Lord's sayings or doings. For he did not hear the Lord or accompany him, but was later, as I said, a companion of Peter, who offered his instruction as occasion required without attempting to frame an ordered account of the Lord's sayings..." Thus Mark's gospel is in a sense the memoirs of Peter concerning Jesus. It is perhaps because of this tradition and the great prestige of Peter in the church, that this gospel, which is so much more meager, in what it reports of the teachings of Jesus, survived in the church, after Matthew and

Luke came into circulation. Add the fact that the gospel was almost certainly written for Gentiles, not Jews, and the tradition that connects it with the Roman church which Peter reputedly founded, and it can well be understood why it was preserved, for very early the Roman church was influential in the affairs of Christendom.

Mark's gospel may well be based upon the memoirs of Peter. It has been pointed out that the narrative begins properly at the point where Peter enters the scene—that incidents in which Peter figures are told in greater detail than others, especially those associated with the period of Capernaum, where he stayed in Peter's house. But scholars think that Peter's memoirs were added to from other sources, including possibly "Q," by others than Mark; that these formed the nucleus of the gospel which was expanded by a later editor to the form in which we have it. Even so this occurred before the writing of Matthew or Luke, who seem to have used Mark substantially in its present form.

Compared with the other gospels, Mark is a more or less straightforward narrative of Jesus' life, with a minimum of teaching material included. There is a directness about its language, particularly in the time sequences, that is lacking in the other gospels. "And straightway on the sabbath." "At even when the sun was set." "And he went forth by the seaside." "And he goeth into a mountain." "And he went out from thence." On the whole, while the Papias tradition asserts that he did not attempt to write "in order," Mark's gospel provides the best historic framework for the life of Jesus, and is generally followed by the other two Synoptics.

Though the narrative is swift and direct with no attempt at literary embellishment, there is a descriptive vividness about it which is striking and refreshing. It is a real experience to sit down with the gospel of Mark and read it through at a sitting without interruption. But if the book is largely narrative, it is narrative with a purpose. Mark is concerned to make clear that Jesus was the Messiah and that he came to preach the Kingdom of God. While probably Mark gives a clearer picture of the human Jesus than any of the gospels, he also presents him as Lord.

Matthew's gospel was for centuries thought to be the earliest of the gospels and still is so regarded by many conservative scholars. Mark was thought to be a shorter resumé of Jesus' life and teachings, more simply written, and based upon Matthew. We have seen that modern scholarship has reversed the order and makes Mark a major source of Matthew who, while generally using Mark's gospel as a framework, has incorporated large bodies of material not known to, or at any rate not contained in Mark. Apart from the other evidences which support this view the literary style of Mark, which is much less refined than that of Matthew, would seem to argue against its being taken from Matthew. It is rarely the case that a well-written work is so revised as to produce a cruder one.[58]

Even a very superficial comparison of Matthew with the others reveals his peculiarities in the handling of his material. Most notable, perhaps, is his very frequent use of the phrase "in order that it might be fulfilled which was spoken by the prophet." He seems anxious to show that Jesus in his life and teaching was the fulfillment of Old Testament prophecy. This would have no meaning for those to whom the Old Testament was either unknown, or of no particular importance. It would be highly significant to Jews, who cherished the Old Testament as the basis of their religious faith. The gospel, therefore, is clearly written primarily, not for Gentiles, but Jews. This Jesus who came and lived among them was not the enemy of the Jewish faith that he was being represented to be. On the other hand, he was the very fulfillment of what the prophets had so long foretold as the hope of the restoration of the people of Israel. When, for example, Jesus entered triumphantly into the city of Jerusalem amid the acclaim of the multitudes, riding upon an ass, he was but fulfilling the word of Zechariah written centuries before, "Behold thy king cometh unto thee, meek, and riding upon an ass and upon a colt, the foal of an ass."[59]

A second peculiar feature is Matthew's way of grouping sayings together, as if in one discourse, which Mark and Luke report as having been uttered on quite different occasions. Now, it is not

[58] Scott, *op. cit.*, p. 33.
[59] Matthew 21:4–5, Zechariah 9:9.

inherently impossible that Jesus might have uttered the same words on various occasions; he probably did; but the more or less obvious relating of sayings together which while similar in import do not necessarily grow one out of the other naturally, makes it much more likely that the author was grouping them for a special purpose—that of teaching. Matthew has well been called the teaching gospel.

The most notable example of such grouping is the so-called Sermon on the Mount, where within the compass of three chapters, is brought together what are generally regarded as the major ethical teachings of Jesus. It begins: "And seeing the multitudes, he went up into the mountain, and when he had sat down his disciples came unto him; and he opened his mouth and taught them, saying:" Then follow the ten beatitudes. Why ten? Could it be because there were ten commandments? It has been pointed out by scholars that the book of Matthew as a whole falls into five main sections each closing with the words, "And when Jesus had finished these sayings," 7:28, 11:1, 13:53, 19:1, 26:1. These, together with the story of the birth and infancy at the beginning and of his death and resurrection, make up the gospel. Why five sections? Could it be in correspondence with the five books of the Law? For Matthew, the gospel constitutes a New Law, which had superseded the Old Law. Would it not be natural to divide the New Law into five books also? There may be nothing to the suggestion; but the ten beatitudes and the five sections of a book by one whose Jewishness stands out throughout the gospel, would not seem at all out of character. If the Bible were not so accessible to most readers of this book, it would be fitting to transcribe here the greater part of the Sermon on the Mount.

If one wishes to get at the heart of Jesus' teaching quickly, he can do no better than to read this so-called sermon. It is quite the most revolutionary document in the entire Bible which has, as a whole, been called a revolutionary book. These three chapters cut sharply across most contemporary practice of the Christian world, especially in respect to our international relationships, which seem to be based primarily on force as the ultimate appeal. Though the Sermon has been publicly acclaimed as the ideal basis for national and international policy, if peace is to be had, there is little in the actual working policy of any so-called Christian nation that remotely approaches it. And even in individual behavior, where does one see it practiced in our day? It will not do to say that no one really takes it seriously, for example in his personal relations with others, for many individuals do live in the spirit of the Sermon on the Mount; but they constitute a very small minority. Let it be suggested that Jesus really meant it when he said "turn the other cheek," and the majority attitude is either that Jesus really did not mean it to be taken literally, or else the frank avowal that at that particular point Jesus was an impractical idealist and, at the most, meant this counsel only for those alive at the time and during the brief interim before the anticipated early end of the age. And many who admire it as an ideal to be achieved in individual behavior, still doubt that it can ever work at the international level.

Mr. Gandhi, a Hindu, who had behind him a long-time and widespread tradition of non-violence or *ahimsa,* loved the Sermon on the Mount. He acknowledged that it was this, indirectly at least, which led to his adoption of the non-violent method of seeking ends he cherished, rather than resorting to violence. The outstanding victories which he won without doing physical violence to any enemy, particularly the winning of independence for India without striking a single violent blow at Britain, has quickened the faith of not a few Christians, who see no way out of the fearful threat of destruction of everything the world values, if violence be man's ultimate reliance. It encourages them in their belief that in the adoption of Jesus' way of non-violence and love lies the only salvation of our very lives and all of our cherished values, from total destruction.

But with the communist world threatening to engulf western civilization, as well as the East, where it has already won signal success as in China, even devout Christian men and women feel driven to fall back upon bigger and better atomic bombs and other means of mass destruction as the only guarantee of self-preservation. It would take great faith, and enormous skill and patience and love, to undertake to deal, let us say, with Russia, on any other basis, but in the end what other hope is there? Does anyone living now believe that security and lasting peace can be had on the basis of ever-increasing destructiveness and terror? Maybe Jesus did have the way out. "Love your enemies!" If one did so, really, one wonders if he would have any enemies very long.

At any rate, it is easy to see that here is a set of sayings which would quite revolutionize human society if they were put into practice. It is a new law Jesus announces. "You have heard that it was said of old time . . . but I say unto you." It is the law of love. He did not go on to spell out in a detailed code exactly what must be done in every situation, and so create the possibility of a new if refined legalism, but he set a new principle, provided a new motivation, which must work itself out in appropriate ways as men face the perplexing problems of individual and social life. Read the whole of it and try to imagine what kind of a world it would be if men lived after the pattern here set forth, rather than on the basis of the conventional morality of our day.

There is undoubted advantage for teaching purposes in this bringing together of matter similar in character, rather than allowing the separate sayings to appear singly, in isolation from the rest. Of course literary arrangement follows the purpose of the author. If it is simply to narrate what happened, when and where, then the other method is quite proper. If the portrayal of a personality is the end, it may be the better way. Matthew seems to have been primarily interested, not so much in the person of Jesus as in his teachings. Other groups of sayings are to be found in chapter 23, where he strikes out at the Pharisees, while his apocalyptic utterances are grouped in chapters 24 and 25. He also groups most of the miracles in one section.

Matthew is unique also among the evangelists in his concern for the church. He is the only one who specifically mentions it.[60] It is clear that he regards the teachings of Jesus as the New Law for the church, just as the Torah was the Law for the synagogue. His gospel probably was used more by the church than either of the other Synoptics.

[60] 16:18; 18:17.

We have already seen that the gospel in its present form is based upon written sources, certainly upon Mark and "Q." The latter may have been originally collected by Matthew, and so have given his name to the gospel. Tradition has it that the gospel was written in Antioch—but there is no proof that the tradition is true. However, no other place of origin can be certainly fixed. It is later than Mark, which would mean certainly some time after 70 A.D. How long a time would be required for the new gospel of Mark to acquire a standing which would warrant the compiler of Matthew to make it really the framework of his own gospel, it is difficult to say. It is variously dated by modern scholars from the late seventies to the early nineties.

The gospel of Luke is really the first of a two-volume history of the rise of Christianity. Volume II is known as the Acts of the Apostles, but deals chiefly with the activities of but Peter and Paul, the most outstanding figures. In the prologue of Acts the writer begins: "The former treatise I made, O Theophilus, concerning all that Jesus began both to do and to teach," etc. This is clearly a description of the gospel of Luke, which, as we have before seen, is dedicated to Theophilus. We may, therefore, speak of Luke-Acts as a literary unit, in two parts, which carries the story of nascent Christianity from the Annunciation of the birth of Jesus down to a time when Paul was a prisoner in a Roman prison, awaiting consideration of his case by the emperor, to whose judgment he had appealed the case, tried in the court at Caesarea Philippi. It is just possible that Luke intended writing a third volume to carry the story on to a later period, possibly including the further itineraries of Paul, should he indeed be set at liberty. But Paul was executed, probably without being freed for further work, though a tradition exists that he was set free, went to Spain, as he had hoped, and continued preaching until he was again arrested, and this time put to death.

Scholars, both conservative and liberal, are agreed that Luke was the author of both books, though there is no indication in either as to whose pen it was that wrote it. A very old tradition attributes them to Luke, a physician, known from Paul's letters to have been a companion in some of his journeys, though his name does not appear in the Acts at all. There are, however, some sections of the Acts which are written in the first person plural, indicating that the author was one of the travelling companions of Paul during part of the time. Without the tradition it would have been difficult, if not impossible, to fix upon the one individual of all his company who might have written both documents. But with the tradition given, it is not difficult to find evidence supporting the Lukan authorship. Luke was a physician, therefore an educated man. He did accompany Paul on some of his journeys. Luke was a Greek. He would, therefore, have been able to write Greek more easily and correctly than a native Jewish companion. The Greek of Luke-Acts is the finest to be found in the New Testament. Others point out the extreme interest the gospel of Luke shows in the diseases of which Jesus healed people. This would be natural in a physician. So one evidence after another tends to corroborate the tradition. Furthermore, no one else has been suggested as so likely a possible author. Of course, there is always the possibility that Luke had only kept a diary of the events which occurred while he was with Paul, and that someone may have had access to this, as well as to other materials, when he sat down to write. But this seems most unlikely, since linguistic specialists agree very well that there is no substantial variation in literary style in the "we" sections and the rest of the Acts and the gospel—and no one seriously distinguishes stylistic differences between Acts and the gospel.

We have already seen that Luke made a frank use of sources—several of them, none adequate, as he felt. Hence he himself would, having carefully looked over the field, put the whole in order. He comes nearest to the method of a modern scientific historian of any of the gospel writers. He made large use of Mark, as a framework, though his independent judgment is shown now and then in his variations from the Marcan sequence, or, for example, as to where Jesus' ministry was begun; he puts it in Nazareth while Mark puts the Nazareth incident at a much later period of his ministry. He makes large use of "Q," for we may confidently assign all the parallels to Matthew's material to the "Q" source. But he has a great deal besides. His infancy stories differ from those of Matthew. He alone tells the story of Jesus as a lad in the temple, the only glimpse of him afforded by any gospel between infancy and his baptism by John the Baptist, and the beginning of his public ministry. There is so large a body of material peculiar to Luke, about two-fifths, all told, that sometimes scholars, for want of any more adequate explanation, assign it to "L," a special Lukan source.

Regardless of whence it came the author has woven the various strands into perhaps the best biography of Jesus that the New Testament affords. He writes with a literary charm unequalled in the other gospels. His figures live. He seems very much interested in persons, has sympathy for them and understanding. He is noted for the attention given to the women characters who enter the scene. His interest in the poor and the underprivileged is noteworthy. It may not be without significance that the beatitude, "Blessed are the poor in spirit: for theirs is the kingdom," is given in Luke simply as "Blessed are the poor, for theirs is the kingdom of heaven."

One of the questions that has puzzled some scholars is as to why the author, if Luke, and therefore a companion of Paul, shows so little of the influence of Pauline theology in his writings. But as a matter of fact Luke was simply a layman, not primarily concerned with theological questions. He writes not as a partisan, propagandizing for a particular point of view, but as a biographer setting forth the facts as he found them reported in his sources, or in the Acts as an historian, reporting the developments as they occurred. Of course he does follow Paul in his universal view of the gospel, as meant not for a particular people but for the world, and in the book of Acts tells the story of the struggle through which Paul went in emancipating the gospel from the particularism which threatened to limit its outreach, and making it truly a world religion.

As has already been remarked, there is comparatively little poetry in the New Testament. One wonders why. Possibly the rich heritage of poetry in the Old Testament was adequate to express most of the religious emotion of the early Christians, especially since they felt that the coming of Jesus lay not outside the traditional faith, but was rather its fulfillment. But now and then a poem is included, in Luke more often than in the other gospels. Two appear in the birth and infancy sections. One, the Magnificat, is of singular power and beauty. It is the song of Mary:

> My soul doth magnify the Lord
> And my spirit hath rejoiced in God my savior.
> For he hath looked upon the low estate of his handmaid:
> For behold, from henceforth all nations shall call me blessed.
> For he that is mighty hath done to me great things
> And holy is his name.
> And his mercy is unto generations and generations
> Of them that fear him.
> He hath showed strength with his arm,
> He hath scattered the proud in the imagination
>   of their heart.
> He hath put down the princes from their thrones
> And hath exalted them of low degree.
> The hungry he hath filled with good things
> And the rich he hath sent empty away.
> He hath given help to Israel his servant
> That he might remember mercy
> (And he spake unto our father)
> Toward Abraham and his seed forever.[61]

There is a sonorous quality about it reminiscent of some of the great Psalms. Did Luke compose it, or was it already a part of one of his sources? The reference to filling the hungry and sending the rich away empty is definitely in the Lukan spirit.

He also includes another poem, the utterance of Zacharias, father of John the Baptist. He had been deaf and dumb, but at the birth of the child his tongue was loosed and "filled with the Holy Spirit he prophesied, saying:"

> Blessed be the Lord the God of Israel
> For he hath visited and wrought redemption
>   for his people
> And hath raised up a horn of salvation for us
> In the house of his servant David. . . .

[61] Luke 1:46–55, *American Revised Version*.

Salvation from our enemies, and from the hand
    of all that hate us. . . .
Yea, and thou, child, shalt be called the prophet of the Most High
For thou shalt go before the face
    of the Lord to make ready his ways,
To give knowledge of salvation to his people
In the remission of their sins,
Because of the tender mercy of our God
Whereby the dayspring from on high shall visit us
To shine upon them that sit in darkness,
    and the shadow of death
To guide our feet into the way of peace.[62]

The gospel of Luke has been dated by modern scholars all the
way from a little after 70 A.D. to the middle nineties. There is no
certainty as to just when it appeared. The same considerations
mentioned in connection with Matthew lead to its dating thus. The
Acts of the Apostles was written later, but how much later it is
impossible to say. It was a valuable service which Luke performed
in giving us his gospel and history of the early church. It was not
a complete history, and perhaps not even a wholly accurate history.
It is certain that it is not always in agreement with what is found
in the letters of Paul which were written a long time before Luke
wrote, and by a major figure in the early history of the church. But
it is the earliest connected story we have of the movement growing
out of Jesus' appearance, and the only one that was written so close
in time to the events narrated. It was not until the time of Eusebius,
c. 263–c. 340 A.D., that another studied attempt to write a history of
the church was made. Aside from these works the historians of the
church today must reconstruct the unfolding life of the movement
from such scattered notices as may be found in the well-authenticated early writings of Paul and the other apostles and early leaders
of the church in the post-apostolic age, by sifting a great mass of
accumulated tradition, of very uneven value, for some kernel of
fact.

The debt of the church historian to Luke, therefore, is very great

[62] Luke 1:68–80, *passim. American Revised Version.*

for having written the gospel and the Acts. If time does not permit the reading of the entire book of Acts, read at least the story of Pentecost in chapter 2, a turning point in the experience of the discouraged followers of Jesus, and the real beginning of the Christian church. This includes the fiery sermon of the formerly vacillating Peter who is now as bold as a lion. Chapter 7 is the story of Stephen who became the first among many martyrs to the faith. Just at the end of that chapter, Saul, later Paul, is introduced. His conversion is told in chapter 9, certainly one of the most important events in the history of the early church. Chapter 10 tells the story of Peter's conversion from Jewish particularism to a recognition of the universal nature of the gospel. It was a great step for Peter, the Jew, to cry: "Of a truth I perceive that God is no respecter of persons; but in every nation he that feareth him and worketh righteousness is acceptable to him" (v. 34–35). The account of the first council of the church is given in chapter 15. In this council an agreement was reached between Paul and the leaders of the church in Jerusalem that officially broke down the wall of particularism around the growing Christian faith, and made it truly a universal religion. Said James, the head of the church in Jerusalem:

"My judgment is that we trouble not them that from among the Gentiles turn to God, but that we write unto them that they abstain from the pollution of idols and from fornication, and from what is strangled and from blood." That is, they need not become Jews in order to become Christians, but they were cautioned against idolatry and certain other practices, moral and dietary. The elders even set apart Paul and Barnabas and others to go and work among the Gentiles, giving them a cordial letter of introduction and greeting. Christianity was definitely on its way to becoming a world religion. All the rest of the book of Acts is the story of Paul's mission to the Graeco-Roman world—and an interesting one it is. Read his visit to the center of culture, Athens, and his speech on Mars Hill, chapter 17:16–34. His stay in Ephesus, where he was involved in a riot, is interestingly told in chapter 19. Mobbed in the temple at Jerusalem, he was rescued by a captain of the Roman constabulary. He asked for a chance to make a defense of his position and was given permission. Standing on a stairway of the barracks, he addressed the mob, as told in chapter 22, in the course of which he recounts once more his conversion. Most of the remainder of the book deals with his various trials and imprisonment and his appeal to the emperor, which as a Roman citizen he had a right to make. Chapter 26 is his defense before Agrippa, a model of effective public speech.

Why the book ends where it does, with Paul in prison awaiting judgment, it is difficult to say. Even if Luke had had the intention of writing a third volume, it would have been more natural to have ended this one with the apostle's release from prison, unless he had done the writing while the outcome of the appeal was still unknown. But scholars are agreed that the book could hardly have been written so early, since it presupposes the gospel, which is usually dated as late, at least, as 70. It is possible that more was written, but that some accident destroyed the last part of the manuscript, as seems to have happened in the case of Mark, of which the portion from verse nine of chapter 16 to the end is not found in the two oldest Greek manuscripts. It has quite a different ending in some other manuscripts.

Paul's letters form a very substantial part of the New Testament. Thirteen are definitely attributed to him, and for centuries the letter to the Hebrews was also thought to be Paul's. While in the older versions of the New Testament it is still attributed to him, it is now the almost unanimous opinion of scholars, conservative as well as liberal, that he could not have written it. The thirteen are, in the order in which they appear in the canon, the letter to the Romans, two to the Corinthians, one each to the Galatians, Ephesians, Philippians, and Colossians, two to the Thessalonians, two to Timothy, one to Titus, and one to Philemon. The last four named are letters to individuals, the others to various churches.

Paul, whose story is told in the book of Acts, was not one of the original followers of Jesus. He may never have seen him, though it is possible that he was a student in Jerusalem while Jesus was still alive. He was born of Jewish parents, in a provincial city, Tarsus, in Cilicia, but enjoyed Roman citizenship, a fact which was to stand him in good stead many times during his career. He represented in himself the fusion of two great cultures, the Hebrew and the Greek, so that he was well prepared for leadership in turning Christianity into a world religion, rather than allowing it to remain as it might otherwise have done, a Jewish sect. He had gone up to Jerusalem to finish his education as a rabbi. While there, the new movement arose, and became very troublesome from the standpoint of a believer in the status quo. An upstart teacher from a provincial town had ventured to set aside the ancient law and substitute for it his own law. "You have heard it said of old time...but I say unto you." The teacher had been properly liquidated by crucifixion and the threat disposed of—at least that was what they thought—for a little while; then it began to be heard that the crucified one was not dead but alive—that he had risen from the dead. This was non-sense, of course, they said, because people do not rise from the dead except in the general resurrection at the last day. But, strangely enough, people seemed to believe it. Soon there were people preach-ing this strange doctrine and beginning to form a movement around the belief in the crucified Jesus. Clearly, something must be done about it. Young Saul, ardent Pharisee and profound believer in the authority of the law, felt impelled to aid in its suppression, for sup-pression seemed the way to deal with such blasphemies. He was first noticed in Luke's story in the Acts as being present at the stoning of Stephen, for it is there said that they laid down their garments—that is, the men who threw the stones that crushed out Stephen's life—at the feet of a young man named Saul. "And Saul was consenting unto his death." If Saul was not the leader of the group that put Stephen to death, he was at least present when a mob slew him, and did nothing to prevent his lynching. It may have been the memory of Stephen's quiet courage in meeting death and forgiving his slayers which started Saul thinking seriously about the matter and ultimately led to his conversion.

A little later he was leader of a party on the way to Damascus to stir up the local synagogues against a new group of these fanatical followers of Jesus, when a strange thing happened. Suddenly, as he told it later, a bright light shone about him, he fell to the ground blinded and seemed to hear a voice saying to him, "Saul, Saul, why persecutest thou me?" And he answered, "Who art thou, Lord?" The voice replied, "I am Jesus whom thou persecutest." Was it the voice of conscience that had been troubling him ever since the day he saw Stephen done to death for no crime save that of preaching the gospel of Jesus? It was a pivotal point in Saul's career. The number-one persecutor of the new faith was transformed into the greatest of all its propagators and gave the rest of his life, after a brief period of readjustment, to the task of spreading that gospel over the Graeco-Roman world.

It took some time to think the matter through and to work out in his own mind the significance of the new gospel, but once he had made it thoroughly his own, Saul, "who also is called Paul," became the most important single figure in the spread of the new movement and the formation of its ideology or theology. Much of this comes down to us through his letters and through Acts.

His was an itinerant ministry. He made several missionary journeys, planting the church in many centers scattered over the eastern end of the Mediterranean. He seldom stayed long in one place. It was his custom to begin speaking in the synagogue. But as soon as he introduced the revolutionary idea of a risen Christ, he was denied further use of the platform, and had to continue preaching in the home of some individual who had been attracted by his message. Soon a small group formed about him which eventually became a church. He remained with them for a time, usually working at his trade, that of a tent-maker or weaver, until they seemed strong enough to carry on alone, then went on to another center, leaving some helper in charge or sometimes simply some local individual who had shown signs of leadership.

But as he went on to other centers, he never forgot the little groups he had organized. He often wrote letters back to them, or sent words of greeting when some traveller was going in that direction. He was interested not only in their conversion but in their confirmation. This interest of Paul in his new converts is the basis of all his letters, save perhaps one, that to the Romans, a church he had never visited in person. Sometimes the letters are written in response to messages either written to him, or personally conveyed by some member of the groups, asking advice in certain matters, or relating difficulties that had arisen in the churches. To these Paul replied in the letters that have been preserved to us, and probably in a great many more that were lost. There is no space here to discuss the several letters one by one, but only to show something of their general nature.

The very earliest of the letters we have was his first letter to the church at Thessalonica. They were troubled about a very practical matter. Paul apparently believed in and assured them of an early return of Jesus to the earth. But some of those who had believed had died, and would not be there on his return. What of these? To this Paul replies: "But we would not have you ignorant, brethren, concerning them that have fallen asleep. . .if we believe that Jesus died and rose again, even so them also that are fallen asleep in Jesus will God bring with him. For this we say unto you by the word of the Lord, that we that are alive, that are left unto the coming of the Lord, shall in no wise precede them that are fallen asleep. For the Lord himself shall descend from heaven, with a shout, with the voice of an archangel, and with the trump of God; and the dead in Christ shall rise first; then we that are alive, that are left, shall be caught up in the clouds, to meet the Lord in the air; and so shall we be forever with the Lord. Wherefore comfort one another with these words." But he went on to urge them to be watchful, for "the day of the Lord cometh as a thief in the night. When they are saying, peace and safety, then sudden destruction cometh upon them as travail upon a woman with child."[63]

Apparently they took this to mean that the Lord would come very soon, for in the second letter we find him writing further concerning the matter. It is true that the Lord will come; the exact time cannot be known, but certain signs will precede his coming (2:3–12). Meanwhile they are not to leave off their work as some apparently had done in anticipation of the end. "If any man will not work, neither let him eat," he wrote.

In the case of the Galatian letter an attack had been made upon Paul's authority to teach. His answer is a vigorous forthright defense

63 4:13–5:4, *passim.*

of his apostleship. "For I make known to you brethren, as touching the gospel which was preached by me, that it is not after man. For neither did I receive it from man, nor was I taught it, but *it came to me* through the revelation of Jesus Christ" (1:11–12). He then recounts the story of his thorough Jewish background, his persecuting zeal, his conversion and call to preach to the Gentiles. "Straightway," he continues, "I went not up to Jerusalem to them that were apostles before me; but I went away into Arabia; and again I returned to Damascus." Only after three years did he go to Jerusalem to visit Peter and James, the Lord's brother. His gospel was one gotten not from apostles but from Christ directly. So far from receiving it from Peter, he found it necessary to "resist him face to face," for his lack of consistency in being quite liberal and eating with Gentiles until there came emissaries from James, when he withdrew from fellowship with them. "O foolish Galatians, who did bewitch you...having begun in the Spirit are you now perfected in the flesh?" (3:3). Paul is so certain of his gospel that he writes, "But though we or an angel from heaven should preach unto you any gospel other than that which we preached unto you, let him be anathema" (1:9).

The church at Corinth presented a variety of problems. There was first of all division within the church. Some were saying, "I am of Paul, I of Apollos, I of Cephas and I of Christ" (1:12). But writes Paul, "Is Christ divided? Was Paul crucified for you? Or were ye baptized unto the name of Paul? . . . What then is Apollos? And what is Paul? Ministers through whom ye believed, and each as the Lord gave to him. I planted, Apollos watered, but God giveth the increase" (1:11–3:6, *passim*). There is much of self-disclosure in these passionate attempts to correct the errors of his beloved brethren.

It has been reported to him that gross immorality is practiced among the membership, even incest, and litigation, brother going to law against brother. He has been asked about marriage and replies at length in chapter 7. It is thought by some that Paul had not been happy in his own married life. The problem of what to do about eating meat that had been offered to idols was a real one to people who had been converted from pagan ways. Paul himself comes to see no harm in eating such meat. After all, the pagan gods to whom the meat was offered had no reality. But if he or any other by eating such meat should lead another, for whom it was a matter of conscience, to do so, then indeed would it be wrong, "for through thy knowledge he that is weak perisheth, the brother for whose sake Christ died. And thus sinning against the brethren and wounding their conscience when it is weak, ye sin against Christ." Wherefore, Paul declares personally, "If meat causeth my brother to stumble, I will eat no flesh for evermore, that I cause not my brother to stumble" (8:10–13 *passim*), thus stating what has been regarded as the classic principle of Christian liberty.

A good deal of discussion had arisen in the Corinthian church regarding the matter of spiritual gifts. Which was the most important? Some were speakers, some healers, some prophesied, some spoke in tongues as at Pentecost, etc. Writes Paul, "Now there are diversities of gifts, but the same spirit, and there are diversities of ministrations and the same Lord, and there are diversities of workings, but the same God, who worketh all things in all. . . . For as the body is one and hath many members, and all the members of the body, being many, are one body; so also is Christ. For in one Spirit were we all baptized into one body, whether Jews, or Greeks, whether bond or free; and were all made to drink of one Spirit. For the body is not one member, but many. If the foot shall say, Because I am not the hand, I am not the body, it is not therefore not of the body. If the whole body were the eye, where were the hearing? . . . The eye cannot say to the hand, I have no need of thee. . . . Whether one member suffereth all members suffer with it. . . . Now ye are the body of Christ, and severally members thereof."[64] No figure of speech has been more often used of the church than this, the "body of Christ," and in our own day the ecumenical movement is an attempt once again to heal the division that the centuries have created, and so to restore to wholeness the body of Christ.

To be sure, he continued, God has given a variety of gifts. Are all apostles, or prophets, or miracle workers, or healers, or speakers

[64] 1 Cor. 12:4–27, *passim*.

in tongues, or interpreters? But, he cries, "Desire earnestly the greater gifts. And moreover I show you a more excellent way."

If I speak with the tongues of men and of angels, but have not love, I am become sounding brass, or a clanging cymbal. And if I have the gift of prophecy, and know all mysteries and all knowledge; and if I have all faith, so as to remove mountains, but have not love, I am nothing. And if I bestow all my goods to feed the poor and if I give my body to be burned, but have not love, it profiteth me nothing. Love suffereth long, and is kind; love envieth not; love vaunteth not itself, is not puffed up, doth not behave itself unseemly, seeketh not its own, is not provoked, taketh not account of evil; rejoiceth not in unrighteousness, but rejoiceth in the truth; beareth all things, believeth all things, hopeth all things, endureth all things.

Love never faileth: but whether there be prophecies, they shall be done away; whether there be tongues, they shall cease; whether there be knowledge, it shall be done away. For we know in part and we prophesy in part; but when that which is perfect is come, that which is in part shall be done away. When I was a child, I spake as a child, I felt as a child, I thought as a child: now that I am become a man, I have put away childish things. For now we see in a mirror, darkly; but then face to face: now I know in part; but then shall I know fully even as also I was fully known. But now abideth faith, hope, love, these three; and the greatest of these is love.[65]

And so, out of the day's work, in the course of a letter of practical counsel and advice, comes one of the greatest chapters in the whole New Testament, a poem of rare beauty and power. Some have analyzed it in great detail and found it perfect in literary construction and balance.

Was it, therefore, a work of labored composition, carefully thought out and arranged so that it fulfilled all the laws of Greek poetry? Or did it come with a rush from the heart of Paul, and spontaneously take the form it now has? Only speculation is possible here, but it affords an interesting point to ponder. How does inspiration come? Certainly if only one passage in the entire body of Paul's writings could claim inspiration, this would be the one most worthy

[65] I Corinthians 13.

of the claim. The writer's guess is that inspiration quite as often as not comes as a by-product of what one is doing in the course of his ordinary daily work, if what he is doing is worthwhile.

Examples could be multiplied of the practical purposes which the letters were meant to serve. They were the written response to a particular need in most cases. But they do far more than deal with the specific matters which were the occasion of the writing. The letters follow fairly closely a general pattern. They begin with a salutation and with an expression of Paul's regard for those to whom he is writing and often thanksgiving for the good things he has heard concerning them. Often also he recalls how he first came to them, and some of the experiences they have shared. Then in the main body of the letter the matters are dealt with that provoked the letter. In the course of this is to be found a rich vein of insight into the meaning of the gospel as Paul conceives of it. This has been of great influence in the formation of Christian theology. Then toward the end there are varied admonitions and counsel of a practical and usually highly moral character. Finally there is the closing word of personal greeting and farewell. A good many of the letters were probably dictated. In a few cases he signs them personally as in I Corinthians. "The salutation of me, Paul, with mine own hand. If any man loveth not the Lord, let him be anathema. Maranatha. The Grace of the Lord Jesus Christ be with you. My love be with you all in Christ Jesus. Amen" (16:21–24).

The letter to the Romans differs from the rest in that it was written to a church Paul had not yet visited. Even so there must have been a good many members whom he had known elsewhere, who had gone to live in Rome, the capital of the empire. In it there is less that is personal, nor does it seem to have been written in response to any question or any report that had come to him. He had long wanted to go to Rome, had tried several times and was hindered, but he states definitely that it is his purpose to come to them (1:15).

The letter contains the most nearly systematic statement of Paul's theology to be found in any of his epistles. Here he is not held to the discussion of, or emphasis upon, some special topic concerning which inquiry has been made, but is free to set forth in general terms the gospel as he understands it. As a result this letter has probably been more influential in the formulation of Christian theology than any of his other writings. In chapter 5 is set forth his classic idea of justification by faith, as over against the more legalistic conception of salvation which had been taught him, but brought him no peace. It was the recovery of this insight which signalized the Protestant Reformation. In it Luther is said to have found the inspiration for his revolt against the Christianity of his own day, and it has been a chief reliance of Protestant Christianity from that day until now. Whenever Christianity tends to fall back into a formalism and reliance upon "good works" there is usually a recovery of this note by some minority group within the larger church. Methodism had its rise in this way as a revolt against the Anglican church of Wesley's day. And there is something of this involved in the Neo-reformation emphasis in our own day.

Chapter 8 furnishes the basis for the characteristic Augustinian-Calvinist concept of predestination, that some are elected to salvation and some to eternal loss, which has played such a significant role in Christian history. "For whom he foreknew, he also foreordained to be conformed to the image of his Son, that he might be the first-born among many brethren. And whom he foreordained, them he also called; and whom he called, them also he justified; and whom he justified, them he also glorified" (8:29–30). Yet even in this letter he did not fail to add a section of practical advice and moral counsel.

Perhaps chapter 12 has been as often read as the New Testament lesson in Christian worship as any chapter in the entire Bible. The whole section 12–15 is packed with good, sound, moral teaching, which squares absolutely with that of Jesus. "Let love be without hypocrisy. Abhor that which is evil, cleave to that which is good. . . . Render to no man evil for evil. . . . Avenge not yourselves. . . . If thine enemy hunger, feed him; or if he thirst give him to drink. . . . Be not overcome of evil, but overcome evil with good" (12:19–

21 *passim*). "Love worketh no ill to his neighbor, love therefore is the fulfillment of the law" (13:10). "Now we that are strong ought to bear the infirmities of the weak, and not to please ourselves" (15:1).

Of the personal letters two were directed to Timothy, a young preacher, a convert of Paul's, and to Titus also a helper. Some doubt if these letters, as they stand today, are genuine Pauline letters, though containing some material from the hand of Paul. His letter to Philemon was written to a friend who was converted under Paul's preaching, and in whose house he had stayed and preached. A runaway slave of Philemon had come to Rome, been converted and now Paul sends him back with this delightfully precious personal note, asking that Philemon receive him not as a slave but as a brother in Christ, and forgive him. There is no lashing out here against the evils of slavery and a demand that Philemon give up the practice of slave-holding, or even that he set Onesimus, the returned slave, free. But he nonetheless cuts away the foundation upon which slavery finally rests. Brotherhood, love, and slavery simply do not go together, when properly understood. It took the Christian church a long time to see this.

Modern scholarship is doubtful of the authenticity of some of the Pauline letters, though by far the greater body of material attributed to him is undoubtedly genuine. Nor are modern scholars agreed as to how and when they got into anything like general circulation. Some think that there was, from an early date, a tendency to trade letters among the churches. Some have thought that Ephesians and possibly Colossians were intended for more than the one church. Goodspeed holds the opinion that the letters were carefully kept by the churches to which they were addressed, perhaps read and reread from time to time, but that there was no attempt made at collecting them until after the appearance of Luke's early history of the church, the Acts of the Apostles, and that it was this which gave the impulse to a revival of interest in Paul, and led to a search for and collection of his extant writings. Had his writings been in general circulation in the years during which the gospels were taking form, they would surely have exercised some theological influence upon the gospels, it is argued. The question cannot be settled definitely, because we do not have sufficient information concerning the process. Actually there are scholars who profess to find Pauline influence in some of the gospel writings. It is largely a matter of interpretation, into which the subjective element must perforce enter.

It seems to the writer rather unlikely that so dynamic a figure and influence in the early church as Paul was should have faded into near oblivion, only to be revived by the publication of a book about him, nearly a generation after his death. Paul had his devoted followers who continued to circulate among the churches after his passing, and who might well be expected to keep his memory alive by the rereading publicly of his vigorous letters and by their gradual circulation among other churches. What he had written was seen to be not limited to a single locality, but of universal validity and, coming with the prestige of Paul's name, might be very useful in congregations far removed from the churches to which they were originally addressed.

The other letters, Hebrews, and the general epistles, as they are called, were probably written considerably later than those of Paul; some of them, notably that of second Peter, are definitely regarded as products of the second century. They all, save Jude, bear the names of some one of the apostles, but evidence to support the claims of apostolic authorship is at least doubtful. They do reflect at least modes of thought in the early church and are therefore of great historic value.

The Epistle to the Hebrews, for centuries attributed to Paul, is now regarded almost universally as non-Pauline, written by an unknown author to interpret the Christian gospel, on the analogy of the old Hebrew sacrificial system. It is chiefly meaningful to those acquainted with that system. To those who have no such background it speaks almost an unknown language. But even here there are passages of beauty and rare significance. Few chapters are more often read than the eleventh chapter, illustrative of the dynamic quality of faith. If I Corinthians 13 is the great love chapter of the New Testament surely Hebrews 11 is the *faith* chapter *par excellence*:

> Now faith is the assurance of things hoped for, a conviction of things not seen. . . . By faith . . . the worlds have been framed by the word of God, so that what is seen hath not been made out of the things which appear. By faith Abel offered unto God a more excellent sacrifice than Cain. . . . By faith Enoch was translated that he should not see death. . . . By faith Noah . . . prepared an ark. . . . By faith Abraham when he was called obeyed . . . and went out not knowing whither he went. . . . By faith Abraham offered up Isaac. . . . By faith Isaac blessed Jacob and Esau. . . . By faith Moses . . . refused to be called the son of Pharaoh, choosing rather to share ill treatment with the people of God, than to enjoy the pleasures of sin for a season. . . . By faith the walls of Jericho fell down. . . . And what more shall I say, for the time would fail me if I tell of Gideon, Barak, Samson, Jephthah: of David and Samuel, and the prophets: who through faith subdued kingdoms, wrought righteousness, obtained promises, stopped the mouths of lions, quenched the power of fire, escaped the edge of the sword, from weakness were made strong . . . and others had trial of mockings and scourgings . . . of bonds and imprisonment: they were stoned, they were slain with the sword: they went about in sheepskins, in goatskins; being destitute, afflicted, illtreated (of whom the world was not worthy). . . . And these all having had witness borne to them through their faith, received not the promise, God having provided some better thing concerning us that apart from us they should not be made perfect. Therefore, let us also seeing we are compassed round about with so great a cloud of witnesses, lay aside every weight, and the sin which doth so easily beset us, and let us run with patience the race that is set before us . . . (11:1–12:2 *passim*).

The first epistle of John is preëminently the epistle of love—Christian love. In almost every paragraph this note appears. "He that loveth his brother abideth in the light" (2:10). "Love not the world. . .if any man love the world the love of the father is not in him" (2:15). "Behold what manner of love the father hath bestowed upon us that we should be called the children of God" (3:1). . . . "We know that we have passed out of death into life, because we love the brethren" (3:13). "Beloved, let us love one another, for love is of God and everyone that loveth is begotten of God. He that loveth not knoweth not God, for God is love" (4:7–8). "God is love; and he that abideth in love abideth in God, and God abideth in him" (4:6). "There is no fear in love, but perfect love casteth out fear" (4:18).

Whether these little letters were written by the beloved disciple John, as conservative scholars like to believe, or are late products of some member of the Johannine school, is not a matter of primary concern. Particularly 1st John is one of the greatest of the classic Christian writings, deeply in the spirit of Jesus. All three of the letters can be read entire in a few minutes.

The Epistle of James is a book that has been held by some to be not a Christian book at all, but a Jewish tract modified at one or two points to make it appear Christian.[66] By another it is said to come closer to the Synoptic gospels in its type of thought than any other of the early writers. It has been regarded as among the earliest and as quite late. It could be an early Christian sermon in the form of a letter. Generally speaking its emphasis is primarily moral rather than theological or mystical. It puts stress on "work," not to the exclusion of faith, but as the necessary fruitage of a faith that is real. The author is down-to-earth, practical, common-sense in his teaching. Religion is not holding some particular theological beliefs. Incidentally it is in this book only that the word "religion" itself appears in the entire Bible. "Pure religion and undefiled is this—to visit the fatherless and widows in their affliction and to keep oneself unspotted from the world" (1:27).

The whole epistle can be read in but a few minutes. It is packed full of moral maxims which are not distinctively Christian. It has even been suggested that the book was originally written by some Greek ethical teacher. But on the whole it does represent a moralistic Christian outlook, which has been a wholesome note throughout the centuries of mystical, philosophical, theological and ecclesiastical emphasis. "Be ye doers of the word and not hearers only, deluding your own selves" (1:22). James would agree one hundred per cent with the saying of Jesus, "By their fruits ye shall know

[66] Scott, *op. cit.*, p. 213.

them." It is refreshing to pick up the little epistle of James after prolonged immersion in the theological discussions, say, of Paul's letter to the Romans.

The epistle of Jude is undoubtedly late. It was one of the last of the New Testament books to find its way into the canon. On reading some of the books that failed to make the grade, one wonders how it got in at all. It seems less in accord with the spirit of the earlier New Testament writings than any other.

The two epistles of Peter are attributed to the disciple Peter by conservative scholarship, but are almost unanimously held by modern scholarship to have appeared too late to have been written by the great disciple. Internal evidences put the first letter probably during the general persecution of Christians by Domitian near the end of the first century, while the second is generally regarded as a second-century writing. The latter is much inferior to first Peter, much more in the spirit of Jude and, like Jude, only with difficulty, did it achieve a permanent place in the canon. First Peter is in form a circular letter. It is addressed to the Dispersion in Pontus, Galatia, Cappadocia, Asia and Bithynia (1:1) and is largely a message of hope and encouragement to Christians in a time of suffering and persecution. It contains one unique belief with reference to Jesus, not found, at least certainly, in any other part of the New Testament, namely, that Christ between the time of his death and resurrection "went and preached to the Spirits in prison, that aforetime were disobedient" (3:18). Again in 4:6 he speaks of the gospel being preached "even to the dead, that they might be judged indeed according to men in the flesh, but live according to God in the spirit." This is the basis for the phrase, "he descended into Hell" in the Apostles' creed, and has been the basis also of certain doctrines concerning the after-life to be found, for example, in Mormonism.

We have passed over the discussion of the gospel of John until now because it, too, in the belief of modern scholarship, rather generally, but not by any means unanimously, is a product of the second century, and not therefore the work of the beloved disciple to whom tradition assigns it. It is not a simple narrative, as are the

Synoptics, of the life and teachings of Jesus, but represents an interpretive or reflective view of Jesus. Here is no longer the relatively simple figure of a Galilean teacher but an idealized Christ.

In the beginning was the Word, and the Word was with God, and the Word was God. The same was in the beginning with God. All things were made through him; and without him was not anything made that hath been made. There came a man named John. The same came for a witness, that he might bear witness of the light, that all might believe through him. . . . And the Word became flesh and dwelt among us and we beheld his glory, glory as of the only begotten form of the father, full of grace and truth (1:1–14 *passim*).

This prologue to the gospel as a whole seems to be a definite attempt to interpret the Christian gospel in terms of Greek thought. They were familiar with the "Word" or Logos concept. The identification of Jesus as the "Word" was, therefore, designed to make him meaningful to people, in terms familiar to them. Paul had tried to do somewhat the same thing in his speech on Mars Hill in Athens, when he declared of the Unknown God, which he found them worshipping, "Whom ye ignorantly worship, him declare I unto you." Apparently he was not too successful in this approach, for a little later we find him writing to the church at Corinth, "I determined to know nothing among you save Jesus Christ and him crucified."

But this is a most natural process and a necessary one. Religion must always express itself in terms people are capable of understanding, if it is to be meaningful for them. But John does something new to the Logos concept also. It had become a highly speculative idea; he brings it down to earth and links it with the historic Jesus. To be sure, the picture of Jesus in John's gospel is not quite the flesh-and-blood figure which stalks through the Synoptics; often he seems to wear a halo, and there is about him something of an air of physical unreality, save in a few episodes such as the conversation with the woman at the well and that of the woman taken in adultery and brought to Jesus to be judged. This latter, however, is not found in all the ancient manuscripts; in others it is found in a different place or marked as doubtful. Yet the intention to make Jesus a definite historical figure is unmistakable. The method in John's gospel is not that of the Synoptics. He hardly speaks in parables at all, though he does use figurative language, and in such discourses as that of the Vine and the Branches, and the Good Shepherd, he does approach the parable type. In John there are not so many short epigrammatic utterances. He runs to discourses of some length, as for example, concerning the new birth, in his conversation with Nicodemus (chapter 3); on the bread of life after the feeding of the five thousand (6:22 ff); on the true children of Abraham (8:31–59); on the shepherd and the sheep (10:1–18); and particularly his forceful discourse after eating the Last Supper with his disciples, which include some of the most highly cherished utterances recorded of Jesus. Here is the famous passage read almost always at Christian funerals:

Let not your heart be troubled: believe in God, believe also in me. In my Father's house are many mansions; if it were not so I would have told you; for I go to prepare a place for you. And if I go and prepare a place for you I shall come again and will receive you unto myself; that where I am, there ye may be also. And whither I go, ye know the way. Thomas saith unto him, Lord we know not whither thou goest: how know we the way? Jesus saith unto him, "I am the way and truth and the life; no one cometh unto the Father but by me. . . . Philip saith unto him, Lord, show us the Father and it sufficeth us. Jesus saith unto him, Have I been so long time with you, and dost thou not know me, Philip? He that hath seen me hath seen the Father.

All through the gospel there is emphasis upon the relationship personally of the individual to Jesus, and there is almost no mention of the central concept of the Synoptics, namely the kingdom of God.

Chapter 15 contains the discourse on the Vine and the Branches, a kind of allegory rather than a true parable, and quite typical of the Johannine emphasis. It has been a favorite of the mystically minded Christian throughout the whole of Christian history:

I am the vine, ye are the branches. He that abideth in me, and I in him, the same beareth much fruit: for apart from me ye can do nothing.

If a man abide not in me he is cast forth as a branch and is withered, and they gather them, and cast them into the fire, and they are burned. If ye abide in me and my words abide in you, ask whatsoever ye will and it shall be done unto you. Herein is my Father glorified, that ye bear much fruit, and so shall ye be my disciples. Even as the Father hath loved me, I also have loved you. Abide ye in my love. If ye keep my commandments ye shall abide in my love, even as I have kept my Father's commandments and abide in his love.

He stresses the expediency of his going away: "It is expedient for you that I go: for if I go not away the Comforter will not come unto you, but if I go, I will send him unto you. . . . When he, the Spirit of truth is come, he shall guide you into all the truth" (16: 7–13 *passim*). John seems not to hold the apocalyptic view of the physical coming again of Jesus. His coming is as the "Comforter," i.e., in spirit to guide men into the ways of truth. The historic physical body of Jesus is not the important thing, but the spirit of truth, and this they shall have when he has been separated from them.

The so-called high-priestly prayer of Jesus, better, the prayer of consecration, or of intercession, too long to quote here in its entirety, should be read. It is found in chapter 17.

Father, the hour is come: glorify thy Son that the Son may glorify thee. . . . Holy Father, keep them in thy name which thou hast given me, that they may be one, even as we are one. . . . I pray not that thou shouldest take them out of the world, but that thou shouldest keep them from the evil *one*. . . . Sanctify them in truth: thy word is truth (*passim*).

The reiterated prayer, "that they may all be one even as thou Father art in me and I in thee, that they be one in us," is perhaps the best Christian statement of the aims of the mystic, the achievemen of oneness with the divine. This is characteristic of the gospel throughout. It was this fact that led Kenneth J. Saunders to call John the *Gospel for Asia*. In his book under that title he compares it with the Hindu Gita and the Lotus Gospel of Buddhism, and declares that it is preëminently the approach of Christianity to

Asiatics who have come under the sway of the great mystics of Hinduism and Buddhism.

Yet with all its mystic quality, there is genuine historic value in John's gospel. The passion story is rather generally regarded as historically more accurate than the corresponding narratives of the Synoptics.

Who wrote the gospel may never be surely known. The gospel itself says nothing of its authorship, save in the last chapter, which is probably an editorial addition to the main narrative, where it seems to credit it to the "disciple whom Jesus loved," but does not name him. It seems too late in origin to be the work of a direct disciple, think most modern scholars. It may, therefore, have been the work of a certain "presbyter John" of whom there is notice in early tradition, who was perhaps a disciple of John. The plain fact is that all the evidence, both internal and external, leaves the question as to its authorship indeterminate. But it has commended itself to the heart of the Christian church throughout the ages as truly expressive of the spirit of Jesus and his teachings, and has served as the devotional guide *par excellence* to Christians in every century.

The last book to be considered stands last in the New Testament and was the latest to find a secure place in the canon. It, like the gospel and the epistles of John, is assigned traditionally to the authorship of the disciple John. As we have seen, generally speaking, modern scholarship no longer believes that they were all from the same hand, or that the disciple John wrote any of them himself. The book of Revelation may indeed have been the earliest of the five to appear, and could more easily be considered a possible work of the aged disciple, since it almost certainly dates from the time of the Domitian persecution of the church about 96 A.D. But the only certain thing is that it is attributed in the book itself to John.

As we saw in the discussion of the Old Testament, the Apocalypse was a common literary form employed, usually, in times of stress and strain, to bring some hope and encouragement to people who were having a bad time of it. Such writings have been called "tracts for hard times." The essential feature of the Apocalypse is that no matter how dark the outlook may be on any human basis, salvation is possible and certain through the intervention of God in the affairs of the world. He will break through into history and, in some cataclysmic form, bring to pass what man has himself been unable to achieve. It represents an indomitable faith on man's part that seeming danger and defeat are not final. God stands behind, watching, and may be depended upon to come to the rescue.

The Apocalypse is usually cryptic in its language, employing strange figures, weird imagery, and is therefore difficult of understanding to those who do not have the key. Consequently these writings lend themselves to a great variety of interpretation. Written usually to meet an immediately difficult situation, they are made to serve as a blue print for what is to come in distant ages. It is chiefly upon the various apocalypses in the New Testament that the modern prophets of the end of the world, the second coming of Jesus, etc., base their predictions.

There are several apocalypses, or at least apocalyptic passages, in the New Testament besides the book of Revelation.[67] The apocalyptic outlook was a prominent feature in the background of the early church. Aside from the apocalyptic sections of the Old Testament there were other later, but well-known, Jewish apocalypses among the so-called False Writings or *Pseudepigrapha*. It is not strange, therefore, that the New Testament should have its own apocalyptic writings.

From the stoning of Stephen the Christians had experienced persecution. But often it was only local and sporadic in character. Even the drastic treatment of Christians under Nero was probably limited largely to Rome. But under Domitian there seems to have been a well-concerted and empire-wide effort to compel Christians to signify their political loyalty to the emperor by participating in the one and only required ceremony, that of emperor worship. Aside from this, the Romans were extremely tolerant in the matter of religion. But Jews and Christians, believers in one and only one God, were a sore trial to Roman authorities who took their conscientious refusal to worship the emperor as a sign of disloyalty.

[67] See Mark 13, Matthew 24, Luke 21, II Thessalonians 2:1–12, and II Peter 3:8 ff.

They became "subversives," like Jehovah's Witnesses of our own time, when they refused to salute the flag. Then indeed was the church in deep trouble and suffering. The whole church seemed to be threatened with destruction. There was deep need of some message of hope and confidence. The book of Revelation was just that. There was tribulation, yes, and danger and destruction, but the final word lay not in the hands of men but of God, and God would presently bring to naught the devices of evil men, and there would be a new heaven and a new earth.

It was a definite apocalyptic pattern that, before the end, the anti-Christ must come. And he was already present. There is little doubt that the author expected the intervention of God to come very soon. The prophecies of things to come were not to await a distant future unfolding of history for their fulfillment. But that did not happen, so eventually the book, while it had been meant doubtless as a basis for a very early hope of deliverance, has come to be regarded as the revelation of the divine plan for the ages. As such it is studied and restudied, generation after generation, and the answer sought as to when its fulfillment may be expected. The dates have been set many times by Adventists, Millennialists, Jehovah's Witnesses, etc.; but the end delays. Many have seen in the rise of successive figures in history the anti-Christ, or the *Beast*. This figure has been identified as Martin Luther by Catholics, as some particular pope by Protestants, as Kaiser Wilhelm by people on one side in World War I and with Lloyd George or Wilson by people on the other—with Hitler and Mussolini, with Roosevelt and Churchill in World War II; and now every Adventist in the non-Communist bloc is sure that Joe Stalin is the dread figure. Clearly time has about run out. The end of the age is imminent. Jehovah's Witnesses proclaim it incessantly and the Voice of Prophecy tirelessly proclaims it over the ether waves.

Whatever may be its hidden meaning, and there is no indication that it was at all hidden to the people of the times for which it was written, it makes fascinating reading. One very intelligent woman tells how as a child she got hold of it and read it. She thought it the most wonderful fairy-story she had ever read. There are in it passages which are of high poetic quality, and of matchless beauty. The writer once heard the playwright and actor, Charles Rann Kennedy, read aloud the 21st chapter. It was the thrill of a lifetime.

And I saw a new heaven and a new earth: for the first heaven and the first earth are passed away; and the sea is no more. And I saw the holy city, new Jerusalem, coming down out of the heaven from God, made ready as a bride for her husband. And I heard a great voice out of the throne saying: Behold the tabernacle of God is with men, and he shall dwell with them, and they shall be his people and God himself shall be with them, and be their God: and he shall wipe away every tear from their eyes, and death shall be no more, neither shall there be mourning nor crying, nor pain any more: the first things are passed away. And he that sat on the throne said: Behold, I make all things new. . . . I am the Alpha and the Omega, the beginning and the end. I will give unto him that is athirst of the fountain of water of life freely. He that overcometh shall inherit these things, and I will be his God and he shall be my son. . . . And he showed me a river of water of life, bright as crystal, proceeding out of the throne of God and of the Lamb, and in the midst of the street thereof. And on this side of the river, and on that was the tree of life, bearing twelve manner of fruits, yielding its fruit every month: and the leaves of the tree were for the healing of the nations. And there shall be no curse any more . . . and there shall be night no more; and they need no light of lamp, neither light of sun; for the Lord God shall give them light; and they shall reign forever and ever.

There can be little doubt that the book brought a deeper faith and courage to the persecuted Christians and so performed its purpose. Failing of immediate fulfillment, it has continued to bring hope to people in difficult situations. Taken too literally, it has led some believers into strange and bizarre beliefs concerning religion, and has sometimes brought religion itself into disrepute. But it is a permanent witness to an indomitable faith in God, a persistent belief that it is God's world in which we live, that God is the controller of history and that, no matter how dark the day may be, he may be trusted to bring in the end the fruition of men's highest hopes and dreams.

It is not the highest expression of Christian moral teaching. It has, indeed, been thought by some scholars to be an old Jewish apocalypse, adapted to Christian purposes. It is otherworldly to a degree not appreciated particularly by modern Christians for whom life is on the whole good and abundant. But in its central emphasis on the ultimate triumph of God's purposes of good for the world it stands as a solid rock amid the shifting sands of opinion in this, our modern world of relativity. Taken for what it was meant to be, it is by no means unworthy, as some great Christian leaders have thought, of its place in the canon of scriptures.

Now, how did these writings all get together as we have them and come to be regarded as scripture? The process was a long one.

The Bible for early Christians was, of course, the Old Testament. It was constantly read in the churches. The early teaching and preaching of the apostles and their immediate successors was largely from the remembered sayings and doings of Jesus, at first orally transmitted, then written in various forms. Probably this was read at first, not as scripture, but as the source of information about Jesus and his work. Paul's letters were probably read from time to time as bits of practical counsel and instruction in doctrine, but not as scripture. Not only these but other writings were also read in the church. There was a collection called the Didache or Teaching of the Apostles, and another apocalypse, the Shepherd of Hermas, and still another, the Apocalypse of Peter, also letters by early leaders such as Barnabas, Clement of Rome, and others.

About the middle of the second century a ship-owner of Pontus, Marcion, advocated setting aside entirely the Old Testament and making use of only the gospels of Luke and the letters of Paul—ten of them only—as the Christian scripture. Marcion was soon declared a heretic, but it is possible that it was he who gave the real impulse to the formation of a New Testament collection of scripture. By about the end of the second century there is evidence, in the writings of Irenaeus, Tertullian, and a fragment of a manuscript to be dated in that period, known as the Muratorian fragment, that the books advocated as scripture by Marcion, plus the other three gospels and Acts and three other epistles of Paul, I and II Timothy, and Titus, were recognized in widely separated sections of the church as properly to be read in the churches. Each of the three recognized one or more additional books not accepted by the other, e.g., Irenaeus and Tertullian each recognized an epistle of Peter, the Muratorian fragment none; the Muratorian fragment and Tertullian recognized Jude, but Iranaeus did not. Also all three include the Apocalypse of John, but Iranaeus and Tertullian also include the Shepherd of Hermas, while the Muratorian fragment includes the Apocalypse of Peter. Each includes twenty-two books, in contrast to the twenty-seven generally accepted books today.

Clement of Alexandria, a little later, offered a list including in addition to these a letter of Barnabas and one of Clement of Rome to the Corinthians. Origen in the third century listed twenty-nine books all of which he accepted, but divided them into two lists of acknowledged and disputed books, meaning that they were not all universally accepted. His list of acknowledged books includes the four gospels and Acts and, to the thirteen Pauline letters, he adds Hebrews and I Peter, I John and Revelation. The disputed books were James, II and III John, II Peter, Jude, the letter of Barnabas, and the Shepherd of Hermas. Thus he had twenty-nine books, or two more than are now recognized. That is, he had the New Testament as we have it, save for the presence of the letter of Barnabas and the Shepherd of Hermas. The oldest Greek New Testament manuscript, Sinaiticus, contains just these books, and it is dated about the middle of the fourth century.

Eusebius, the church historian, who wrote in the early part of the fourth century, furnishes evidence that some parts of the church accepted still other books, the Acts of Paul, the Teaching of the Apostles, or the Didache, and the Preaching of Peter. In the Eastern Church doubt was cast upon the apostolic authorship of the book of Revelation and it is omitted from about half of the extant Greek manuscripts of the New Testament.

Athanasius, a fourth-century figure, in an Easter letter, in the year 367 A.D., was the first to list the New Testament books exactly as we have them today. He added, as valuable reading for those under instruction for church membership, the Didache and the Shepherd of Hermas.

But this does not mean that acceptance of this list was as yet universal. The great Syriac version, the Peshitto, dated 411 A.D., still contained but twenty-two books. In the West the matter was pretty well fixed by Jerome's revision of the Old Latin version, the famous Vulgate version, which appeared near the end of the fourth century, and included the books of the Athanasian list. But in the East the canon remained fluid for a long time.

Thus came into existence the New Testament, the distinctive scriptures of Christianity. It was a long slow process, from the earliest oral traditions about Jesus and his teachings to the nearly universally accepted twenty-seven books which make it up today. We have seen that other books were accepted for longer or shorter periods in some sections of the church. Many gospels were written, besides the four, many other letters also, and apocalypses. Many of these are still extant and are called collectively the New Testament Apocrypha. They are available in good translations and make interesting reading, especially the gospels. Some of these are of a high order, and save in spots seem quite similar to the canonical gospel stories. But one does not have to read long to discover why the good judgment of the early church rejected them. They do furnish the basis of some beliefs and practices still held in the Christian churches, particularly the Catholic branches. One of the most interesting is the gospel of Thomas which narrates many stories of the childhood of Jesus, obviously the work of the pious imagination of devoted followers who, in every religion we have seen, delight to embroider the life of the beloved founder of their faith. There is, of course, some of this in the canonical gospels themselves, but beside the apocryphal gospels they shine by contrast as serious, relatively factual stories of the life of Jesus. If one believes in a providential element in their writing, he may well believe also that in their collection and preservation the same good providence was at work. But here, as so often, Providence has worked through the normal patterns of human behavior, and the good common sense of the general body of the church, in weighing and testing and finally approving the book as it now stands. Possibly the experience of modern man might lead to a modification of their choice if it were left open to change. But time has already taken care of that, and it is not likely that the canon will be changed, though parts of it may, indeed have already, largely fallen into disuse. In a sense, within the historically determined canon, each individual or group really determines his own effective canon, and may add to or subtract from it at will.

PART III: THE VERSIONS

We have thus far discussed the making of the Old and New Testaments and carried the story down to their completion in the languages of their origin, Hebrew and Greek, allowing for the possibility but not certainty of an original Aramaic version for some of the gospels. How did they get to us in the versions we today use? Briefly the story is this—and it must be very brief.

The Old Testament was first translated into the Greek language to meet the needs of Jews who lived outside of Palestine and had lost their use of the mother tongue. This was the great Septuagint version of the Seventy, so-called from the legend that it was translated in seventy days by seventy elders. It was made in Alexandria and includes a number of books not acknowledged by Palestinian Jews. These extra books, as indicated above, are known as the Apocrypha, and constitute the difference between the Roman Catholic Bible, which includes them as scripture, and the Protestant Bible, which, if it includes them at all, sets them apart from the usual order of books and indicates that they are to be read for instruction and inspiration but not as a basis of dogma.

Jerome in the fourth century was the first to distinguish them as Apocrypha, i.e., hidden or secret books, but he did not separate them from the other books in the Vulgate. The earliest English version, that of Wycliffe in 1382, contained them. Luther was the first to segregate them, in his translation of the Bible into German. They were published separately to complete the Bible which had appeared in various installments. Luther did some rearranging of material in the New Testament and in the full edition of the Bible placed the Apocrypha between the Old Testament and the New. This custom was followed in English translations generally, except in the Catholic versions. Under Puritan influence they were dropped out completely from most versions. Today they are seldom found in Protestant Bibles except in large pulpit editions where they are segregated between the Testaments. (The so-called Chicago Bible published by the University of Chicago Press contains the Apocrypha.)

The vernacular versions of the Bible have had a great influence on the languages. The rise of literary German was greatly influenced by Luther's translations and the English language has been tremendously influenced by successive English translations notably the King James or Authorized version.

In English, Wycliffe's version is the first of which we have any definite evidence. It was translated from the Vulgate. It makes very strange reading to modern English-speaking people. What would you make of this? "Nye yee deme, that yee be not demede, for in what dome yee demen, yee schulen be demede." It is Matthew 7:2 and in present-day speech reads, "Judge not that ye be not judged, for with what judgment ye judge, ye shall be judged."

William Tyndale, an English scholar, like Luther made his translation not from the Vulgate but from the original Greek text as published by Erasmus. Attempts were made by the Roman Catholic authorities to prevent its publication, but in 1525 the New Testament was issued at Worms, in Germany, to which Tyndale had been forced to flee. Every attempt was made by the church to prevent its circulation in England but it was eagerly welcomed by the people and became very influential on all subsequent English translations. Goodspeed says that ninety-two per cent of the King James version is still just as Tyndale wrote it.[68]

Tyndale did not complete the translation of the whole Bible, but did publish the Pentateuch in 1530. He was hounded by those who sought to prevent his work and was finally imprisoned and executed in 1536, for no other crime than that of translating and publishing a vernacular translation of Holy Writ. Truly this Bible, taken so much for granted by people of our own day, was not easily come by. There is a romance about its history that makes fascinating

[68] Edgar J. Goodspeed, *How Came the Bible*, Abingdon-Cokesbury, N. Y., 1940

reading. One author wrote the story under the title, *The Romance of the English Bible.*[69]

But the execution of Tyndale did not keep the Bible from the people. Indeed, even before his execution and while he was in prison, Myles Coverdale in 1535 printed the complete Bible in English using Tyndale's New Testament and Pentateuch, and translating the remainder from the German and Latin versions. Just two years later Matthew's Bible appeared. It included not only Tyndale's New Testament and Pentateuch, but also a hitherto unpublished translation of the further books of the Old Testament from Joshua through Chronicles. The remainder was a revision of Coverdale's work. This became the first licensed Bible in English and could be circulated without interference from the state. Two years later, in 1539, the Great Bible appeared, designed particularly to be read in the churches, and from that time forward the Bible might be read to the people in their own tongue instead of in the Latin. It was the first authorized version. Not only was it read in public worship, but it was permissible for people to read it privately. A copy was made available to the public but, to prevent its being stolen, it was secured by a chain, so it has come to be called the Chained Bible.

The next great version was the Geneva Bible, so called because it was prepared and published by Puritans who had fled England and found a home in Geneva, Switzerland. This, besides being an improvement on former editions, was divided into verses. This system was introduced by a French printer in the Greek text. Chapter divisions had been made in the Vulgate as early as the twelfth century. This version is often called the Breeches Bible from the translation of Genesis 3:7, which reads "And when they knew that they were naked they sewed figtree leaves together and made themselves breeches." It was very popular and went through a hundred editions. It was the version current in Shakespeare's time, and his numerous Biblical quotations appear to have come from it.

The Bishop's Bible, 1568, was an authorized revision of the Great Bible and superseded it for use in public worship.

[69] Laura H. Wild, Doubleday Doran and Co., Inc., Garden City, N. Y., 1929.

All the Bibles thus far noted were of Protestant origin. But by this time the Catholics, too, desired it in their own language. The Douay version was the result. The translation which was made, not from the Greek text but from the Latin Vulgate, was begun at the Catholic College at Douay, but completed at Rheims, France, whither the school had fled on being banished from Douay. The New Testament was published there in 1582, so it is called the Rheims New Testament. The publication of the Old Testament was delayed some seventeen years, appearing in 1609–1610. Meanwhile, the College had returned to Douay. The Bible as a whole is, therefore, referred to usually as the Douay Version. This has been revised many times—so often indeed that it is said that "scarcely any verse remains as it was originally published." The revision of Bishop Challoner, near the middle of the eighteenth century, has been the basis of most subsequent English versions. For example, one of the most recent Catholic translations of the New Testament, the so-called Confraternity Edition, is "a revision of the Challoner-Rheims Version, edited by Catholic scholars under the patronage of the Confraternity of Christian Doctrine."[70] This has appeared separately from the Old Testament, but has also appeared recently bound up with the Douay version of the Old Testament, with newly edited Annotations of Bishop Challoner, etc.

Another completely new Catholic translation of both Old and New Testaments has been published recently by Monsignor Ronald A. Knox. This is a fresh translation from the Vulgate, but "where the Vulgate yields no tolerable sense," says the translator, "or yields a sense which evidently quarrels with the context," he has rendered the passage from the Hebrew text and given the literal translation of the Latin Vulgate in a footnote.

The great Protestant English version that has come down into our own times is the so-called King James, an authorized version which appeared in 1611 and held its place securely for almost three centuries before an important rival version appeared. It was a work of real scholarship, performed coöperatively by representative scholars and clergy of the day, though largely only a careful revision of

[70] Catholic Book Publishing Company, Chicago, 1948.

the Bishop's Bible. No single other work has had greater influence upon English language and literature than this. It became the basis of the liturgy of most of the churches, as well as being the version used by ministers in preaching and in the devotional as well as scholarly reading of individuals for well over two hundred and fifty years before a new version was undertaken. When this did appear as the English Revised version, in which American scholars participated to some degree, it was resisted firmly, and neither it nor the American Revised version which in this country displaced largely the English Revised, has even yet succeeded in replacing it, especially in the liturgical literature of the churches. Most of the very conservative churches still use the King James version and it is this version which is distributed in such vast numbers by the British and American Bible Societies.

The English and American revisions represented a distinct improvement over the King James version. Its language has been from time to time modernized since 1611, but it is still extremely archaic in many of its expressions and therefore not easily intelligible to the ordinary reader. The intervening years had seen the discovery of numerous ancient manuscripts which had made possible a great improvement in the Greek and Hebrew texts. There changes are reflected in the later versions. Very recently a new version has been undertaken by American scholars and the New Testament was published in 1946 as *The Revised Standard Version*.[71] The Old Testament is nearing completion. Whether this latest version will succeed in weaning readers away from both the newer version and the King James, it is impossible to predict with assurance. It is not so difficult to get it accepted for private use, but it is extremely difficult to substitute its newer language in the liturgies, for these things acquire a near sanctity which resists innovation very strongly.

In general, English-speaking Jewish people have made use of the King James version or the Revised version, being content to make modifications in it, or to supplement it by commentaries. But in England partial translations did appear in the nineteenth century, and in America an English version was produced in 1853, by Isaac

[71] Thomas Nelson and Sons, N. Y., 1946.

Leeser. By the end of the century this had come to be regarded as inadequate and a new version was projected by the Jewish Publication Society. It was not, however, until 1917 that the version currently in use among the Jews made its appearance.

Meanwhile, the modern world has seen a number of private translations. Only two of the better-known versions include the whole Bible, the Moffatt and the so-called Chicago Bible, but of New Testament translations there have been many. Most widely circulated of these perhaps have been the Moffatt and Goodspeed versions. A list of other such translations appears at the end of the chapter.

In what version shall one read the Bible? English teachers are likely to say the King James, since it is the version whose language is so woven into the warp and woof of English and American literature that an understanding of the literature requires some knowledge of the Bible.

If one wishes an accurate understanding of what the original writers of the Bible were trying to say, he will do best to read the newer translations, though he will do well to read and compare several, rather than rely upon just one version. Some of them are translated by persons or groups who have special doctrinal emphases to set forth, and this is likely to color the translation. Latest of all versions to appear is the one published by Jehovah's Witnesses. One would do well to investigate the peculiar biases of the individual or group which publishes a version, before putting too much confidence in it. This doctrinal bias is almost completely absent in the latest American revision, for the participation of scholars of widely differing points of view has tended to cancel out the biases that might affect privately issued translations.

For the convenience of the reader a list of versions briefly annotated is found below.

BIBLE VERSIONS

The King James, or *Authorized, Version.*
The Revised Version (English).
The American Standard Bible, Thomas Nelson & Sons, N. Y.
The Bible: A New Translation, by James Moffatt, Harper & Brothers, N. Y.

The Complete Bible: An American Translation, by J. M. Powis Smith and others and Edgar J. Goodspeed, University of Chicago Press, 1939.

The Douay Version (Roman Catholic).

The Old Testament, translated by Ronald A. Knox, 2 vols. Sheed & Ward, N. Y., 1948, 1950.

The New Testament, translated by Ronald A. Knox, Sheed & Ward, 1944.

The Holy Bible: A New Catholic Edition translated from the Vulgate. The Old Testament is the Douay version with newly edited annotations by Bishop Challoner and a new translation of the Psalms from the new Latin version. The New Testament is the Confraternity edition. See below—Catholic Book Publishing Company, N. Y., 1948.

There are many special editions of the Bible, most of them based on the King James version. Among these are:

The Bible, Designed to Be Read as Living Literature, ed. by E. S. Bates, Simon and Schuster, New York, 1936. Much of the duplicated material is omitted. It is beautifully printed and bound, and all chapter and verse markings are left out. Poetry is printed in poetic form. In this it resembles an earlier edition,

Richard G. Moulton's *Modern Reader's Bible,* The Macmillan Company, New York, 1895, which has been widely used.

The Dartmouth Bible, edited by Roy B. Chamberlin and Herman Feldman, Houghton Mifflin Company, Boston, 1950, is likewise an attempt to eliminate duplicated material. A new feature is the blending of the four gospels into a single connected story. Chapter and verse indications are retained, but are made very inconspicuous, and do not interfere with the logical division into paragraphs and sections. Also a great deal of introductory material and explanatory notes are introduced, reflecting a moderate liberal attitude toward the Bible.

NEW TESTAMENT VERSIONS

The New Testament: An American Translation, by Edgar J. Goodspeed, University of Chicago Press, 1923.

The New Testament in Modern Speech, translated by Richard Francis Weymouth, Pilgrim Press, Boston, 1914.

The New Testament: A New Translation, by James Moffatt, Harper & Brothers, N. Y., 1935.

The New Testament, translated by Ronald A. Knox, Sheed and Ward, New York, 1944 (Roman Catholic).

The New Testament in Basic English, Cambridge University Press, England, 1941.

The Revised Standard Version, Thomas Nelson and Sons, 1946.

The Rheims New Testament—revised by Catholic scholars under the patronage of the Episcopal Committee of the Confraternity of Christian Doctrine (Roman Catholic), St. Anthony Guild Press, Paterson, N. J., 1947.

The Apocrypha are found published separately in various editions, e.g., by

Thomas Nelson and Sons—Revised 1894.

The Apocrypha: An American Translation, by Edgar J. Goodspeed, University of Chicago Press, 1938.

They are included usually in large pulpit Bibles, bound between the Old and New Testaments.

The Goodspeed translation is bound with the Old and New Testaments in *The Complete Bible,* University of Chicago Press.

They are found, of course, in the Douay version, but not separated out from the other books.

Selections from the Apocrypha may be found in:

The Dartmouth Bible, pp. 736–840.

Ballou, *The Bible of the World,* pp. 1027–1050.

Browne, *The World's Great Scriptures,* pp. 432–435.

S. E. Frost, *Sacred Writings of the World's Great Religions,* pp. 219–226.

THE TALMUD

Complete Editions of the Babylonian Talmud are:

The Babylonian Talmud, Translated and edited by Michael L. Rodkinson, 20 Volumes, Boston, 1896–1903.

The Babylonian Talmud, Edited by Rabbi Dr. I. Epstein, 11 Volumes, Soncino Press, London, 1948–.

SELECTIONS FROM THE TALMUD

The Wisdom of Israel, translated and edited by Edwin Collins, E. P. Dutton & Co., N. Y., 1908.

A. Cohen, *Everyman's Talmud,* J. M. Dent and Sons, London, 1934.

The Babylonian Talmud in Selection, edited and translated by Leo Auerbach, Philosophical Library, N. Y., 1944.

Talmudic Anthology, Selected and edited by Louis I. Newman and Samuel Spitz, Behrman House, N. Y., 1945.

Lewis Browne, *The World's Great Scriptures,* pp. 438–447.

CHAPTER XIII

The Sacred Literature of the Moslems

The sacred book of the Moslems or, as more commonly if less correctly known, the Mohammedans, is the Koran. It is unique among sacred books in several particulars. First of all, it is distinctly a one-man book. All the other sacred literatures include the writings or reputed sayings of many people, usually produced over a comparatively long period of time, but finally collected and regarded as sacred or authoritative. The Koran contains only the purported revelations of Allah, given through his prophet, Mohammed.

Second: Most scriptures abound in historic accounts of a people or the life of the founder of the religion and his contemporaries or successors. In the Koran there is reference to only two of the people of Mohammed's own time, and no information at all concerning his own life experiences. There is, of course, much self-revelation as to the nature of the Prophet in what he includes, but of local setting or circumstances under which he received the revelations there is nothing. The name of Mohammed appears only five times in the entire book. The revelations are introduced simply by the word *Say*, more or less the Biblical equivalent of the phrase so frequently found in the prophets, "Thus saith the Lord."

Third: The Koran was practically completed as a book during

the lifetime of the Prophet, although apparently not written down until after his death. Certainly it assumed definitive form more quickly after Mohammed's death than did any other of the sacred literatures after the passing of the founder of any of the other religions. Thus while there are some textual problems in connection with the Koran, there are relatively many less than in the case of other scriptures.

The Koran is the latest of the great scriptures. Only one other of those considered in this study, save those discussed in the chapter on the Modern Sacred Book, appeared later, namely the Sikh, in India.

Mohammed, the founder of Mohammedanism, or Islam, the term used by Moslems for their faith, was born in 576 A.D. in Mecca, Arabia. Of good family, he was early orphaned, and was obliged as a boy to go to work for a living, journeying with caravans of Meccan merchants sometimes to distant places. This travel gave him his first contact with people of different religions, especially Christians and Jews. These latter he was to know better as he met both Jewish and Christian residents of Mecca, and travellers of these faiths who visited Mecca. All this is thought greatly to have influenced his religious outlook as it appears later in the Koran. He was a dependable worker. He was sometimes called *El Amin*, the trustworthy. His success led finally to his marriage with Khadija, a wealthy woman for whom he worked. Although she was fifteen years his senior, this union was a very happy one and was to have a profound effect upon his future.

Already he had become something of a mystic. He liked to be alone. In his solitude there came to him visions which he little understood. Freed from the necessity of constant journeying and preoccupation with business, he had time and leisure to go apart in the mountains, and it was thus that he began to get what he later regarded as revelations from God, or Allah, as he came to be known among Moslems. At first he was not certain of the source of these visions and insights which came to him. It was not until he had confided some of them to his wife who encouraged him, that he felt sure whence the visions came, and so came to believe that he was called to be the prophet of God, the human voice through whom the will of Allah might be made known to men. Once this was accepted, the Koran was on the way to being born, for it purports to be nothing else than the very word of the all-wise, all-powerful God to humanity, as given through Mohammed.

At first only a few believed. The people of Mecca scoffed at his pretensions of being the mouthpiece of God. In the first place most of them believed not in one God, but in many, and their faith was affronted by the thunderings of their fellow-townsman in the name of Allah, whom he proclaimed to be the one and only God of the universe. He was resisted, ridiculed, persecuted, and finally forced to flee from Mecca to preserve his life. This flight, known as the *Hegira*, marks the beginning of the new age for Moslems who count 622 A.D. as their year 1, from which all other time references are calculated—before the *Hegira* or after it.

The revelations did not cease, but their character changed, for Mohammed, at the invitation of the tribesmen of Medina, now became the head of its government which gradually spread during his own lifetime to include the whole of Arabia. Gone was the leisure for silent contemplation and prayer. He was now concerned, of necessity, with the everyday affairs with which a political chief must deal. The revelations now take on the form of regulations for community living—laws of inheritance, responsibilities in marriage, care of orphans and the helpless. Less of poetry now, more of prose —befitting the prosier aspects of life with which he must perforce deal. But this is none the less the revelation of God. God was through him setting up his rule on earth. The government under him and his successors was for many a year to be a true theocracy, the rule of God—and the Koran was to be the basis for that rule. It still is so regarded in truly Moslem states until now—as we shall presently see.

After ten years of active direction of this new movement, Mohammed died and the revelations ceased. All the materials for the creation of the Koran were now in existence. It only remained for them to be collected and issued in book form.

Mohammed himself probably never wrote a word. It is rather

generally recognized that he neither knew how to read or write![1] Moslems believe and assert that he memorized the messages as they were given to him, then quickly thereafter dictated them to an amanuensis who put them in writing for him in the exact form in which they were given to the prophet by Gabriel. Mohammed is then supposed to have taught these to his increasing number of followers, some of whom were known as reciters, those who could recite the revelations. It was their function also to teach them to other Moslem followers. It does seem to be true that portions of the Koran, as we know it today, formed a part of the Mosque service that Mohammed established, which consisted largely of rituals and passages from the Koran.

There are interesting traditions as to how Mohammed received his revelation. One modern Moslem scholar, Maulana Muhammad Ali, distinguishes three types of inspiration: first there is simply a suggestion that comes into the mind of a man who then speaks it under the influence of the Holy Spirit. The second is described as if one were speaking from behind a veil. It comes generally in the sleeping or trance state, through dreams or visions. The third is that kind where a messenger from God is sent to the prophet with a Divine Message delivered in particular words. This is said to be the highest form of revelation. This he thinks is the form and the only form of revelation the Koran exhibits![2]

Of course, there undoubtedly exist a number of ideas among Moslems as to what inspiration means. There is some beginning among them of a liberal attitude toward the Koran such as that represented by liberal modern scholarship toward the Bible. In general, however, it is a dogma of the Moslem faith that the Koran is the *ipsissima verba*, the very, very word of God. Muhammad Ali says, "It was not the Prophet who spoke under the influence of the Holy Spirit; it was a Divine Message brought by the Holy Spirit, or Gabriel, and delivered in words to the Holy Prophet who delivered it to mankind."[3] It was revealed in the Arabic tongue, says Ali,

[1] Dr. Richard Bell, distinguished translator of the Koran, believes that Mohammed himself wrote most of it. *The Koran,* Vol. 1, p. vi.

[2] *The Religion of Islam,* Lahore, 1936, pp. 20 ff.

[3] *Id.,* pp. 20–21.

citing Sura 26:192–195, "That thou mayest be of the warners, in plain Arabic language." Moslems, generally, until now use the Arabic as the cult language regardless of the nationality to which they themselves belong. There is a special sacredness which attaches to Arabic. Only quite recently and chiefly by non-Moslems, has the Koran been translated into other living vernaculars. Even an English Moslem in the twentieth century, in publishing an English translation, felt obliged to call it not a translation but *The Meaning of the Glorious Koran*.

The impulse to bring together and put in written form the mate- *Koran* rial of the Koran, came as a result of the killing off in warfare of *copies* many of those who were able to recite it from memory. About a *made* year after the prophet's death, his brother-in-law, Omar, later to be the second Caliph or successor of Mohammed, suggested to Abu Bekr, one of the earliest and most influential of the prophet's converts and his immediate successor, the wisdom of making a written collection of all the prophet's sayings. Abu Bekr agreed and at once commissioned one of those who had served as secretary to Mohammed, Zaid by name, to make the collection and put it into written book form. This was done. The testimony varies as to just how he went about the task. One modern Moslem writer seems to think it involved no more than simply having the Koran, as it was already in existence in the memories of living men, copied down in written form. More critical scholars think that a systematic collection was made of all that could be found of the words of the Prophet, both written and remembered by his followers. A tradition says that fragments were gathered together "from date leaves and tablets of white stone, and from the breasts of men."

The question arises at this point as to the order of the material as it was written down. Was it simply collected, the longest first, and so on down to the shortest at the end, a sort of mechanical process carried out by Zaid, or was the Koran essentially completed in its present order in Mohammed's time and perhaps so arranged by him? At this point, violent differences of opinion emerge. There seems to be no sure way of settling the issue. Those who hold that Mohammed had already arranged the chapters essentially as they now exist cite passages from the Traditions to support their claims. One of the Traditions declares that when Mohammed received a message, he usually dictated it to a secretary and told him specifically at what point in any given chapter the new revelation should appear. The dependability of the traditions[4] is a matter of distinct difference of opinion so that the citation of the Traditions as a source is not too convincing.

√ At all events, it does seem to be certain that a version was completed by Zaid, and that copies of it began to circulate among the Moslem faithful. It remained as the standard text all during the Caliphates of Abu Bekr and of Omar, a period of over ten years.

But after a time differences in the text began to be reported, one copy apparently differing from another in some respects. During the Caliphate of Othman, it is reported, an important leader came to him beseeching him to do something about the matter lest the Moslems come to "differ in the Holy Book as the Jews and Christians differ in their scriptures."[5] Whereupon, Othman sent for the original copy which was in the possession of one of the wives of Mohammed (Hafsa), and ordered Zaid once more to make perfect copies from the original. He associated with him three men of Mecca in order to insure that the language in the perfected copies be in accord with the Quraish language which was the original speech of Mohammed. Zaid was himself a native of Medina. When this was done, copies were sent to various quarters of the world and all other copies were ordered to be burned, thus insuring the correctness of all the extant copies of the sacred book.

Critical scholarship, it hardly need be said, does not accept the orthodox view as representing what actually happened. Critical scholars do not think that the material was collected by Mohammed himself, nor by any one else during his lifetime, although some of them do believe that he may have collected some portions of it. Some of the legislative portions may well have been in written form, and certain individuals may have memorized considerable amounts of the revealed material, those known as the Reciters, but

---

[4] For a discussion of the Traditions see below, pp. 452 ff.
[5] Muhammad Ali, *The Religion of Islam*, p. 30.

that they all memorized the same identical collections is not regarded as likely.[6]

Arthur Jeffery—one of those who has worked most critically in the field in recent years—is doubtful whether Abu Bekr ever made an official recension as tradition declares. Rather he thinks that Abu Bekr was one of those who collected revelation material—and that, by reason of his close relationship with the Prophet, he may have inherited the materials the Prophet had collected, perhaps with a view to their official publication. But, he thinks, others of the companions of the Prophet may also have made like collections. There are certainly traditions relating to such collections, but they do not always agree as to just who were the collectors. As the empire expanded, some of these collections became important sources of Moslem teaching, and acquired a degree of authority in limited areas. These would be, naturally, the more complete collections. Thus, according to Jeffery, the people of Damascus and Homs followed the Codex of Miqdad b. al-Aswad, those of Kufa that of Ibn Masud, etc.[7] The recension of Othman then becomes not simply a recopying of Abu Bekr's edition with the removal of its dialectical variants, but a strategical canonization of the collection current in Medina, and requiring that all others be destroyed. Certainly it was politically desirable to have one authoritative text accepted over the empire, when one recalls how much of the actual legislation depended upon it.

Jeffery says, "There can be little doubt that the one canonized by Othman was only one among many in existence at the time."[8] Some of the centers resisted the order to destroy their own collections. In Kufa the community was divided between those who accepted the Othmanic text and those who upheld Ibn Masud, who had refused to give up his codex to be burned.

Evidence is found in various commentaries of variant readings which have been preserved from the earlier codices. Much scholarly work must yet be done before a real history of the development of

[6] Arthur Jeffery, *Materials for the History of the Text of the Qur'an*, Leiden. E. J. Brill, 1937.

[7] *Op. cit.*, p. 7.

[8] *Id.*, p. 8.

the text of the Koran can be written. Moslems have given little attention to such study. But beginnings have already been made and, in the course of time, such a history will be written.

Meanwhile there is no single authoritative text of the Othmanic ✓Koran. The most widely used, perhaps, is an Egyptian text of 1342.[9]

The Koran as it stands today contains one hundred and fourteen chapters or *Suras*. These are quite unequal in length, the longest having two hundred and eighty-six verses, accounting for about a twelfth part of the entire book, the shortest having but three verses. These chapters are given not only numbers but names. A few typical chapter names are "The Cow," the longest of all, "The Spider," "The Night Journey," "Cattle," "The Sun," "He Frowned." This does not mean that the cow Sura treats of cows at all, but that the word occurs somewhere in the Sura and it has simply come to be known by that name. Actually, there is a chapter called "Women," but more material appears concerning women in the chapter called "The Cow." Every Sura save one begins with the same words "In the name of Allah, the Compassionate, the Merciful." This is known as the *Bismillah*. In an interesting statement reflecting the ultra-conservative theory of inspiration of the book, a Mohammedan writer declares that the whole of the Koran may be found in the Bismillah, that the whole of the Bismillah can be found in the initial letter and that the whole of this can be found in the vowel point placed beneath the initial "B."

Much of the Koran is made up of poetry, especially the earlier revelations. Mohammed was a poet of genuine power and ability. Indeed, its poetic style is regarded among Moslems as the noblest of all and it becomes a norm for subsequent Mohammedan verse. Some of the quite early Suras are little more than pious ejaculations. They are the authentic expression of a deeply religious spirit. For example Sura 92, "The Unity," given in Mecca is as follows:

> Say: He is God alone.
> God the Eternal!

[9] For a good statement with reference to the Koran and its sources see: Arthur Jeffery, *Materials for the History of the Text of the Qur'an*, Leiden, E. J. Brill, 1937.

He begetteth not and he is not begotten
and there is none like unto him.[10]

Sura 1, also given in Mecca contains seven verses:

In the Name of God, the Compassionate, the Merciful,

Praise be to God, Lord of the worlds!
The compassionate, the merciful!
King on the day of reckoning!
Thee *only* do we worship, and to Thee do we cry for help.
Guide Thou us on the straight path,
The path of those to whom Thou hast been gracious;—with
   whom thou art not angry, and who go not astray.[11]

In general, the Meccan Suras incline to be shorter since they represent for the most part merely the reported revelation of some aspects of religious truth.

The Medina Suras tend to be longer, more didactic, and concerned with the detailed regulation of the society of which he has now become the political head. Early in his career as prophet, Mohammed is commanded by Allah to make his will known to the people, and the judgment that will fall upon them should they not obey his commandment. Unbelievers stand under God's judgment and in imminent danger of the fire of hell as for example in Sura 52, "The Mountain":

In the Name of God, the Compassionate, the Merciful

By the Mountain,
And by the Book written
On an outspread roll,
And by the frequented fane,
And by the lofty vault,
And by the swollen sea,
Verily, a chastisement from thy Lord is imminent,
And none shall put it back.
Reeling on that day the Heaven shall reel,
And stirring shall the mountains stir.

[10] *The Koran,* translated from the Arabic by the Rev. J. M. Rodwell, J. M. Dent & Co., London, 1909, p. 63.
[11] *Id.,* p. 28.

And woe, on that day, to those who called the apostles liars,
Who plunged for pastime into vain disputes—
On that day shall they be thrust with thrusting to the
      fire of Hell:—[12]

But God is also merciful and compassionate toward those who believe. Again and again he details the joys that wait upon those who yield allegiance to the Prophet's God. There is for example Sura 56, "The Inevitable":[13]

In the Name of God, the Compassionate, the Merciful . . .

And they who were foremost on earth—the foremost still.
These are they who shall be brought nigh to God,
In gardens of delight;
A crowd of the former
And a few of the latter generations;
On inwrought couches
Reclining on them face to face:
Aye-blooming youths go round about to them
With goblets and ewers and a cup of flowing wine;
Their brows ache not from it, nor fails the sense:
And with such fruits as shall please them best,
And with flesh of such birds, as they shall long for:
And theirs shall be the Houris, with large dark eyes,
Like pearls hidden in their shells,
In recompense of their labours past.
No vain discourse shall they hear therein, nor charge of sin,
But only the cry, "Peace! Peace!"
And the people of the right hand—oh! how happy shall be
      the people of the right hand!
Amid thornless sidrahs
And tall trees clad with fruit,
And in extended shade,
And by the flowing waters,
And with abundant fruits,
Unfailing, unforbidden,
And on lofty couches.

[12] *Id.*, p. 63.
[13] Rodwell, *op. cit.*, p. 65.

Of a rare creation have we created the Houris,
And we have made them ever virgins,
Dear to their spouses, of equal age with them. . . .

Or Sura 76, "Man":[14]

In the Name of God, the Compassionate, the Merciful . . .

A stern and calamitous day dread we from our Lord.
From the evil therefore of that day hath God delivered
      them and cast on them brightness of face and joy:
And hath rewarded their constancy, with Paradise and
      silken robes:
Reclining therein on bridal couches, nought shall they
      know of sun or piercing cold:
Its shades shall be close over them, and low shall its
      fruits hang down:
And vessels and silver and goblets like flagons shall be
      borne round among them:
Flagons of silver whose measure themselves shall mete.
And there shall they be given to drink of the cup
      tempered with zendjebil (ginger)
From the fount therein whose name is Selsebil (the
      softly flowing).
Aye-blooming youths go round among them. When thou
      lookest at them thou wouldest deem them scattered pearls;
And when thou seest this, thou wilt see delights and a
      vast kingdom:
Their clothing green silk robes and rich brocade: with
      silver bracelets shall they be adorned; and drink of a
      pure beverage shall their Lord give them.
This shall be your recompense. Your efforts shall meet
      with thanks.
We ourselves have sent down to thee the Koran as a
      missive from on high.
Await then with patience the judgments of thy Lord, and
      obey not the wicked among them and the unbelieving:[15]

Literal-minded Moslems have, no doubt, often enough taken

[14] *Id.,* p. 86.
[15] *The Koran Translated from the Arabic* by the Rev. J. M. Rodwell, pp. 87, 88.

these as literal pictures of the future life just as Christians have taken literally the pictures of immortal existence as given in their sacred book; but many Moslems, like many Christians, believe that these words are but symbols through which the Prophet attempts to give some conception of the life hereafter, which he obviously believes may be one of bitter judgment or of supernal delight.

On the other hand, the Medina Suras tend to be less poetic, more didactic and frequently plain legal enactments for the governance of the people of the growing state which Mohammed has now come to rule. They were given to him from time to time as necessity called them forth, but faithful Moslems regard these detailed rules of living as nonetheless inspired and authoritative, the very word of God. These often reveal a somewhat different attitude toward various elements of the social whole than are held in Western lands, but the Moslem believes that they nevertheless represent Allah's holy will. Mohammed in the name of Allah legislates concerning the matter of family inheritance, concerning the care and responsibility for orphans, reflecting herein, no doubt, a concern born of his own experience as an orphan. The regulation of the family life, the matter of marriage, the responsibilities of men to their wives and wives to husbands are set out in no little detail. The law as to the number of wives, which Mohammed placed at four, is found in Sura 4.

And if ye are apprehensive that ye shall not deal fairly with orphans, then, of other women who seem good in your eyes, marry but two, or three, or four; and if ye still fear that ye shall not act equitably, then one only; or the slaves whom ye have acquired: this will make justice on your part easier. Give women their dowry freely; but if of themselves they give up aught thereof to you, then enjoy it as convenient, and profitable.[16]

Mohammed's ideas with reference to the place of women are no doubt somewhat different from those held in some other parts of the world, but they are set forth with perfect clarity. He obviously regards men as superior to women as for example in Sura 4:

[16] *The Koran Translated from the Arabic* by Rev. J. M. Rodwell, from Sura IV, pp. 410, 411.

Men are superior to women on account of the qualities with which God hath gifted the one above the other, and on account of the outlay they make from their substance for them. Virtuous women are obedient, careful, during the husband's absence, because God hath of them been careful. But chide those for whose refractoriness ye have cause to fear; remove them into beds apart, and scourge them: but if they are obedient to you, then seek not occasion against them: verily, God is High, Great![17]

Yet at certain other points he did definitely lift the position of women to a considerably higher level than that current in Arabia before his own time. For example, female infanticide was forbidden; the number of wives a man might have was limited; a woman's dowry could not be taken from her, and she was given the right to own property and dispose of it at will, quite independently of her husband.

THE BIBLE IN THE KORAN

One of the notable features of the Koran, from the standpoint of Jewish and Christian readers, is the amount of Biblical lore that appears throughout. Whole books have been written about the Bible in the Koran, but here we only deal with the relationships between the two books. One of the most obvious things to say is that Mohammed knew a great deal about the Bible. The probabilities are that he could not read, and that what he included of it had come to him at second-hand. He had many contacts with both Jews and Christians in his travelling about the country with caravans as a young man, and in his contacts with Jews and Christians in Medina and Mecca during his maturer years. It was in these contacts that he picked up what he knew about the Bible. Mohammed did not feel himself very different from the Jews and Christians. He believed definitely that the Arabian people were just as much descendents of Abraham as were the Jews—they stemming from Ishmael, half-brother of Isaac, son of Hagar, one-time serving maid of Sarah but given by Sarah to Abraham as a secondary wife. Thus all of the pre-Abrahamic Biblical figures are a part of Islam's back-

[17] *Ibid.*, p. 415.

ground as well as of the Hebrews', and he makes constant use of those who came after Abraham and who had a significant part in developing the Hebrew faith.

As one reads the Koran, he finds himself often enough in familiar territory. But Mohammed quotes *verbatim* from the Bible only once. Many of the Biblical stories are garbled and scarcely recognizable. He makes frequent references to the great prophets, and today Moslems declare their belief in all the prophets, among whom they rate Jesus very high. He occupies a very important place in the Koran. There is at least one whole book dealing largely with the subject, *Christ in Islam*.[18] To be sure Mohammed never believed in him as divine. His belief in the oneness of God led him to scorn the idea that Jesus could be God or even Son of God. How could God, who was without parts, have a son? In general, his use of scripture is about what might be expected from one who did not have direct access to it, but got his knowledge of it at second-hand.

Some Moslem writers make a great deal of the Old Testament in the Koran, and perhaps even more of the Koran in the Old Testament. Again and again they see in Biblical passages a great foreshadowing of the coming of the Prophet of Allah.[19]

THE TRADITIONS

While the Koran is the one completely sacred book of the Moslems, there exists alongside it a considerable body of supplementary material which is almost as important as the Koran itself in the determination of Moslem belief and practice. It will be recalled that the Koran is regarded as a revelation, given word by word to Mohammed direct from God. In it there is almost nothing concerning Mohammed, the Prophet himself, nothing of his informal teaching outside the moments when he was definitely speaking under direct inspiration from Allah. Yet one of the very important factors in determining Moslem belief and practice has come to be not only

[18] James Robson, John Murray, London, 1929.

[19] See Muhammad Ali, *The Holy Koran With English Translation and Commentary*, pp. lviii to lxxxiii. Also an article of mine on "Some Contemporary Moslem Interpretation of the Bible." *Crozer Quarterly*, Vol. 22, pp. 246–259. Also Sufi M. R. Bengalee, *Life of Muhammad*, Chicago, 1941, pp. 262–280.

what God has revealed directly in the Koran, but whatever it can be certainly known that Mohammed himself either said or practiced. As one modern Moslem writer expresses it, the Koran contains largely broad general principles of action and belief but gives very little in the way of detail as to how this should be worked out in daily life. If it could only be known what the Prophet himself said or did as he went about his daily labors, met people, resolved difficult situations, this indeed would be guidance to his followers.

It is precisely this which the Traditions or as they are known, the *Hadith* and the *Sunnah* provide. The Hadith means literally the saying; Sunnah, the actions or customary practices of the prophet. A single reported Hadith sometimes may relate more than one Sunnah, since they tell what the Prophet did as well as said. So the two terms are practically synonymous. During the Prophet's own lifetime the respect in which he was held and the authority which he enjoyed among his followers made them eager to treasure everything that he said and to note and remember whatever he did.

A comparable modern case is that of Father Divine who is regarded by his followers as God. Being God, whatever he says is, of course, important and to be treasured. Therefore, there surround him constantly stenographers with pads and pencils to preserve his every word as he speaks it. There were sixteen such persons at his beck and call, I recall, when I personally visited him in 1945; and literally everything that he said was faithfully recorded by one or more of this secretarial staff. Later it was transcribed and published, so that there is now a vast body of reported utterances of Father Divine in relatively permanent written form.

During the lifetime of Mohammed probably very little was written down, but the Companions undoubtedly made it a point to remember and to retell again and again to others what they who were privileged to be near him, heard him say or saw him do. There is one Tradition at least which says that Mohammed discouraged writing such things down, lest this record be confused with the Koran itself. There is, however, another Tradition which specifically authorized a person to write down what he was saying.

The fact is, however, that very little was written down during the Prophet's lifetime. After his death the Companions, i.e., those persons who were close to and knew the Prophet personally, probably became centers for the collection of sayings and actions attributed to him, reported by various persons; and became the transmitters to many others, who had not had the privilege of seeing the Prophet, of these sayings and acts of Mohammed. It is related that one of the Companions had as many as eight hundred disciples to whom he imparted the Traditions which he regarded as authentic. Some Moslem writers speak of these Companions as essentially schools for the transmission of the Traditions. Probably some of the material was reduced to writing during this period, but it was not until after the passing of the generation of the Companions that their writing became common. Now clearly the necessity for their recording would become more evident.

By this time the spreading Moslem empire was bringing under its domination wholly new cultures and attempting to teach them the Moslem way of life. Some authoritative source of detailed instruction beyond that furnished by the Koran became imperative so that probably larger and larger numbers of Traditions were committed to writing. Caliph Omar II, about one hundred years after the *Hegira* is reported to have written to an under-officer, ordering him to collect and write down the Traditions for fear many of them might be lost; but he cautioned, "Do not accept anything but *Hadith* of the Holy Prophet."[20] Collections during this period, even those made in writing, were probably by no means general but comprised only those held in certain localities or transmitted through only certain ones of the Companions. Thus there was no general collection available.

It was not until the third century after the *Hegira* that anything like a systematic attempt was made to bring together a general body of Traditions, and of those that were attempted at this time there were two kinds. One was the collection of the Hadith according to the particular Companions of the Prophet to whom they could be traced back. Since a great many could be attributed to a comparatively few of the Companions and these were upon all sorts of sub-

[20] Muhammad Ali, *op. cit.*, pp. 71—72.

jects, the result, while better than no collection at all, was not too helpful. It was of little aid to one who might be seeking a saying on some particular topic. The other type of collection known as *Jami,* arranges the Hadith according to subject matter, and is definitely more critical in tone. Six orthodox collections of Traditions are generally recognized as authentic, though there are several others of which use is frequently made by Moslems. These six are the collections of Bukhari (d. 256 A.H.); Muslim (d. 261 A.H.); Abu Dawud (d. 275 A.H.); Tirmidhi (d. 279 A.H.); Ibn Maja (d. 283 A.H.); and Nasai (d. 303 A.H.). For a more complete list of collections see Muhammad Ali, *Religion of Islam,* pp. 72–76. Of these quite the most important are those of Bukhari and Muslim. Bukhari is recognized as perhaps the most authoritative. He undertook a systematic sifting of a great mass of Traditions, said to number 600,000, but ended up with selecting something less than 9,000 as authentic. Of these about one in three is a variant of some other saying in the collection so that the total number of different recognized sayings in his collection is under 3,000.

The elimination of such vast numbers of reputed sayings of the prophet has led Western scholars to question seriously the validity of any of them. However, Muhammad Ali, a contemporary Moslem scholar, says that among the 600,000 were included hundreds of variants of the same sayings, since it was customary to present as separate Traditions any sayings that differed by as much as one word from any other saying. He thinks that Bukhari's screening of the Traditions was done in a manner, "in no way inferior to modern methods."[21] Many tests were applied to each independent Tradition. First, each transmitter must be authenticated. In the printing of the Traditions it is customary to give the line of transmitters through whom the Tradition has been handed down, e.g., Ibn Omar reported that the Prophet said, "When your women ask to go to the Mosque at night, give them permission." Here the report is that of one of the Companions of the Prophet.[22] But another may read "A" said that "B" reported to him that he heard Mohammed

[21] Muhammad Ali, *op. cit.,* p. 86.
[22] Muhammad Ali, *A Manual of Hadith,* B 10:162, pp. 106–107.

say, or a third or a fourth person may be mentioned as a transmitter. All these must be duly authenticated before the Hadith is accepted as valid. Ali lists ten rigorous tests which each one must pass before it is accepted.[23] But most important of all, is that it must be in accordance with the Koran.

Bukhari in his collection ordinarily heads each section with a Koranic verse, showing, says Ali, that he considered the Traditions simply as an explanation of the Koran, and in no sense a substitution for it. The content of the Traditions is highly varied, some of it is of the most commonplace or seemingly trivial nature. Such, for example, as this:

'A'isha said, I used to comb the hair of the Messenger of Allah, peace and blessings of Allah be on him.[24]

'A'isha was the youngest of his wives and his favorite. Or:

Abu Huraira said. The Messenger of Allah, peace and blessings of Allah be on him, said: "It is the sunna that a man should accompany his guest to the door of the house."[25]

Or:

Ibn 'Umar reported. The Messenger of Allah, peace and blessings of Allah be on him, said: "When one of you is invited to a marriage feast, he should go to it."[26]

'A'isha said, She conducted the bride to a man from among the Ansar. And the Prophet of Allah, peace and blessings of Allah be on him, said, "O 'A'isha! Why had you no music with you, for the Ansar love music. . . ."[27]

'Umar said. The Messenger of Allah, peace and blessings of Allah be on him, said: "Eat together and do not eat separately, for the blessing is with the company."[28]

But if such single Traditions seem of little importance, in the aggregate they do provide a very good picture of the Prophet him-

[23] Muhammad Ali, *Religion of Islam*, pp. 86–87.
[24] Muhammad Ali, *A Manual of Hadith*, p. 366 (Bukhari 6:2).
[25] *Ibid.*, p. 358 (IM-Msh. 20:1).
[26] *Ibid.*, p. 278 (Bukhari 67:72).
[27] *Ibid.*, p. 276 (B. 67:64).
[28] *Ibid.*, p. 356 (IM-Msh. 20:1).

self and of what he was accustomed to do. The Koran, itself, furnishes almost no information concerning the Prophet. It is only through the Traditions that the man himself emerges.

If some of the Traditions seem to be of slight importance, others contain some of the more profound ethical and religious teachings of Mohammed. For example, the following Tradition from the *Mishkat* collection reveals a side of Mohammed not often discovered in the Koranic teachings. It is quite reminiscent of the Sermon on the Mount.

Say not, if people do good to us, we will do good to them, and if people oppress us, we will oppress them: but resolve that if people do good to you, you will do good to them, and if they oppress you, oppress them not again.[29]

Another from the same collection reveals rather a different concept of God from that usually found in the Koran. At least Western interpreters of the Koran find the Moslem God to be a distant, austere, relatively unapproachable figure. Here one finds an active, seeking God not so frequently associated with Moslem teaching.

God saith: Whoso doth one good act, for him are ten rewards, and I also give more to whomsoever I will; and whoso doth ill, its retaliation is equal to it, or else I forgive him; and he who seeketh to approach me one cubit, I will seek to approach him two fathoms; and he who walketh towards me, I will run towards him; and he who cometh before me with the earth full of sins, but joineth no Partner to me, I will come before him with an equal front of forgiveness.[30]

Another story setting forth somewhat the same teaching, is found in three different collections of Traditions. In the Koran there is very little in the way of story material, most of it is made up of the forthright commands of Ali, or directives for the conduct of human affairs in the Theocracy, or poetic expressions of religious insight given to the prophets. But the Traditions abound in good stories, somewhat like the stories found in the gospels. Here is one:

[29] Stanley Lane-Poole, *The Speeches and Table-Talk of the Prophet Mohammad,* London, Macmillan and Company, 1905, p. 147.
   [30] *Ibid.*

Abu Huraira, said. The Messenger of Allah, peace and blessings of Allah be on him, said: a prostitute was forgiven—she passed by a dog, panting with its tongue out, on the top of a well containing water, almost dying with thirst; so she took off her boot and tied it to her head-covering and drew forth water for it; she was forgiven on account of this.

It was said: Is there a reward for us in (doing good to) the beasts? He said:

In every animal having a liver fresh with life there is a reward.[31]

One of the collections brings together a number of interesting sayings by the Prophet concerning women, which have undoubtedly had very great influence on Islamic culture in its attitude toward women.

The world and all things in it are valuable, but the most valuable thing in the world is a virtuous woman.

I have not left any calamity more hurtful to man than woman.

Verily the best of women are those who are content with little.

Admonish your wives with kindness; for women were created out of a crooked rib of Adam, therefore if ye wish to straighten it, ye will break it; and if ye let it alone, it will be always crooked.

Every woman who dieth, and her husband is pleased with her, shall enter into paradise.

A widow shall not be married until she be consulted; nor shall a virgin be married until her consent be asked, whose consent is by her silence.

Do not prevent your women from coming to the mosque; but their homes are better for them.

O assembly of women, give alms, although it be of your gold and silver ornaments; for verily ye are mostly of Hell on the Day of Resurrection.[32]

Slavery was a universally recognized institution in the time of Mohammed, not alone in Arabia but all over the world. It was but natural that he should have had something to say concerning slaves and their treatment. If from the standpoint of today Mohammed's countenancing of the practice seems an evil thing, it should be remembered that Christian people held slaves in America until less

[31] Muhammad Ali, *A Manual of Hadith*, p. 211.
[32] Stanley Lane-Poole, *Speeches and Table-Talk of the Prophet Mohammad*, pp. 161–162.

than a century ago. Actually Mohammed by his teaching did a great deal to ameliorate the harsh conditions under which slaves lived.

God has ordained that your brothers should be your slaves: therefore him whom God hath ordained to be the slave of his brother, his brother must give him of the food which he eateth himself, and of the clothes wherewith he clotheth himself, and not order him to do anything beyond his power, and if he doth order such a work, he must himself assist him in doing it.

He who beateth his slave without fault, or slappeth him in the face, his atonement for this is freeing him.

A man who behaveth ill to his slave will not enter into paradise.

Forgive thy servant seventy times a day.[33]

Although the basis of the Theocracy was laid in the direct revelation recorded in the Koran, Mohammed spoke often of government and the obligations of ruler and subject.

Government is a trust from God, and verily government will be at the Day of Resurrection a cause of inquiry, unless he who hath taken it be worthy of it and have acted justly and done good.

Verily a king is God's shadow upon the earth; and every one oppressed turneth to him: then when the king doeth justice, for him are rewards and gratitude from his subject: but, if the king oppresseth, on him is his sin, and for the oppressed resignation.

There is no prince who oppresseth the subject and dieth, but God forbiddeth Paradise to him.

If a negro slave is appointed to rule over you, hear him, and obey him, though his head should be like a dried grape.

When one of you getteth angry, he must sit down, and if his anger goeth away from sitting, so much the better; if not, let him lie down.[34]

Also of war and fighting he speaks often, aside from that which is found in the Koran.

When the Prophet sent an army out to fight, he would say, March in

[33] Stanley Lane-Poole, *Speeches and Table-Talk of the Prophet Mohammad*, p. 163.

[34] Stanley Lane-Poole, *Speeches and Table-Talk of the Prophet Mohammad*, pp. 166, 167.

the name of God and by His aid and on the religion of the Messenger of God. Kill not the old man who cannot fight, nor young children nor women; and steal not the spoils of war, but put your spoils together; and quarrel not amongst yourselves, but be good to one another, for God loveth the doer of good.[35]

On fighting for the Faith:

I swear to God, in whose hand is my life, that marching about morning and evening to fight for religion is better than the world and everything that is in it: and verily the standing of one of you in the line of battle is better than supererogatory prayers performed in your house for sixty years.[36]

Probably no sacred book has been more influential, not alone upon the religion derived from it, but upon the total culture of the people who embrace the faith, than the Koran. And Islam, it should be said, is not simply a religion, it is a culture. One can hardly speak of Christianity thus, though at certain periods, notably in medieval Europe, the term would have been more applicable than at any other time. But Islam has always been more than religion, it has also been government, indeed almost every aspect of life, both individual and social, has been colored by it. Wherever Islam has gone, among whatever people, it has carried certain patterns of thinking and acting which have molded the total culture of the people into what is distinctly recognizable as Islamic.

Quite the most important factor in effecting this result has been the Koran, and to a lesser extent the Traditions. The Koran is of course the basis of Islamic worship. Most of the rituals and prayers both in the mosque and in private are taken from the Koran. People learn to recite great portions of it. The sermons in the mosque—for in this respect they follow Jewish and Christian custom—are based upon the Koran mainly, though frequently upon the Traditions as well. It is in the latter that the warmer, more personal elements in Moslem teaching are found, and its stories are told and retold as are the Gospel and Old Testament stories in the Christian churches. These form, of course, the basis for all religious education. What-

[35] *Ibid.*, p. 159.
[36] *Ibid.*, p. 159.

ever may have happened within Christianity to remove the Bible from the center of religious education, Moslem religious education is still Koran-centered. Much of it consists in memorizing passages from the Koran. The pupils may or may not understand it, but they learn it, great quantities of it, much as in our earlier days children memorized the Bible.

The Koran is likewise the chief basis of instruction for those who are to exercise leadership in the mosque. Islam does not have priests, for like Protestant Christianity it insists upon the universal priesthood of believers, but there are *Imams, mullahs, ulemas,* who perform many of the functions of ministers, teachers, leaders in Islam, and these must be trained in the knowledge and understanding of the Koran.

The basis of all Moslem ethical teaching is the Koran. The good is what Allah wishes. What Allah wills is revealed in the Koran, supplemented by what Mohammed is reported in the Traditions to have said or done. Questions, then, of right or wrong must be decided on the basis of the Koran. Men, therefore, to live righteously, must know the Koran.

But it is not the basis of religious education alone. It is the chief basis of all education. To say this is of course to speak from the point of view of a secularist age, which sets religion apart from general culture, as only one aspect of it. In an integrated culture such as that existing in the wholly Moslem states, one simply does not talk about religious education as something apart from general education. In a real sense, all education is religious and definitely follows the Moslem pattern. And for this the Koran is basic. Children learn to read from the Koran, not from secular readers such as American children use, where the "I see a cat," type of text is so frequently found. In an older day in New England, it will be remembered, children learned to read from the Bible.

Of course there are few, if any, completely Moslem states now. Modern influences from the West tend to modify the educational process, but there are still parts of the world where the greater part of education, from the primary school through the university, finds its basis in the Koran. Grammar, syntax, poetry, prosody, rhetoric, literary style—from what better source may be drawn the materials of instruction?

But it was perhaps in the realm of legislation that the Koran and the supplementary Traditions most vitally affected the everyday life of Moslem peoples. From the beginning of the Mohammedan period, in Medina, religion and the state became one and the same thing. Mohammed established a theocracy, the rule of God among men. He provided the laws, many of them in the form of direct revelation from Allah; those now found in the Koran. Tradition has it that a part of every day Mohammed set aside to receive the complaints and suggestions of the citizens of Medina, and by his often simple and homely settlement of the important or unimportant issues brought before him, he set the pattern for ages to come in Moslem jurisprudence. Sooner or later, the entire civil and criminal codes of law, known as the *Sharia,* were built solidly upon a Koranic background. This continues to be the case in some Moslem states until the present day. In other states which have lost their independence and have fallen under the rule of foreign powers, modifications have of necessity been made. Modern Turkey, under influence from the West, in 1924 definitely abandoned the Moslem legal system and substituted for it criminal and civil codes taken from the West. But in the greater part of the world in which the Moslems are the majority, the influence of the Sharia is still very great.

The personal rule of Mohammed was confined to a comparatively small area, more or less homogeneous as to its inhabitants— all of them Semitic in background, and dwellers in desert or semi-arid lands. A relatively simple legal system sufficed to govern such a culture, but after the death of Mohammed, the spread of Moslem power was very rapid and soon came to include peoples very different in background and custom from the Arabians. Situations began to arise that Mohammed had never had to meet. How were they to know how to answer questions that Mohammed had never faced? The basic rule was to follow what either had been revealed through the Koran or had come down through the Traditions as having been uttered or performed by Mohammed. But by what means could the extension be made to wholly new situations as they arose?

It was almost inevitable that differences as to the interpretation of the Koran itself as well as the Traditions should arise. Influential individual interpreters created schools of interpretation, some of which came to be regarded as orthodox by the general body of Moslems, and some as heretical. The four recognized as orthodox were the Hanifite, founded in Iraq by a Persian, Abu Hanifa, who died in 767 A.D.; the Malikite, founded in Medina by Malik-ibn-Anas (about 715–795 A.D.); the Shafite, founded by an Arab, al-Shafi'i, born in Persia; and finally the Hanbalite, most conservative of the four, founded in Baghdad, by Ibn-Hanbal. The service they performed was not greatly different from that of the creators of the Jewish Talmud whose commentaries on the Mishnah were designed to guide the Jews in the diaspora, and help them to adjust to the foreign environment in which they found themselves, and still hold fast to their traditional faith.

It was because of the necessity of meeting such problems that two principles were evolved which have been of very great importance in the development of Moslem law. These were the principles of *Ijma,* or agreement, and that of *Qiyas,* or analogy.

The principle, Ijma, is based in part upon an important tradition to the effect that what Moslems agree upon is right—that is, the principle of consensus, "My people shall never agree on an error." The problem, however, is to get consensus of all Moslems. This was comparatively simple in the period immediately following Mohammed's death, but it became exceedingly difficult as Islam spread across the world, so some further definition had to be found. The earliest seems to have been that if the Companions could agree upon anything, that would become authoritative. But after the generation of the Companions disappeared from the scene, who then would represent the consensus? There was much difference of opinion on this question. And no single, everywhere accepted definition was to be found. Perhaps the nearest thing to consensus, one which did become practically effective, was the consensus of the learned doctors of Islam; and this has been still further reduced to the agreement among the learned doctors of the four accepted schools of thought in Islam.

Actually, since the very early period, consensus has played a very important role. But it is possible in almost any given legal decision to invoke as authority those who refuse to abide by the decisions of others. Therefore, there is no completely accepted body of Ijma to which one may turn.

The other principle, and a very far-reaching one, is what is known as *Qiyas,* or analogy. If there were no specific saying in the Koran or in the Traditions, and no Ijma or agreement existed with respect to a situation which arose in the course of Islam's rapid spread beyond Arabia, how could it be met? For it must be remembered that Islam was not simply a way of life for individuals, but for the whole social body. Some principle had to be determined which would make such necessary decisions possible within the framework of Moslem teaching. The principle which emerged was that of analogy, a principle which has been employed informally at least if not formally all through Christian history. Not so many years ago a Christian minister, Charles M. Sheldon, wrote a book which has been one of the most widely circulated volumes in the world, next to the Bible. It was entitled *In His Steps, What Would Jesus Do?* It was the story of a man who undertook to follow in Jesus' footsteps, and do just what Jesus would do. But how would he know what Jesus would do? The author once challenged a daily newspaper to let him run the paper for one week as he thought Jesus would do it—and was given the chance. Circulation for the week zoomed to an all time high—for that particular week—showing the interest people had in such a venture.

Well, obviously, Jesus lived in a different age, amid different surroundings. He knew nothing about modern industrial and urban life. How could Mr. Sheldon know what he would do? Only by invoking the identical principle used by Moslems in the extension of their faith into new and radically different cultures, namely that of analogy. If Mohammed had said or done nothing precisely bearing upon the problem of the moment, what had he said or done in an analogous situation?

Naturally, people might well differ, first, as to whether the situations were really analogous, also as to just how far the analogy might be carried. It is clear that unanimity of judgment would not easily be found, and it has not been. Think for a moment of the difficulties people get into in trying to follow Jesus. Shall one go to war? To be sure Jesus said some things very closely related to it. "They that take the sword, shall perish by the sword." But is it to be taken literally or only figuratively? Moslems have had the same difficulty. Yet the principle has been extensively used in extending the teaching of Mohammed into new areas. When sufficient agreement, Ijma, can be reached as to such extensions, even if only in a limited region, they become effective in providing a basis for an extension of the Sharia.

The Koran has been translated into English and other modern vernaculars many times, though some Moslems, especially the orthodox Egyptians, frown upon it. An annotated list of these will be found at the end of the chapter. Unfortunately only a very small portion of the Traditions has as yet been made available to English readers. It is to be hoped that other selections will appear and that at least the entire collections of Bukhari and Muslim will be translated for the use of modern readers of English.

What has been said thus far has been largely true of Islam in general, but in particular of the larger of the two major Moslem divisions, the Sunnites. All the sects accept the Koran, but they differ in some degree as to their acceptance of the Traditions. The Shiahs, for example, recognize five collections which are not found in the generally accepted Sunnah list. Also it may be said that just as in Christianity and Judaism different elements emphasize some books of the Bible more than others, naturally the ones that support their own peculiar views, so it is within Islam. But all alike, the rigidly orthodox Wahabis, the Persian Shiahs, the Sufi mystics, the modern Ahmadiyya Movement in Islam, which has its own Promised Messiah whose writings have for them the value of scripture, and numerous other branches, find their bases somewhere in the Koran, the various collections of Traditions and their extension through the *agreements* and the *analogies*. And they all are to some extent still involved in adjusting their faith to the changing modern world as it increasingly impinges upon them. For Islam is a living faith.

THE SACRED LITERATURE OF THE MOSLEMS
Sources for Further Reading

TRANSLATIONS OF THE QUR'AN

The Qur'an translated by George Sale has appeared in several editions since its original appearance in 1734.

The Koran, translated from the Arabic by J. M. Rodwell first published in 1876. At present available in Everyman's Library, J. M. Dent and Co., London, E. P. Dutton and Co., N. Y., first printing, 1909.

Marmaduke Pickthall, *The Meaning of the Glorious Koran,* A. A. Knopf, N. Y., 1930, an explanatory translation by an English Moslem.

Richard Bell, *The Qur'an,* translated with a critical rearrangement of the Surahs. 2 Vols., T. & T. Clark, Edinburgh, 1937.

Muhammad Ali, *Translation of the Holy Qur'an with Commentary (and text),* 1917.

The Holy Qur'an with English Translation and Commentary projected to appear in 3 Volumes published at Quadian, India, under the auspices of the Second Successor of the Promised Messiah, by the Sadr Anjuman Ahmadiyya, 1947–1949.

TRANSLATIONS OF THE HADITH OR TRADITIONS

Muhammad Ali, *A Manual of Hadith,* Lahore, 1945, Ahmadiyya Anjuman isha-at-i-Islam.

A brief selection of Traditions is included in Stanley Lane-Poole, *The Speeches and Table-Talk of the Prophet Mohammad,* Macmillan & Company Ltd., London, 1905.

IN THE ANTHOLOGIES

Sacred Books of the East, Vol. 6, translated by E. H. Palmer.

Sacred Books and Literature of the East, Vol. 5, translated by George Sale.

The Harvard Classics, Vol. 45, pp. 885–1021. Translation of E. H. Palmer.

The Bible of the World (Ballou), pp. 1289–1325.

The Bible of Mankind (Sohrab), pp. 515–588.

The World's Great Scriptures (Browne), pp. 511–554.

The Tree of Life (Smith), pp. 445–468.

Tongues of Fire (Turnbull), pp. 391–406.

The Sacred Writings of the World's Great Religions (Frost), pp. 305–346.

CHAPTER XIV

Modern Sacred Books

It is abundantly evident from the reading of the previous chapters on the sacred books of the various peoples of the world that the definition of a sacred book is not a hard and fast one. Thus far I have taken a body of literature which has become recognized historically as sacred and therefore authoritative, for one reason or another, and discussed it. The task in this final chapter is somewhat less fixed for me by history.

Ordinarily time is an important factor in the making of a sacred book, particularly when the book turns out to be of composite authorship, less important when it is a one-man book. Even here, however, only time is able to prove whether the movement founded by the revealer will live and attain to more than limited significance. Most of the scriptures thus far discussed are ethnic in character. Will any one of those I mention here ever arrive at that distinction? Only time will tell. It may be said, however, that in some cases the number of people who have come to esteem the writings here to be mentioned as sacred is much greater, in proportion to the elapsed time since their first appearance, than was the case in some of the world religions as now recognized. This may, of course, be due chiefly to the fact that modern methods of propaganda have greatly increased the ease with which a new teaching can be brought to the attention of the world. Even so, it is not a little startling to discover that some modern movements which purport to be based upon a new revelation from God have been able in the short space of a decade to claim in excess of a million followers.

Since insufficient time has passed to assure to the books here discussed a permanent place among the sacred books of the world, such as that enjoyed by the ones that have so far been discussed, I feel it necessary to draw up a definition of a sacred book which will enable me to pick out of our modern world what may be called its sacred books. I propose as that definition, realizing that it would probably exclude some of those already discussed, the following: The sacred book contains writings that purport to have been produced under divine or extra human inspiration or impulse, and which have come to be recognized by a substantial number of people as the basis of their religious faith, since it is regarded by them as the authentic revelation of God to them and to the world.

Are there, under this definition, any modern sacred books? The answer is, "Yes, many." They are found all over the world. Most of them are local in their significance—so far. Some of them are doubtless more or less ephemeral, but some have already achieved the dignity of world religions. Let me first mention two from Japan, both of them the product of the last hundred years.

The Japanese Shinto sect, Tenrikyo, which before the war ranked among the recognized Shinto sects, with a membership of some three million, was founded by a woman known simply as the Foundress, whose prophecies constitute the basic scriptures of the movement. She died in 1886 at the age of ninety. She was the incarnation of God, as stated by one of their publications. God had never before, it declares, "come down to the world to lead the people," but, "after a long waiting, the time at last came and God showed himself to the World, taking the body of The Foundress as the incarnation, at the sacred place of Jiba in October, 1838. The Foundress taught the world, and led men, high and low, to the salvation for the reconstruction of the world. Through the mediation of the Foundress, after a long separation, i.e., since the creation of the world, God and men met again."[1] It was not, however, until 1869 that she began the composition of the prophetic poems known by the name O-fude-saki. Thenceforth, according to the book *Tenrikyo,* "almost for twelve years the Foundress wrote down the holy prophecies piece by piece by the dim light of a kerosene lamp, as they came flashing through her mind that was filled with heavenly inspiration. She sometimes wrote them down in the dark, but there was no need to change the characters."[2] Only a few of the poems are available in English translation, known as the Dancing Psalms.[3]

Konkokyo is another Shinto sect which was founded by one Ikigami Konko Daijin in 1859 "in accordance with the divine command of Tenchi-Kane-no-Kami." At that time the founder "enlightened by inspiration from God, indicated the path of true belief and his practical solutions, based on his own spiritual experience, brought relief to people suffering from disease, misfortune, and all other miseries of life."[4] The movement was recognized by the Japanese government in 1900 and took its place among the officially approved Shinto sects. "Dependence upon salvation through the founder is the cardinal point of the (our) teaching,"[5] for, having "set himself to the task of accomplishing the divine work, he (The Founder) attained the rank of *Ikigami,* the living God, who though in the flesh was one with the God, and was given the divine name *Ikigami Konko Daijin,* Living God Konko Daijin."[6]

It is his teachings that form the sacred book of Konkokyo. Unfortunately, there is no indication in available sources as to how extensive it is nor how it was collected. It is found in English, probably only in part, in the little volume *The Sacred Scriptures of Konkokyo,* translated and edited by Konkokyo Hombu (Headquarters of Konkokyo) Konko-cho, Okyama-kin, Japan 2593, 1933. The Konkokyo sect was represented at the World Parliament of Religions at Chicago, 1933.

[1] *Tenrikyo,* Doyusha, Tenrikyo Head Church, Tsuchisaburo Itakura, Moderator, Tambaichi, Japan, n.d., pp. 4–5.
[2] *Ibid.,* p. 131.
[3] *Ibid.,* pp. 151–176.
[4] *The Sacred Scriptures of Konkokyo,* p. iii.
[5] *Ibid.,* p. xx.
[6] *Ibid.,* p. xii.

America has been prolific in its production of scriptures, some already completed, some still in the process of being revealed. The relative unimportance of many of them makes them of little interest, for example, the inspired utterances of the founder of the House of David, Benjamin Purnell. Timothy Drew, better known as Noble Drew, Ali, a Negro, Founder of The Moorish Science Temple of America, was the medium through whom a new Holy Koran was revealed to serve as the scripture for the group. It has only a few centers in the larger cities.

Father Divine gives new revelations every day which are duly recorded in *The New Day,* a weekly newspaper. There has as yet been no collection of these revelations, other than scattered selections published by a follower, Walter C. Lanyon, in England.[7] But, here is a scripture in the making. If the movement survives the passing of the founder, it may become one as truly as any of those that now exist. Here, his followers believe, is God himself speaking. His words are recorded verbatim by a corps of stenographers. There were sixteen of them when I visited him. Even now where groups meet outside of the Eastern area, where Father Divine appears before them in person, his messages are read from *The New Day,* very much as scripture is read in other religious groups.[8]

The I Am groups regard the writings of Mr. and Mrs. Guy Ballard, their founders, as given them direct from some divine source, chiefly the Ascended Masters, of whom St. Germain is the principal one. Ballard published his earliest revelations from St. Germain in *Unveiled Mysteries,* a most unusual account of his adventures out of the body, in both space and time, in the course of which the basic teachings of the cult appear. This was followed by other volumes of similar nature. It is difficult to say just what will be the outcome of all this. As long as Ballard lived—he died in 1939—both he and Edna Ballard, his wife, continued to receive messages in public and in private via the Ascended Masters, includ-

---

[7] *Behold The Man,* London, 1933; *The Eyes of the Blind,* London, 1932; *It Is Wonderful,* London, 1934; *Out of the Clouds,* London, 1934.

[8] For a description of Father Divine's movement and a more detailed discussion of his revelations, see Charles S. Braden, *These Also Believe,* Macmillan, N. Y., 1949.

ing Jesus. Since his death and consequent elevation to the state of an Ascended Master himself, Mrs. Ballard continues to receive messages from them and from him. The fact of still-current revelations, of course, prevents the closing of the canon. Whether on the death of Mrs. Ballard, one of the three only Accredited Messengers to this age, the messages will be continued through the third Messenger, son Donald Ballard, it is impossible to predict surely. I personally think it doubtful. In this case there may be a closing of the book, and eventually a gathering of all of this mass of revealed material into a single collection. It has so far been published in various books and in the monthly magazine, *The Voice of I Am.* Again, it is a sacred book in the making.[9]

Another prophetic revealer was Dr. Frank B. Robinson of Moscow, Idaho, founder of Psychiana. He called himself a prophet. One of his books bears the title *The Prophet Speaks.* In dozens of places in his writings he asserts categorically that he speaks under divine inspiration. He died in 1948, so it is too early to predict what may eventually come of his revelation. During most of twenty years Dr. Robinson steadfastly refused to organize his numerous followers. His work was almost exclusively by mail or radio, so no church developed which might naturally be expected to carry on after his death. In his latter years, he informed me, that policy was changed and they had begun to organize as rapidly as possible. With what success they met I have not heard. If it does become a well-organized movement and develops deep loyalties to Dr. Robinson and his teachings, it may yet result in the creation of another modern sacred book to serve as the basis of the new faith. He has written a great deal. There is much repetition in what has come from his pen. But some process of selection might well take place in the course of time which would provide a solid core of teachings which the group would recognize as authoritative.[10]

Among the modern forms of religion that have developed their own sacred literatures may be found two variant types: (1) Those which, besides acknowledging as their own some already established

[9] Braden, *op. cit.*, pp. 257–308.
[10] Braden, *op. cit.*, pp. 78–127.

scripture, add to it a supplementary scripture, the product of the inspiration of their own founder. (2) Those which recognize no other basic scriptural authority than the revelation brought to light by their founder. Examples of the first type are Christian Science and Mormonism; of the second, Bahai. We deal first with Bahai. It is a world religion, found widely scattered among the nations.

Bahai was born in Persia just a little more than a century ago, 1844. There was within the Shiah Moslem group a lively expectation of the return of the Twelfth Imam who had disappeared, promising that he would one day come back. There was likewise a belief, probably influenced by Jewish thought, that there must first appear a Forerunner, in the manner of John the Baptist, before the coming of the expected one. In 1844 such a one announced himself, called by Bahais the Bab. He gained a considerable following, but after only a few years was put out of the way by the Persian government. But only a short time after this, arose one claiming to be the one foretold, and he was so received. He became known as Baha'u'llah, the Splendor of God, and his movement as Bahai. He spent a great part of his life as a prisoner—not always in prison, but obliged to live in a prison colony. All during these years he taught and wrote what have since come to be known as "The Tablets of Baha'u'llah." These have come to be regarded as the basic scripture of the movement, though the writings of the Bab and of the prophet's son and successor, Abdul Baha, are likewise considered on almost, if not, the same level as those of the founder. Says one who was for many years a leader of the movement, Albert Vail:

The Bahais who make a practice of reading as far as possible the sacred books of all religions, declare the words of the Bab, Baha'u'llah and Abdul-Baha possess the same recreative power (as other sacred books). They illumine, exalt them, reveal to them the presence of God and set them aflame with His love.[11]

Esselmont says that the founder's utterances "like other divine manifestations, may be divided into two classes, in one of which he

[11] "The Bahai Movement," reprinted from *Harvard Theological Review*, July, 1914, Vol. VII.

writes or speaks simply as a man who has been charged by God with a message to his fellows, while in the other class the words purport to be the direct utterance of God himself." But he admits that "no hard and fast line can be drawn between the human and divine element in his life or teachings." For even when he speaks as a man, says Esselmont, he "speaks as God's messenger, as a living example of entire devotion to God's will. His whole life is actuated by the Holy Spirit."[12] His writings were very extensive and only a part of them have been translated into English or other European languages, so few can know the whole of them. For practical purposes, a brief selection known as *Hidden Words* has been widely circulated as expressing the more important teachings of the prophet. It is issued in vest-pocket size. This selection, plus a much larger number of passages, have been translated and published under the title *Bahai World Faith*. This has appeared in various editions, each larger than the previous one. The 1943 version carries the following statement. "This replaces the work published in 1923 under the title *Bahai Scriptures* and contains later and more accurate translations, as well as Tablets and prayers not then accessible in English." It contains 465 pages and is arranged topically. It, as well as a number of other publications of Bahai, is issued with the approval of the Bahai Central Commission.[13]

It appears that the canon is not yet fixed. Nor does it seem likely that it will ever be completely closed, for one of their beliefs is in the continuing revelation of God for which they have made provision in their scheme of organization. In this it resembles Roman Catholicism and Mormonism, both of which have a definite concept of continuing revelation, and machinery through which revelation is supposed to be received, namely, the church represented in the person of the Pope in the case of the Roman Catholic Church and the First Presidency in the case of the Mormons.

There remain two modern American sacred books to be considered at somewhat greater length, viz., *Science and Health with*

[12] *Baha'u'llah and the New Era*, Rev. 2nd ed., G. Allen and Unwin, London, 1940, p. 53.

[13] National headquarters of the movement are at Wilmette, Illinois, where their magnificent and unique temple is located.

Key to the Scriptures, and the peculiar sacred writings of the Church of Jesus Christ of Latter Day Saints.

Let it first be said that Christian Science accepts the Protestant Christian Bible, just as other Protestant Christians do. Furthermore, Christian Scientists read their Bibles, I suspect, with more regularity than most other Protestants. Article I of the Statement of Belief, which must be signed by all who seek membership in the First Church of Christ Scientist in Boston, the Mother Church, reads: "As adherents of Truth, we take the inspired word of the Bible as our sufficient guide to eternal life." This article was handed down by Mrs. Eddy, and there is no word in the remaining five articles which even refers to any other scripture. No mention is therein made of *Science and Health.* However, in Article IV, on church membership, it is specifically stated that a member must be a "believer in the doctrines of Christian Science according to the platform and teaching contained in the Christian Science textbook, *Science and Health with Key to the Scriptures,* by Reverend Mary Baker Eddy. The Bible, together with *Science and Health* and other works by Mrs. Eddy, shall be his only textbooks for self instruction in Christian Science and for teaching and practicing metaphysical healing." Are we then justified in regarding *Science and Health* as a sacred book? May it not be merely a peculiar interpretation of the Bible which is held to by the church in accordance with good Protestant custom? Presbyterians are supposed to regard the Westminster Confession as an authoritative interpretation of the true meaning of the Bible at crucial points, yet that famous confession would hardly be held to be a sacred book.

Here we must recall the definition of a sacred book with which we began. It must be first regarded as of divine inspiration, and secondly, be held as authoritative by the group in matters of faith. Does *Science and Health* fit these requirements? As to the second requirement there can be little doubt. One only needs to recall the place given to it in the public and private worship of Christian Scientists to be convinced that it does meet this requirement. In public worship there are two readers. One reads a passage from the Bible, selected ahead of time by a committee which determines for all Christian Science churches what shall be read in the churches on each Sunday of the year. The other reads correlative passages from *Science and Health*. Some think there is significance in the fact that the second reader—there are two in every church—reads from the Bible, while the first reader reads from *Science and Health*. As is well known there is no sermon. The reading from *Science and Health*, which is of course the word of Mrs. Eddy, is effectively the sermon, and historically did take the place of sermons by the pastors which were regularly preached in the earlier Christian Science churches, until done away with by order of Mrs. Eddy. That is to say, independent study and interpretation of the Bible is not enough. It is always the Bible interpreted by Mrs. Eddy in her various writings which is regarded as the true statement of doctrine. It is she who determines for her followers the effective meaning of scripture. It would seem, therefore, that the inspiration of Holy Writ is dependent on its interpreter for its effectiveness in reaching the mind of the Christian Scientist. Does this then mean that her own writings are themselves inspired? If they are, then clearly they meet the first requirement of the definition of scripture.

That Mrs. Eddy herself considered them inspired, there can be no doubt. "No human pen nor tongue taught me the Science contained in this book, *Science and Health*," she declares (10:18). Or, again she writes: "God certainly revealed the Spirit of Christian Science" (495:29), which is, of course, known only through *Science and Health*. She speaks too of "the divine origin and operation of Christian Science" (272:25), of the "divine basis of Christian Science" (388:8), and asserts that "Christian Science is unerring and divine" (99:15). But Christian Science can only be known through the textbook; therefore, is it not also "unerring and divine"? For *Science and Health,* she states, "is the voice of Truth to this age and contains the full statement of Christian Science." On a number of occasions she spoke or wrote concerning the writing of the book. In *Miscellany* she wrote: "I should blush to write of *Science and Health with Key to the Scriptures* as I have, were it of human origin, and were I, apart from God, its author" (p. 115). A follower reports that, once visiting Mrs. Eddy, he was asked if he had seen a certain painting in her room at the Mother Church. It pictured a chair in which she sat while writing the textbook. Sheets of manuscript were scattered on the floor beside it. Said Mrs. Eddy to him: "The picture is true to life. When the ideas of Truth poured into my thought, I was so careful not to miss anything, that I let my papers fall to the floor. When the moment of revelation passed, I gathered them up and arranged them."[14]

In *Miscellany*, she tells a bit about writing:

I could not write these notes after sunset. All thoughts in the line of Scriptural interpretation would leave me until the rising of the sun. Then the influx of divine interpretation would pour in upon my spiritual sense as gloriously as the sunlight on the material senses. It was not myself, but the divine power of Truth and Love, infinitely above me, which dictated *Science and Health with Key to the Scriptures*.[15]

And her followers have accepted its inspiration. Dakin quotes from the *Christian Science Journal* (unfortunately he fails to give chapter and verse) a statement made by the editor in answer to a query concerning *Science and Health*: "Would it not be too material a view to speak of *Science and Health* being *based* upon any edition of the Bible. . . . The Chosen One, always with God in the Mount, speaks face to face. In other words, *Science and Health* is a firsthand revelation."[16] Another who knew Mrs. Eddy personally writes: "Perhaps we sometimes read *Science and Health* without a thought of the author. May we not rather realize that we are not only reading the word of God, but that our communion with Him (God) is through the Message written by His chosen scribe."[17] Sibyl Wilbur, official biographer of Mrs. Eddy for the movement, indicates again and again the inspired nature of her writings: (Italics mine)

It is no refutation of her sublime discovery in 1866 or of *her divine guidance in preparing and presenting its principles,* that the work was a growth and did not spring full blown into her mind.[18]

---

[14] *We Knew Mary Baker Eddy*, Christian Science Publishing Company, Boston, 1943, pp. 42–43. Used by permission.
[15] *We Knew Mary Baker Eddy*, p. 43.
[16] *Mrs. Eddy*, Charles Scribner's Sons, N. Y., 1930, p. 195.
[17] *We Knew Mary Baker Eddy*, p. 41.
[18] *Life of Mary Baker Eddy*, p. 182. Used by permission.

Her dissertations as well as her writings were beginning to unseal the fountains of her *inspiration*.[19]

Her authorship of the *Manual* was as much inspired as her authorship of *Science and Health with Key to the Scriptures*.[20]

One who was her personal secretary for a time notes several sayings of Mrs. Eddy, which he wrote down immediately on returning to his desk. They were, he writes, confirmed by other members of the household as substantially correct. One of them was:

"Every by-law in the *Manual* is inspired. I did not write them any more than I wrote *Science and Health*" (showing, says the reporter of the utterances) that both came to her through revelation.[21]

Surely no other citations are necessary to establish the fact that these writings are regarded as inspired. Thus we are fully justified in classifying *Science and Health* as a modern sacred book, according to our definition.

Mormonism, like Christian Science, accepts the Bible in its Protestant form. Article 8 of its Articles of Faith states simply, "We believe the Bible to be the word of God," but adds, "as far as it is correctly translated." The phrase, "as far as it is correctly translated," means that the Mormons have their own version of the Bible, which was made by Joseph Smith between June, 1830, and July, 1833.

In the *Book of Mormon* (1 Nephi iii, 40) it is asserted that "many plain and precious parts" have been removed from the Bible; and again in a revelation of Joseph Smith given June, 1830, God, speaking to Moses, declares, "I will speak unto you concerning this earth upon which thou standest and thou shalt write the things which I shall speak and in a day when the children of men shall esteem my words as naught and take many of them from the book which thou shalt write, behold I will raise up another like unto thee, and they shall be had again among the children of men, among even as many as shall believe."[22] This is the evident authorization for a correction of the received version of that time.

[19] *Ibid.*, p. 181.
[20] *Ibid.*, p. 368.
[21] *We Knew Mary Baker Eddy*, p. 22.
[22] *Doctrines and Covenants*, Sec. 22, p. 9.

In the preface to the 1944 edition of the Bible published by the Reorganized Church of Jesus Christ of Latter Day Saints at Independence, Missouri, this statement appears:

This work is given to the Church of Jesus Christ of Latter Day Saints and to the public in pursuance of the commandment of God. As concerning the matter of translation and correction, it is evident from the manuscripts and the testimony of those who were conversant with the facts that it was done by direct revelation from God.

A few of the differences observed on comparing this version with the regular King James version may be indicated.

The first verse of Chapter I of Genesis in the corrected version reads:

(v. 1) And it came to pass that the Lord spake unto Moses, saying, Behold, I reveal unto you concerning this heaven and this earth; write the words which I speak. (v. 2) I am the Beginning and the End, the Almighty God. By mine Only Begotten I created these things.

All of this precedes what is ordinarily verse 1 in the standard versions. Verse 3 of the Mormon version continues:

Yea, in the beginning I created the heaven and the earth upon which thou standest (v. 4) and the earth was without form, and void; and I caused darkness to come upon the face of the deep, etc.

Note that it is all expressed in the first person instead of the third person, and this follows clear through the creation story.

The narratives run fairly close together through chapters 3 and 4. At the introduction of Enoch in the Mormon version, there is a long section continuing through chapter 6, with 71 verses, and chapter 8 with 85 verses, dealing with Enoch's ministry, his prophecies, visions, prayers, etc. The flood narrative is substantially the same, and at chapter 11 the two narratives are once again parallel. From there on, there seems to be very slight difference between the versions.

Space does not permit an examination of the whole Bible. It is significant that there are changes, sometimes rather substantial indeed, in comparison with the regular authorized version.

One sample from the New Testament must suffice. In chapter 12 of St. Luke, the versions are identical through verse 9, which reads: "But he who denieth me before men shall be denied before the angels of God." In the Mormon version is then inserted the following two verses.

Now his disciples knew that he said this because they had spoken evil against him before the people for they were afraid to confess him before men and they reasoned among themselves, saying "He knoweth our hearts and he speaketh to our condemnation and we shall not be forgiven." But he answered them and said unto them.

Once again the two versions run parallel.

Between verses 30 and 31 of the regular version is inserted the following:

And ye are sent unto them to be their ministers and the laborer is worthy of his hire for the law sayeth that a man shall not muzzle the ox that treadeth out the corn.

By the end of the chapter, the Mormon version has gained a total of nine verses.

Article 8 further adds: "We also believe the Book of Mormon to be the word of God"[23] But the revelation has not ceased, as they believe, for the 9th Article of Faith reads: "We believe all that God has revealed, all He does now reveal, and we believe that He will yet reveal many great and important things pertaining to the Kingdom of God." In accord with this article, Talmage wrote: "The canon of scripture is still open: many lines, many precepts, are yet to be added: revelation surpassing in importance and glorious fulness any that has been recorded, is yet to be given to the church and declared to the world."[24]

The Articles of Faith themselves were, according to Mormon belief, "given by inspiration" by Joseph Smith about 1841, in a short history of the church which he furnished at the request of a Chicago editor. The history was published first in *Times and Season*, March 1, 1842.

[23] Talmage, *Articles of Faith*, p. 2.
[24] *Ibid.*, p. 311.

Actually, Mormons accept as authoritative revelation not only the *Book of Mormon,* but also the *Book of Doctrines and Covenants* and *The Pearl of Great Price.* These are quoted constantly by Talmage in his discussion of the Articles of Faith, which is really a study of Mormon theology, alongside the Bible and the *Book of Mormon.* Thus it may be said that these together constitute the historic canon of scripture as received by the church of Jesus Christ of Latter Day Saints.

The channel through which continuing revelation reaches the church is the First Presidency which is the head of the church, very much in the same sense as the Pope in Roman Catholicism. Says Talmage: "By divine direction, a president is appointed from among the members of the High Priesthood to preside over the entire church. . . . He is called to be 'a seer, a revelator, a translator, and a Prophet, having all the gifts of God which he bestows upon the head of the church.' " This latter quote is the precise expression used to describe Joseph Smith himself. Talmage continues: "His station is compared by the Lord to that of Moses of old, who stood as the mouthpiece of God unto Israel." To him belong "the keys of the kingdom."[25]

The story of the *Book of Mormon* is too familiar to require detailed retelling here. It is believed to have been written on gold plates, whose whereabouts was revealed to Joseph Smith as a very young man, but written and hidden away centuries earlier by Moroni, last remnant of the people who had migrated from the old world to the new. The greater part of the story is that of Laman and Nephi, sons of the prophet, Lehi, who migrated from Jerusalem about 600 B.C. From them descended the Lamanites and Nephites, the former becoming the American Indians. The two peoples warred against each other, and finally about 400 A.D., the Nephites were destroyed in a battle in Upper New York near where the tablets were found. In the course of the narrative is found the account of Jesus' appearance to the Nephites shortly after his ascension. The golden age of the Nephites followed this appearance. All this had been recorded on plates of gold. These

[25] *Op. cit.,* p. 210.

the prophet Mormon abridged on other plates of gold and left to his son, Moroni, to be added to as he deemed necessary, and hidren away in the earth. He made some modifications and added to the book of Ether, in which is told the story of the Jaredites, who at the time of the building of the Tower of Babel migrated to the Western world. They, too, were finally destroyed, but the record had been written by Ether, the last prophet of the Jaredites, and hidden away. Found later by one of the rulers of the Nephites, it was shortened and added to the *Book of Mormon* by Moroni.

Alleged to have been written in hieroglyphics, it was translated by Joseph Smith, a very meagerly educated young man, by means of the Urim and Thummim found along with the plates. The work of translation is reported to have been done by Joseph, who was separated by a curtain from the amanuensis who wrote it down. In all the successive versions of the *Book* a statement signed by eight witnesses is included, witnessing to their having seen and handled the golden plates. This is held by Mormons to be proof positive of the truth of the reputed origin of the *Book*. Naturally it has been doubted by those outside the faith and every effort has been made to find a more plausible explanation of the sources of this scripture. While absolute certainty is, of course, impossible at this late date, non-Mormon scholars are pretty well convinced that its basis was an historical novel by a one-time Presbyterian clergyman by the name of Spaulding, which he intended calling *The Manuscript Found in the Wilds of Mormon* or, *Unearthed Records of the Nephites*. It was offered for publication to a printer in Pittsburgh, without title affixed. The manuscript was left with the printer, the author agreeing to provide the title page and a preface. Sickness caused a delay, and on his return the manuscript had disappeared. But what is the connection of all this with the Book of Mormon and Joseph Smith? The link is found in the fact that Sidney Rigdon was employed in the print shop at the time and that he was a primary figure in the early days of the founding of Mormonism. Arbaugh[26] goes so far as to declare that the real founder of Mormonism was Rigdon, rather than Joseph Smith, and that the latter

[26] G. B. Arbaugh, *Revelation in Mormonism*, University of Chicago Press, 1932.

was used rather as a tool in effecting his purpose. Naturally Mormon writers deny this and defend the book as a genuine revelation received through the prophet Joseph Smith.[27] It is impossible to enter here into the merits of the controversy, but there is much circumstantial evidence to support the claim of non-Mormon scholars. In an age such as ours, critical of all claims that run counter to what may be scientifically proven, the Mormon has a heavy burden of proof upon him. Mormon children who grow up under the careful tutelage of the church entertain no more serious doubts about the inspiration of Joseph Smith than they do that of Isaiah, Jeremiah or Paul. But older Mormon youth have their difficulties as they move out, as many of them do, into the larger community of the world and catch something of the critical spirit of the age.

Mormon educators seem to be quite hospitable to the work of critical scholarship as applied to the Bible. For example, various professors from the University of Chicago, including Dr. Goodspeed, Dr. Graham and others, have been invited to lecture on the Bible at Brigham Young University. I have never seen any work of a critical nature on the Mormon revelation specifically done by Mormon scholars. It will be strange if eventually such work is not attempted.

The Book of Doctrines and Covenants contains a series of lectures on faith delivered at Kirtland, Ohio. It is not stated that they were given by Joseph Smith. But the remainder of the book consists chiefly of revelations given to Joseph Smith, the Seer or Revelator. Each revelation is dated and a title states to whom it was directed, and in some cases under what circumstances. Some are general, some to specific individuals, including at least one directed to his wife, Emma. There is one given through Brigham Young.

The Pearl of Great Price contains *The Book of Moses,* which purports to be visions of Moses as revealed to Joseph Smith in

[27] A good example of the way in which Mormons support their belief in the Book of Mormon is Vol. 17, No. 4 of *The Gospel Quarterly,* an Adult Study Course, published by The Herald Publishing House of the Reorganized Church at Independence, Mo., under the title "External Evidences of the Book of Mormon."

1830. *The Book of Abraham,* which is described as "a translation of some ancient records that have fallen into our hands from the catacombs of Egypt, the writings of Abraham while he was in Egypt," is also included. In addition, there are other writings of Joseph Smith, a short account of the beginnings of his work, and the *Articles of Faith*.

These two books then contain in the main the revelations which came to Joseph Smith during the early years of the movement—those probably referred to in the phrase "all that He does now reveal." They are basic to the whole movement, and far more important in their bearing upon the organisational life of the Mormons than either the Bible or *The Book of Mormon,* for it was in these successive revelations of the prophet that the growing movement took shape, and their most characteristic beliefs and practices were determined.

Limitation of space precludes an adequate discussion of the cultural role of these numerous modern sacred books. Since there is not one of them which represents other than a minority group within a larger whole, one cannot here write, as has been done in the case of some of the great ethnic scriptures, of their molding influence upon a total culture. But it may be said that each scripture does play an important part in the lives of the members of the various groups. Only in the Mormon group has there been a profound social effect upon the adherents. Here, perhaps due more than to any other single factor, to the doctrine set forth in their scriptures, of the "Gathering of the Saints," they tended to draw together into a compact social body, building their own communities as they did at Kirtland, Ohio; in Jackson County, Missouri; at Far West, Missouri; at Nauvoo, Illinois; and finally in Utah. Converts came from all over the United States, Canada and England to join the Mormon community. This concentration of Mormons, their unfamiliar religious beliefs, their different patterns of living, and their economic solidarity, which constituted something of a threat to the non-Mormon community, even on the frontier, brought upon them the bitter persecution which drove them from one place to another in search of peace and the opportunity to live according to their revealed way of life. It became finally evident that only in the complete isolation of the West could they enjoy this freedom, so they braved the hardship of the long trek across the plains and desert mountains to the valley of the Great Salt Lake.

Here in relative isolation from a restrictive majority, they did develop a culture of their own in which the influence of their revealed scriptures was very great. Here they formed what was practically an ideal theocracy according to their scriptures and built a great self-sufficient community.

Brigham Young was the great organizing genius of this new empire. He derived whatever authority he had from the new revelation and governed, as he thought, certainly, according to the teachings of the faith.

With the coming of the Gentiles to Utah, the political direction of the state has, of course, passed from the church as church, but even today the economic and social life of the Mormon community is still to an amazing degree determined by the principles taught in their sacred book.

It would be a great mistake to suppose that those mentioned thus far in the chapter are the only modern sacred books. Within the year a new one from Japan and another from Cambodia have come to the writer's attention. Almost every movement mentioned in the appendix of *These Also Believe* has something like a sacred book, either already formed, or in the making. And others will yet appear. So long as men believe in a higher power who is believed capable of revealing himself to man, there will arise those who believe that God has spoken to them and will become his mouthpiece just as the prophets of older religions have done. Which of these will live and become the authoritative bases of great religions, only time can disclose. It will undoubtedly be the intrinsic values in the writing themselves and their ability to speak to the universal heart of humanity which will determine the spread of their influence and their ultimate survival.

MODERN SACRED BOOKS
Sources for Further Reading

The more recent sacred books are not usually represented in the anthologies. In the case of Bahai there is a substantial section of the writings of Baha'u'llah and Abdul Baha included in Sohrab, *The Bible of Mankind,* pp. 590–733.

S. E. Frost, *Sacred Writings of the World's Great Religions,* has sections from the *Book of Mormon, Doctrines and Covenants* and the *Pearl of Great Price,* pp. 367–377; and a few excerpts from *Science and Health,* pp. 379–388.

The Christian Science textbook, *Science and Health with Key to the Scriptures* and the *Book of Mormon,* will be found in most libraries. The other sacred books have been mentioned in the footnotes throughout the chapter.

INDEX

Abdul Baha, 472
Abhidhamma, 157, 161, 170, 191, 192
Abraham, 61, 339, 404, 418, 451
Abu Bekr, 443, 444, 445
Abu Hanifa, 463
Accredited Messengers, 471
Activism, 280, 282
Acts, 401, 403, 405, 406, 416, 428, 429
Acts of Paul, 429
Adi Granth, 229
After life, 374; Egyptian, 37
Agamas, 123
Agni, 89, 90, 98, 101, 137
Agreements, the, 463, 466
Ahimsa, 174, 204, 207, 399
Ahmadiyya Movement in Islam, 465
Ahura-Mazda, 308, 309, 310
Akhnaton, 53; hymn of, 55–58
Allah, 220, 440, 446
Amar Das, 231
Amaterasu, 293, 298, 301
American Standard Version, 318
Amida, 200
Amitabha, 200
Amos, 47, 317, 324, 344, 347, 348, 349, 356
Amritsar, 222, 223
Analects, 238, 261, 263, 267, 270, 299
Analogies, the, 463, 466
Anga, 207, 210, 211
Angas, 206
Angra-Mainyu, 310
Anguttara-Nikaya, 161
Ani, The Instructions of, 49
Annals of Lu, 259
Anthologies, ix, xi, xii
Anthropologists, 292, 321
Apastamba, 122
Apocalypse, 324, 375, 380, 424, 425, 428
Apocalypse of Peter, 429
Apocrypha, 8, 323, 325, 376, 431
Apocrypha, New Testament, 430
Apocryphal Gospels, 430
Arabia, 411, 440, 441, 458

Aranyakas, 83, 110, 111, 121
Archaeology, 329; Babylonian, 60; Chinese, 238; Egyptian, 35
Archer, J. C., 219, 220, 222, 229, 235
Arhantship, 155, 163, 182, 183, 184, 186
Arjun, 223, 228, 229, 233
Arjuna, 125, 126, 132, 140
Arnold, Sir Edwin, 130, 132, 139, 140, 144, 198
Articles of Faith, 477, 479, 483
Aryans, 83, 85, 102, 188, 311
Arya-Samaj, 85
Ascended Masters, 470, 471
Aston, W. G., 294, 301
Asvaghosa, 198
Atharva-Veda, 83, 102
Atman, 114, 117, 118
Aton, hymn to, 55–58
Avesta, 306, 307, 310, 314
Aztecs, 12, 19, 169

Bab, the, 472
Babylon, 343, 350, 355, 359, 377
Badarayana, 120
Bahai, 472; Central Commission, 473; Scriptures, 473; World Faith, 473
Baha'u'llah, 472
Ballad, 214, 246
Ballard, Donald, 471; Edna, 470; Guy, 470
Barnabas, 395, 406
Barnabas, Epistle of, 428, 429
Baudhayana, 122
Beal, Samuel, 198
Beatitudes, 389, 398
Bell, Richard, 442, 466
Bewer, Julius A., 334, 335, 342, 356
Bhadrabahu, 205
Bhagavad, Gita, 121, 124, 130, 139, 201, 219; date, 144
Bhakti, 195, 200, 218
Bhikkunis, 154, 158, 185
Bhikkus, 154
Bhima, 120, 125

487